# Press Law in Modern Democracies

## A COMPARATIVE STUDY

**Pnina Lahav, Editor**

*Boston University*
*School of Law*

# Longman

New York & London

D1255542

**Press Law in Modern Democracies**
*A Comparative Study*

Longman Inc., 1560 Broadway, New York, N.Y. 10036
Associated companies, branches, and representatives
throughout the world.

Developmental Editor: Gordon T. R. Anderson
Editorial and Design Supervisor: Russell Till
Production Supervisor: Ferne Y. Kawahara

*343.0998*
*P935*

**Library of Congress Cataloging in Publication Data**

Lahav, Pnina, 1945–
   Press law in modern democracies.

   (Annenberg/Longman communication books)
   Includes index.
   1. Freedom of the press.   2. Press law.   I. Title.
II. Series.
K3255.L33     1983      343'.0998      83-19595
ISBN 0–582–28478–3      342.3998

MANUFACTURED IN THE UNITED STATES OF AMERICA
9  8  7  6  5  4  3  2  1      92  91  90  89  88  87  86  85

To Moshe, Alexandra, and Absalom

# Contents

## PART I. THE ANGLO-AMERICAN APPROACH

One
Press Law in the United Kingdom
**Michael Supperstone**

# Contributors

**Thomas I. Emerson** is Lines Professor of Law Emeritus at Yale University. He held various legal posts in the United States government from 1933 to 1946 and taught constitutional law at the Yale Law School from 1946 until he retired in 1976. He is the author of *Toward a General Theory of the First Amendment* (Random House 1966) and *The System of Freedom of Expression* (Random House 1970), and co-author of *Political and Civil Rights in the United States* (Little, Brown: 4th ed. 1976).

**Roger Errera** is "Maître des requêtes" at the French Conseil d'Etat in Paris. He teaches civil liberties at the Institut d'Études politiques in Paris and is a member of the Human Rights Committee of the United Nations Covenant on Civil and Political Rights. He has written a number of articles on the legal status of human rights in national and in international law, and a book, *Les Libertés à l'Abandon* (1975).

**Masao Horibe** is a professor of law at Hitotsubashi University, Japan. He holds an LL.M. degree from the University of Tokyo. He has written extensively in the area of mass communications. His writings include: *The Right of Access* (in Japanese) (University of Tokyo Press, 1977); *The Contemporary Privacy* (in Japanese) (Iwanami Shoten, 1980).

**Helmut Kohl** is Professor for civil law in the Johann Wolfgang Goethe-University School of Law, Frankfurt, Federal Republic of Germany. His publications include *Die "Verwässerung" berühmter Kennzeichen;* (with Hoffmann-Riem, Kübler/Lüscher) *Medienwirkung und Medienverantwortung;* he is coauthor of the *Alternativkommentar zum BGB.*

**Pnina Lahav** is associate professor at Boston University School of Law. She holds an LL.B. degree from the Faculty of Law at Hebrew University in Jerusalem and LL.M. and J.S.D. degrees from Yale Law School. She taught Israeli constitutional law at the Hebrew University, and since 1979 has been teaching American constitutional law at Boston University. She is the author of several articles on constitutional law and civil liberties. She recently was awarded a Rockefeller Fellowship and is currently writing the intellectual biography of Israel's former chief justice, Simon Agranat.

**Aviam Soifer** received his B.A., M. Urban Studies and J.D. from Yale University. He is a professor of law at Boston University, where he has taught since 1979. After law school, he served as law clerk to Federal Judge Jon O. Newman; he began teaching at the University of Connecticut School of Law. He was the recipient of a major grant from Project '87, sponsored by the American Historical Association and the American Political Science Association, as well as fellowships from the American Bar Foundation and the Legal History Program at the University of Wisconsin. In 1976–1977 he spent a year at Harvard University as a law and humanities fellow. He is the author of numerous articles about constitutional law, legal history, and federal courts, and is currently at work on a book about the Thirteenth Amendment.

**Håkan Strömberg** has been professor of public law at the University of Lund, Sweden, 1962 to 1981. He has written several monographs in constitutional and administrative law, the latest of which deals with the power of legislation according to the Swedish Constitution of 1974 (Lund, 1983). He has also written a number of textbooks in constitutional and administrative law, one of which treats Swedish press law. All his books are written in Swedish.

**Michael Supperstone** practices law as a barrister of the Middle Temple in London, England. He holds M.A., and B.C.L. degrees from Oxford University. He is author of *Brownlie's Law of Public Order* and *National Security* (1980), and of *Immigration: The Law and Practice* (1983). He is currently writing a book on the law relating to discrimination.

# Foreword

Freedom of the press is a key element in any system of individual rights, now or in the future. The press can serve an indispensable function in informing the public, criticizing the institutions and practices of a society, exposing abuses in government, and generally acting as a counterweight to established centers of power. Indeed, the extent to which a society is open and democratic can be measured in great part by the degree to which the press in that society is independent and vigorous. This crucial role played by the press in the democratic process is, at least in the United States, attributable to a number of factors.

First, the concept which the press holds of itself has tended to shift over the years from that of representing exclusively private or partisan interests to that of representing the public interest. One need only examine the vitriolic newspapers being published at the time of the adoption of the First Amendment, or the yellow journalism of the Hearst era, to be acutely aware of the difference in outlook and attitude. The growing insistence on professionalism, the acceptance of "investigative reporting" as a routine feature of publishing a newspaper, even the claims made by the press for special treatment, as in shield laws protecting the confidentiality of sources, are indications that the ideal which the press seeks to have acknowledged is that of functioning in the public interest. This is not to say that all sectors of the press share this ideal or that any sector of the press really achieves it. Yet the existence of the concept is important, and at times the goal is at least partially realized.

Second, the concept of the press as operating in the public interest has become the popular as well as the legal justification for protecting freedom of the press. The support which the press receives in the legislatures, in the organs of opinion, and among the general public is founded on the premise that the press adds independent voices to public deliberations, voices that are worth hearing. Likewise, the constitutional basis for keeping the press free of governmental restraint was put by Justice Hugo Black in the Pentagon Papers case in the following terms:

> In the First Amendment the Founding Fathers gave the free press the protection it must have to fulfill its essential role in our democracy. The press was to serve the governed, not the governors. The Government's power to censor the press was abolished so that the press would remain forever free to censure the Government. The press was protected so that it could bare the secrets of government and inform the people. Only a free and unrestrained press can effectively expose deception in government. . . . In revealing the workings of government that led to the Viet Nam war, the newspapers nobly did that which the Founders hoped and trusted they would do.*

Third, the press, as an institution, constitutes a viable base from which to oppose governmental and private power. The modern expansion of state power, the concentration of nongovernmental power in ever-larger aggregates, and the relationship of major sectors of the press to those sources of power do operate of course to diminish the likelihood that the press can or would maintain a position independent of the establishment. Nevertheless, a significant potential for independence remains. The press provides services for which a continual demand exists, in addition to what governmental facilities may undertake to supply. People are eager to write and publish, people want to be informed, and people will strive to have their needs and desires expressed. Hence, a workable commercial or interest basis for press enterprises can be found. Moreover, the press is a source of power in its own right. It can influence public opinion, affect the outcome of elections, and create pressures that shape the activities of governmental or private centers of power. If the press is not constrained by government, and if democratic procedures are maintained, the press is a major source for the generation of political and other power.

Finally, it should be remembered that the constitutional and other legal doctrines that protect the press are stated in universal terms. They apply to all sectors of the press, at least in theory. The rights and privileges accorded those sectors that represent the established order must be extended equally to the unorthodox and dissenting sectors. Of course, that part of the press which reflects the domi-

---

*New York Times Co. v. United States, 403 U.S. 713,717 (1970).

nant views in a society will always have a louder voice. Yet the legal framework of press freedom also allows a minority to seek an audience and attempt to expand its influence.

For those reasons, among others, freedom of the press is a central requirement for any democratic society, regardless of whether the society is based on free enterprise or more collectivist institutions. On the other hand, freedom of the press does not exist in isolation; press powers must be reconciled with other interests of the society in which the press functions. Thus, there are potential conflicts or tensions between freedom of the press and certain general social interests, such as national security, internal order, and racial justice. Similarly, freedom of the press may impinge on rights essential to the welfare of particular persons, such as the right to preserve one's reputation, the right of privacy, the right to an unprejudiced trial, and the right of access to the means of communication. Moreover, it may be that the system of press freedom ought to be supported or encouraged in certain ways, such as by ensuring greater access to government information, by honoring a reporter's pledge of confidentiality, or by affording relief from intrusive forms of government investigation. Conversely, the society may decide that certain forms of limitation, such as antitrust laws forbidding concentration in the mass media, are essential to effective functioning of the system.

Efforts to deal with these complex problems have produced a multiplicity of statutes, regulations, court decisions, practices, and institutions. These devices can be used to strike an honest balance between freedom of the press and those interests with which it is in tension. On the other hand, they can be designed or administered to smother a free press or suppress it altogether.

The chapters of this book undertake to describe how these issues have been resolved in seven democratic countries, and to assess the results. Their findings are of vital concern not only to lawyers, judges, and political scientists but to everyone who depends on the press for information or looks to it for some measure of opposition to abuses of power—which is to say all of us.

*Thomas I. Emerson*

# Acknowledgments

The idea of this book was conceived years ago, when during my research of the Israeli press law I looked for comparative materials. I discovered that there was no volume in English which coherently and comparatively analyzed the press laws of modern democracies, and realized the need for a book which would focus on the statutory and judicial approaches of the various democratic legal systems to the press but would remain sensitive to political theory and social reality.

Credit for turning this idea into a realizable project is owed to Professor Ithiel de Sola Pool of the Massachusettes Institute of Technology. He not only encouraged me to undertake the project but also introduced me to the Modern Media Institute at St. Petersburg, Florida. His untimely death in March 1984 is a sad loss to the Communications Community.

I am very grateful to the Modern Media Institute and its director, Mr. Donald K. Baldwin, for financially assisting me and my fellow contributors, and for their patience, encouragement, and good spirits in seeing me through the organizational and editorial hardships of writing this book.

I wish also to thank the administration of the Boston University School of Law, whose generous help made this undertaking possible. Dean William Schwartz and Ms. Margo Hagopian were especially forthcoming with assistance.

Special thanks go to my research assistants, Gail Strassfeld, Karen Kepler, William Abbott, Mindy Hertz (who translated the French essay), Andrew Schwartz, and Cynthia Weigel. Their diligence in research and editorial assistance greatly facilitated the process of turning the essays, written mostly by scholars for whom English is a foreign language, into a readable manuscript, while at the same time retaining the authenticity and cultural flavor of the different countries. This is also the right moment to thank my fellow contributors for their patience and endurance during the lengthy and tedious editorial process.

Many good friends assisted with encouragement, support, and advice, as well as in providing fruitful comments in reading portions of the manuscript. Thanks go to Peter Arenella, Victor Brudney, Alan Feld, Eric Green, Harry Hirsch, Anthony Lewis, Ira Lupu, Frances Miller, Henry Monaghan, David Phillips, Aviam Soifer, and the late Ithiel de Sola Pool.

Special appreciation goes to my secretary Kenneth Westhassel, whose intelligence and competence were invaluable throughout the years of research and writing. I also wish to thank Diane Jackson and Linda Tedesco for patiently typing so many drafts, and Sandra L. Wilfong for processing them.

Thomas I. Emerson introduced me to American constitutional law and taught me the art of thinking about freedom of speech. For me he has since served as a fountain of inspiration and faith in the human spirit. I cannot praise him enough.

My husband, Moshe, and my children, Alexandra and Absalom, have been wonderful companions in this enterprise, and this book is dedicated to them.

*Pnina Lahav*

# Introduction

**Pnina Lahav**

Freedom of the press is an elusive concept. What makes the press "free"?[1] Can there be a free press absent the inclusion of a commitment to press freedom in a constitution? Can a society have a statute that clearly defines the privileges and obligations of the press and still maintain a "free" press? Can the press be "free" under a regime of censorship? Can the state interfere with editorial discretion, by providing for a statutory right of reply for example, and still maintain a free press? Can the press fulfill its role as watchdog of the government and yet be sued for defamation by public officials?

In the United States, the conventional answer to these questions in all probability would be that the First Amendment is essential for press freedom, and that a special statute which regulates the press, censorship, and the right of reply, or a defamation law which ignores the importance of uninhibited criticism of public officials, are all incompatible with the notion of a free press. Indeed, the American legal system reflects just this set of answers to the questions posed above.[2]

But America has no monopoly over democracy or press freedom. The United Kingdom and Israel have neither a constitution nor an explicit commitment to press freedom engraved on a basic charter. Sweden, France, and the Federal Republic of Germany have special press statutes which define the legal status of the press. Yet all of these countries are generally recognized as democracies and their press is considered free. It is this phenomenon—the basic similarity between these countries in the sense that they are all operational democracies and in the sense that they all consider the freedom of the press as both a fundamental and a viable value—that triggers the need to compare the way by which different democratic legal systems treat their press.

This volume provides the foundations for such an inquiry. It brings together essays about the press laws of liberal democracies, and thereby

1

provides the groundwork for a future, more comprehensive examination of the features of press law essential for a functioning democracy. The essays focus on the press in general and thus address issues which are relevant to both the printed press and the electronic media. They do not, however, address the unique features of broadcasting law, primarily because a meaningful discussion of broadcasting regulations merits a volume specifically dedicated to such issues.[3]

The essays have two distinctive characteristics, which should make them valuable for students of the press. First, they are authentic; the scholars who authored them wrote about their own legal systems. Thus, the essays reflect both the familiarity and the bias of the particular culture toward its press—qualities that are not easily accessible to an outsider. Second, these essays are uniformly structured; within the general body of press law they discuss similar topics, such as the press and national security and reporters' privilege. This uniformity in structure should further facilitate a comparative inquiry.

Beyond their contribution to the comparative study of press law, the essays are significant because of the rich base of information they provide for the development of a general theory of press law in democracy. Later in this volume I suggest that, rather than focus on formal structural dissimilarities, a theory of press law should probe the underlying dialectics which dominate all democratic press laws. I try to show that the key to understanding any particular press law is the political ideas which animate the particular democratic country.

The essays are organized into three divisions, the Anglo-American, the Continental, and the non-Western groups, each representing a unique feature of democratic press law.

The Anglo-American group is represented by the United Kingdom and the United States. What distinguishes both legal systems is "the common law tradition," an approach whereby the judiciary evolves the substantive content of norms over time. Both systems are reluctant to accord the press a special legal status, and both insist on giving newspapers and private individuals equal treatment, at least in theory. Both systems consider the Blackstonian doctrine against prior restraint as the foundation on which their press laws are built.[4]

The Continental group—France, the Federal Republic of Germany, and Sweden—share the basic Anglo-American aversion to censorship. Jurisprudentially, they differ from the Anglo-American group in the sense that their legal systems are part of the civil law tradition. That tradition is structured around legal codes, where an effort is made to organize and explicate the legal content of norms and where the judiciary does not play as central a role in developing the law. Additionally, in each of these countries there is a special statute devoted exclusively to newspapers and periodicals.

Both Anglo-American and Continental societies share the history and humanistic tradition of the Enlightenment, encompassing the ideas of liberalism, individualism, and constitutionalism. They also share philosophical and political justifications for freedom of expression and freedom of the press. Not so the third group in this study. Israel and Japan received, rather than generated, the institution of the modern press and the liberal philosophy of press freedom. The press laws in these two countries, while reflective of their authentic cultures, also reflect Western influence. Israel, which gained sovereignty in the mid-twentieth century, was previously under British control. Its laws represent a peculiar mix of the British common law tradition and an authoritarian colonialist approach to the press which contradicts the formal commitment to press freedom. The history of the Japanese press law parallels Japanese history in the twentieth century. Until the end of the Second World War, Japan had an authoritarian government. Its press laws were strongly influenced by the repressive press laws of Imperial Germany. Following the war, as Japan accepted a democratic form of government, its public law—including its press law— assumed the distinctive characteristics of American law.

The division of this study into three basic groups emphasizes the basic dissimilarities between the Anglo-American, the Continental, and the non-Western groups. However, it is important to note that these groups also differ among themselves. The United States seems to be much more permissive toward the press than the United Kingdom. As Professor Soifer's essay demonstrates, the combination of the First Amendment to the United States Constitution, which guarantees freedom of speech and of the press, and an activist judiciary, possessing both the power to invalidate statutes and the will to give the value of free speech a preferred status, has made American law more sympathetic toward freedom of expression. This concern for freedom of expression is also manifested in legislation, for example, the federal Freedom of Information Act of 1967 and the enactment of press shield laws by many of the states.[5]

The best illustration of the difference between the American and English approach to press freedom is the Pentagon Papers case.[6] There, the United States Supreme Court refused to enjoin the *New York Times* from publishing official documents which were classified as top secret. Mr. Supperstone's discussion of the press and national security reveals that such a decision, in all probability, would not occur in the United Kingdom. The Official Secrets Act, coupled with the rather deferential stance of the courts toward governmental policies, might deter journalists from a similar undertaking, and spur the courts to prevent an unauthorized disclosure of top secret materials.[7]

Sweden provides an interesting comparison. As Professor Strömberg's discussion shows, the elaborate and original Swedish press statute, which dates back to 1809, guarantees formal protection to journalists. That guarantee, combined with the Swedish tradition of permitting substantial popular access to official information, seems to resemble the contemporary

American attitude toward the press and the American conception of press freedom.[8] Conversely, the United Kingdom, whose legal system and judiciary displays a more elitist attitude toward the press, more resembles the French and German attitudes toward the press.[9] Professor Kohl's essay on the Federal Republic of Germany and Mr. Errera's essay on France reveal that the rhetoric of press freedom is as vigorous in these countries as it is in the United States or Sweden, but that these legal systems more readily will tilt the balance against expression when major interests of the state appear to be threatened.[10]

Within the third group, the non-Western democracies of Israel and Japan, there are also significant dissimilarities. My own essay on Israel points to a very interesting phenomenon in that the Jewish (consensus) press is relatively free and robust, whereas the Arab (pro-Palestinian) press is strictly regulated and occasionally suppressed.[11] Unlike Israel, which retained the pre-independence authoritarian press laws, Japan discarded similar statutes that it had borrowed from Imperial Germany. After the Second World War, Japan adopted a democratic form of government and followed the American model, which eschewed formal regulation of the press. Yet it is important to note that the Japanese press, while free and critical, observes an unwritten code of Japanese cultural tradition concerning what can and what cannot be said in public.[12]

The press laws of these non-Western countries illustrate the transformation that Western press laws undergo as they are transplanted into a different culture (Japan), or particularly into Israel's volatile political context.

Finally, my own comparative essay attempts to develop a general theory to explain the relationship between democracy and freedom of the press and the reasons why the relationship appears in many diverse legal forms. Drawing on the essays in these volumes, I argue that the press law of any particular democracy is not so much determined by the availability of a commitment in the constitution, or by the presence of a special press statute, as by the particular resolution, in the given democratic regime, between two sets of tensions. One is the tension between universal liberal values and the nation state. The other is the tension within journalism, between the press as a partisan political organ and the reporter as a disinterested professional. All democracies share these dialectics. The resolution of the tensions depends on the particular political and legal culture.

## NOTES

1.   The attempt to define the "free" press as that which is not licentious, immortalized by Lord Kenyon in his famous statement "freedom of the press is

dear to England, the licentiousness of the press is odious to England," *Trial of John Cuthell*, 27 How. St. Tr. 642, 647 (1799), is at best circular. It only suggests that the decision makers, whether public officials or judges, should utilize their discretion (subjective values) in order to find the speech licentious and then legitimize its suppression by invoking the distinction between licentiousness and freedom. This technique should not be confused with the philosophical premise that freedom of speech cannot be absolute, which leaves open to rigorous inquiry the question of what speech can be suppressed, why, and under what circumstances.

2.  *See, e.g., The Pentagon Papers Case*, 403 U.S. 713 (1971); *Miami Herald Pub. Co.* v. *Tornillo*, 418 U.S. 241 (1974); *New York Times Co.* v. *Sullivan*, 376 U.S. 254 (1964).

3.  For an important discussion *see* I. de Sola Pool, *Technologies of Freedom* (1983). *See also* R. Cass, *Revolution in the Wasteland; Value and Diversity in Television* (1981).

4.  W. Blackstone, Commentaries*, 151–152. In the United States, the doctrine against seditious libel appears *alongside* the doctrine against prior restraint as the key to understanding First Amendment jurisprudence.

5.  Soifer, *Press Law in the United States, infra*, pp. 105, 112.

6.  403 U.S. 713 (1971).

7.  *See* Supperstone, *Press Law in the United Kingdom, infra* p. 13.

8.  *See* Strömberg, *Press Law in Sweden, infra* p. 231.

9.  *Compare* the British approach, which holds that exposure of public officials to criticism by the press "would tend to deter sensitive and honorable men from seeking public positions of trust and responsibility and leave them open to others who have no respect for their reputation," G. Gately, *Libel and Slander* 223, (7th ed. 1974) *with* the American approach expressed by Justice Brennan in *New York Times* v. *Sullivan, supra* note 2 at 273:

> If judges are to be treated as "men of fortitude, able to thrive in a hardy climate" [citation omitted], surely the same must be true of other government officials, such as elected city commissioners. Criticism of their official conduct does not lose its constitutional protection merely because it is effective criticism and hence diminishes their official reputations.

10.  *See* Kohl, *Press Law in the Federal Republic of Germany, infra* p. 185; Errera, *Press Law in France, infra* p. 137.

11.  Lahav, *Press Law in Israel, infra* p. 265.

12.  *See* Horibe, *Press Law in Japan, infra* p. 315.

# PART 1

# The
# Anglo-American
# Approach

# One

# Press Law in the United Kingdom*

**Michael Supperstone**

## GENERAL FRAMEWORK

In the absence of a constitutional guarantee[1] or a special regime of law regulating the press, an English newspaper is, generally speaking, as protected as a letter—neither more nor less.[2] The main feature of liberty of the press consists, as Lord Mansfield described it, "in printing without any previous license subject to the consequence of law."[3] Under English law,[4] press offenses are tried and punished only by ordinary courts.[5] Affirming this position, the Royal Commission on the Press of 1977 (the 1977 Commission) expressed its belief that "the press should not operate under a special regime...but should...stand before the law in the same way as any other organisation or citizen."[6] The 1977 Commission continued:

> Our firm belief is that the press should be left free to be partisan and restrained as at present only by the law and by the voluntary system of a Press Council greatly strengthened in the ways which we recommend....[7]

Prior to 1855 the situation was very different. The Crown controlled all presses. It allowed no one to print except under special license and kept all presses subject to regulations issued by the Star Chamber. Press offenses were a special class of crimes cognizable by a special tribunal—the Star Chamber—which sat without a jury and administered severe punishment. The Star Chamber collapsed in 1661, but censorship survived and under the Restoration was given a strict statutory foundation.[8] Subsequent enactments continued the censorship until 1695, when the House of Commons refused to continue the Licensing Act.[9] After the system of

---

* The term "United Kingdom" refers to England, Wales, Scotland, and Northern Ireland. In the text reference will be made to the law of the United Kingdom or English law. Where the law in Scotland differs from the law in England this will be made clear.

licensing was terminated,[10] the government had no formal hold over newspapers. Nonetheless, indirect control in the form of the Newspaper Stamp Duties Act[11] lasted until 1855. Thereafter, the state played only a small role in the control of the newspaper business.[12] The growth of advertising helped distance the press from both government and political parties. Advertising funds reduced the importance of subsidies provided by political parties and progressively displaced direct funding by government. Thus, "the view that advertising is the midwife of press freedom contains an element of truth."[13] Advertising, however, was to carry with it its own dangers.[14]

Freedom of the press has diverse meanings.[15] The 1977 Commission defined it as the "freedom...which is essential to enable...journalists to advance the public interest by publishing the facts and opinions without which a democratic electorate cannot make responsible judgments."[16] This definition represents an interesting shift from the view of earlier Royal Commissions, which defined the freedom as a property right of publishers to conduct their newspapers as they saw fit subject to the law.[17]

The 1977 Commission saw the need for individuals in a democratic society to have access to a wide range of accurate information and opinion.[18] It was forced to recognize, however, the deficiency in serious coverage of news and opinion from the left-wing standpoint.[19] It recognized that "the monopolist, by its selection of the news and the manner in which it reports it, and by its commentary on public affairs, is in a position to determine what people shall read about the events and issues of the day, and to exert a strong influence on their opinions."[20] Nevertheless, while abandoning the classic liberal theory that the free market provides access to a variety of competing views,[21] the 1977 Commission, like its predecessors, rejected suggestions to introduce some form of subsidy in order to maintain a variety of competing newspapers. All three Royal Commissions on the Press have opposed any significant government intervention in the press industry.[22] Still, they recommended that positive action be taken against the growth of press concentration.[23]

Although the 1977 Commission properly criticized the free marketplace of ideas theory of the press, its silence about the positive guarantee of press freedom is disappointing.[24] Clearly, the absence of a constitutional guarantee of press freedom has prevented the English courts from grappling with the constitutional dimensions of many of the issues before them.[25] In the *Sunday Times* case[26] the European Court of Human Rights asserted that the principle of freedom of expression is subject only to a limited number of narrowly defined exceptions. By contrast, English law fails to recognize and affirm the primacy of freedom of expression. Incorporating the European Convention for the Protection of Human Rights and Fundamental Freedoms into English law or adopting a suitable alternative text as part of a Bill of Rights is the only way that the United

Kingdom can meet "the standards of human rights declared by international instruments to which [it] is a party."[27]

Disappointing as well is the courts' consideration of the theoretical justifications for freedom of the press. Three cases illustrate that in general the opinions of the English courts lack a theory of freedom of the press that adequately reflects the values at issue.

In the *Sunday Times* case, the issue before the courts was whether a national newspaper could be restrained, on the ground of contempt of court, from publishing an article discussing pending litigation. The *Sunday Times* published an article concerning the plight of the deformed children born to women who had taken the drug thalidomide during pregnancy. The Attorney General obtained an injunction restraining publication of a second article on the ground that publication might prejudice the administration of justice and thus would amount to a contempt of court. The Court of Appeal discharged the injunction but the House of Lords reinstated it. Only two opinions, those of Lord Denning, M.R., in the Court of Appeal, and Lord Salmon, in the House of Lords, discussed the theoretical justifications for press freedom and their connection with contempt of court.[28]

In the *Crossman Diaries* case,[29] the Attorney General attempted to restrain publication of the first volume of the diaries of Richard Crossman, a cabinet minister from 1964 until 1970. The Attorney General argued that the obligation of secrecy and confidentiality concerning cabinet information precluded publication. Although Lord Widgery, C.J., refused to grant the injunction, the decision was devoid of any discussion of the right of the press to inform the public and the corresponding right of the public to be properly informed. Nor was there any real appreciation of the importance of press freedom or of the proposition that the government's power to protect secrets should be complemented by the citizen's right to know.[30] Instead, Lord Widgery found that because the matters related to events occurring 10 years earlier, free discussion by the present cabinet would not be inhibited by their disclosure, even though some members might be the same and the problems discussed distressingly similar.[31]

Notwithstanding the outcome of the case, the decision is not sensitive to press freedom. The court accepted uncritically the Attorney General's argument that the publication of a cabinet member's views would seriously affect the doctrine of ministerial responsibility.[32] Lord Widgery also failed to indicate the interval of time necessary to preclude any potential detrimental effect on current cabinet discussions. Finally, and most important, the court did not delineate the type of material that might breach the law of confidence.

Similarly, in the *Granada* case,[33] although the court applied a balancing test, it gave no guidance to the weight to be granted to the different interests. Granada Television broadcasted a program devoted to a steel strike. The program quoted from secret or confidential documents of the British Steel Corporation. Pursuant to British Steel's order of discovery, the lower court ordered Granada to reveal the source of the confidential documents. The Court of Appeal dismissed Granada's appeal, and the House of Lords affirmed. It held, *inter alia*, that the press had no immunity based on a public interest from the obligation to disclose its sources in court when the interests of justice required disclosure. The courts considered neither the importance of newsgathering nor the need for any special interest concerning protection of sources.[34]

The courts have occasionally protected journalists. However, at the same time the courts have not been slow to condone the recent resurrection of long-forgotten crimes. Blasphemous libel, a subspecies of criminal libel, was revived by a charge against the magazine *Gay News* in December 1976.[35] Criminal libel, too, turned out to be alive and well in the mid-1970s when it was invoked against the magazine *Private Eye*.[36]

By contrast with American law,[37] there is no English doctrine that entitles expression that exposes governmental misbehavior to a higher level of protection than other expression. It is hardly surprising therefore that English libel law has not developed any special rule to encourage the right of free public discussion of the stewardship of public officials. Indeed, the position is to the contrary. Undoubtedly the libel laws in their present form have had a chilling effect on press freedom.[38]

Criticism of the present state of English law relating to the press is directed at several levels. The main criticism is that the courts have failed to provide any proper analysis of the basic values underlying freedom of the press and as a consequence have developed no coherent doctrinal criteria for regulating press freedom with a libertarian spirit. I believe that only the enactment of some form of constitutional guarantee of press freedom[39] will stimulate judicial sensitivity to free speech jurisprudence.

## THE PRESS AND THE GOVERNMENT

Few deny the need for protecting certain information in the interests of national security. Similarly, few consider the present state of the law in the United Kingdom on the disclosure of information to be satisfactory. As one commentator has observed, "In recent decades there has been a marked tendency on the part of the executive to interpret the public interest more in terms of its own efficiency than in terms of popular control, and a by-product of this tendency has been a growth in executive secrecy."[40] Despite demands for change, those tendencies have become even more marked during the last decade. A new balance must be struck between secrecy and security on the one hand and the legitimate demands for an informed public opinion on the other.

## The Offical Secrets Acts, 1911–1939[41]

Until 1889 no legislation prohibited disclosure of official secrets. The present law is contained in the Official Secrets Acts of 1911, 1920, and 1939. The Acts have two distinct purposes: to protect the state against espionage and other activities that might aid an enemy, and to guard against the unauthorized disclosure of information held by public employees in their official capacity, whether or not the information is related to national security. The 1911 Act was passed as "emergency legislation,"[42] "aimed mainly at espionage."[43] There is no doubt, however, that the legislation has, and was intended to have, a wider scope. Despite its innocuous title,[44] "An Act to re-enact the Official Secrets Acts, 1889, with Amendments," the 1911 Act, together with the Acts of 1920 and 1939, constitutes a formidable obstacle to the free communication of information regarding governmental activity and the free expression of opinion.[45]

Section 1(1) of the 1911 Act prohibits the process of gathering or communicating official information. Under section 1(2) if such information is proved to have been obtained or communicated by any unauthorized person, the accused carries the burden of proving that the purpose was not prejudicial to the safety or interests of the state. If no evidence exists to show a prejudicial purpose, the accused may still be convicted "if from the circumstances of the case, or his conduct, or his known character as proved, it appears that his purpose was...prejudicial to the interests or safety of the State."[46]

Both the section's marginal note, "Penalties for spying,"[47] and the parliamentary debates make clear that section 1 was directed against spying.[48] Nevertheless, the section is open to a wider interpretation.[49] It clearly bites on the publication of information about defense matters.[50]

In practice, section 1 charges are usually laid only in cases involving spying for a foreign power. In the recent case of *R. v. Berry, Campbell and Aubrey*,[51] however, espionage was not an issue. Rather, the charges under both sections 1 and 2 of the Official Secrets Act arose out of an interview with Berry, a former corporal in the Intelligence Corps, conducted by Aubrey and Campbell, both journalists. The section 1 charge against Campbell rested on a massive volume of documents found in his possession relating to the country's defense communications system. The defense established that a considerable proportion of the material was publicly available in various publications[52]; it argued that since each individual piece of information was not protected by the Act, it would be contrary to common sense to assert that the mere possession and compilation of this information should amount to an offense.[53] The trial judge was not prepared to limit the applicability of section 1 to spying or sabotage cases. He held, however, that section 1 should be invoked only in the clearest and most serious cases,[54] and this was not such a case. During the proceedings, the section 1 charges were dropped. Subsequently, both the initial section 1 charges and their withdrawal led to criticism of the Attorney General.[55] His consent to the withdrawal of the charges called into question his original decision to lay the charges.[56]

Section 2 of the 1911 Act[57] is designed to prevent the wrongful communication of certain types of information. The main offense is the unauthorized communication of official information by any person who holds or has held office under Her Majesty,[58] including government contractors and their employees. Catching all information without distinction, it plainly extends beyond crown secrets to information that bears no relation to the security of the state.[59] Moreover, the information need not be secret or confidential. Indeed, the language is broad enough to cover any information which anyone holding office, however humble, receives in confidence.[60] Section 2 creates over 2,000 differently worded offenses,[61] and even "makes it a crime, without any possibility of defence, to report the number of cups of tea consumed each week in a government department."[62] Further, any person who comes into possession of official information "which has been made or obtained in contravention of the Official Secrets Act" is prohibited from disclosing it without authorization. The difficulty for the press is that journalists obtain an important part of their information about government business from personal investigation, intelligent deduction, and unauthorized leaks from within the government or defense industries. Thus, the law can be used to prohibit newspapers from printing information that they have obtained through their own resources.[63]

Section 2(2) prohibits the receipt of information by anyone with knowledge or with reasonable grounds to believe that the information is being communicated in contravention of the Act. The only defense available is for the accused to prove that the communication to him was contrary to his desire. That the accused did not intend to do anything to prejudice the safety or interests of the state is no defense.[64] Clearly, section 2 is very far reaching and it has been heavily criticized as striking at "the very foundation of journalism."[65]

It is still uncertain whether, and if so, what, *mens rea* must be proved. The Act "contains nothing to imply directly that mens rea is an ingredient of the offence."[66] It may well be that no *mens rea* is required beyond an intention to cause the *actus reus* of the offense. In the *Sunday Telegraph* case,[67] four defendants, including a military officer, a journalist, and a newspaper editor, were prosecuted under section 2. The charges arose out of the communication and receipt of a confidential assessment of the Nigerian Civil War written by a defense adviser at the British High Commission in Lagos ("the Scott Report"). The court directed the jury that an intention to commit the offense had to be proved on the part of all the persons involved in the chain of communication.

Hundreds of technical contraventions of the section occur every day, yet prosecutions have been few. Since 1945, they have averaged about one a year.[68] One reason for the small number of prosecutions is that the Attorney General must consent to each prosecution.[69] The other, and perhaps more important, reason is that ministers and civil servants "authorize themselves" to convey information about matters of government. By this practice of self-authorization many officials decide for themselves how much information to disclose depending on the nature of their job and the circumstances of the case.[70]

In *R.* v. *Berry, Campbell and Aubrey*,[71] all three defendants were convicted of section 2 offenses.[72] Berry[73] was convicted of communicating information without authority and sentenced to six months imprisonment suspended for two years. The two journalists, Campbell and Aubrey, were convicted of receiving information and abetting the receipt of information respectively. Each was given a conditional discharge for three years, and ordered to pay heavy costs.[74]

Section 2 has been vigorously criticized. In the *Sunday Telegraph* case the court commented that the section should be "pensioned off."[75] Its broad scope allows a claim of public interest not involving any issue of national security to interfere with the freedom of the press. The Franks Committee criticized its "extreme width" and "considerable uncertainty." It viewed the section "as an ancient blunderbuss, scattering shot in all directions, need[ing] replacement by a modern weapon."[76]

A general theme of the evidence before the Franks Committee was the important distinction between espionage and leaks. The former concerns those who intend to help an enemy. The latter concerns those who disclose information with no such intent. The Official Secrets Acts should be confined to the former. Journalists in particular find it offensive that performing their job may place them in peril of prosecution under Acts meant for spies and traitors.[77] As the Franks Committee noted, "Section 2 is rarely activated in the courtroom, but it is seen by many as having a pervasive influence on the work and behavior of hundreds of thousands of people."[78] Too often the Official Secrets Acts are used to muzzle criticism.[79]

The Franks Committee proposed that section 2 be repealed and replaced by a separate statute containing narrower and more specific provisions which would be known as the "Official Information Act."[80] Following the repeal of section 2, the remaining provisions of the Official Secrets Acts would be more appropriately called "the Espionage Act." While the committee's proposals would restrict the ambit of the criminal law, they are in no sense radical.[81] The types of conduct most commonly selected for prosecution under section 2 would be covered by one or more of the exceptions to disclosure in any Official Information Act, and the breadth of the exceptions themselves would create problems.[82] Overclassification would still occur, and the difficulties inherent in the concept of self-authorization would remain.

The Franks Committee recommended the establishment of an advisory committee on classification. This would be some safeguard against political control.[83]

Mere receipt of information would not be an offense under the Franks Committee's proposals. Legislation to implement these reforms has been promised repeatedly since 1972.[84] Had these promises been kept, the journalists in *R. v. Berry, Campbell and Aubrey* could not have been prosecuted.[85]

## The D Notice System[86]

There is no formal system of censorship in the United Kingdom. There is, however, an informal system in the form of a nonstatutory Services, Press and Broadcasting Committee, which has a senior civil servant as chairman.[87] The primary function of the committee is to approve and issue D Notices.[88] These are letters sent by the secretary of the committee to editors[89] requesting that material relating to military matters not be published because of a prejudicial effect on the national interest.[90] The secretary of the committee may then advise editors on the interpretation of notices. The system is aimed at preventing publication of top secret defense matters. Thus, D Notices relate primarily to defense.[91]

Noncompliance with a D Notice is not an offense in itself. The system is entirely voluntary and has no legal effect.[92] Failure to comply, however, may result in prosecution for breach of the Official Secrets Acts.[93] Although nothing in the system relieves an editor of his responsibilities under the Acts, compliance with the request is, in practice, a safeguard against prosecution.[94]

The system depends on "the essential element of trust."[95] A number of alleged and actual breaches of the system have received considerable publicity. For example, the names of the head of M.I.5. and M.I.6.[96] have been published in contravention of a D Notice. Further, an alleged breach in 1967 led to what became known as the "D Notice Affair."[97] The *Daily Express* published a report that private cables and telegrams sent overseas from the United Kingdom were regularly intercepted and made available to the Security Services for examination.[98] A committee of three privy councillors under the chairmanship of Lord Radcliffe was appointed to look into the matter. Their report concluded that "there had been a misunderstanding."[99] Certainly when a D Notice is vaguely worded it may be unclear as to where the line should be drawn between information which can be disclosed and that which cannot. It was partly with this problem in mind that in 1971 the D Notices were rewritten and reduced in number to 12.[100]

There can be little doubt, however, that the relationship between the government and the press was strained by the D Notice Affair. It highlighted the danger of overextending the concept of security.[101] Three years earlier, the Court of Appeal observed "a desire in the official mind to push ever forward the frontiers of secrecy."[102] The Radcliffe Committee saw no alternative to the D Notice system other than compulsory censorship[103]; and direct press censorship would probably be unacceptable in Britain except in times of great emergency.[104] More recently, the Commons Select Committee on Defence recommended reform of the D Notice system.[105] The committee was highly critical of the system:

> [I]t is clear that the [D Notice] system...is failing to fulfill the role for which it was created. If...the system is not used by newspapers; if major newspapers do not know what part of the D Notices is classified and have not consulted the D Notices for a number of years; and, in one case, admitted to having lost them; if some categories of sensitive information are not covered; if both foreign and fringe press are outside the system; if the wording of the D Notices is so wide as to render them meaningless; if the D Notice Committee only finds it necessary to meet twice a year and then does not seriously review the Notices themselves, having had no single amendment proposed from the press side in nearly 10 years; we are forced to the conclusion that...the system hardly serves a useful purpose.[106]

There are two main criticisms of the system. First, it is a form of censorship, stimulating secrecy in a society that is already over secretive. Second, it can be used by the government to suppress information for reasons of political convenience, when publication would not endanger national security.[107] Thus, allegedly national security information often includes items merely of national interest, such as foreign relations and the conduct of the economy. It is a system peculiar to the United Kingdom and appears to be a remnant from the days when "the men in Whitehall" knew what was best for the country. Experience has proved they are not always correct.[108] Certainly it is difficult to understand why D Notices should be used to prevent the press and the public from knowing what our enemies or potential enemies already know. The result is a serious lack of informed public discussion on the important issues of defense, technology, and foreign affairs.[109] Furthermore, the general language of the D Notices has led to criticism that they are out of touch with modern circumstances. One useful reform would be to publish confidential appendices to the D Notices, detailing specific advice on particular matters and updating current developments in the defense field.[110]

## Other Statutes

### Treason

Treason, the most serious offense against the state, carries a mandatory sentence of the death penalty. Although the Treason Act of 1351 remains the basis of the present law of treason,[111] the concept of treason has been transformed. It has changed "from that founded upon a breach of a feudal and personal duty of loyalty to the reigning monarch into the modern concept which regards treason as 'armed resistance made on political grounds to the public order of the realm.' "[112] One form of treason is to adhere to the King's enemies in his realm, giving them aid or comfort.[113] Considering that treason carries a heavy penalty and that its most important form concerns acts of disloyalty in time of war, it has been suggested correctly that the offense and the persons to whom it applies be defined precisely.[114]

### Sedition

The law of sedition is of the common law.[115] The 1951 Canadian decision, *Boucher* v. *R.*,[116] probably representing good English law,[117] reflects the modern doctrinal approach to sedition. Boucher, a Jehovah's Witness, was convicted of seditious libel for publishing a pamphlet alleging persecution of Jehovah's Witnesses. The pamphlet referred to individual and mob attacks, to police animosity to the sect, and to public officials and Roman Catholic clergy who were allegedly behind the prosecutions lodged against members of the sect.[118] On appeal, the Supreme Court quashed the defendant's conviction and directed an acquittal.[119] The court referred to the historical vagueness of the offense of sedition and emphasized that the modern law of sedition requires more than proof of an intention to promote feelings of ill will and hostility between different classes. To convict of sedition, there must be "an intention to incite to violence...for the purpose of disturbing constituted authority."[120]

Despite the narrowing interpretation of sedition, one important and difficult question remains unresolved: the *mens rea* that must be proved to constitute the offense. In *R.* v. *Caunt*, Devlin J. indicated that the mental element should not be diluted and he cautioned the jury that "nothing should be done in this court to weaken the liberty of the press."[121] Both the press and the principle of free speech would be served best by limiting the offense of sedition through application of the incitement doctrine. Thus, conviction would follow only if a person (1) has intended to incite violence or public disorder or disturbance (2) with the intention thereby of disturbing constituted authority.[122]

There have been few prosecutions for sedition. The standard reference works cite only three post-1909 cases[123]: *Boucher* v. *R.*[124]; *Wallace-Johnson* v. *R.*[125]; and *R.* v. *Caunt*.[126] In *Wallace-Johnson*, the defendant had been convicted of seditious libel for publishing an article critical of colonial rule in a Gold Coast Colony newspaper. The Privy Council affirmed the West African Court of Appeal's dismissal of the defendant's appeal. In *R.* v. *Caunt*, the editor of a local paper in North Lancashire was prosecuted for having published an article attacking British Jewry shortly after the bodies of two British sergeants were discovered in Palestine. He was acquitted of the charge of seditious libel. In the last 18 years there has been only one proceeding brought for sedition.[127]

The offense is not obsolescent, however. It appears in the Criminal Law Act of 1967, which punishes "offences against the Queen's title, prerogative, person or government."[128] Further, recent experience in relation to other offenses generates caution.[129] More important, as has occurred in modern times in areas under British colonial rule, an insecure executive might resort to it again in times of crisis.[130] The relative disuse of the offense of sedition owes much to its vagueness, to the possible unpopularity of the crime with juries, and to its unhappy historical associations with a palpably undemocratic past. Furthermore, use of the offense is not necessary to protect the government. In times of real crisis, defense regulations and emergency powers are more readily invoked. The provisional view of the Law Commissioners is that there is no need for an offense of sedition in the criminal code.[131] If the definition of sedition is restricted to that expressed in *Boucher* v. *R.*,[132] then in any event proof of incitement or conspiracy to break the law would be required, and these elements exist as offenses independent from the offense of seditious libel. In view of twentieth century developments, it seems quite improbable that the law of sedition will be used to suppress political dissent.[133]

### Incitement to Disaffection and Mutiny[134]

English law protects the armed forces and the police from attempts to subvert their allegiance or persuade them to disobey orders.[135] The Incitement to Mutiny Act of 1797 was passed following the mutiny of the Navy at Nore.[136] The Incitement to Disaffection Act of 1934[137] creates two offenses. Section 1 proscribes attempts to subvert members of the armed forces from their duty or allegiance.[138] Under section 2 it is an offense to possess, with the intent to violate section 1, any documents that, if disseminated, would constitute such an offense.[139] The law does not require that the expression be directed against any named individuals; it may be addressed to the forces generally. "Knowledge" is, however, required. An accused may be convicted only if he knew the person was a member of the armed forces.[140] Furthermore, the expression must be addressed "wilfully and maliciously"; recklessness does not suffice.

The Act passed in Parliament against vociferous opposition.[141] The government denied that it was a panic measure and claimed that it was merely designed to prevent sedition without having to rely on the 1797 Act.[142] Nonetheless, the Act broadened the scope of the 1797 Act.[143]

The Act is of wide application. Any advocacy of a policy which conflicts with a government policy relative to specific duties can be regarded as an "endeavour to seduce." The Act could be invoked against persons distributing pacifist literature, left-wing literature, poems, or even the Bible to members of the forces.[144] Some critics point out that the law is not likely to be effective since servicemen may, on their own initiative, read literature which may lead to disaffection. Others insist that as a matter of principle soldiers should be allowed to form their own opinions.

Prosecutions had been rare until the 1970s. Between 1973 and 1975 members of a campaign for the withdrawal of British troops from Northern Ireland were prosecuted because of certain leaflets they had prepared. In 1974, Pat Arrowsmith, a pacifist and leader of the campaign, was convicted of possessing and distributing literature in the army barracks at Warminster. The literature included leaflets entitled "Some Information for Discontented Soldiers." In 1975, fourteen persons were prosecuted for conspiracy to seduce soldiers from their duty or allegiance and for possession of documents similar in content to those in the *Arrowsmith* case. All were acquitted. In the opinion of Professor Street, "their acquittal shows that juries can be relied upon to acquit where the accused do nothing more than express their views on the Government's military policy in Ulster and give advice about how soldiers may legally obtain their discharge."[145]

Despite assertions that the Act is no longer a serious threat to liberty,[146] it needs reform. It should clarify its purpose of penalizing only those who endeavor to seduce and explicitly require an intention to seduce a member of the forces from his allegiance.[147]

## Access to Governmental Information

### *Public Records Acts, 1958 and 1967*

The Public Records Acts, 1958 and 1967,[148] lay down procedures for the preservation and availability of official records, including cabinet papers, for public inspection.[149] Under the normal practice, documents are transferred to the Public Record Office and become available for public inspection after 30 years.[150] The Lord Chancellor has the power to vary the period for nondisclosure at the request of the relevant minister or other person primarily concerned. Each case is also considered by the Advisory Council on Public Records, the Chairman of which is the Master of the Rolls.[151] Regrettably, the period of nondisclosure for documents that may be of real interest is usually lengthened rather than shortened. Discussion of public issues is thereby inhibited even further.[152]

In practice, documents falling into certain categories, and certain individual documents selected ad hoc by reference to their contents, are retained beyond 30 years.[153] Among the 1947 cabinet papers that were not made available in 1978, on the expiration of the 30-year period, were minutes of the historic meeting at which a select group of ministers decided to manufacture a British atomic bomb.[154]

The decision to postpone disclosure is not always conscious and rational. Recently, cabinet papers relating to the last years of the British Mandate in Palestine were withheld. On investigation it was discovered that the fault lay with the bureaucracy. After reading the papers that were subsequently released, Lord Bethell, the historian, commented: "The idea that they contain anything...harmful to national security or even to our diplomatic position is quite absurd. The whole thing leads one to question what other totally harmless but very interesting documents are still closed or being held...."[155] Too often "national security" is invoked to preserve the decision making process from scrutiny when no real danger to the security of the country would result from publication.[156] Reportedly, steps now have been taken to ensure that the withholding of any cabinet papers beyond 30 years be approved at the highest level within the Cabinet Office.[157]

Concern has also been expressed over the preservation of public records in general. The quantity of paper involved and the lack of available storage space has resulted in destruction of many documents.[158]

### Cabinet Papers

Present or former cabinet ministers who wish to refer to cabinet papers during the period when the documents are protected by the Public Records Acts are required by convention to obtain the consent of the Secretary to the Cabinet.[159] Powerful political forces operate to prevent current cabinet ministers from publishing cabinet documents or releasing details of cabinet discussions to the press. Until 1975, it was not clear that a minister had any legal obligation not to reveal "secrets" of the cabinet which did not fall within the prohibition of the Official Secrets Acts.[160]

In 1975, the Divisional Court declared in the *Crossman Diaries* case[161] that the courts can restrain publication of cabinet secrets in certain limited circumstances. In this case, the Attorney General failed to obtain an injunction restraining publication of the first volume of the diaries of the late Mr. Richard Crossman, a cabinet minister from 1964 until 1970. Throughout that period Mr. Crossman was candid about keeping a diary containing details of discussions held in the Cabinet and in cabinet committees. It was his ambition "to write a book which fulfilled for our generation the function of Bagehot's 'English Constitution' 100 years ago by disclosing the secret operations of Government which are concealed by the thick mass of foliage which we call the myth of democracy."[162]

The Divisional Court declined to ban the publication. Lord Widgery, C.J., stated: "I am far from convinced that the Attorney General has made out a case that the public interest requires such a Draconian remedy when due regard is had to other public interests, such as the freedom of speech."[163] The court did, however, recognize an obligation of secrecy and confidentiality for cabinet information.[164] That obligation, the court held, stemmed not from the secrecy oath but from the doctrine of collective responsibility, whereby a policy decision reached by the Cabinet must thereafter be supported by all members of the Cabinet, whether they approve of it or not.[165] The confidentiality of cabinet discussions promoted the doctrine of collective responsibility. In balancing the interests in confidentiality and free speech, the issue of timing was crucial. The court rejected the proposition that despite an interval of 11 years the publication of the diaries "would inhibit free discussion in the Cabinet of today."[166] In a dictum, however, the court did add that in extreme cases, for example those involving matters affecting national security, the courts can restrain publication, and further that "[s]ecrets relating to national security may require to be preserved indefinitely."[167] To prompt court intervention the government must demonstrate that the overriding public interest in nondisclosure is still valid. This was not such a case. The *Crossman Diaries* decision is grounded in ad hoc considerations and fails to give any real guidance as to how and when the courts will intervene.

### The Radcliffe Committee on Ministerial Memoirs

After the *Crossman Diaries* case, the government set up the Committee on Ministerial Memoirs under the chairmanship of Viscount Radcliffe to review the existing conventions. The government accepted the committee's proposals in 1976.[168] The new system was used recently in connection with the publication of Professor A.V. Jones' book, *Most Secret War*.[169] In his book, Professor Jones, a former scientific advisor to M.I.6 and associate director of intelligence at the Air Ministry, referred to Britain's secret scientific intelligence operations during the Second World War. When documents containing wartime intelligence information were released under the "30 year rule,"[170] former intelligence officers were given permission to write their memoirs but were asked to submit their manuscripts to their former departments and to the D Notice Committee of the Ministry of Defence.[171] Professor Jones submitted his book to the present head of M.I.6, who suggested various deletions. For example, he was asked to omit the names of the security service agents with whom he had collaborated in 1944. They had planted false information in German counter-intelligence in London. He agreed to the requested deletions and was given permission to publish.

### Conclusion

Disclosure of information is an area in which "it is exceedingly difficult to maintain a just equilibrium between competing interests."[172] For there to be effective government, the principle of confidentiality cannot be abandoned completely. Yet, it is most unfortunate that, as Professor Street has observed,

> the government and the senior members of the opposition agree on one thing: that the less the public knows about the process of decision making the better. Whether this is an understandable confusion of what is politically and administratively convenient with what is in the public interest may well be asked.[173]

It may be proper for the balance to continue to be tilted in favor of national security rather than in favor of disclosure. Too often, however, the system "installs as the judges of what ought to be revealed men whose interest it is to conceal."[174] Nevertheless, the decisions in *Conway* v. *Rimmer*, the *Crossman Diaries* case, and *Burmah Oil Co. Ltd.* v. *Bank of England*,[175] at least have established two points: the principle of judicial review and the balancing of interests as the proper judicial approach. Those who desire a right of access similar to that existing in the United States were disappointed by the failure of the Franks Report to recommend such legislation. The continued refusal of successive governments to introduce a Freedom of Information Act has led to increased criticism and demand for reform.[176]

## THE PRESS AND THE JUDICIAL PROCESS

### Free Press and Fair Trial

The law relating to contempt of court[177] has developed over the centuries as a means whereby the courts may prevent or punish conduct that tends to obstruct, prejudice, or abuse the administration of justice either in relation to a particular case or generally.[178] Any conduct tending to bring the authority and administration of the law into disrespect or to interfere with litigation is a contempt of court.[179] In the past, the contempt power has evoked concern on a number of points. First, the law, especially as it affects the press, is quite vague. Second, the contempt power may unduly inhibit freedom of expression. Finally, the summary process may lack the procedural fairness thought essential for orthodox criminal proceedings.[180]

Uncertainty as to the scope of the law of contempt stems in part from the law's historical development. Until 1960 a finding of contempt was not appealable.[181] Thus, the law, which was judge-made common law with a few statutory modifications, had to be gleaned from a large number of first instance decisions covering a wide variety of conduct. Moreover, contempt is triable summarily by judge alone and, until recently, was punishable by an unlimited period of imprisonment or fine.[182] Uncertainty in the law had created a "chilling effect" on the press. As one leading editor commented, "I probably spend more time worrying about the possibility of contempt of court than I do about all the other legal restrictions put together."[183] No better illustration of the uncertain state of the law, prior to the Contempt of Court Act, 1981, exists than the variety of judicial opinions expressed in the *Sunday Times* case.[184]

In September 1972, the *Sunday Times* published a leading article on the tragedy of the deformed children born to women who had taken the drug thalidomide during pregnancy. The article stated that the story shamed English society and English law and that Distillers, the manufacturer of the drug, "should offer much, much more" than they were offering in settlement of pending legal actions. The Attorney General decided not to move against the newspaper over the first article. He did, however, attempt to prevent the paper from publishing a second article that discussed the manufacturing and marketing of the drug and suggested there was a strong case in negligence against Distillers. The government argued that publication of the second article would be a criminal contempt of court as it might affect the long-standing pending civil litigation between the thalidomide victims' parents and Distillers.

The Divisional Court granted the injunction on the ground that the article was a contempt of court. The Court of Appeal unanimously reversed the lower court, but on further appeal, the House of Lords reimposed the injunction.[185] Although agreeing with the Divisional Court that litigants must be protected from "scurrilous abuse," the majority of their Lordships held that private and even public persuasion was permitted. Nevertheless, each member of the House ruled against the proposed article. The House of Lords balanced the interests in freedom of speech and in the administration of justice, and formulated an absolute rule: publication that prejudges any issue in pending proceedings is in contempt, even if it only created a small risk of interference with the course of justice.

The *Sunday Times* filed an application with the European Commission of Human Rights, claiming that the injunction violated its right to freedom of expression guaranteed by Article 10 of the European Convention for the Protection of Human Rights and Fundamental Freedoms.[186] The commission referred the case to the European Court of Human Rights, which upheld the claim of the *Sunday Times* by a majority of 11 to 9.[187] Unlike the House of Lords, the European Court of Human Rights found it was "faced not with a choice between two conflicting principles, but with a principle of freedom of expression that is subject to a number of exceptions which must be narrowly interpreted."[188] The court held that Article 10 guarantees not only the freedom of the press to inform the public, but also the right of the public to be properly informed.[189] It further found that because the families of numerous victims had a vital interest in disclosure, they could be deprived of the information "only if it appeared absolutely certain that its diffusion would have presented a threat to the 'authority of the judiciary.'"[190] The court concluded that the reasons given for the injunction were insufficient under Article 10(2) of the Convention: "it was not necessary in a democratic society for maintaining the authority of the judiciary."[191]

The *Sunday Times* case showed again[192] that it is difficult to reconcile English law with international obligations undertaken by the United Kingdom as a party to the European Convention.[193] The case was also the focus of criticism before the Phillimore Committee, appointed in 1971 to consider the law of contempt.[194] The committee criticized the prejudgment test formulated by the House of Lords as excessively vague[195] and proposed that any definition of contempt refer directly to the "mischief which the law . . . is and always has been designed to suppress . . . the risk of prejudice to the due administration of justice."[196]

Parliament adopted many of the Phillimore Committee's proposals in the Contempt of Court Act, 1981 (the 1981 Act). Yet the 1981 Act is far from clear. It does not define a contempt of court.[197] Furthermore, it yields two very different forms of criminal contempt. The first category is defined by the Act. By section 1 it consists of conduct which tends to interfere with the course of justice, in particular, legal proceedings. By section 2(2) a publication[198] is a contempt if it "creates a substantial risk that the course of justice in the proceedings in question will be seriously impeded or prejudiced," regardless of any intent to interfere with the legal proceedings. A person who makes such a publication is strictly liable for it. The second category comprises all other forms of criminal contempt, including publications which fall outside the definition of the 1981 Act. *Mens rea* is a necessary constituent of this category of contempt.[199] It is sufficient if the "contempt" complained of creates a definite but small likelihood of interference with particular proceedings or the administration of justice in general.[200] Although the 1981 Act is purported to bring the law into conformity with the European Convention on Human Rights, whether it has in fact succeeded remains uncertain.

Section 5 of the 1981 Act provides that it is not a contempt if a publication is made "as or as part of a discussion in good faith of public affairs or other matters of general public interest . . . if the risk of impediment or prejudice to particular legal proceedings is merely incidental to the discussion." In *Attorney General* v. *English*,[201] the House of Lords considered the effect of this section. In October 1981, while the trial of Dr. Arthur, a consultant pediatrician charged with the murder of a baby suffering from Down's syndrome, was in progress, the *Daily Mail* published an article[202] in support of an independent pro-life candidate at a parliamentary by-election. The article was concerned in general terms with the moral question of allowing handicapped babies to die. There was no mention in the article of Dr. Arthur's trial. The Divisional Court, taking a very narrow view of section 5, had found the newspaper guilty of contempt. However, the House of Lords disagreed and allowed the appeal. Lord Diplock said that the section was not intended to prevent the suppression of bona fide discussion in the media of controversial matters of public interest merely by reason that contemporaneous legal proceedings existed in which some particular instance of those controversial matters might be at issue.[203] Moreover it was for the Attorney General to prove that a publication did not fall within section 5 and that the risk of prejudice to a fair trial was not "merely incidental" to the discussion. In the present case, the proposition that pediatricians commonly allowed severely handicapped children to die was integral to the cause for which the pro-life candidate was campaigning and to the wider public discussion on the moral justifiability of mercy killing and of allowing newly born, hopelessly handicapped babies to die. The risk of the article prejudicing the fair trial of Dr. Arthur was no more than an incidental consequence of expounding the main theme of discussion on a matter of general public interest.[204] However, it would not seem that section 5 would have protected the *Sunday Times* from contempt in respect of their second article on Distillers. Lord Diplock described the article that was the subject of the case in *Attorney General* v. *English* "to be in nearly all respects the antithesis of the article" in the *Sunday Times* case.[205]

A matter of real concern is that the House of Lords in *English* agreed with the Divisional Court that the article did "create a substantial risk that the course of justice in the proceedings in question will be seriously impeded or prejudiced."[206] The risk that has to be assessed is that which was created by the publication at the time it was published without regard to the ultimate result of the proceedings.[207] Lord Diplock interpreted the words "substantial" and "seriously" as "intended to exclude a risk that is only remote."[208] Since the article suggested that it was a common practice among pediatricians to do what Dr. Arthur had been charged with doing, the risk that it would seriously prejudice the course or outcome of the trial was not remote, and accordingly section 2(2) was satisfied. However, such an interpretation would appear to rob the words and the subsection of all meaning.[209]

The 1981 Act redefines and delimits the time during which the law of contempt obtains. Previously, contempt could be found for comment on matters that were *sub judice*, pending or imminent,[210] even though not yet initiated.[211] Those time periods were ambiguous. For example, in 1967, David Frost interviewed Dr. Savundra on television concerning his management of the Fire, Auto and Marine Insurance Company. The matter concerned thousands of car insurance policy holders. Seven days later, Dr. Savundra was arrested and subsequently tried and convicted of conspiracy to defraud. He appealed his conviction on the ground that the interview amounted to "trial by television" and prejudiced his defense. The Court of Appeal dismissed the appeal but added that the television program was intolerable and deplorable. The court was heard to say that if it was "obvious to all" that an arrest was about to be made, the proceedings were "imminent."[212]

The Phillimore Committee found these rules unfair and sought clearer criteria. The 1981 Act, following the committee's recommendations, applies the "strict liability rule"[213] only when the proceedings in question are "active," and establishes criteria for determining that stage.[214] Separate criteria are created for criminal, civil, and appellate proceedings.

"Criminal proceedings" are active from the taking of the "initial step" in the proceedings until they are concluded. Included in the "initial steps" are arrest without warrant and the issue of a warrant for arrest.[215] In two respects the new law is less satisfactory than before. Previously, the strict liability rule attached only when an arrest or a charge was imminent; now it attaches as soon as the warrant has been issued, even if no imminent arrest is contemplated. This rule may lead to suppression of information vital to the public interest between issue of a warrant for arrest and an actual arrest, which may be months later.[216] It would be preferable if the "initial step" was the charge, rather than the arrest. A journalist may not know whether a person who is with the police, after a crime has been committed, has actually been arrested, or is merely helping the police with their inquiries.

Civil proceedings are active from the time when arrangements for the hearing are made; if no such arrangements are made, they are active from the time that the hearing begins until the proceedings are disposed of, discontinued, or withdrawn.[217] Although it provides a considerable improvement over the previous law, arguably the period should be further limited, perhaps to two weeks before trial, since months may pass between the setting down of a case for trial and the actual hearing date.[218]

Certainly, however, these new rules should end the justifiable complaints from the press about "gagging" writs. Only too often at the very moment a newspaper publishes the first in a series of investigative reports, its subject issues a writ for libel against the newspaper, intending to prevent publication of further incriminating matter. In the *Sunday Times* case, the House of Lords followed previous judges in condemning this practice.[219] Yet the press was understandably hesitant about continuing their series of articles after the issue of the writ for libel. However, as Lord

Denning has observed, "No professionally trained judge should be influenced by anything he reads in the newspapers or sees on television. Thus in the case of a civil action which is to be tried by a judge it should be very rare indeed that a newspaper would be guilty of contempt by making comments on it."[220]

Finally, "appellate proceedings" become active from the time when they commence, either by application for leave to appeal or for review, or even by notice of such application, until they are disposed of, abandoned, discontinued, or withdrawn.[221] It is to be regretted that the law of contempt may fetter free comment merely because an application for leave to appeal has been made. Arguably, strong adverse criticism of long sentences, such as those following the Great Train Robbery trials, now could not be made with guaranteed immunity. In a criminal case, an intimation to the court that an appeal is under consideration may be interpreted as preservation of the proceedings as "active" for purposes of the 1981 Act.[222] Even though appeal is possible, once a case has been decided no substantial reason for prosecution of contempt seems to remain. Experienced judges of the Court of Criminal Appeal would alone decide the appeal and they should be relied upon to be completely uninfluenced by press reports.[223] Indeed, the law of contempt should not extend to appellate proceedings at all.

Section 2(3) of the 1981 Act merely restricts the application of the strict liability rule. It does not provide that prejudicial publications outside the active period cannot be contempts, although they will only be so if *mens rea* is shown. Section 6(1) of the Act specifically provides that nothing in the foregoing provisions of the Act restricts liability for contempt of court in respect of conduct intended to impede or prejudice the administration of justice. At common law the restraints of contempt apply to imminent criminal proceedings. Prejudicial publications in this period may still be a contempt if *mens rea* is present. On principle the contemnor must know the publication contains matter capable of prejudicing particular proceedings. He must know the proceedings are pending or imminent, and he must intend to prejudice those proceedings. It may be that if he is reckless as to any or all of these requirements he will also be guilty.[224]

However, if a contempt may be committed by recklessness[225] this may cause difficulties where investigative journalism is involved. There are instances where a newspaper investigates a crime of which the police know nothing; but once the details of the investigation are published proceedings may be considered imminent. Indeed it does not appear that the proceedings affected in *Attorney General* v. *Times Newspapers* had been set down for trial at the time of publication.[226] For that reason the strict liability rule would not have applied. Yet it seems plain that the article would be held to be an intentional contempt for raising a real, although small, risk of prejudice to proceedings.[227] Thus the only basis on which the case would have been differently decided is if the defense of fair and temperate pressure on a litigant applies to intentional contempt.[228]

The present state of the law is quite unsatisfactory. The 1981 Act omitted any general defense that the publication complained of was in fact a public benefit. For example, under the 1981 Act a series of connected frauds could not be exposed while a single related case is awaiting trial. This would result in the fact that the public would remain unwarned.[229] The Phillimore Committee considered a public benefit defense too vague and it was not included in the 1981 Act. Neither the committee nor the 1981 Act, however, deals adequately with one situation in which the defense of public interest should be accepted. The police frequently ask the press and television authorities to help them by publishing photographs of wanted criminals. Unless a special defense of public interest is recognized, the press would have no answer to a contempt charge if, at police request, they published a photograph of a prisoner who had escaped from custody while awaiting trial.[230] During passage of the bill, the Attorney General observed that it was proper for the police to be able to warn the public through the press and that the press should not fear publishing matter calculated to assist in the apprehension of a wanted man.[231] Nevertheless, in the absence of a public interest defense, investigative journalism such as uncovering of insurance frauds or revealing the unsafe nature of certain goods on sale to the public is still a risk.

The European Court of Human Rights, in the *Sunday Times* case, asked whether the injunction imposed on the *Sunday Times* corresponded to a social need so pressing as to exclude the general principle of freedom of speech. In effect, therefore, they were asking whether the injunction was for the public benefit.[232] Their answer involved balancing a variety of considerations, an exercise which the House of Lords rejected in the interests of certainty. The question whether the Act brings English law into line with the Convention may depend not on the provisions of the Act but on the existence of a defense of fair and temperate criticism of a litigant, and also on the degree to which, if at all, it is permissible to go beyond criticism and apply more practical pressure on litigants.[233] The Phillimore Committee recommended that bringing influence or pressure to bear on a party to proceedings should not be held to be a contempt unless it amounts to intimidation or unlawful threats to person, property, or reputation.[234] This recommendation is another important omission from the 1981 Act.[235]

Apart from the 1981 Act, there are other statutory provisions restricting the reporting of certain proceedings. Essentially, public policy reasons underlie these restrictions. These rules, as well as the procedures and penalties for their breach, are clear. Such restrictions include reporting details of (1) cases involving juveniles (persons under the age of 17) when names, photographs or particulars may lead to identification of the juvenile concerned[236]; (2) evidence of indecency and evidence in matrimonial proceedings[237]; (3) domestic proceedings[238]; (4) committal proceedings in which a preliminary hearing decides whether a sufficient case exists for a defendant to answer in a higher court[239]; (5) matters affecting national security[240]; and (6) under certain circumstances, the name of a defendant or complainant in rape trials.[241]

Section 4(2) of the 1981 Act affects the fourth of these categories, that is, committal proceedings. That subsection grants the court disturbingly broad discretion to postpone publication of any report of the proceedings for such period as the court thinks necessary.[242] No convincing case for this new power has been made.[243] In any event, such discretionary powers should be considerably more qualified and precise. The absence of any time limit is wholly unacceptable. Moreover, the section covers all proceedings in all courts. In a recent case involving committal proceedings before a Magistrates' Court,[244] the magistrates at the outset of the proceedings banned reporting of any information, including names, addresses, charges, and the decision of the justices until the case came to trial.[245] On appeal the courts held that the order was broader than necessary to protect the fair administration of justice and remitted for further consideration. Nevertheless, the press is likely to feel inhibited by this section. Although the magistrates' blanket ban was struck down, they were still permitted to make other orders prohibiting the reporting of the proceedings.[246]

The 1981 Act fails to address problems that can arise in the practice of journalism. For example, tacit assumptions of guilt may be prejudicial to a defendant. Criticism was made, although no proceedings were taken, of the conduct of both the police and press following the arrest of Peter Sutcliffe, the "Yorkshire Ripper."[247] After Sutcliffe's arrest, the police held a congratulatory press conference. The press then published photographs of the "Yorkshire Ripper," and detailed interviews with his family. Occasional injection of cautious phrases did not dispel the tacit assumption of guilt. The Solicitor General reminded editors "of the vital principle... that [an] accused...is presumed to be innocent and is entitled to a fair trial, and of the responsibility which the law...places upon editors...."[248]

Another problem arises from "checkbook journalism," despite the Press Council's attempts to crush the practice. Matters came to a head over the Moors murder trial. David Smith, the leading prosecution witness, stated that he was paid by the *News of the World* for giving his story to the newspaper, and that the size of the eventual payment depended on whether the accused were convicted. The newspaper acknowledged the agreement, but denied that payment was contingent on a guilty verdict. The Attorney General refused to prosecute the newspaper, expressing doubt whether payments to witnesses during a trial, in return for exclusive information after a trial, was contempt.[249] The 1977 Commission on the Press urged the Press Council to keep a special watch to ensure that such behavior is deterred.[250] However, the difficulty in framing any legislation on this subject without excluding the normal Fleet Street practice of paying for news is considerable.[251]

The Phillimore Committee recommended that the law of contempt no longer should apply to criticism of judges. Rather, there should be a new offense for imputing improper or corrupt judicial conduct, with a defense if the allegations were made for the public benefit. These proposals should be enacted. There is no need for a special crime of contempt in order to protect a judge's reputation.[252] In any event, if a judge's character is blackened, a defamation action is available. It is desirable that the performance of judges be subject to examination and comment. Even more obviously, the accuracy of the law laid down by them in their decisions should be subject to fearless scrutiny. In 1968, Mr. Quintin Hogg, now the Lord Chancellor, criticized the Court of Appeal in *Punch* magazine. In dismissing the application for contempt of court, Lord Denning stated: "No criticism of a judgment, however vigorous, can amount to contempt of court, provided it keeps within the elements of reasonable courtesy and good faith."[253] Nevertheless, the strict law is that to attribute a particular decision to the personal weakness of a judge is to suggest that he is incapable of administering impartial justice.

Another area in need of reform relates to contempt of Parliament. A citizen, whether a member of Parliament or not, who violates a parliamentary privilege or casts aspersions on the dignity of the House of Commons commits a contempt. The House of Commons views seriously any newspaper comments reflecting on the character of the House. For example, the introduction of gasoline rationing after the Suez expedition of 1956 brought forth a spate of cases. The *Sunday Express* suggested that politicians had allowed themselves to be unduly favored over supplementary petrol. The House of Commons held this to be a grave contempt by the editor.[254] The severity of the parliamentary law of contempt becomes evident when its procedures are examined. A person may be found guilty without a hearing and the House may issue a warrant and arrest anybody whom it suspects of committing contempt without giving any reason. Further, there is no right to representation or to cross-examine witnesses. When found guilty, the contemnor is expected humbly to apologize; his punishment is likely to be more severe if he does not. The powers of punishment are wide and include imprisonment. Yet trials of citizens should not be a function of the House of Commons: disciplining its members is one thing, punishing outsiders is another.[255]

The justifications that have developed for the law of contempt are an intrinsic part of the definition of contempt itself. Underlying any conflict is the partial emphasis given by the press and the judiciary respectively to goals that all agree are fundamental to political and social democracy. For the press, freedom of speech and the right to know are paramount. For the judiciary, it is the protection of the administration of justice, especially the right to a fair trial. Paradoxically there is only one case in which a conviction was quashed because of prejudicial publicity.[256]

The peculiar nature of the summary procedures that are followed when an alleged contempt is committed adds weight to the various criticisms of the contempt power.[257] In every sense the procedures are most unusual.[258] The Phillimore Committee recommended that certain criminal contempts be punishable only on indictment. In particular, it proposed that press interference with the administration of justice prior to the case be dealt with as contempt only if no other offense covers the conduct, or if there are particular reasons of urgency or practical necessity.[259] Regrettably, this approach is not reflected in the 1981 Act.

The rules formulated in the nineteenth century were a reaction to the growth of mass circulation newspapers, an increasingly powerful press, and many instances of flagrant abuse.[260] Hopefully, the 1981 Act will redress the balance by establishing that the public has a right to know and that the press must be free to gather and impart information subject only to the limited controls necessary to preserve a democratic society.

### Reporters' Privilege

In 1963 Parliament ordered an inquiry into newspaper allegations that there was a spy in the Admiralty. Two journalists were asked for the source of their allegations that "it was the sponsorship of two high-ranking officials which led to Vassall avoiding the strictest part of the Admiralty security vetting."[261] When they refused to reveal their source, the Attorney General moved to punish them for contempt of court. They were each sentenced to six months imprisonment. Lord Denning, M.R., observed: "[T]here is no privilege known to the law by which a journalist can refuse to answer a question which is relevant...and...which, in the opinion of the judge,... is proper...."[262]

In *British Steel Corp.* v. *Granada*, [263] the House of Lords confirmed this view. It held that journalists had no immunity based on public interest protecting them from the obligation to disclose their sources in court when such disclosure was necessary in the interests of justice.[264] Quite regrettably the House of Lords stated that the case did not "touch upon the freedom of the press even at its periphery."[265] Technically this view can be explained in light of the fact that Granada did not dispute that British Steel, if it had acted in time, could have obtained an injunction against publishing or reproducing the contents of the documents.[266] What is depressing about their Lordships' judgments is the emphasis on private as opposed to public rights.[267] Only Lord Salmon, in a minority of one, was prepared to consider the case in constitutional terms. His judgment concluded:

The immunity of the press to reveal its sources...save in exceptional circumstances is in the public interest, and has been so accepted by the courts for so long that I consider it is wrong now to sweep [it] away. The press has been deprived of that immunity only twice...[in matters of national security].... Moreover, there are no circumstances in this case which have ever before deprived or ever should deprive the press of its immunity.... The freedom of the press depends upon this immunity....[268]

The *Granada* case had proved the importance of the press role as watchdog of the government: the "Steel Papers" revealed serious mismanagement within British Steel and the government's covert intervention into the affairs of British Steel. It is difficult to understand how management of a huge, nationalized industry, which had lost billions of pounds of taxpayers' money, is not a matter of the utmost public interest.[269] Even in the absence of legislative immunity, these powerful arguments should have led the House of Lords to a contrary conclusion.

The common law position was recently restated in *Attorney General* v. *Lundin*.[270] It is not a contempt of court for a journalist to refuse to reveal his sources of information even when ordered to do so by a judge unless the answer to the question is both relevant and necessary to the issue before the court.

Section 10 of the 1981 Act provides that

no court may require a person to disclose, nor is any person guilty of contempt of court for refusing to disclose, the source of information contained in a publication for which he is responsible, unless it be established to the satisfaction of the court that disclosure is necessary in the interests of justice or national security or for the prevention of disorder or crime.[271]

As of yet, there is no significant case law interpreting this definition.

## THE PRESS AND THE INDIVIDUAL

### Defamation

The law of defamation has two purposes: to protect individual reputation and to preserve free speech. A sound law should strike a proper balance between these two often conflicting aims.[272] In fact, the vast majority of published news stories are free from libel. Nevertheless, the law does inhibit public enlightenment on a number of issues.[273] The Faulks Committee identified two principal criticisms of the present state of the law: litigation is too long and too costly, and the findings as to liability and damages are unpredictable.[274] In addition, because of the complicated body of law, an unsuccessful litigant can often find some arguable point on which to appeal. The Faulks Committee itself had been established in part as a result of the severe criticism of many aspects of defamation law by

Diplock, L.J., in *Slim* v. *Daily Telegraph*. Describing the tort of libel as "artificial and archaic," he recommended inquiry into this field by the Law Commission since "[i]t has passed beyond redemption by the Courts."[275]

The law of defamation is basically common law with statutory modifications. It provides two separate civil actions for the publication of defamatory matter: libel and slander. In general terms, libel concerns a writing or other permanent recording; slander is concerned with dissemination by word of mouth or some other transient mode.[276] The most important consequence of the distinction between libel and slander is that libel is actionable per se, that is, without proof of special damage.[277] In slander, special damage must be proved except in a limited number of cases.[278]

### Elements of the Action

Subject to any defense, a plaintiff in a defamation action must establish that the words complained of (1) are defamatory; (2) refer to the plaintiff; and (3) have been published.

### The words must be defamatory

In practice the real difficulty is deciding whether the words are defamatory. Ascertainment of the meaning of words has been a source of much confusion and difficulty.[279] Given its critical importance, the complexity of deciding the meaning of words is unfortunate. As the Faulks Committee pointed out:

> If the [words] are statements of fact, the defendant...must prove they are true...; if they consist essentially of...opinion the defence of fair comment can succeed only if the defendant proves that in their meaning they are fair comment on a matter of public interest. Even if the defence is that the words were published on a privileged occasion, a question may arise with regard to the meaning of the words. Finally, if the plaintiff succeeds...the assessment of damages [will] depend substantially on the gravity of the defamation, which also hinges on the meaning of words.[280]

In construing words in a defamation action, a court does not use the rules of interpretation that obtain for the construction of, for example, contracts. Rather, it explores the effect of the words on ordinary people, postulating that "the layman's capacity for implication is much greater than the lawyer's."[281] Further, the court is willing to narrow the group of ordinary persons to those who give the particular words used a special meaning because of certain facts or circumstances.[282]

No one test determines what constitutes a defamatory statement. Various formulae have been suggested: a statement that may tend to lower the plaintiff in the estimation of right-thinking members of society generally[283]; a statement that exposes him to hatred, ridicule, or contempt; a statement that causes him to be shunned or avoided; or a statement that has a tendency to injure him in his office, profession, or trade.[284] In the absence of a satisfactory and comprehensive definition in the case law, the Faulks Committee proposed the following statutory definition:

> Defamation shall consist of the publication to a third party of matter which in all the circumstances would be likely to affect a person adversely in the estimation of reasonable people generally.[285]

The law has developed two types of meaning in a defamation action, natural and ordinary meanings and innuendo meanings.[286] The former applies when the words would be reasonably understood by ordinary people using their general knowledge and common sense.[287] This seemingly straightforward rule has been burdened by legalistic complexities. For instance, the sense in which the words were intended is irrelevant.[288] Moreover, the sense in which the words were in fact understood is irrelevant. It seems, however, that regard will be paid to the sort of people to whom the words were or were likely to have been published.[289] In this context, the different functions of judge and jury are important.[290] If a defendant claims the words are not capable of bearing the particular meaning alleged, the judge decides that question. If they are so capable, the jury must then decide whether they actually bear that particular meaning.

If the words are not defamatory in their natural and ordinary meaning, or if the plaintiff wishes to rely on a traditional defamatory meaning in which they were understood by persons having knowledge of particular facts, proof of innuendo is required.[291] The plaintiff must provide the meaning that he attributes to the words, and prove the existence of facts to support that meaning.[292]

### The words must refer to the plaintiff

If the statement mentions the plaintiff by name, there is no difficulty in proving this requirement. However, material may be defamatory even though it does not mention the plaintiff by name and even if it contains no "key or pointer" indicating that it refers to him. The question is then whether reasonable persons would reasonably believe that the words refer to the plaintiff. As the intent and knowledge of the defendant are irrelevant, the dangers for the journalist and the editor are very real. Indeed, in *E. Hulton & Co.* v. *Jones*, the court held that a statement may be defamatory even though neither of the defendants knew of the existence of the plaintiff.[293] If reasonable persons would reasonably believe the words refer to the plaintiff, the defendant is liable, despite an attempt to disguise his reference to the plaintiff by using initials, asterisks, fictitious names, or some other subterfuge. Nor will the defendant escape liability if he intended to refer to someone else. Although the decision in *E. Hulton & Co.* v. *Jones* has not escaped criticism,[294] the principle announced in that case seems to be so well established that it is now too late for any but statutory modification. A journalist's difficulty is compounded because the average reader often does not read a sensational article with cautious, critical, and analytical care. Indeed, in deciding whether reasonable persons would understand the words as referring to the plaintiff, courts do not expect such persons to consider the matter in detail. The Faulks Committee recommended no change in this rule.[295]

### The words must be published

Publication is the communication of the words to at least one person other than the person defamed. The plaintiff carries the burden of proof. If the publication is in a newspaper and the claim is that defamation inheres in the ordinary meaning of words, there is a presumption of communication. If the plaintiff relies on innuendo, he must show that publication was to specific persons who knew of special facts enabling them to understand the innuendo, and that the words referred to the plaintiff.[296]

Every person who takes part in the publication of defamatory matter is prima facie liable.[297] Thus, the writer of the article, the publisher, the editor, and the printers of the newspaper are liable.[298]

### Defenses

For journalists the most important aspect of the law of defamation is the various procedural and substantive defenses.[299] It is in the defense that the law strikes a balance between the need to protect reputation and free expression.[300]

### Justification—the defense of truth

The essence of this defense is truth. "Justification" has a quite different meaning in modern parlance. The Faulks Committee recommended retitling this defense "Truth" so as to avoid any risk of a jury being confused by archaic terminology.[301] It is a complete defense to show that the defamatory statement is true in substance and fact.[302] To succeed, the defendant must prove the truth of the words complained of, not only in their literal meaning but also in such inferential or innuendo meaning as the jury may find them to bear.[303] It is no defense that the defendant was merely repeating what he had been told.[304] In practice, this defense is attended with difficulties. A newspaper may believe that a statement is true, but to adduce evidence in court to prove it may not be easy.

Under the present law the meaning of the specific text is not judged in reference to the text as a whole. The Faulks Committee recommended that a defendant be entitled to rely on the whole publication in answering a claim by a plaintiff that complains only of part of it. This would ensure that in assessing the truth of a defamatory publication the effect of the whole, not merely the sting of a selected part, can be taken into account.[305]

It should be noted that a defendant need not show that the publication is both true and for the public benefit. Although the Faulks Committee considered such a proposal, it rejected it for several reasons. First, it would be unjust to allow a plaintiff to recover for defamatory statements that were true. Second, the term "public benefit" in this context is too vague. Third, such a requirement would produce a chilling effect on the press. Sympathy for an individual case should not lead to the adoption of a rule detrimental to the interests of the community as a whole. "Muckraking" may be more properly dealt with by self-regulation through the Press Council. Arguably, a law of privacy, if one were enacted,[306] would more adequately protect the reputation of a now respectable individual who had committed indiscretions in the past.

### Fair comment

Another defense obtains if the defamatory text amounts to a fair comment on a matter of public interest. The defense may be defeated, however, by proof that the defendant was motivated by express malice.[307]

To qualify for this defense the comment must be based on fact and a defendant must have delineated the facts on which he based his statements. If the comment is fair with regard to the facts that are true, the defense will not fail merely because every fact relied on is not true.[308] Comment must satisfy the following test: Could any man honestly express that opinion on approved facts? The very wide breadth of this main criterion for the defense of fair comment is generally regarded as a bulwark of free speech. The Faulks Committee did not receive any suggestion to restrict the test in any way and it recommended no change. The committee did propose, however, that the adjective "fair" be deleted from the phrase "Fair Comment," since prejudiced or exaggerated views may be protected and still seem extremely unfair to an average person. It also proposed retaining the requirement that the comment be on a matter of public interest.[309]

The real difficulty with this defense arises from the complexity of cases in which a defendant alleges malice. To simplify the problem substantially, the term "malice" should not be used. Instead, the defense should be defeated if the plaintiff proves that the comment did not represent the defendant's genuine opinion.[310] Duncan and Neill submit that an imputation of dishonesty or of dishonorable conduct or motives can be defended as fair comment provided the imputation is presented as an expression of opinion; however, the authorities are not in agreement on this matter.[311]

The Faulks Committee recommended that the defense apply generally in all cases involving expression of opinion.[312]

## Privilege

In balancing the individual's right to protect his reputation and the right of freedom of speech, the law protects certain categories of content from legal action. It is "probable" that the defense of absolute privilege[313] applies to fair and accurate reports of judicial proceedings in the United Kingdom if published contemporaneously. Qualified privilege[314] protects, *inter alia*, fair and accurate reports of judicial proceedings, whether made contemporaneously or not, and reports of parliamentary proceedings. The defense of qualified privilege can be defeated on proof that the defendant was actuated by malice.[315] Section 7 of the Defamation Act, 1952, provides for a qualified privilege to protect the publication of certain items specified in the schedule to the Act. The section, however, has no application to, for example, the reports of courts or bodies of the European Economic Community, foreign legislatures or courts, or the proceedings of a number of important bodies such as the Council of the Stock Exchange, the Press Council, and the Panel of Takeovers and Mergers.[316]

It was suggested to the Faulks Committee that a qualified privilege be created to protect expression if it is in the public interest, if the publisher believed the facts to be true, if the publisher exercised all reasonable care in relation to such facts, and, insofar as the publication consisted of comment, if the comment was capable of being supported by any fact and was made in good faith.[317] The committee rejected the proposal. In particular, it stated that no concrete evidence was presented that newspapers or broadcasting authorities are handicapped in their porper functions without this extra protection. Moreover, it concluded that the proposal would not work as long as newspapers and television and broadcasting authorities held to the principle of nondisclosure of confidential sources.[318]

## Other defenses[319]

Notwithstanding the general rule that defamation does not depend on the intent to defame, in certain circumstances the defendant may escape liability by proving that the defamation was published by him innocently and that he has made an offer of amends. Section 4 of the Defamation Act, 1952, creates this defense. In practice, however, it does not appear to provide any wide measure of protection to a defendant. Witnesses before the Faulks Committee agreed that the purposes that section 4 were designed to achieve are extremely valuable; they were almost equally unanimous that the section as drafted is difficult to operate, if not unworkable.[320]

The distributor of defamatory matter may rely on the defense of innocent dissemination. This defense is particularly important to wholesalers, booksellers, news agents, and libraries, who may otherwise be liable for libels contained in reading materials that they market.[321] Although the law places a burden on distributors to make proper checks in doubtful cases, the task involved is not unduly onerous or expensive. The committee recommended no change in this defense to grant greater freedom from liability to distributors; however, it proposed extension of this defense to printers, subject to the same or similar conditions applying to distributors.[322]

The committee rejected the United States rule relating to public officials as set out in *New York Times* v. *Sullivan*. Apparently no English witness advocated the adoption of that principle. Nevertheless, there is continuing support from the press and some academics for protecting the publication of matters in the public interest in the absence of knowledge of their falsity or a reckless disregard for the truth.[323]

## *Juries*

Considerable controversy surrounds the question whether jury trials should continue to be available in defamation cases. The Faulks Committee recommended that trial by jury be retained, but as the exception rather than the rule.[324] The traditional arguments against juries—inconsistency of verdict, expense, and length of time—are more an indictment of the complexities of the law rather than of juries themselves. Many leading defamation lawyers, both past and present,[325] I believe correctly favor retaining the jury system. As Lord Gardiner, a former Lord Chancellor, observed: "English is a living language; juries know better than judges...what words mean."[326] The meaning of words is not a question of law, but of the meaning they convey to the average reasonable man. Moreover, the issue of malice, which is often raised against the defense of fair comment, involves an attack on the defendant's good faith. If the defendant is a journalist, his professional honesty, reputation, and his whole livelihood may be at stake. This again is a matter that should be determined by a jury of ordinary people. Questions affecting reputation have a close relationship with questions affecting liberty and, as such, are proper matters to be determined by juries.[327]

## *Damages*

Damages can fall within a wide bracket. Generally, they are to be assessed on a compensatory basis. In certain circumstances, however, exemplary or punitive damages can be awarded.[328] The largely subjective element in damage awards in defamation actions makes it impossible to present an objective standard by which to gauge the correct figure in any particular case.[329]

The Faulks Committee recommended no change for assessing compensatory damages.[330] They did recommend, however, that Parliament remove the power to give exemplary damages in defamation actions in England and Wales.[331]

If awarded, damages may be very high, especially when compared with personal injury awards, and very difficult to appeal. An appeal will be denied unless the award is manifestly incorrect. With so many newspapers financially weak, the risks involved are considerable.[332] One former editor commented:

> This lottery of damages really brings the national passion for gambling too far into the arena of public policy.... At the moment, the uncertainty regarding possible damages weighs heavily on newspapers as they consider whether to fight or not.... When this gamble...is added to the question of costs...the readiness of newspapers to settle actions out of court can easily be understood.[333]

### Criminal Libel

Historically, libel was both a crime and a tort. Actions for criminal libel, however, are extremely rare. Nevertheless, they are serious since the fine that can be imposed is unlimited and the maximum period of imprisonment is two years. Newspapers are safeguarded from criminal libel actions because no prosecution may be commenced without permission of a High Court Judge.[334] In *Goldsmith* v. *Pressdram Ltd.*,[335] the court set out the relevant factors to be considered in an application to commence a prosecution. There must be a clear prima facie case; the libel must be serious and the proceedings should be in the public interest. The question whether damages afford the plaintiff an adequate remedy[336] is irrelevant. In this case, the court did allow a private prosecution to be brought by Sir James Goldsmith against the publishers of *Private Eye*.[337]

The Faulks Committee recommended both maintaining criminal libel and extending it to broadcasting.[338] Yet the institution and subsequent withdrawal of proceedings in the Goldsmith case led to renewed criticism of the offense.[339] More recently, in *Gleaves* v. *Deakin*, Lord Diplock spoke of "the present sorry state of the law of criminal libel in this country." He was convinced that it departed from the accepted principles of modern criminal law in England. Moreover, the offense was difficult to reconcile with the United Kingdom's international obligations as a party to the European Convention of Human Rights.[340]

### Conclusion

The law of defamation is in considerable need of reform. In 1975, the Faulks Committee presented its report to Parliament. In general, its recommendations[341] have been welcomed. Indeed, the 1977 Royal Commission on the Press was "not aware of widespread disagreement with any of them."[342] Nevertheless, the law remains unchanged.

## Privacy

There is no legal right to privacy as such in the law of England and Wales.[343] The Younger Committee on Privacy rejected proposals for a general remedy protecting privacy although it did recommend new remedies to cover certain specific ways in which privacy may be invaded.[344] Further, it drew attention to the action for breach of confidence, which it considered potentially capable of affording greater protection to privacy than had hitherto been realized.[345]

The committee agreed that the concept of privacy embodies values essential to a free society.[346] It recognized that under modern conditions the growing interdependence and organization of individuals, together with technological developments, have subjected privacy to dangerous pressures, and that therefore privacy required additional protection. In lieu of any general right to privacy, however, it recommended specific legislation to prohibit activities that unreasonably frustrate individual privacy.[347]

Yet, since the European Convention of Human Rights recognizes the right of privacy in general terms, English law will have to change if the United Kingdom is fully to honor its international obligations.[348]

The committee was forced to admit that its piecemeal approach to press law leaves several gaps. First, there exist certain intrusions in the private sector, most obviously by journalistic investigators or prying neighbors, for which its recommendations provide no new legal remedy.[349] Second, some of the proposals rely overoptimistically on the readiness of the press to respond not to legal sanctions but to the pressure of public and professional criticism.[350]

A further criticism of the committee's report is that it places too great an emphasis on the extent to which privacy is already protected by English law. Certainly, the law of defamation affords a strong protection against the publication of defamatory false statements.[351] The legal remedy against physical intrusion into privacy by the press, however, is limited. The laws of trespass to land and nuisance provide a right of action for invasion of privacy only to the legal occupier of the property. Furthermore, in the absence of actual damage, the remedy is usually an empty one.[352] Thus, in cases in which the press have entered hospitals surreptitiously to interview or photograph a patient, the hospital authorities could bring proceedings in trespass, but the patient or his family could not.[353] There is in fact no right at all to prevent the taking of one's picture.[354]

The Younger Committee considered the law on breach of confidence as offering the best protection of privacy.[355] However, it is apparent from the Law Commission's report that even this area of the law is inadequate. In particular, there is uncertainty as to the fundamental principles on which the action for breach of confidence is based; there are problems relating to the initial creation of the obligation of confidence; and there are doubts as to the position of the person acquiring information without actual or constructive knowledge of its confidential character. Additional problems exist concerning the information capable of protection and the remedies available for breach of confidence.[356]

## PRIVATE ARRANGEMENTS THAT AFFECT THE ROLE OF THE PRESS IN SOCIETY

### Individual Access to the Media

Classical liberal theory postulates that press freedom exists because anyone who does not find his views expressed in the press has the right to start his own newspaper. The United Kingdom indeed has a considerable range of newspapers. There are national newspapers, foreign newspapers and periodicals, provincial morning and evening newspapers, local weekly newspapers, the immigrant press,[357] and the alternative press.[358] Yet despite the number of publications, fewer alternative sources of information exist today, and control of the media has become concentrated in fewer hands.[359]

Neither the libel law nor press taxes prevented the rise, from the 1790s to the late 1820s, of a press that reflected the interests of the working class.[360] Finances, however, proved more of a hindrance. The left-wing *Daily Herald* went from one crisis to another despite reaching a circulation of over 250,000 at its height before the First World War.[361] After the repeal of the Stamp Duty in 1853, the role of advertising became increasingly important. Radical newspapers often could survive only by moving up market to attract an audience desired by advertisers.[362] Advertising is now the most important source of revenue for all classes of publication except national popular newspapers and "consumer" periodicals dealing with general and leisure interests.[363] Seventy percent of all advertising is done in the press,[364] and its influence on the national press has been significant. In 1964 the *Daily Herald* was compelled to close, primarily due to its inability to attract sufficient advertisers. The *News Chronicle*, a leading liberal newspaper, closed for similar reasons. It had a circulation many times that of the *Guardian*, the only other liberal newspaper, but did not have the affluent readership nor the number of advertisers that the *Guardian* had.[365] The alternative press suffers considerably from the lack of advertising revenue, as well as from the rapid increase in the cost of newsprint since 1973.[366]

The first half of the twentieth century saw press barons create and rule empires as if they were personal fiefdoms. During the interwar period, four men—Lords Beaverbrook, Rothermere, Camrose, and Kemsley—established dominant positions. At one time the combined circulation of their newspapers was in excess of 13 million; they owned nearly one out of every two national and local daily newspapers as well as one out of every three Sunday papers sold in Britain.[367] In the Victorian period proprietors were concerned only with the general politics of their papers. By contrast, these press barons exercised personal and close control over both the content and administration of their key papers. Lord Beaverbrook told the 1949 Royal Commission on the Press that he ran the *Daily Express* "merely for the purpose of making propaganda with no other motive."[368] In a memorable sentence, Mr. Baldwin commented: "What proprietorship of these papers is aiming at is power, and power without responsibility—the prerogative of the harlot throughout the ages."[369] However, today the scene is different. The personal influence of individual proprietors on the content of their newspapers has diminished as the press barons have been replaced by corporate proprietors.[369a]

Britain is alone in the world in having nine newspapers circulating across the country. Nevertheless, it is said that there is a gap in the national press that could be' filled by a newspaper which generally supported the left-wing line and provided fuller coverage than is available.[370] Certainly the disappearance of the *News Chronicle* and the *Daily Herald* marked a significant loss in diversity, style, and content, as well as in political outlook. Despite the perilous financial state of the newspaper industry, the 1977 Royal Commission opposed any scheme of government subsidies. Nor did it support establishing any public body that could, or might have to, discriminate among publications in the sense of supporting selected publications.[371]

Groups of union members have occasionally sought to control newspapers by industrial action. In the early 1970s, newspaper workers dissatisfied with certain editorial matter interfered with newspaper production on a number of occasions.[372] In *Associated Newspapers Group Ltd.* v. *Wade*,[373] the General Secretary and other officers of the National Graphical Association were restrained from organizing a *blacking*\* of certain advertisements in the press. In upholding the interlocutory injunction, the Court of Appeal emphasized the illegality of the union's action:

> The press should be free.... A trade union has no right to use its industrial strength to invade the freedom of the press. They have no right to interfere with the freedom of editors to comment on matters of public interest.... Interference with the freedom of the press is so contrary to the public interest that it is to be regarded as the employment of unlawful means....[374]

---

\* Refused to print.

To strengthen their industrial bargaining position the unions have adopted the controversial "closed shop."[375] Most journalists view the "right to write" as absolute and, in a democratic society, as superior to the right of the National Union of Journalists to bargain collectively on the same terms as other trade unions. The present law is neutral: the closed shop is not prohibited, but it is equally not made compulsory. Lord Goodman's proposal to introduce a legally enforceable code of industrial relations for the press was rejected.[376]

In the past the press has been criticized on the ground that advertisers exercise too much influence over the content of newspapers. But the 1977 Commission concluded that the overall balance of content in newspapers was not unduly influenced by advertisers. It is doubtful, though, whether the commission received a correct picture, since advertisers could be expected to suppress evidence of successful influence on the press.[377]

The commission did, however, recognize that the press failed to cover adequately or accurately industrial relations and trade union affairs, and recommended that they improve and broaden their coverage.[378] Yet the issue of accurate coverage is fraught with difficulty. The commission pointed this out when it considered the allegations, published by the *Daily Mail*, that British Leyland maintained a slush fund. The commission recognized that the quest for unbiased coverage may conflict with the ideal of a free marketplace of ideas: "There is no escape from the truth that a free society which expects responsible conduct must be prepared to tolerate some irresponsibility as part of the price of liberty."[379]

## Media Concentration

The 1949 Commission identified press monopolies as the main danger to free public opinion.[380] The monopoly publisher is in a position to determine who should be criticized in his papers.[381] The commission observed that "[e]ven if this position is not consciously abused, a paper without competitors may fall below the standards of accuracy and efficiency which competition enforces."[382] Nevertheless, publishers oppose regulation, arguing that monopoly gives financial security, which in turn enables them to give a better service by allocating greater resources to newspapers than would be possible under competition.[383]

The 1949 Commission followed a debate on press monopoly in the House of Commons. However the commission found there was nothing approaching monopoly in the press as a whole.[384] Moreover, the 1962 Royal Commission identified competition (not monopoly) as the real killer,[385] but it remained, albeit unenthusiastically, in favor of the free market.[386] The 1977 Commission also rejected all proposals for government assistance to newspapers but recognized that there may be circumstances in which market forces threaten the proper fulfillment of social and political functions for the press.[387]

The 1962 Commission recognized that a large circulation newspaper is more likely to flourish, "and to attract still more readers, whilst a newspaper which has a small circulation is likely to be in difficulties."[388] It recommended that newspapers of "smaller circulation...differentiate themselves in a way which will appeal to special types of readers and of advertisers, and so reduce the intensity of competition with their more powerful rivals."[389] The reality of the newspaper world supports this view. For example, the *Daily Telegraph* is the paper for commercial and industrial job advertisements, while the *Guardian* is the paper for civil service and local government jobs.[390]

There has been little increase in concentration of ownership of national newspapers since 1962.[391] On the other hand, no new national daily newspaper has been launched recently.[392] All evening newspapers launched since 1961 have been in towns that did not previously have a local evening newspaper. Moreover, there is little prospect of a local monopoly being challenged by new entrants, since the launching cost of a directly competing newspaper would be prohibitively high.[393]

The 1977 Commission was required to consider the issue of media concentration and its relationship to "other interests and holdings, within and outside the communications industry."[394] Prior to 1950, most newspaper publishing companies depended primarily on newspaper interests. In some cases newspaper publishing activities now have become subsidiaries of much larger organizations whose interests include television and radio, travel, North Sea oil, paper, and banking and financial services.[395] In a few instances, newspapers suffering losses are subsidized by the organization's other activities. However, the 1977 Commission did not receive or unearth specific evidence of abuse or biased editorial comment as a result.[396] More commonly, the subsidy comes from profitable newspapers. For example, the *Guardian* is subsidized by the *Manchester Evening News*. Because both the *Guardian* and the *Times* might have closed long ago without cross-subsidies, or might exist in very different forms, the commission accepted the lack of any preferable alternative to an assured subsidy.[397] They were, however, concerned to ensure the separation of newspaper from broadcasting companies[398] in order to maintain diversity of voices.[399] Apart from what they recommend elsewhere regarding ownership, the commission did not believe that special legislation on the interests of companies that own newspapers was required.[400]

Both the 1962 and 1977 Commissions emphasized the desirability of greater public knowledge about the ownership of newspapers and periodicals.[401] They considered that public knowledge should extend beyond ownership of other publishing interests to knowledge of the other main business interests of groups that publish newspapers and periodicals.[402] The 1977 Commission recommended amending the Companies Acts, 1967 and 1976, so that every newspaper and periodical should state not merely, as at present, the name and address of the publisher, but also, if the publisher is a subsidiary company, the name and country of incorporation of its ultimate holding company. Moreover, it recommended that this information be displayed with reasonable prominence[403] and that the Press Council police this obligation.[404] In addition, newspapers and periodicals should declare their interests when reporting or commenting on the affairs of an associated company or on an industry in which they have a significant direct or indirect financial interest.[405]

Following the 1962 Commission, monopoly and merger legislation was strengthened in 1965 by provisions now contained in the Fair Trading Act, 1973.[406] Under the 1973 Act transfers of controlling interests in daily, Sunday or local newspapers to persons with newspaper interests require the consent of the Secretary of State for Prices and Consumer Protection* if such persons already control, or as a result of the transfer would obtain control over, daily, Sunday, or local newspapers having an average daily circulation in the United Kingdom of 50,000 copies or more. The Secretary of State may either authorize the merger or refer the matter to the Monopolies and Merger Commission.[407] The policy recommended by the 1977 Commission recognizes that at times mergers and acquisitions are necessary, but aims to discourage acquisitions by the biggest companies and by companies already strong in a particular region.[408] The commission recommended reversing the practice whereby consent is granted by the authorities unless they are satisfied that the merger will operate against the public interest, since it had proved impractical to expect such evidence. Instead, consent should be withheld unless the authorities are satisfied that the merger will not operate against the public interest.[409] They also recommended that, in exercising discretion, the Secretary of State should consider the aggregate circulation of the group of papers to be acquired. The requirement that an individual newspaper have a circulation of 25,000 was not considered sufficient.[410]

## Self-Regulation

A central recommendation of the 1949 Commission was the creation of a Press Council. It was not established, however, until 1953, and then only after the threat of legislation. Its membership was restricted to press representatives, it was run with very limited finances, and functioned primarily as a public relations agency for the press and harmless grievance

---

* Now, the Under-Secretary of State for Corporate and Consumer Affairs.

system for angry individuals.[411] The 1962 and the 1977 Commissions criticized the council's lack of independence and impartiality.[412]

After 1962, the Press Council redrafted its constitution so that its purposes became, *inter alia*:

(a)  To preserve the established freedom of the British press.

(b)  To maintain the character of the British press in accordance with the highest professional and commercial standards.

(c)  To consider complaints about the conduct of the press or the conduct of persons and organisations towards the press, to deal with these complaints in whatever manner might seem practical and appropriate and record result and action.[413]

. . .

(g)  To publish periodical reports recording the Council's work and to review, from time to time, developments in the press and the factors affecting them.[414]

Regrettably the council has failed to persuade the public that it deals satisfactorily with complaints about newspapers, notwithstanding that this is seen as its main purpose.[415] Its predominantly professional membership tends to be satisfied with less than rigorous standards and looks for excuses for the press.[416] The 1977 Commission recommended that the council be constituted with an equal number of lay and press representatives under an independent chairman.[417] That recommendation has now properly been implemented.[418]

Most of the work of the Press Council concerns complaints and most of the comments to the 1977 Commission centered on the council's complaint procedure.[419] The commission acquitted the Press Council staff of the charge that they delay cases.[420] Nevertheless, it recommended that the Press Council change its procedure for handling complaints. In particular, it recommended that the council undertake as a primary responsibility a duty of mediation and conciliation in the preliminary stage of its investigation of a complaint; that this be done by a named conciliator; and that only after failure to conciliate should a formal complaint be brought before the Complaints Committee.[421] Because the council receives complaints dealing with a wide range of matters,[422] it would clearly be better if it sought to obtain a satisfactory result before going through the quasi-judicial procedures leading to an adjudication. It is easy for attitudes to harden once those procedures begin.[423]

Press Council adjudications constitute a body of case law; yet it is not always clear on which basis they are made.[424] The 1977 Commission criticized this condition and recommended that the council draw up a code of behavior on which to base its adjudications. Such a code would enable the public to judge the performance of the press by known and accepted standards.[425]

Notwithstanding the risk of adverse adjudication by the Press Council, flagrant breaches of acceptable standards continue.[426] The 1977 Commission rejected the plea to give statutory teeth, such as fines or suspensions, to the council's sanctions.[427] It felt that these remedies would represent a potentially dangerous weapon of control over the press.[428] Nevertheless, it made two recommendations to assist in improving the situation. First, the Press Council should approach the various organizations representing publishers, asking them to publish adjudications that uphold complaints on the front page of the newspaper in question, or in the case of periodicals, with a prominence at least equal to that of the offending passage.[429] Second, the Press Council should undertake a wider review than it presently does of the record of the publication or journalist concerned.[430] The commission also recommended that the Press Council change its position on accuracy and bias.[431] Council practice does not appear to be strict enough in protecting the public against the dangers of partisan opinion exacerbated by factual inaccuracy. Contentious opinions based on inaccurate information should be grounds for censure.[432]

Regrettably, it seems unlikely that the Press Council will develop the civic responsibility expected of it.[433] Apart from further enlargement of its lay membership under an independent chairman and the adoption of certain proposals relating to mediation and conciliation, the Press Council failed to implement any of the key proposals of the commission.[434]


## CONCLUSION

The Royal Commission on the Press of 1977 noted that its terms of reference were sufficiently wide to permit it "to examine and make recommendations on any aspect of the law which relates to the press."[435] Yet it deliberately chose not to do so. The reason it gave was that between July 1972 and March 1975 reports of four committees were presented to Parliament which together covered all the important areas of interaction between the law and the press. The commission considered and rejected a general law of the press. In its broadest form this would involve a written constitutional provision guaranteeing press freedom. A particular disadvantage of this, according to the commission, would be that the courts would acquire jurisdiction over matters which it believed were more suitable for deliberation by Parliament.[436]

A decade has now passed since the first of those reports, and with the exception of the Contempt of Court Act, 1981, little has changed. Legislation to reform the Official Secrets Acts has been promised repeatedly since the Franks Report in 1972. The commission considered the whole subject to be a matter of urgency. In the area of defamation the story is the same. The Faulks Committee made its recommendations to the commission in 1975. Two years later the commission observed that "in general the recommendations have been welcomed and we are not aware of widespread disagreement with any of them."[437] Nevertheless the law remains unaltered.

In the area where Parliament has taken action it has been only after considerable delay and the result is less than impressive. The Phillimore Committee reported on the law of contempt in 1974. Yet it was not until the decision of the House of Lords in the *Sunday Times* case was overturned by the European Court of Human Rights in 1979 that Parliament was stirred into action. Incredibly, it is now uncertain whether the Contempt of Court Act, 1981, has in fact brought law in the United Kingdom into line with the European Convention on Human Rights.

Certainly there is need for increased Parliamentary activity in many areas of the law involving the press. However such action can be no substitute for the courts developing a proper approach to regulating press freedom in a libertarian spirit; and this will only be achieved with the assistance of some form of constitutional guarantee of press freedom. It is here that Parliament must ultimately act.

## NOTES

1.   There is no constitution in the United Kingdom. The United Kingdom is, however, a party to the European Convention for the Protection of Human Rights and Fundamental Freedoms. *See infra* note 27 and accompanying text, notes 186–93.

2.   "It is hardly an exaggeration to say...that liberty of the press is not recognised in England." A. Dicey, *Introduction to the Study of the Law of the Constitution* 247 (10th ed. 1965). On press law generally, *see* Royal Commission on the Press, Final Report, Cmd. 6810 (1977) (hereinafter cited as the 1977 Commission); H. Street, *Freedom, the Individual and the Law* 97–107 (5th ed. 1982); C. Wintour, *Pressures on the Press* (1972); H.P. Levy, *The Press Council* (1967); J. Whale, *The Politics of the Media* (2d ed. 1980); J. Curran and J. Seaton, *Power Without Responsibility* (1981).

3.   *R. v. St. Asaph Dean*, [1784] 3 T.R. 428 (Notes). *See* 4 W. Blackstone, *Commentaries* 151.

4.   There are areas of general law which relate predominantly, and in some cases almost exclusively, to press activities.

5.   A. Dicey, *supra* note 2, at 250. This has in reality contributed much to free the press from control. As Dicey has commented:

If the criterion whether the publication be libellous is the opinion of a jury and a man may publish anything which twelve of his countrymen think is not blameable, it is impossible that the Crown or the Minister should exert any stringent control over writings in the press unless (as indeed may sometimes happen) the majority of ordinary citizens are entirely opposed to attacks on the Government.

*Id.*

6.   The 1977 Commission, *supra* note 2, at Addendum, para. 9 at 107.

7.   *Id.* at paras. 10–11.

8.   14 Charles II, c. 33.

9.   *See* A. Dicey, *supra* note 2, at 260, 269.

10.   "Terminated" rather than "abolished." *See* A. Dicey, *supra* note 2, at 261.

11.   The stamp was a special postage rate which newspapers had to pay whether they were mailed or not. In particular, it "operated against the founding both of provincial newspapers, (swamped by competition from London through the mails) and of papers which working people could afford." *See* J. Whale, *supra* note 2, at 11–12.

12.   Postal subsidy continued, however. During 1975, 12 million national newspapers carrying second-class stamps were delivered as first-class mail. Thereby, the press industry saved no more than £240,000—"not an annual sum whose withdrawal would bring the press to its knees...The other concession made by the State looked more substantial. When the United Kingdom introduced Value Added Tax in April 1973, it did not join certain other member countries of the European Economic Community in applying the tax to newspapers. By 1975, the remission was worth £20 million a year to national newspapers." However, the threat to withdraw this concession "is too generalised and permanent to have any practical effect on conduct." *See id.* at 120–121

13.   *See* J. Curran and J. Seaton, *supra* note 2, at 19. The last known English paper to receive Secret Service subsidies was the *Observer* in 1840.

14.   *Id. See also* C. Wintour, *supra* note 2, at 35–44 and text accompanying notes 362–366 *infra.*

15.   It may mean the freedom of publishers to market their publications; or the freedom of all individuals to address the public through the press; or the freedom of editorial discretion. The 1977 Commission considered all these as elements of the right of freedom of expression. *See* the 1977 Commission, *supra* note 2, at ch. 2 ("Functions and Freedom of the Press"). A quotation illustrating the freedom of editors begins chapter 2:

"The press is a mighty engine, Sir," said Mr. Pott. Mr. Pickwick yielded his fullest assent to the proposition.

"But I trust, Sir," said Pott, "that I have never abused the enormous power I wield. I trust, Sir, that I have never pointed the noble instrument which is placed in my hands, against the sacred bosom of private life, or the tender breast of individual reputation;—I trust, Sir, that I have devoted my energies to endeavours—humble they may be, humble I know they are—to instill those principles of—which—are—." Here the editor of the *Eatanswill Gazette*, appearing to ramble, Mr. Pickwick came to his relief, and said— "Certainly." [C. Dickens, *The Pickwick Papers* (1836).]

16. The 1977 Commission, *supra* note 2, at para. 2.3.

17. *See* Royal Commission on the Press, 1947–1949, Report, Cmd. 7700, at para. 58 (1949) (hereinafter cited as the 1949 Commission): "it is undoubtedly a great merit of the British press that it is completely independent of outside financial interests and that its policy is the policy of those who own and conduct it." *See also* J. Curran and J. Seaton, *supra* note 2, at 290–309.

18. The 1977 Commission, *supra* note 2, at para. 2.9.

19. *Id.* at para. 11.4. *See* Sir Dennis Hamilton, *Who Is To Own the British Press* 9 (1976).

20. The 1977 Commission, *supra* note 2, at para. 14.5, quoting with approval the 1949 Commission *supra* note 17, at para. 274.

21. *See* J. Curran and J. Seaton, *supra* note 3, at 290–309.

22. The majority report of the 1977 Commission argued that "[N]o public body should ever be put in a position of discriminating like a censor between one applicant and another." However, this is exactly what the Independent Broadcasting Authority has always done when awarding radio and television franchises. *See* J. Curran and J. Seaton, *supra* note 2, at 327–331.

23. *See* Monopolies and Mergers Legislation, *infra* text accompanying notes 406–407. The 1977 Commission concluded: "there is...a consensus...that the press should neither be subject to strict control nor left entirely to the unregulated forces of the market." The 1977 Commission, *supra* note 2, at para. 2.12.

24. The terms of reference of the 1977 Commission were wide and permitted it to examine and make recommendations on any aspect of the law that related to the press. The 1977 Commission, *supra* note 2, at para. 19.2.

25. *Brownlie's Law of Public Order and National Security* 339 (M. Supperstone, 2d ed. 1981).

26. *Sunday Times* v. *United Kingdom* (1979), Eur. Ct. of Human Rights, series A, No. 30, *reprinted in* 2 Eur. Hum. Rts. Rep. 245 (1979).

27. L. Scarman, *English Law—The New Dimension*, 19–20 (Hamlyn Lectures 1974). Detailed legislation can supplement the broad expression of rights. *Brownlie's Law of Public Order and National Security, supra* note 25, at 339. On the European Convention of Human Rights *see generally* J. Fawcett, *The Application of The European Convention on Human Rights* (1969); F. Jacob, *The European Convention on Human Rights* (1975).

28. *See Attorney General* v. *Times Newspapers Ltd.*, [1973] Q.B. 710; [1974] A.C. 273, (at the national level, before the case went to the European court).

29. *Attorney General* v. *Jonathan Cape Ltd.*, [1976] 1 Q.B. 752. *See* further discussion *infra* at notes 161–167 and accompanying text.

30. *See* 1975 Pub. L. 277, 279.

31. [1976] 1 Q.B. at 771.

32. 1975 Pub. L. at 279.

33. *British Steel Corp.* v. *Granada Television, Ltd.*, [1980] 3 W.L.R. 774.

34. *But see* [1980] 3 W.L.R. at 804 (Lord Denning, M.R. (C.A.)); *id.* at 846 (Lord Salmon (H.L.)). *See also* discussion *infra*, text accompanying notes 263–269.

35. *R.* v. *Lemon, sub. nom. Whitehouse* v. *Lemon*, [1979] A.C. 617, [1979] 2 W.L.R. 281 (H.L.).

36. *See infra* text accompanying notes 335–337.

37. *New York Times* v. *Sullivan*, 376 U.S. 254 (1964); *see* Blasi, *The Checking Value in First Amendment Theory*, 1977 Am. Bar Found. Research J. 526, 551.

38. *See infra* section IV.A.

39. *Brownlie's Law of Public Order and National Security, supra* note 25, at 337–340.

40. D.G.T. Williams, *Not in the Public Interest* 9 (1967). The view of the intelligence service as to what constitutes an "official secret" was summed up in the evidence of the then-head of Military Intelligence 5 to the Franks Committee: " 'It is an official secret if it is on an official file.' " Departmental Committee on §2 of the Official Secrets Act 1911, Cmd. 5104, vol. III at 249 (1972) (hereinafter cited as "Franks Report").

41. *See* D.G.T. Williams, *supra* note 40; Williams, *Offences against the State 1964–1973*, 1974 Crim. L. Rev. 634, 639; H. Street, *supra* note 2, at 221–227; J.C. Smith and B. Hogan, *Criminal Law* 808–812 (4th ed. 1978). E. Wade and G. Phillips, *Administrative and Constitutional Law* 523 (9th ed. 1977). These Acts apply throughout the United Kingdom.

42. D.G.T. Williams, *supra* note 40, at 26.

43. Franks Report, *supra* note 40, at para. 50. Indeed there was no discussion whatsoever during the debates of section 2. The bill passed all its stages in a single afternoon.

44. *See* H. Street, *supra* note 2, at 222.

45. P. O'Higgins, *Censorship in Britain* 36 (1972). D.G.T. Williams has described the Official Secrets Acts as "one of the most ubiquitous, far reaching and all purpose blocks of statute law ever perpetrated in this country!" D.G.T. Williams, *supra* note 40, at 38.

46. Official Secrets Act, 1911 §§ 1(1), 1(2), as amended by the Official Secrets Act 1920, §§ 9, 10, sched. 1. Section 1(1) provides:

> If any person for any purpose prejudicial to the safety or interests of the State (a) approaches [inspects, passes over] or is in the neighbourhood of, or enters any prohibited place within the meaning of this Act; or (b) makes any sketch, plan, model or note which is calculated to be or might be or is intended to be directly or indirectly useful to an enemy; or (c) obtains [collects, records, or publishes] or communicates to any other person [any secret, official code word, or password, or] any sketch, plan, model, article or note, or other document or information which is calculated to be or might be or is intended to be directly or indirectly useful to an enemy he shall be guilty of a felony.

*Id.*

Under section 3, a prohibited place includes any defense establishment and any other place "declared [by order of a Secretary of State] to be a prohibited place...on the ground that information with respect thereto, or the destruction or obstruction thereof, or interference therewith would be useful to an enemy." *Id.* §3. The word "enemy" includes a potential enemy with whom there might be war. *R.* v. *Parrott [1913] 8 Cr. App. Rep. 186. See also R.* v. *Sutch*, [1975] 2 N.Z.L.R. 1. The breadth of subsection 1(1)(b) is enormous. "Anyone can be sent to prison for a minimum period of three years for making a note of information which might be indirectly useful to an enemy." P. O'Higgins, *supra* note 45, at 37.

47.  The maximum sentence for a section 1 offense is 14 years imprisonment.

48.  *See* Thompson, *The Committee of 100 and the Official Secrets Act 1911*, 1963 Pub. L. 201; P. O'Higgins, *supra* note 45, at 36.

49.  *See Chandler* v. *DPP*, 1964 A.C. 763, [1962] 3 A11 E.R. 142. *See also* D.G.T. Williams, *supra* note 40, at 106–109.

50.  Third Report from the Defence Committee (Session 1979–1980) HC 773, 640 i-v ('The D Notice System') para. 13 (hereinafter cited as "Third Report from the Defence Committee").

51.  This case is known as the 'ABC' case. *See Times* 18 November 1978; Nicol, *Official Secrets and Jury Vetting*, 1979 Crim. L. Rev. 184.

52.  The same tactics were adopted in the defence of Daniel Ellsberg and Anthony Russo when they were prosecuted for releasing the Pentagon Papers. *See* P. Schragg, *Test of Loyalty* 243 (1974).

53.  *See* Nicol, *supra* note 51, at 285–286.

54.  *Id*. at 288 (per Mars-Jones, J.).

55.  *Id*. at 286.

56.  *See* 128 N.L.J. 1133 (1978). Significantly the Attorney General did not thoroughly check the official and semi-official sources of the information. Admittedly it would have been a considerable task. But when charges that may result in 30 years imprisonment are laid against a defendant, this is not an excuse. At the outset of the trial the three defendants faced a total of nine charges, five of which were under section 1. All section 1 charges were withdrawn after Mars-Jones, J., indicated that he found them to be "oppressive." *Times*, 18 November 1978. *Cf.* Progressive Case, *New York Times*, 13 September 1979.

57.  Section 2(1) prohibits any person who possesses or controls certain information (a) to communicate it "to any person, other than a person to whom he is authorised to communicate it, or a person to whom it is in the interest of the State his duty to communicate it"; (b) to use it "for the benefit of any foreign power or in any other manner prejudicial to the safety or interests of the State"; (c) to retain it when he has no right to do so or when it is contrary to his duty to do so; and (d) to fail to take reasonable care of it, or so to conduct himself as to endanger the safety of the information." Official Secrets Act, 1911, §2, as amended by Official Secrets Act, 1920, §§9, 10, Sched. 1.

The information falling under this subsection includes:

[any secret official code word, or password, or] any sketch, plan, model, article, note, document or information which relates to or is used in a prohibited place or anything in such a place, or which has been made or obtained in contravention of this Act, or which has been entrusted in confidence to him by any person holding office under Her Majesty or which he has obtained [or to which he has had access] owing to his possession as a person who holds or has held office under Her Majesty, or as a person who holds or has held a contract.

*Id*.

The European Communities Act, 1972, §11(2), extends the Acts to cover persons involved in "Euratom" who communicate or disclose classified information.

58.  A police officer is also included within its scope. *Lewis* v. *Cattle*, [1938] 2

K.B. 454, [1938] 2 All E.R. 368 (a journalist was convicted for failing to reveal the source of a statement); *see also* Parliamentary Commissioner Act, 1967, §11; Nuclear Installation Act, 1965, sched. 1, para. 2; Atomic Energy Authority Act, 1971, §§17, 19.

59.    D.G.T. Williams, *supra* note 40, at 84.

60.    *See R. v. Crisp and Homewood*, [1919] 83 J.P. 121, 15 Digest (Reissue) 935.

61.    Franks Report, *supra* note 40, at para. 16.

62.    Letter from Sir Lionel Heald Q.C. to the *Times*, 20 March 1970.

63.    Third Report from the Defence Committee, *supra* note 50, at paras. 14 and 425.

64.    *R. v. Fell* [1963] Crim. L. Rev. 207.

65.    41 Law Society's Gazette 1 (1978). *See The Law and the Press* (Report of a Joint Working Party of "Justice" and the British Committee of the International Press Institute) 18–23 (1965); D.G.T. Williams, *supra* note 40, at 69–93; *see generally* Franks Report, *supra* note 40.

At no time did the prosecution allege in *R. v. Berry, Campbell and Aubrey*, that the two journalists, Campbell and Aubrey, had communicated secret information to anyone. In fact they received such information by perfectly acceptable and legitimate means; nevertheless, their actions fell within the ambit of the Acts.

66.    Franks Report, *supra* note 40, at para. 20.

67.    (Per Caulfield, J.) reported in J. Aitken, *Officially Secret* 79–206 (1971).

68.    *See* Franks Report, *supra* note 40, appendix II.

69.    Official Secrets Act, 1911, §8.70.

70.    Authorization is nowhere defined in the Acts. *See* D.G.T. Williams, *supra* note 40, at 46; Franks Report, *supra* note 40, at para. 21 and appendix II, at 116; *infra* note 160.

71.    *See* text accompanying notes 51–56 *supra*.

72.    The maximum penalty for this offense is three months imprisonment and/or a fine of £1,000 on summary conviction. On conviction on indictment the maximum sentence is two years imprisonment and/or an unlimited fine.

73.    Because of his former membership in the Intelligence Corps, Berry was a Crown office holder.

74.    They did not hold office under the Crown and were therefore in a very different position than Berry. Campbell was ordered to pay £2,200 toward the prosecution costs and £2,500 towards his own costs. Aubrey was ordered to pay £2,500 toward the prosecution costs and a third of his own costs. *Times*, 18 November 1978; 28 November 1978.

75.    *See supra* text accompanying note 67. It was this case, and Mr. Justice Caulfield's summing up to the jury in particular, that made the demand to change section 2 irresistible. A "not guilty" verdict was returned for all the defendants.

76.    Franks Report, *supra* note 40, at paras. 13 and 105, respectively.

77.    Franks Report, *supra* note 40, at para. 41. Journalists and members of Parliament have been threatened with prosecution in order to prevent the dissemination of information. *See* P. O'Higgins, *supra* note 45, at 39; C. Pincher, *Inside Story* (1978).

78.    Franks Report, *supra* note 40, at para. 26. *See also Times*, 20 May 1980 (At the request of the Independent Broadcasting Authority, Granada Television

withdrew a scheduled "World in Action" program concerning allegations about the Hong Kong station of the Government Communications Headquarters. The Independent Broadcasting Authority said that the program breached the Official Secrets Acts "in ways which could be prejudicial to national security.").

79.   *See* P. O'Higgins, *supra* note 45, at 39–40.

80.   The Official Information Act would protect defined classes of information against improper disclosure. These classes would comprise (a) classified information relating to defense, national security, foreign relations, or to the currency or reserves, the unauthorized disclosure of which would cause serious injury to the national interest; (b) cabinet papers; (c) information which is likely to assist criminal activities or to impede law enforcement; and (d) information that has been entrusted to the government by a private individual or concern. Only material classified as "Top Secret" or "Secret" (or "Defence—Confidential") would be protected in category (a). However, a 1978 government White Paper suggested that the test of criminality should be the likelihood that the disclosure of information will seriously damage the nation's interests and not simply the fact that a document has been classified. The White Paper extended "Defence—Confidential" to a wider range of defense information than the Franks Committee envisaged; it also considered that security and intelligence information should form a separate category of any proposed bill. This recommendation was made to guard against the gradual accumulation of small items of such information, apparently trivial in themselves, which, when added together, could constitute a serious threat to the interests of the nation. Cmd. 7285, paras. 16–32 (1978).

81.   *See* S. de Smith, *Constitutional and Administrative Law* 473, (4th ed. 1981).

82.   *See supra* note 80.

83.   *See* text accompanying note 68.

84.   In 1979, the government introduced the Protection of Information Bill, but as a result of heavy criticism, *see Times*, 14 November 1979, and the "Blunt Affair," *see Times*, 16 November 1979, the government was forced to withdraw it.

85.   *See Times*, 18 November 1978; 128 N.L.J. 1133 (1978).

86.   *See generally* Security Procedures in the Public Service, Cmd. 1681, ch. 9 (1962); Report of the Committee of Privy Councillors appointed to inquire into 'D' Notice matters, Cmd. 3309 (1967); The "D" Notice System, Cmd. 3312 (1967); D.G.T. Williams, *supra* note 40, at 80; 1967 Pub. L. 271–272; Franks Report, *supra* note 40, at para. 65; P. O'Higgins, *supra* note 45, at 56–59.

87.   The Services, Press and Broadcasting Committee was originally established in 1912 as the Admiralty, War Office and Press Committee. During the Second World War, the Ministry of Defence issued D Notices "agreed with representatives of the Press." Under Defence Regulation 2B (1940) the Home Secretary had power to forbid publication of a newspaper if he was satisfied that the newspaper was systematically publishing matter calculated to ferment opposition to the successful prosecution of the war. In 1941 the *Daily Worker* was suppressed under this Regulation. In 1942 the *Daily Mirror* received a formal warning. After the war the committee was reconstituted in its present form.

In fact, the general public was not aware of the existence of the D Notice system until 1961, when a D Notice was issued requesting newspapers not to report certain evidence given in court during the prosecution of George Blake. *See R.* v.

*Blake*, [1962] 2 Q.B. 377, [1961] 3 All E.R. 125. Since then two independent committees have reported on the workings of the system. *See* Cmd. 1681 (1962); Cmd. 3309 (1967). In addition, there has been a government White Paper on this issue. *See* Cmd. 3312 (1967).

The Services, Press and Broadcasting Committee is composed of five officials from government departments concerned with defense and national security and 11 representatives of the press and broadcasting organizations. There is a full-time secretary, usually a retired senior officer from the armed services.

88.   The committee also issues P and C Letters (private and confidential), which explain the relevance of old D Notices to new matters. *See* P. O'Higgins, *supra* note 40, at 56.

89.   A minister of a government department may send a draft of a D Notice that he wishes to have issued to the secretary, who will then advise on the form that is most likely to be acceptable to the press. A notice may only be issued on the authority of the committee. In an emergency, the government may ask the committee to issue a special D Notice. Such a notice requires the approval of at least three of the press and broadcasting members of the committee. Subsequently it must be reviewed by the whole committee. The notices are sent to newspapers, periodicals, radio and television, and to some publishers. Every editor receives two copies, one for himself and one for the news editor.

90.   Regrettably, however, D Notices have been issued in circumstances unrelated to national interests. *See Times*, 19 February 1979; P. O'Higgins, *supra* note 40, at 57. One former cabinet minister, Mr. George Wigg, commented: "[T]here has been a tendency in recent years towards too much secrecy in...matters which are not a question of national security but of political expediency." "Politicians and the Press," *The Listener*, 21 September 1967, at 363–366. It is too easy to use the D Notice system to cover up departmental error and inefficiency.

91.   D.G.T. Williams, *supra* note 40, at 83. In 1962, the Radcliffe Committee on Security Procedures in the Public Service (hereinafter cited as Radcliffe Committee) recommended that D Notices should not be issued for non-defense matters except "on special occasions when the subject is one of grave and obvious importance." Cmd. 1681, para. 143 (1962). *But see supra* note 90. At present there are 12 D Notices. The D Notice titles disclosed to the House of Commons Select Committee on Defence are as follows: (1) defense plans, operational capability, and state of readiness; (2) classified military weapons, weapons systems, and equipment; (3) Royal Navy, warship construction, and naval equipment; (4) aircraft and aero engines; (5) nuclear weapons and equipment; (6) photography; (7) prisoners of war and evaders; (8) national defense, war precautions, and civil defense; (9) radio and radar transmissions; (10) British intelligence services; (11) Cyphers and communications; and (12) whereabouts of Mr. and Mrs. Vladimir Petrov. Third Report from the Defense Committee, *supra* note 50, at 3.

92.   Yet only the British would describe the system as "voluntary." C. Pincher, *supra* note 77, at 229. Mr. Andrew Wilson, then defense correspondent of *The Times*, highlighted the practical dangers of noncompliance to a working journalist: "Everybody...is aware that there would be serious consequences. For example, a defence correspondent could be denied all Ministry of Defence facilities, such as visits to military establishments, transport in service aircraft, and

most important of all, off-the-record talks in Whitehall. Without these facilities most correspondents would find it extremely hard to do their job." *Times*, 26 February 1967. *See also* Franks Report, *supra* note 40, at para. 65.

93.    The D Notice system was introduced after the passing of the Official Secrets Act of 1911 because:

> Almost as soon as the Act of 1911 reached the statute book, the Government had to seek ways and means of clarifying and alleviating the position of the Press. Their solution was to set up in 1912 a Committee whose object was to let the Press know unofficially when they could commit an offence without risk of prosecution.

H. Street, *supra* note 2, at 218. *See also* Cmd. 3309 (1967), para. 6.

94.    One important reason for the paucity of prosecutions of journalists under the Official Secrets Act is no doubt the existence of the system. Between 1911 and 1972 there were only four such prosecutions. *See* Franks Report, *supra* note 40, app. II. *But see R. v. Berry, Campbell and Aubrey*, discussed *supra* at text accompanying notes 51–56.

95.    Cmd. 3312, para. 29 (1967). Its continued existence was explained by the Radcliffe Committee, Cmd. 1681, para. 135 (1962), in the following terms:

> It suits the official side, because it provides a centralised and quickly working means of communicating requests and warnings to the Press before the damage is done... it suits the Press side because, without it being mandatory, it enables an editor to know before publication that a news item is regarded by the Government as unfit for use without prejudice to the national interest... and it does give him the kind of guidance in respect of matters that may be affected by the Official Secrets Acts that he would have to look for somewhere, for his own protection, if there were no "D" Notices to rely on.

96.    *See Times*, 18 October 1967. The security service is commonly known as M.I.5 (Military Intelligence 5) and is concerned with security within the United Kingdom. The Secret Intelligence Service is commonly known as M.I.6 (Military Intelligence 6) and is concerned with security abroad. For criticism of two D Notices urging newspapers and broadcasting organizations to refrain from publishing details about British intelligence services and government ciphers and communications, *see Times*, 2 April 1980; *New Statesman*, 3 April 1980.

97.    *See* 748 H.C. Official Report (5th series) cols. 1972–2100; 284 H.L. Official Report (5th series) cols. 767–846.

98.    The Official Secrets Act 1920, §4, does authorize this practice in limited circumstances. Then-Prime Minister Mr. Harold Wilson claimed the article violated two D Notices. The author claimed that the D Notices did not apply to this information. *See* C. Pincher, *supra* note 77, ch. 23.

99.    The Radcliffe Committee, *supra* note 86. The Report found no deliberate intention by the *Daily Express* to evade or defy the D Notice procedure; moreover, the story was accurate. On the same day that the Report was published, the Prime Minister issued a White Paper (Cmd. 3312) rejecting its findings.

100.    *See Times*, 16 May 1980.

101.    *See* Williams, *Official Secrecy in England*, 1968 3 Fed. L. Rev. 20, 35 (1968). *See also Times*, 12 June 1980; *Times*, 3 July 1980.

102.    *In Re Grosvenor Hotel, London (No. 2)*, [1965] Ch. 1210, 1248 [1964] 3 All E.R. 354, 363 (per Harman, L.J.).

103.    Cmd. 3309, para. 66 (1967).

104.    The D Notice system was suspended in both world wars and replaced by direct government censorship. *See Times*, 9 July 1980. *See also* D.G.T. Williams, *supra* note 40, at 76. Press censorship was, however, in keeping with British colonial practice. *See, e.g.,* E. Summerlad, *The Press in Developing Countries* (1966). On censorship during the Falklands war, see M. Hastings and S. Jenkins, *The Battle for the Falklands* (1983).

105.    Third Report from the Defence Committee, *supra* note 50, at para. 3a; *see also Times*, 23 July 1980; *Times*, 8 August 1980.

106.    Third Report from the Defence Committee, *supra* note 50, at para. 24.

107.    *Id.* at paras. 654 and 17 and app. 12, p. 138.

108.    *Id.* at para. 17.

109.    *Id.* at paras. 497 and 11.

110.    *Id.* at para. 30.

111.    Treason Act, 1814, §1. The Act covers (a) compassing and imagining the death of the King, his queen, or their eldest son and heir; (b) violating the King's wife, or his eldest daughter unmarried or the wife of his eldest son and heir; (c) levying war against the King in his realm; (d) being adherent to the King's enemies in his realm; and (e) killing the Chancellor, Treasurer, or the King's justices, in their places doing their offices. *See generally* 1 *Russell on Crime* 207 (12th ed. 1964); *Kenny's Outlines of Criminal Law* 295 (19th ed. 1966); J.C. Smith and B. Hogan, *supra* note 41.

112.    Law Com. Working Paper no. 72, para. 14 (1977) (hereinafter cited as "Law Com. Working Paper").

113.    This form of treason was invoked to deal with acts of disloyalty in the two world wars. Apart from cases in wartime, there is in fact no modern instance of prosecution in the United Kingdom courts for treason. Law Com. Working Paper, *supra* note 112, at para. 47. The King's enemies are foreign states in actual hostility against him, whether there has been a declaration of war or not. *Kenny, supra* note 111, at 399.

114.    Law Com. Working Paper, *supra* note 112, at para. 3. The committee also recommended that a specific offense apply in peacetime to prohibit the overthrow, or the supplanting by force, of constitutional government. *Id.* at para. 6.

115.    *See* 2 J. Stephen, *History of the Criminal Law of England* 298 [1883].

116.    [1951] 2 D.L.R. 369, 382 (Kellock, J.).

117.    *See* H. Street, *supra* note 2, at 214; Law Com. Working Paper, *supra* note 112.

118.    [1951] 2 D.L.R. at 389–390.

119.    *Id.* at 393.

120.    *Id.* at 389. Although the House of Lords has cast doubt on whether there is a distinct crime of effecting a public mischief, publication of, for example, an anti-Semitic article, may now constitute an offense under the Race Relations Act of 1976.

Even the modern interpretation of sedition leaves certain difficulties. First, it cannot be claimed that it is related in all respects to the genuine likelihood of disorder. If the latter requirement stands, publication is necessary. Second, there is some support for the view that the accused must take his audience as he finds it. In deciding whether the words have a tendency to incite public disorder, it is proper to look at all the circumstances, including the nature of the audience addressed, the place, the state of public feeling, and so on. Third, there still may be room for the view that advocacy of violent methods is seditious even if no violent action results or is likely to result. Fourth, statements published that are defamatory of the sovereign seem to be regarded, as it were, as seditious per se; but on this subject there are no modern cases.

121. *R.* v. *Caunt*, [1948] 64 L.Q.R. 203, *noted* in 64 Law Q. Rev. 203 (1948); *see* J.C. Smith and B. Hogan, *supra* note 41, at 804–805; *see also R.* v. *Aldred*, [1909] 74 J.P. 55; *R.* v. *Burns*, [1886] 16 Cox C.C. 355, 362, 364, (Cave, J.); *R.* v. *Burdett*, [1820] 1 State TR NS, 1, 122, 123, 128, 139.

122. *See Boucher* v. *R.*, [1951] 2 D.L.R. 369, 389; Law Com. Working Paper, *supra* note 112, at para. 77.

123. The date of *R.* v. *Aldred*, [1909] 74 J.P. 55.

124. [1951] 2 D.L.R. 369; *see supra* text accompanying notes 116–120.

125. 1940 A.C. 231, [1940] 1 All E.R. 241.

126. *See* 64 Law Q. Rev. 203 (1948).

127. Law Com. Working Paper, *supra* note 112, at para. 76. *See R.* v. *Callinan, Quinn and Marcantonio, Times*, 20 January 1973, CCC. After the charges alleging treason-felony were quashed, Callinan pleaded guilty to two charges, and Marcantonio to one charge, of unlawfully and seditiously uttering certain words in Hyde Park.

128. *See* Criminal Law Act, 1967, sched. I, List B. The Police Offences Amendment Act of 1951, indicates that the New Zealand legislature considers that the offence is still of significance.

129. Note, for example, affray; and also misprision of felony, and conspiracy to corrupt public morals. *See Brownlie's Law of Public Order and National Security*, *supra* note 25, at 140–146.

130. Post-1909 charges include the following: McLean, Maxton, McDougall and Jack Smith (1916); Muln, Bell and Gallacher (1916); Ramsay (1919); Pollitt and others (1925); Mann and Pollitt (1934); Spence and others (1966). The latter case involved charges of seditious conspiracy. *See Times*, 26 August 1966. *Cf.* 2 J. Stephen, *supra* note 115, at 377.

131. *See* Law Com. Working Paper, *supra* note 112, at para. 78.

132. [1951] 2 D.L.R. 369.

133. *See* H. Street, *supra* note 2, at 212.

134. On incitement at common law, see J.C. Smith and B. Hogan, *supra* note 41, at 212–215.

135. Mutiny by members of the armed forces is punishable under the Army Act of 1955, the Air Force Act of 1955, and the Navy Discipline Act of 1957.

136. Originally, the Act applied to the Army and Navy. It was extended to include the Air Force in 1918. Air Force (Application of Enactments) (No. 2) Order 1918, Stat. R. & O. 1918 No. 548.

137. Incitement to Disaffection Act, 1934, 24 and 25 Geo. 5, ch. 56.

138. Section 1 of the Act provides: "If any person maliciously and advisedly endeavors to seduce any member of Her Majesty's forces from his duty or

allegiance to Her Majesty, he shall be guilty of an offence under this Act."

139.   Section 2(1) provides:

If any person, with intent to commit or to aid, abet, counsel, or procure the commission of an offence under section 1 of this Act, has in his possession or under his control any document of such a nature that the dissemination of copies thereof among members of His Majesty's forces would constitute such an offence, he should be guilty of an offence under this Act.

140.   *See R.* v. *Bowman*, (1912) 76 J.P. 271; *R.* v. *Fuller*, (1797) 2 Leach 790; J.C. Smith and B. Hogan, *supra* note 41, at 807.

141.   *See* I. Jennings, *The Sedition Bill Explained* (1934); H. Street, *supra* note 2, at 215–218; D.G.T. Williams, *supra* note 40, at 102–103.

142.   That Act necessitated trial on indictment in every case with a maximum penalty of life imprisonment. The 1934 Act made it possible either to charge offenders for a summary offense before magistrates or to indict them and have them tried before a jury.

143.   The 1934 Act replaced "duty *and* allegiance" with "duty *or* allegiance." A further objection to the Act is that no act by the possessor need be proved for a section 2(1) offense. Once possession and intention are established the accused is guilty. No seduction of any soldier need take place, nor any act of seduction.

144.   *See* de Smith, *supra* note 81, at 470. *See also* European Convention for the Protection of Human Rights and Fundamental Freedoms, Art. 10(1). *But see* Law Com. Working Paper, *supra* note 112, at paras. 92–93 for comments.

145.   H. Street, *supra* note 2, at 220; *see R.* v. *Arrowsmith*, [1975] Q.B. 678, [1975] 1 All E.R. 463; *R.* v. *Williams, Times*, 11 December 1975, CCC.

146.   *See* H. Street, *supra* note 2, at 220. Law Commissioners propose that if the Act is retained it should be amended. Law Com. Working Paper, *supra* note 112, at para. 96(8).

147.   This could be furthered by replacing the words "maliciously and advisedly" in section 1 with words more in accord with modern usage.

148.   12 Statutes 883; 12 Statutes 909. *See* Grigg Committee Report, Cmd. 9163 (1954), which led to the 1958 Act.

149.   The Public Records Act of 1958 and 1967 apply to England and Wales. Scotland has its own public records law. Since 1968, however, access to government records in Scotland has been controlled by the same rules that cover Whitehall departments. *See Times*, 22 April 1980.

150.   The 1967 Act reduced the presumptive period from 50 years in the 1958 Act to 30 years. The 30-year period has been criticized as "an unnecessarily long time." Anderson, *Liberty, Law and Justice* 114 (Hamlyn Lectures, 1978).

151.   *See* D.G.T. Williams, *supra* note 40, at 67.

152.   In 1967 Lord Gardiner, then-Lord Chancellor, explained the criteria on which extensions to the basic 30-year period are likely to be made:

[F]irst, those containing information about individuals whose disclosure would cause distress or embarrassment to living persons or their immediate descendants (such as criminal or prison records, records of courts martial, records of suspected persons and certain police records); secondly, those containing information obtained under a pledge of confidence, such as the census and various individual returns used in publishing statistical compilations; thirdly, certain papers relating to Irish Affairs; fourthly, certain exceptionally sensitive papers which affect the security of the State. In addition certain papers the ownership of which is shared with "old" Commonwealth countries, cannot be released until all the Governments concerned have given their consent.

282 H.L. Official Report (5th Series) cols. 1657–1658.

153.   *See* H. Street, *supra* note 2, at 238. Some documents are classified for up to 100 years.

154.   *Times*, 3 January 1978.

155.   *Times*, 11 May 1977.

156.   *See* E. Wade and G. Phillips, *supra* note 41, at 250–252. The Public Records Committee, established in 1978, is examining the operation of the Public Records Acts. *See Times*, 7 February 1980.

157.   *Times*, 11 May 1977. *But see Times*, 19 February 1980 (delay may simply be caused by the lack of reviewers to sift the material and prepare it for release).

158.   *Times*, 3 May 1977; *see* Cmd. 6677 (1976) Report of the Committee of Privy Counsellors on Cabinet Security; P. O'Higgins, *supra* note 45, at 153.

159.   The convention permits former ministers to have access to such papers, but not to photocopy or remove them. *See Times*, 7 February 1980. But "[f]ormer Cabinet Ministers...[can] side-step the bars on publication of official Cabinet documents by talking about Cabinet activities rather than quoting Cabinet documents." *Times*, 29 November 1968; *see* P. O'Higgins, *supra* note 45, at 154.

160.   *See* section II.A. *supra*. No minister has ever been prosecuted for breach to the Acts. In 1934, George Lansbury's son was convicted of receiving Cabinet memoranda which he had used in writing a book about his father. "He could only have broken section 2 [of the Official Secrets Act, 1911] by receiving the documents, if they had been communicated to him in contravention of the section." His father was recognized as having given them to him, but was not prosecuted. Franks Report, *supra* note 40, app. II, at 116.

161.   There were two actions: one against the literary executors of Richard Crossman; the other against the *Sunday Times* newspaper. *Attorney General* v. *Jonathan Cape Ltd., Attorney General* v. *Times Newspapers Ltd.*, [1976] 1 Q.B. 752, [1975] 3 All E.R. 484. *See* H. Young, *The Crossman Affair*, 1975 Pub. L. 277.

162.   R. Crossman, *Diaries of a Cabinet Minister* [1975] [preface].

163.   [1976] 1 Q.B. at 767.

164.   The Attorney General sought to restrain publication of three classes of communications: discussions in the Cabinet or in cabinet committees; policy communications between ministers or between ministers and civil servants; and discussions concerning the appointment, transfer, or fitness for office of senior civil servants. *See* Comment, 1975 Pub. L. 277.

165.   [1976] 1 Q.B. at 764. The doctrine of collective responsibility is, however, only a "convention," not law. "There is no conflict between the proposition that governments have a right or liberty to protect their secrets whilst others have a right to find them out." Comment, *supra* note 164, at 279.

166.   [1976] 1 Q.B. at 771. "If free and frank discussion really rests upon the confidence principle it will hardly survive in the same form if the participants are aware that present confidences may well share the same fate as past confidences." Comment, *supra* note 164, at 278.

167. [1975] 1 Q.B. at 768, 770. *Compare New York Times* v. *United States*, 403 U.S. 713 (1971). The courts have considered the problem of disclosure at the request of a party to legal proceedings. *Compare Duncan* v. *Cammell Laird & Co. Ltd.*, 1942 A.C. 624; *Conway* v. *Rimmer*, 1968 A.C. 910; *Burmah Oil Co. Ltd.* v. *Bank of England*, [1979] 3 W.L.R. 722; *Science Research Council* v. *Nassé, BL Cars Ltd.* v. *Vyas*, [1979] 3 W.L.R. 762. *See Air Canada* v. *Secretary of State for Trade* [1983] 2 W.L.R. 494 (H.L.).

168. *See generally* H. Street, *supra* note 2, at 231–234; Report of Committee of Privy Councillors on Ministerial Memoirs. Cmd. 6386 (1976). The proposals resembled submissions of the Attorney General that had been rejected by the Divisional Court the previous year.

169. *Times*, 10 May 1977. *See also* C. Pincher, *supra* note 77, at 216–219 (concerning the publication of Lord Russell of Liverpool's book *The Scourge of the Swastika.*)

170. *See* text accompanying note 150 *supra.*

171. They were also reminded of the Official Secrets Act.

172. N. Anderson, *supra* note 150, at 114.

173. H. Street, *supra* note 2, at 238.

174. N. Anderson, *supra* note 150, at 114 (quoting Lord Devlin).

175. [1968] 1 All E.R. 874; [1976] 1 Q.B. 752, [1975] 3 All E.R. 484; [1979] 3 All E.R. 700.

176. The Franks Committee stated that it had not investigated fully the possibility of legislation in the United Kingdom along the lines of the Freedom of Information Act as it was not entirely within the committee's terms of reference. Franks Report, *supra* note 40, at para. 85. The 1978 government White Paper reiterated the principle of the right to know but made only minor modifications to the Franks Report proposals. *See supra* note 80. Also, Lord Scarman recommended a British Freedom of Information Act modelled on American and Swedish legislation and the establishment of judicial review of the right of access. Under the government's proposals made on the Franks Report, Cmd. 7285 (1978), there would be more prosecutions but no greater right of public access to information. The same criticism can be made of the Protection of Information Bill, 1979. For an alternative proposal, *see* the Report of "Justice," Freedom of Information (1978), which recommends a Code of Practice, the first principle under which is that "as much information as is reasonably and practicably possible relating to government and administration should be disclosed." *Id.* at para. 8. *But see id.* annex. 2, para. 9 (Proposed Code of Practice) for breadth of exemptions. *See also Times*, 10 March 1980; *Open up!* (Fabian tract 467, 1980).

177. Criminal contempt of court can be grouped under five separate headings:

(i) publications prejudicial to a fair criminal trial;
(ii) publications prejudicial to a fair civil trial;
(iii) scandalising the court;
(iv) contempt in the face of the court; and
(v) acts which interfere with the course of justice.

*See* G. Borrie and N. Lowe, *The Law of Contempt* (2nd ed. 1983). The press is primarily concerned with the first two categories and occasionally with the third.

The question of civil contempt of court—breach of an order of court—normally concerns the press only on the question of reporter's privilege. *See infra* section III.B.

178.   Report of the Committee on Contempt of Court, Cmd. 5794, para. 1 (1974) (hereinafter cited as Phillimore Committee).

179.   *See Morris* v. *The Crown Office*, [1970] 1 All E.R. 1079, 1087 (Salmon, L.J.).

180.   *See* S.H. Bailey, B. Harris and B.L. Jones, *Civil Liberties, Cases and Materials* 243 (1980).

181.   Such a right was introduced by the Administration of Justice Act, 1960.

182.   *See* Contempt of Court Act, 1981, §14(1). The maximum sentence is two years in the case of committal by a superior court or one month in the case of committal by an inferior court.

183.   *See* C. Wintour, *supra* note 2, at 129.

184.   *Attorney General* v. *Times Newspapers Ltd.*, [1973] 1 Q.B. 710 (D.C. and C.A.), 1974 A.C. 273 (H.L.). *See Generally Suffer the Children—The Story of Thalidomide* (1979) (a history of events surrounding the case written by Philip Knightley and other *Sunday Times* journalists).

185.   [1974] A.C. 273.

186.   Article 10 provides, in pertinent part:

1.   Everyone has the right to freedom of expression. This right shall include freedom to hold opinions and to receive and impart information and ideas without interference by public authority....

2.   The exercise of these freedoms, since it carries with it duties and responsibilities, may be subject to such formalities, conditions, restrictions or penalties as are prescribed by law and are necessary in a democratic society...for maintaining the authority and impartiality of the judiciary.

European Convention on Human Rights and Fundamental Freedoms, 4 November 1950, 1955 Gr. Brit. T.S. No. 71 (Cmd. 8969) (hereinafter cited as "European Convention on Human Rights").

187.   *Sunday Times* v. *United Kingdom* (1979), Eur. Ct. of Human Rights, Series A, No. 30, *reprinted in* 2 Eur. Hum. Rts. Rep. 245 (1979).

188.   *Id.* at para. 66, reprinted in 2 Eur. Hum. Rts. Rep. at 281.

189.   *Id.* at para. 65, reprinted in 2 Eur. Hum. Rts. Rep. at 280.

[F]reedom of expression constitutes one of the essential foundations of a democratic society;.... it is applicable not only to information or ideas that are favourably received...but also to those that offend...the State or any sector of the population....

[T]he courts cannot operate in a vacuum. Whilst they are the forum for the settlement of disputes, this does not mean that there can be no prior discussion of disputes elsewhere, be it in specialised journals, in the general press or amongst the public at large. Furthermore, whilst the mass media must not overstep the bounds imported in the interest of the proper administration of justice,... it is incumbent on them to impart information and ideas concerning matters that come before the courts...[and] the public also has a right to receive them.

190. *Id.* at para. 66 (quoting Article 10(2) of the European Convention on Human Rights), *reprinted in* 2 Eur. Hum. Rts. Rep. at 281.

191. *Id.* at para. 67, *reprinted in* 2 Eur. Hum. Rts. Rep. at 282.

192. *See, e.g., Handyside* v. *United Kingdom* (1976), Eur. Ct. of Human Rights, Series A, No. 24; *Golder* v. *United Kingdom*, 1970 Y.B. Eur. Conv. on Human Rights 416; *Ireland* v. *United Kingdom*, 2 Eur. Hum. Rts. Rep. 25 (1978). *See also* Mann, *Contempt of Court in the House of Lords and the European Court of Human Rights*, 95 Law Q. Rev. 348; Gray, *European Convention on Human Rights—Freedom of Expression and the Thalidomide Case*, (1979) C.L.J. 242.

193. The *Sunday Times* case strengthens the argument for the incorporation of the Convention into English Law. *See Brownlie's Law of Public Order and National Security, supra* note 25, at 338.

194. *See supra* note 178.

195. Phillimore Committee, *supra* note 178, at paras. 111, 113. In two cases subsequent to the *Sunday Times* case, lower courts held that prejudgment would amount to contempt only when it creates a real risk of prejudice to the fair and proper trial of the pending proceedings. *See Blackburn* v. *B.B.C., Times,* 15 December 1976; *R.* v. *Bulgin ex parte B.B.C., Times,* 14 July 1977.

196. Phillimore Committee, *supra* note 178, at para. 111.

197. *See* A. Aldridge and D. Eady *The Law of Contempt* (1982), para. 2–01a.

198. A publication includes "any speech, writing, broadcast or other communication in whatever form, which is addressed to the public at large or any section of the public." Contempt of Court Act, 1981.

199. Contempt of court is a crime of general intent. A. Aldridge and D. Eady, *supra* note 197 at para. 2–80.

200. The Contempt of Court Act, 1981, does not create any new offense but merely limits the application of the strict liability rule (section 6). Thus the decision in *Attorney-General* v. *Times Newspapers Ltd.* "may still be good law in relation to these cases which fall outside the rule." *See* A. Aldridge and D. Eady, *supra* note 197, at para. 2–13.

201. [1982] 3 W.L.R. 278.

202. The article included the statement: "Today the chances of such a baby surviving would be very small indeed. Someone would surely recommend letting her die of starvation, or otherwise disposing of her...." [1982] 3 W.L.R. 278, 283.

203. [1982] 3 W.L.R. 278 at 287–288.

204. *Id.*

205. *Id.* at 288.

206. [1982] 3 W.L.R. 278.

207. *Id.*

208. *Id.* at 286.

209. Comment: Fair Trial and Free Press, [1982] Pub. L. 343 at 344.

210. *See R.* v. *Savundranayagan and Walker*, [1968] 1 W.L.R. 1961.

211. *See, e.g., R.* v. *Parke*, [1903] 2 K.B. 432, 437–438 ("It is possible to effectively poison the fountain of justice before it begins to flow.") (Wills, J.).

212. Notwithstanding the Court's criticism, David Frost later wrote that he did not know that Savundra's trial was pending although he had gone to some lengths to find out. *See* H. Street, *supra* note 2, at 177. The problem of "trial by

television," as it affects Tribunals of Inquiry, was expressed well in the Report of the Committee on Contempt Cmd. 4078, para. 31 (1969): "The real danger...is that the witnesses whose evidence is vital to the matter under investigation are questioned without any of the safeguards which are obtained in our courts...or before Tribunals of Inquiry." Compare this with the Phillimore Committee's finding that "responsibly conducted, they make a useful contribution to public information." Phillimore Committee, *supra* note 178, at para. 55.

213.    Under the Act, the "strict liability rule" means that "conduct may be treated as contempt of court as tending to interfere with the course of justice in particular legal proceedings *regardless of intent to do so*." Contempt of Court Act, 1981, §1 (emphasis supplied).

214.    *Id.* §2(3) and sched. I.

215.    *Id.* sched. I, paras. 3, 4.

216.    P. Carter-Ruck, *Contempt of Court Act, 1981*, Law Society's Gazette, 28 October 1981, at 1184. Proceedings are not active if no arrest is made pursuant to a warrant within 12 months; they become active when arrest is effected.

217.    Contempt of Court Act, 1981, ch. 49, sched. I, para. 12.

218.    Lord Salmon told the Phillimore Committee that he thought criminal contempt completely irrelevant in civil proceedings if the case would be tried only by a judge: "I think the law of libel takes care of anything you may say about a civil case, and if a judge is going to be affected by what is written or said, he is not fit to be a judge." Evidence to the Phillimore Committee, *supra* note 178.

219.    *See, e.g.,* (1974) A.C. 273 at 301 (Lord Reid).

220.    *Wallerstein* v. *Moir*, [1974] 1 W.L.R. 991, 1005; *Thompson* v. *Times Newspapers Ltd.*, [1969] 1 W.L.R. 1236, 1239–1240 (Salmon, J.). *See also Attorney General* v. *B.B.C.* [1979] 3 W.L.R. 312, 319.

221.    Contempt of Court Act, 1981, sched. I, para. 15.

222.    The Law Society's Gazette, 28 October 1981, at 1185.

223.    *R.* v. *Duffy*, [1960] 2 Q.B. 188, 198 (Lord Parker).

224.    A. Aldridge and D. Eady, *supra* note 197 at para. 4–46.

225.    *Id.* at para. 4–34.

226.    [1974] A.C. 277 (H.L.).

227.    *See* [1974] A.C. 277 at 307.

228.    Aldridge and Eady can see "no reason in principle why [the defence] should not apply to all contempts" *supra* note 197, at para. 3–91. However the matter is not free from doubt. *Id.* at para 3–90.

229.    *See* J. Whale, *supra* note 2, at 133.

230.    *See* H. Street, *supra* note 2, at 178–179. This is despite section 5 which permits publication made "as part of a discussion in good faith of public affairs" if the risk to particular legal proceedings "is merely incidental to the discussion." Contempt of Court Act, 1981, ch. 49, §5.

231.    The Law Society's Gazette, 28 October 1981, at 1184.

232.    A. Aldridge and D. Eady, *supra* note 197, at para. 3–93.

233.    *Id.* at para 3–92.

234.    Cmd. §794, para. 62.

235.    A. Aldridge and D. Eady, *supra* note 197, at para. 3–95.

236.    Children and Young Persons Act, 1933, as amended by Children and Young Persons Act, 1969.

237.   Judicial Proceedings (Regulation of Reports) Act, 1926.

238.   Magistrates Courts Act, 1980, §71; and Domestic and Appellate Proceedings (Restriction of Publicity) Act, 1968.

239.   Criminal Justice Act, 1967, §3, now replaced by Magistrates Courts Act, 1980, §§8(4).

240.   Official Secrets Act, 1920, §8(4).

241.   Sexual Offenses (Amendment) Act, 1976, §§4, 6.

242.   Contempt of Court Act, 1981, §4(2). Under subsection 4(1) the strict liability rule is not applied to "a fair and accurate report of legal proceedings held in public, published contemporaneously and in good faith." *Id.* §4(1). Under subsection 4(2), however, the court may order the postponement of publication of any report if "it appears to be necessary for avoiding a substantial risk of prejudice to the administration of justice in those proceedings, or in any other proceedings pendent or imminent." *Id.* §4(2). Where reporting restrictions at committal proceedings have been lifted under section 8 of the Magistrates Courts Act, 1980, the court can still restrict publication under section 4(2) of the Contempt of Court Act, 1981. However, an order under that section should be no wider than is necessary for the prevention of prejudice to the administration of justice: *R. v. Horsham J.J., ex p. Farquharson,* [1982] 2 W.L.R. 430.

243.   Comment, *Contempt of Court,* (1981) Pub. L. 145, 146.

244.   *R. v. Horsham Justices ex parte Farquharson and Another, Times,* 22 December 1981 (C.A.).

245.   The court relied on its power under subsection 4(2) of the Contempt of Court Act, 1981.

246.   *Times,* 22 December 1981, at 3. *Also see* Practice Direction (Contempt Reporting Restrictions) [1982] W.L.R. 1475. For the first time, the confidentiality of jury deliberations is preserved by statute. *See* Contempt of Court Act, 1981, §8 which supercedes the decision in *Attorney General* v. *The New Statesman* [1980] 2 W.L.R. 246 (D.C.).

247.   Subsequently he has been convicted of the murder of 13 women and the attempted murder of 7 more.

248.   *Times,* 7 January 1981. In general, publishing photographs is an area of danger for the press. *See, e.g., R. v. Thomson Newspapers Ltd.* ex parte Attorney General, [1968] 1 All E.R. 268. *See also R. v. Evening Standard Ltd. ex parte Attorney General, Times,* 3 November 1977 (D.C.) (Company fined £1,000 for publishing a photograph of the defendant together with an article on the front page of the *Evening Standard* on the day that he was to take part in an identification parade after being charged with theft of £490 from a bank in Putney. He was ultimately acquitted.) *See* P. Hain, *Mistaken Identity* 21–22, 39, 40, 42–85 (1976).

249.   H. Street, *supra* note 2, at 179.

250.   The 1977 Commission, *supra* note 2, at para. 10.150.

251.   *See* the "Crumbles" case: *Evening Standard ex parte D.P.P.,* [1924] 40 T.L.R. 833.

252.   H. Street, *supra* note 2, at 180.

253.   *R. v. Metropolitan Commissioner ex parte Blackburn,* [1968] 2 Q.B. 150, 155. *See also R. v. Chandler, Randle and Foley, The Guardian,* 9 November 1967. This was not always so. *See R. v. Gray,* [1900] 2 Q.B. 36; *R. v. New Statesman (Editor),* [1928] 44 T.L.R. 301.

254.   Second report from the Committee of Privileges, 1956–1957, 20 December 1956. *See also* H. Street, *supra* note 2, at 189–190.

255.   H. Street, *supra* note 2, at 192. If an M.P.'s character is attacked, his remedy is an action for defamation. Serious attacks on institutions of government may be punishable as libel, either seditious or defamatory. *See also Attorney General* v. *Leveller Magazine Ltd.*, [1979] 1 All E.R. 745 (H.L.); and 1978 CLJ 196, 198 (case and comment).

256.   Dyson, [1943] 29 Cr. App. R. 104. For examples of the English courts' usual approach, *see Thomson Newspapers Ltd. ex parte Attorney General*, [1968] 1 All E.R. 582 (the *Sunday Times* was fined for contempt for references to a defendant's unsavory past, yet the Court of Appeal refused to quash his subsequent conviction); *R.* v. *Savundramayagam and Walker, supra* note 210.

257.   3 W. Holdsworth, *A History of English Law* 393 (5th ed. 1942). The jurisdiction is essentially without rule, regulation or safeguard, except as modified by statute. It was criticized as early as 1877 as "arbitrary and unlimited." *In re Clements and the Republic of Costa Rica* v. *Erlanger*, [1877] 46 L.J. Ch. 375, 383.

258.   The procedures apply even when the offender is in prison. *See* G. Borrie and N. Lowe, *supra* note 177.

259.   Phillimore Committee, *supra* note 178, at para. 21.

260.   *See* R. Williams, *The Long Revolution* 217–218 (1965); R. Williams, *Dangerous Estate* 109–110 (1959).

261.   *Attorney-General* v. *Mulholland, Attorney-General* v. *Foster* [1963] 2 Q.B. 477.

262.   *Id.*

263.   [1980] 3 W.L.R. 774. Granada Television broadcast on a national television network a current affairs program devoted to a strike in the nationalized steel industry. The strike was of great concern to the government and to the public. The program quoted from a number of secret or confidential documents (the "Steel Papers"), the property of British Steel which had been leaked to Granada Television by an employee of British Steel. The documents revealed various faults in the corporation's management. *See* discussion *supra* text accompanying notes 33–34.

264.   Only Lord Salmon, who emphasized the importance of the press in informing the public, dissented. In the Court of Appeal, Lord Denning, M.R., recognized a qualified privilege, subject to the condition that the newspaper act with a due sense of responsibility. *Id.* at 805. He came to the unreasonable conclusion that Granada had not acted with a due sense of responsibility, thereby forfeiting its claim to protect its sources of information. *See also id.* at 842 (Lord Salmon, dissenting).

265.   *Id.* at 821 (Lord Wilberforce).

266.   *Id.* at 821 (Lord Wilberforce), 829 (Viscount Dilhorne), 853 (Lord Fraser).

267.   *Id.* at 852 (Lord Fraser).

268.   *Id.* at 846 (Lord Salmon, dissenting).

269.   [1980] 3 W.L.R. at 836, 843 (Lord Salmon, dissenting).

270.   [1982] Crim. L.R. 296.

271.   Contempt of Court Act, 1981, §10.

272.   Report of the Committee on Defamation, Cmd. 5909, para. 19 (1975) (hereinafter cited as Faulks Committee).

273.  C. Wintour, *supra* note 2, at 109, 111–112.

274.  Faulks Committee, *supra* note 272, at para. 20.

275.  [1968] 2 Q.B. 157, 179. Despite the Faulks Committee's various suggestions for reform, no action has been taken.

276.  *See* P. Winfield and J. Jolowicz, *Winfield & Jolowicz on Tort* 276 (11th ed. 1979). Moreover, broadcasting and theatrical performances are treated as publication in permanent form, i.e., as libel. *See* C. Duncan and B. Neill, *Defamation* 3 (1978).

277.  P. Winfield and J. Jolowicz, *supra* note 276, at 278. "Special damage" is a phrase that has been criticized as either meaningless or misleading. "Actual damage" is a more accurate expression. Whatever the adjective used, it signifies that no damages are recoverable merely for loss of reputation by reason of the slander, and that the plaintiff must prove loss of money or of some material advantage which can be compensated in money.

278.  The Faulks Committee recommended abolishing the distinction and assimilating slander to libel for purposes of civil proceedings. Faulks Committee, *supra* note 272, at para. 91.

279.  C. Duncan and B. Neill, *supra* note 262, at 4.01.

280.  The Faulks Committee, *supra* note 272, at para. 92.

281.  *See Lewis* v. *The Daily Telegraph Ltd.*, [1964] A.C. 234, 277 (Lord Devlin).

282.  C. Duncan & B. Neill, *supra* note 276, at 4.01.

283.  *Sim* v. *Stretch*, [1936] 52 T.L.R. 669, 671 (Lord Atkin).

284.  H. Fraser, *Libel and Slander* 1 (7th ed. 1936).

285.  Faulks Committee, *supra* note 258, at para. 2. Duncan and Neill opposed this definition since it further complicates interpretation. C. Duncan and B. Neil, *supra* note 276, at 7.07.

286.  *Id.* at 4.01.

287.  The natural and ordinary meaning of words is determined in accordance with the following principles. The court decides the meaning as a question of fact by attributing to the words the meaning that the court considers they would convey to ordinary reasonable persons. This meaning is not limited to the literal meaning of words but includes any inference or implication which could reasonably be drawn. The words are to be construed in their context. *Id.* at 4.04. In *Lewis* v. *Daily Telegraph Ltd.*, [1964] A.C. 234, Lord Reid put the matter as follows: "Sometimes it is not necessary to go beyond the words themselves, as where the plaintiff is being called a thief or a murderer. But more often the sting is not so much in the words themselves as in what the ordinary man will infer from them, and that is also regarded as part of their natural and ordinary meaning." *Id.* at 258.

288.  *See E. Hulton & Co.* v. *Jones*, [1910] A.C. 20, 23 (Lord Loreburn L.C.); *Cassidy* v. *Daily Mirror Newspaper*, [1929] 2 K.B. 331, 354 (Russell L.J.).

289.  C. Duncan and B. Neill, *supra* note 276, at 4.04. *See Hough* v. *London Express Newspaper Ltd.*, [1940] 2 K.B. 507, 515 (Goddard L.J.). It follows, therefore, that a man may be defamed even though the publishee does not believe the imputation against him or knows it to be false. *See Morgan* v. *Odhams Press Ltd.*, [1971] 2 All E.R. 1156, 1168 (Lord Morris); *id.* at 1163 (Lord Reid).

290.  *See Lewis* v. *Daily Telegraph Ltd.*, [1964] A.C. 234, 259 (Lord Reid); *Morgan* v. *Odhams Press Ltd.*, [1971] 2 All E.R. 1156, 1168 (Lord Morris); *Jones* v. *Skelton*, [1963] 3 All E.R. 952, 958 (Lord Morris).

291. P. Winfield and J. Jolowicz, *supra* note 276, at 287.

292. One of the best known cases concerning the successful use of the innuendo is *Tolley* v. *Fry & Sons Ltd.*, [1931] A.C. 333. The plaintiff, a famous amateur golfer, was portrayed by the defendants, without his knowledge or consent, in an advertisement for their chocolate. The advertisement depicted him with a packet of the chocolate protruding from his pocket. Mere juxtaposition to noxious matter may make an otherwise innocent representation defamatory. The famous instance of this is *Monson* v. *Tussauds Ltd.*, [1894] 1 Q.B. 671. The defendants, who kept a waxworks exhibition, exhibited a wax model of the plaintiff with a gun in a room which adjoined the "Chamber of Horrors."

293. *E. Hulton and Co.* v. *Jones*, 1910 A.C. 20. *See* Defamation Act, 1952, §4 (defence of "Unintentional Defamation"). *See also Morgan* v. *Odhams Press Ltd.*, [1971] 1 W.L.R. 1239; Holdsworth, 57 Law Q. Rev. 74.

294. *See, e.g.*, Holdsworth, *supra* note 293.

295. Faulks Committee, *supra* note 272, at paras. 121–123.

296. *See Hough* v. *London Express Newspapers Ltd.*, [1940] 2 K.B. 507.

297. Although each communication is a separate publication, a plaintiff will probably not be allowed to bring more than one action regarding different copies of a newspaper. *See Jones* v. *Pritchard*, [1849] 6 D.O.W. and L529; *Goldsmith* v. *Sperrings Ltd.*, [1977] 1 W.L.R. 478, 489. The Faulks Committee recommended that if proceedings regarding a defamation have been concluded, the plaintiff should not be allowed to bring proceedings, or continue further proceedings in the same matter, without leave of the court. Faulks Committee, *supra* note 272, at para. 29.

298. Subject to the defense of innocent dissemination, news agents who sell the newspaper to the public are also liable. *See infra* text accompanying notes 321–322.

299. C. Duncan and B. Neill, *supra* note 276, at 8.12.

300. R. Callender-Smith, *Press Law* 16 (1978).

301. Faulks Committee, *supra* note 272, at para. 129.

302. This is now subject to an exception if details of a person's "spent" conviction are published maliciously. Whether convictions can become "spent" or the length of time that elapses before they do, depends on the gravity of the sentence. For example, a sentence of imprisonment of over two and one-half years can never be rehabilitated. A fine on the other hand, is a conviction which may become "spent" after five years. *See* Rehabilitation of Offenders Act, 1974.

303. The defendant need not prove the truth of every detail of the words.

304. *Lewis* v. *Daily Telegraph Ltd.* 1964 A.C. 234, 283 (Lord Devlin).

305. Faulks Committee, *supra* note 272, at para. 134.

306. *See infra* section IV.B..

307. *London Artists Ltd.* v. *Littler*, [1969] 2 Q.B. 375, 391 (Lord Denning M.R.). *See infra* text accompanying note 296.

308. *Kemsley* v. *Foot*, [1952] A.C. 345, 356 (Lord Porter). Defamation Act, 1952, §6.

309. Faulks Committee, *supra* note 272, at paras. 151, 152.

310. *Id.* at para. 155.

311. C. Duncan and B. Neill, *supra* note 276, at para 12.26. *See Silkin* v. *Beaverbrook Newspapers Ltd.*, [1958] 2 All E.R. 516; *Campbell* v. *Spottiswoode*, [1863] 3 B and S 769.

312. Faulks Committee, *supra* note 272, at para. 169.

313. C. Duncan and B. Neill, *supra* note 276, at 13.02. The Faulks Committee recommended that fair and accurate reports of judicial proceedings should be declared absolutely privileged by statute. Faulks Committee, *supra* note 272, at para. 191.

314. *Id.* at ch. 14.

315. *See supra* text accompanying notes 310–312.

316. C. Duncan and B. Neill, *supra* note 276, at 14.28.

317. *See* Report of the Committee of Justice (the Law and the Press) at 38, para. 119. The publisher would also have to exercise all reasonable care to establish the truth of facts supporting comments.

318. Faulks Committee, *supra* note 272, at para. 215. *See also supra* section III.B. Nevertheless, the committee recommended a qualified privilege for technical and scientific articles, published in genuine technical and scientific journals, e.g., doctors should be free to publish in medical journals without undue worry over libel actions. *Id.* at para. 232.

319. *See* C. Duncan and B. Neill, *supra* note 276, at ch. 16.

320. Faulks Committee, *supra* note 272, at paras. 281, 287.

321. *See Vizetelly* v. *Mudie's Selecter Library Ltd.,* [1900] 2 Q.B. 170; *Emmens* v. *Pottle,* [1933] 150 L.T. 211; *Weldon* v. *Times Book Club* [1911] 28 T.L.R. 143.

322. Faulks Committee, *supra* note 272, at para. 315 (C).

323. *See* H. Street, *supra* note 2, at 164; *See* 376 U.S. 254 (1964).

324. Faulks Committee, *supra* note 272, at para. 19.35.

325. *See id.* (Minority Report by Mr. Kimber and Mr. Grisewood) Also, Lord Gardiner, Viscount Dilthorne, Lord Salmon, and Mr. Justice Shaw (as he then was) *see generally id.* at paras. 454–477.

326. *Id.* at para. 466.

327. *Id.* at Minority Report E, Annex 1, at para. 7 and para. 474.

328. Exemplary damages may be awarded in three circumstances: (a) if the plaintiff has been injured by oppressive, arbitrary, or unconstitutional governmental action; (b) if the defendant has deliberately committed a tort to gain some advantage; and (c) if expressly authorized by statute. *See* C. Duncan and B. Neill, *supra* note 276, at 18.26.

329. *Cassell and Co. Ltd.* v. *Broome,* [1972] A.C. 1027. In assessing damages, the seriousness of the libel is always relevant. Other factors are special damage, injury to the plaintiff's feelings, including aggravating circumstances, mitigating factors, and extent of publication. *See* C. Duncan and B. Neill, *supra* note 276, at ch. 18.

330. Faulks Committee, *supra* note 272, at para. 350. The committee did not receive substantial criticism of the existing system. *Id.*

331. *Id.* at para. 360.

332. *Savalas* v. *Associated Newspapers Ltd., Times,* 16 June 1976. (Telly Savalas was awarded £34,000 for a report in the *Daily Mail* that represented him as a man unable to cope with super stardom). *See also infra* section V.A.

333. C. Wintour, *supra* note 2, at 128.

334. *See e.g.,* Libel Act, 1843; Law of Libel Amendment Act, 1888.

335. [1977] Q.B. 83.

336.  *Id.* at 88.

337.  *Id.* at 92–93. In May 1977, the prosecution was abandoned after an out-of-court settlement. *See* Ingrams and others (Defendants), *Times*, 17 May 1977, CCC.

338.  Faulks Committee, *supra* note 272, at para. 448. One commentator has, however, observed that "a disquieting feature of some of the [old] cases studied is the fact that the law has occasionally been used to punish persons who in good faith sought to raise issues of public importance." Spencer, *Do We Need a Crime of Defamatory Libel at All?* 1977 Crim. L. Rev. 383, 391–393.

339.  *See* H. Street, *supra* note 2, at 164–165; *Times*, 17 May 1977; *Brownlie's Law of Public Order and National Security, supra* note 25, at 195–199.

340.  [1979] 2 All E.R. 497, 499; *see* Article 10 of the European Convention on Human Rights, *supra* note 186.

341.  The report contained a draft bill of approximately 40 clauses.

342.  1977 Commission, *supra* note 2, at paras. 19, 37.

343.  Younger Committee on Privacy, Cmd. 5012, para. 83 (1972) (hereinafter cited as Younger Committee). Scotland has no recorded case recognizing the right. *See id.*, app. 2, para. 72. The position in the United Kingdom contrasts sharply with that in the United States, where the courts in most jurisdictions have, sometimes with the aid of legislation, developed a tort of invasion of privacy. Ironically, the article by Warren and Brandeis, *The Right to Privacy*, 4 Harv. L. Rev. 913 (1890), which was the inspiration for this development, argued for the existence of the right of privacy in tort largely on the basis of English precedents such as *Prince Albert* v. *Strange*, [1849] 1 Mac. & G. 25, 44 Eng. Rep. 1171 (ch. 1849).

344.  For example, it envisaged a criminal offense of "surreptitious surveillance," Younger Committee, *supra* note 343, at para. 563, and a civil remedy to cover overt and surreptitious surveillance. If in either case the surveillance was carried out by a "technical device" in "circumstances in which, were it not for the use of the device, [the] person would be justified in believing that he had protected himself or his possessions from surveillance by overhearing or observation." *Id.* at para. 565. *See* Report of the Royal Commission on Criminal Procedure, Cmd. 8092, at paras. 3.52–3.60 (1981) (where the use by the police of surreptitious surveillance devices is examined).

345.  *Id.* at para. 630; *id.*, app. 2, paras. 29–32. Because it found the action for breach of confidence vague, it suggested that the Law Commission clarify the action by statute. In October 1981, the commission delivered its report, including a draft bill to "impose obligations of confidence . . . on persons acquiring information in certain circumstances and otherwise to amend the law . . . as to civil liability for the disclosure or use of information and for connected purposes." Law Commission on Breach of Confidence, Cmd. 8388, No. 110 (1981) (hereinafter cited as Law Commission).

346.  Younger Committee, *supra* note 343, at para. 651 and ch. 6.

347.  *Id.* at paras. 651, 664, 663. The committee's main recommendations were:

(i) a criminal offence of surreptitious, unlawful surveillance by means of a technical device;

(ii) a tort of unlawful surveillance by such means;

(iii) a tort of disclosure or other use of information unlawfully acquired; and

(iv) a legally enforceable right of access to information held by a credit agency about one.

This last recommendation was implemented by the Consumer Credit Act, 1974, §158. The committee also recommended changes in the working of the Press Council, *see infra* section V.C., and improving the confidentiality of personal information held by banks, universities and employers. *See* Computers and Privacy, Cmd. 6353 (1975) and Report of the Committee on Data Protection (the Lindop Committee). Cmd. 7341 (1978).

348.  *Id.* at para. 662. *See also Brownlie's Law of Public Order and National Security, supra* note 25, at 337–339.

349.  Younger Committee, *supra* note 343, at para. 659.

350.  *Id. See* C. Wintour, *supra* note 2, at 56–66; Press Council Declaration on Privacy, April 1976, *reprinted in* P. O'Higgins, *Cases and Materials on Civil Liberties* 360–361 (1980). A person aggrieved by the press may complain to the Press Council. The Press Council deals with a substantial number of complaints of all kinds each year. *See infra* text accompanying notes 419–423.

351.  Younger Committee, *supra* note 343, at para. 663. *See id.*, app. 1, at paras. 82–91 and *supra* section IV. A.

352.  *See Hickman* v. *Maisey*, [1900] 1 Q.B. 752 (C.A.); Younger Committee, *supra* note 343, at para. 85.

353.  *See* S.H. Bailey, B. Harris, and B.L. Jones, *supra* note 180, at 305–308. *See also* Younger Committee, *supra* note 343, at 290.

354.  *Sports & General Press Agency* v. *Our Dogs Publishing Co., Ltd.,* [1916] 2 K.B. 880.

355.  Younger Committee, *supra* note 343, at para. 87. Both the civil and criminal law were included in this assessment.

356.  *See* Law Commission, *supra* note 345, at paras. 5.2, 5.3, 5.7, 5.10–5.15, 5.16–5.22.

357.  There are a number of publications for various groups of people who have settled in the United Kingdom, including West Indians, Indians, Pakistanis, Poles, Cypriots, and Irish. *See* the 1977 Commission, *supra* note 2, at para. 3.19.

358.  The alternative press probably includes at least 500 titles. Most are devoted to radical politics, to religion and the occult, and to science and ecology. A directory of alternative publications for the years 1969–1974 lists over 1,250 titles launched between those years, although many have collapsed since. *Id.* at para. 3.32. *See* also "Periodicals and the Alternative Press," Cmd. 6810–6 (1977).

359.  J. Curran and J. Seaton, *supra* note 2, at 12.

360.  *Id.* at 34.

361.  *Id.* at 49.

362.  *Id.* at 54.

363.  The 1977 Commission, *supra* note 2, at para. 5.10.

364.  *Id.* at para. 4.1.

365.  J. Curran and J. Seaton, *supra* note 2, at 82–83, 118–121. "In the early 1930s, the *Daily Mirror* seemed to be a dying paper. Its circulation was declining by about 70,000 a year and by 1933 was below 800,000." A change in editorial

direction in 1933 led to "the paper being skillfully steered towards a gap in the market...The paper's relaunch was essentially a marketing one...This was reflected in the close involvement of a leading advertising agency, J. Walter Thompson, in every stage of the paper's rebirth. A change in market direction required a corresponding shift in the paper's politics."

366.  The 1977 Commission, *supra* note 2, at para. 5.36. Newsprint was 30 percent of the total cost of printing a popular daily in 1972; the proportion reached 36 percent by 1975, and was higher still in 1976.

367.  J. Curran and J. Seaton, *supra* note 2, at 65.

368.  Evidence to the Royal Commission, Cmd. 7700.

369.  J. Curran and J. Seaton, *supra* note 2, at 62. *See* H. Cudlipp, *The Prerogative of the Harlot. Press Barrons and Power* (1980).

369a.  But see H. Evans, *Good Times and Bad Times*, 1983.

370.  The 1977 Commission, *supra* note 2, at para. 11.4. *Se also id.* at paras. 10.11–10.71; "Analysis of Newspaper Content," Cmd. 6810–4, (1977). The study of content relating to industrial relations was the most extensive. The same industrial relations topics appeared with similar frequency in different newspapers. Strikes was the largest category, constituting one-fifth of all topics. This was followed by other disputes and actions or settlements by unions or the T.U.C. By contrast, the settlement of strikes and negotiations tend to go unreported. Trade unions are presented as bodies concerned with starting but not ending disputes. *Id.* at para. 10.49. The commission treated the extent and degree of dissatisfaction with the coverage of industrial relations and trade union affairs as a significant weakness in newspapers. They recommended that they should act to improve and broaden their coverage. *Id.* at para. 10.131.

371.  "Subsidies would make the continuance of publications contingent upon the government's willingness or, in difficult times, its ability to maintain them." The 1977 Commission, *supra* note 2, at para. 11.15.

372.  *See* J. Whale, *supra* note 2, at 104.

373.  [1979] 1 W.L.R. 697.

374.  *Id.* at 709 (Lord Denning, M.R.); *see* P. O'Higgins, *supra* note 350, at 314–316. Also *see Daily Mirror Newspapers* v. *Gardner*, [1966] 29B 762, 785. Over the last decade the "industrial strength" of the unions has prevented the introduction of modern technology and the reduction of costs that Fleet Street so urgently requires. Strikes and stoppages in the newspaper industry have increased to an alarming extent. *See* S. Jenkins, *Newspapers, the Power and the Money* (1979).

375.  A closed shop is a place of work where either as a condition or as a consequence of being hired everyone must belong to a certain trade union.

376.  Parliament sought to resolve the sharp differences of opinion by section 2 of the Trade Union and Labour Relations (Amendment) Act, 1976. This provided that the parties must try to agree to a charter "containing practical guidance for employers, trade unions and editors and other journalists on matters relating to the freedom of the press." The 1977 Commission, para. 17–12. Since the parties failed to agree by 24 March 1977, the Secretary of State was to consult with them and with organizations representing workers and employers and submit his own draft before Parliament. The 1977 Commission recommended that the Secretary of State's draft include certain safeguards protecting the freedom of journalists and editors. *Id.* at para. 17–20. Regrettably no charter was laid before Parliament and by section 19(a) of the Employment Act, 1980, section 2 of the 1976 Act ceased to have effect.

377. The 1977 Commission, *supra* note 2, at para. 10.158. *See also* J. Whale, *supra* note 2, at 90. In July 1976, the asbestos industry was attacked on the ground that working with asbestos could cause cancer. The industry defended itself in a full page advertisement in the *Sunday Times*. In the same issue, two staff reporters gave reasons for dissenting from several of the advertisement's claims.

378. The 1977 Commission, *supra* note 2, at para. 10.131.

379. *Id.* at Addendum, para. 11.

380. The 1949 Commission, *supra* note 17, at para. 274.

381. The 1977 Commission, *supra* note 2, at para. 14.6.

382. The 1949 Commission, *supra* note 17, at para. 274.

383. The 1977 Commission, *supra* note 2, at para. 14.7.

384. The 1949 Commission, *supra* note 17, at paras. 664–679. The largest single group, Kemsley's, owned 17 percent of daily and Sunday newspapers and 24 percent of provincial morning newspapers. In 58 out of 66 towns in Britain where daily newspapers were published, there was a local monopoly, but its importance was qualified by the fact that national newspapers circulated throughout the country. *See* J. Whale, *supra* note 2, at 16.

385. In 1960, two minor Sunday papers in the Kemsley Group—the *Sunday Graphic* in London and the *Empire News* in Manchester—disappeared in the Thomson reorganization. Financial troubles then came to a head at *Odhams*, a magazine empire which owned the *Daily Herald* and the *Sunday People*. The closure in October 1960 of the *News Chronicle* was a special case. *See generally*, J. Whale, *supra* note 2.

386. Royal Commission on the Press, 1961–1962 Report, Cmd. 1811 at para. 313 (1962) (hereinafter .cited as The 1962 Commission). "We are all forced to the conclusion—which we regret because of our clear realisation of the dangers which exist—that there is no acceptable legislative or physical way of regulating the competitive and economic forces so as to ensure a sufficient diversity of newspapers. The only hope of the weaker newspapers is to secure—as some have done in the past—managers and editors of such enterprising originality as will enable these publications to overcome the economic forces affecting them."

387. The 1977 Commission, *supra* note 2, at para. 13.48. "We hope, perhaps optimistically, that by arguing the pros and cons we may have finally laid them to rest." This is unlikely.

388. The 1962 Commission, *supra* note 386, at para. 221.

389. *Id.* at para. 225.

390. The 1977 Commission, *supra* note 2, at para. 6.9. The 1977 Royal Commission reaffirmed the conclusions of the 1962 Report that "the ability of newspapers to specialise has helped them to resist the strong pressures towards concentration." *Id.* at para. 6.12.

391. In 1977, nine national daily newspapers under nine ownerships and seven Sunday newspapers under six separate ownerships were published. The 1977 Commission, *supra* note 2, at para. 9.8. In 1980 the two evening London newspapers were merged. These newspapers were generally considered to be part of the national press because their finances were intimately linked with those of the nationals. The 1977 Commission, *supra* note 2, at para. 3.10. The greatest degree of concentration and of monopoly is found nationally among periodicals. However, the provincial newspaper industry is where the 1977 Commission considered the problem of growing concentration to be most serious. *Id.* at paras. 14.1–14.11.

392.  *Id*. at para. 6.26.

393.  It may take four to five years before a new evening newspaper breaks even. By then, the accumulated losses for a paper of average circulation may amount to a million pounds. By contrast, the cost of entry into weekly newspaper publishing is relatively modest. *Id*. at para. 6.36. *Id*. at para. 9.8. To set up a completely new plant to publish an evening newspaper of average circulation costs at least £2 million. *Id*. at para. 6.30.

394.  *Id*. at para. 15.1.

395.  *Id*. at para. 15.2. In 1977, 220 separately controlled companies published newspapers, compared with over 490 in 1961. In some large international concerns, newspaper publishing is one activity among many. On the other hand, the publishing company may be a small family business. At one end of the scale, Reed International has an annual turnover of over £1,000 million and its main activity is paper manufacture and paper products. In 1961 there were about 460 publishers of weekly newspapers; in 1977 there were 180. The number of publishers of both daily and weekly newspapers has remained about the same. *Id*. at para. 4.7.

396.  *Id*. at para. 15.31.

397.  *Id*. at para. 15.3.

398.  *Id*. at para. 15.26.

399.  *Id*. at para. 15.19.

400.  *Id*. at para. 15.33.

401.  *See id*. at paras. 15.35–15.36. "There may be more than one view on the question whether the public interest is actually injured by the degree of concentration of ownership and control existing at any one time. But no reliable view can be formed at all unless the facts are known." *Id*. at para. 15.35, citing 1962 Commission, *supra* note 386, at para. 314.

402.  The 1977 Commission, *supra* note 2, at para. 15.36.

403.  *Id*. at para. 15.40.

404.  *Id*. at para. 15.42.

405.  *Id*. at para. 15.44.

406.  *See* The 1977 Commission, *supra* note 2, at para. 14.15.

407.  A controlling interest is a holding of 25 percent or more of the voting shares. The Secretary of State is required to refer all such proposed transfers to the Monopolies and Mergers Commission within one month of application. However, if he is satisfied that the newspaper concerned is not economic as a separate newspaper, he may give his consent without reference to the commission if the paper is to continue as a separate newspaper and the case is one of urgency. He may also consent without reference to the commission if the paper has an average daily circulation of not more than 25,000 copies. On a reference, the commission is required to report whether the transfer may be expected to operate against the public interest, taking into account all relevant matters and in particular "the need for accurate presentation of news and free expression of opinion." The 1977 Commission, *supra* note 2, at paras. 14.15, 14.16. Between 1965 and 1977, 50 cases falling within the terms of the legislation came to the notice of the Secretary of State. Seven were referred to the commission—the merger of *The Times* with *The Sunday Times*, and six involving local newspapers. In the remaining 43 cases, consent was given without reference to the Monopoly and Mergers Commission. One of these was the acquisition of *The Sun* by *News International*. *Id*. at para. 14.17. On the acquisition of the *Times* by *News International* see H. Evans, *supra*

note 369a, pp. 80–167. In none of the six cases of local newspaper acquisition examined by the commission has the commission concluded that, if consent to acquisition were refused, the alternative would likely be closure of the papers. In four of the six cases, they concluded that substantial improvements in commercial efficiency would be unlikely but, in each case, they gave their consent. More than once, however, they have expressed concern that, even though there might be no harm to the public interest in the proposal under reference, it would be impossible to judge the cumulative effect of the total of such mergers. *Id.* at para. 14.19.

408.    *Id.* at para. 14.27. According to the 1977 Commission the objectives of public policy are to secure:

(a) a prosperous industry;
(b) the maximum diversity of titles and of ownership locally and nationally which is compatible with prosperity;
(c) as many independent publishers throughout the country as are compatible with economic production of newspapers; and
(d) the independence of editors and journalists irrespective of the extent of monopoly or concentration of ownership.

*Id.* at para. 14.23.

409.    *Id*, at para. 14.28.
410.    *Id*, at para. 14.33.
411.    J. Curran and J. Seaton, *supra* note 2, at 301.
412.    The 1977 Commission, *supra* note 2, at ch. 20.
413.    The Press Council requires that in certain cases, the complainant should waive his right to sue a newspaper as a condition of an agreement to consider the complaint. The 1977 Commission correctly took the view that such a demand displays a misunderstanding of the true role of the Press Council. Its role is to maintain proper ethical standards by adjudicating complaints of alleged breaches of those standards that are brought to its attention. For it to refuse to adjudicate because the breach of ethical standards is so serious that it may also give rise to the possibility of legal proceedings seems strange. The newspaper is not placed in double jeopardy any more than is anyone faced with criminal or civil proceedings concerning the same act. The 1977 Commission, *supra* note 2, at para. 20.46. The commission recommended that a waiver is not justified and should be abolished. *Id.* at para. 20.48.

414.    *Id.* at para. 20.10. The objects of the Press Council are set out in clause 2 of the articles of association. *See* P. O'Higgins, *supra* note 350, at 303.

415.    The 1977 Commission, *supra* note 2, at para 20.12.

416.    *Id.* at para. 20.13. The Press Council initially consisted of 25 representatives drawn only from the profession. The 1962 Royal Commission recommended the appointment not only of lay members, but also of a lay chairman. As a result, the Press Council was reconstituted to have an independent chairman and five lay members out of the 25 members that were appointed. Following the report of the Committee on Privacy the membership of the Press Council was changed again in 1973. An independent commission, the Press Council Appointments Commission, was established for appointing lay members. The number of lay members was increased to 10 out of 30. The constitution of the Complaints Committee was changed to give it six lay members and six press members under the chairmanship

of the chairman of the Press Council. For present composition of the Press Council, *see* note 404 *infra*.

417. The 1977 Commission, *supra* note 2 at paras. 20.17, 20.18. The public will not believe that a council dominated by journalists and other members of the press can keep an effective watch on the standards of the press or can deal satisfactorily with complaints by citizens. *Id*. at para. 20.1.

418. The Press Council now consists of an independent chairman and 36 members, consisting of an equal number of press and lay members. *See* S.H. Bailey, B. Harris and B.L. Jones, *supra* note 180, at 212–218.

419. The 1977 Commission, *supra* note 2, at para. 20.25.

420. *Id*. at para. 20.26.

421. *Id*. at paras. 20.32, 20.34. Any procedure for handling complaints should aim to: "(a) provide independent machinery with a clear duty to the general public; (b) promote the improvement of standards by initiating investigations and complaints; and (c) give those who handle complaints an explicit duty to mediate between a complainant and a publication complained of, with the object of securing rapidly any correction which is justified." *Id*. at para. 20.29.

422. The list includes misreporting, sensationalizing, distortion, publication of corrections and apologies, and unethical methods of obtaining information. *See* S.H. Bailey, B. Harris and B.L. Jones, *supra* note 180. at 212–218. *See also* an adjudication by the Press Council on a complaint by Ms. Maureen Colquhoun, M.P., that the *Daily Mail* had intruded into her privacy in a story in its gossip column. Complaint rejected. *See* P. O'Higgins, *supra* note 350, at 306–310.

423. The 1977 Commission, *supra* note 2, at para. 20.32. The Press Council put into effect the recommendations of the Royal Commission concerning concilia- tion in 1978. *See* Annual Report of the Press Council, 1977, at 99, 114.

424. The 1977 Commission, *supra* note 2, at para. 20.51. *See also* H. Levy, *The Press Council* X1 (1967).

425. *See* the 1977 Commission, *supra* note 2, at paras. 20.51, 20.52, 20.56, 20.58.

426. *Id*. at para. 20.64. The examination of the methods used in a 1974 case, in which a television personality's romance with a much younger woman was featured at great length in the popular press, led the Royal Commission to the view, on the basis of the admissions of the newspaper concerned, that inexcusable intrusions into privacy were involved. *See id*. at para. 20.64.

427. *Id*. at para. 20.69.

428. *Id*. Fines on journalists would involve turning the occupation into a "closed" licensed profession. Only in this way could a sanction beyond a fine and a suspension of the right to have work published be provided. Suspension from publication of a paper would be tantamount to censorship and the suppression of opinion. *Id*. at para. 20.61.

429. *Id*. at para. 20.73. The Press Council has issued adjudications that have established conventions approximating a right of reply. However, the Royal Commission was not in favor of creating a legal right of reply. *Id*. at para. 20.39. The commission did recommend that, as part of the process of conciliation, the Press Council should actively involve itself in promptly obtaining the publication of counter-statements on behalf of people who have been criticized unfairly through inaccurate information. The counter-statements should be of equal prominence

and space. Furthermore, the Commission recommended limiting an editor's right of refusal to publish counter-statements to legal grounds. *Id*. at para. 20.40.

430.  *Id*. at para. 20.74.

431.  *Id*. at para. 20.76.

432.  *Id*. at para. 20.80.

433.  Indeed, the National Union of Journalists decided to withdraw from the Press Council in 1980 on the grounds that it was neither effectively nor genuinely independent of press management. J. Curran and J. Seaton, *supra* note 2, at 302, G. Robertson, *People against the Press*, (1983).

434.  For an assessment of the achievements of the Press Council during the first 25 years, *see* Lord Shawcross, *Past Performance, Future Tasks—A Personal View*, Annual Report of the Press Council, ch. 1 (1977).

435.  The 1977 Commission, *supra* note 2, at para. 19.2.

436.  *Id*. at para. 19.8

437.  *Id*. at para. 19.37.

# Two

## Freedom of the Press in the United States

Aviam Soifer

## GENERAL FRAMEWORK

### Introduction

Freedom of the press in the United States is much more than a legal concept—it is almost a religious tenet. The United States Constitution, as interpreted by the Supreme Court, is itself virtually a sacred text, and the First Amendment is an integral part of the value system proclaimed by most Americans.

Reverence for a free press in the United States is identified with the English tradition of John Milton and John Stuart Mill; but Americans like to celebrate the writings of Thomas Jefferson and James Madison as unique American contributions to that freedom. Moreover, as a matter of constitutional law, judges have held that freedom of the press enjoys a favored position among constitutional rights.[1]

There may be good reason to doubt that tolerance for freedom of the press always prevailed in the United States, but freedom of each citizen to communicate and to choose among diverse opinions is near the core of basic American individualism. Undoubtedly, the American press is less inhibited by legal constraints than is the press in other countries. This relatively broad press freedom probably is attributable more to the beliefs of American citizens than to the success of reporters and publishers in litigation. In fact, legal cases involving claims based on freedom of the press are almost entirely a twentieth century phenomenon, and by no means do these decisions always uphold press claims.

The history of freedom of the press in America reveals significant gaps between the ideals of tolerance and free choice and the harsher reality. Defeats as well as victories for freedom of the press have occurred in American streets and editorial offices, as they have in courthouses. Even if freedom of the press is sometimes honored in the breach at crucial moments, the presence and power of the ideal persists.

To recognize the tendency of Americans to invoke First Amendment rights in ways that are partially mythic and mostly symbolic does not necessarily diminish the vitality of the ideal. Myths often contain vital truths; as Justice Holmes once wrote, "We live by symbols."[2] Kurt Vonnegut recently provided what may be the best description of the elusive, yet essential quality of the First Amendment in American life. Vonnegut wrote:

> [T]he first amendment reads more like a dream than a law, and no other country, so far as I know, has been crazy enough to include such a dream among its fundamental legal documents.* I defend it because it has been so successful for two centuries in preserving our freedom and increasing our vitality, knowing that all arguments in support of it are certain to sound absurd.[3]

Both the history and the jurisprudence of freedom of expression in America contain important discontinuities. It is clear that those who first constitutionalized freedom of speech and press in the First Amendment did not even begin to contemplate many of today's practical problems in maintaining and encouraging freedom of the press.

Even when accepted, the basis of a claim of primacy for First Amendment rights in any hierarchy of constitutional values changed greatly over time. Moreover, an array of special legal rules evolved on a case-by-case basis typical of American constitutional law. Intermediate types of judicial rulemaking included: abhorrence of prior restraints; acceptance of reasonable regulation of the time, place, and manner of speech; and judicial application of formulae for balancing governmental interests against those of citizens, journalists, and publishers who seek to express themselves.

Much of this chapter is devoted to scrutiny of cases and contexts where there is an obvious gap between America's dedication to freedom of the press and actual court judgments. Yet it must be emphasized that the dream expressed by Vonnegut is widely shared in fact, and the ideal influences action in vast but subtle ways. To possess constitutional language considered fundamental and to be able to invoke an eloquent legal and philosophical tradition explicating the need for an unfettered press is important. Advocates of freedom of expression certainly do not win all their battles in court or before the American public; however, they are able to appeal to a central American theme. Complete commitment to an

---

* This attitude illustrates one reason why a comparative study of freedom of expression is important. As this study shows, many other countries have made strong commitments to freedom of expression. (Editor's note)

unfettered press may be utopian, but today a utopian vision appears to be practically a necessity.

## The Jurisprudence of Freedom of Expression

In the United States there is no definitive source nor reliable *grundnorm* for the basic theory supporting legal protection for freedom of the press. A tradition of separate and overlapping governmental powers and of federalism, combined with devotion to pluralism and rampant individualism, helps ensure that controversy goes on about how far freedom of expression should extend, and for what reasons.

The work of Thomas I. Emerson contains the most complete and thoughtful review of competing theories and analysis of freedom of expression, encompassing freedom of speech as well as freedom of the press.[4] Emerson suggests four major justifications for the preferred position that is generally assigned to freedom of expression in the United States:

### *Individual Self-Fulfillment*

The concept of self-fulfillment usually is tied to the work of John Stuart Mill and to arguments in support of individual liberty. This rationale is related directly to the dominant American belief in individualism; it is evident in many constitutional provisions in addition to the First Amendment.

### *Search for Truth*

Justice Holmes argued that "the best test of truth is the power of the thought to get itself accepted in the competition of the market."[5] This "market-place of ideas" notion may be traced to earlier sources, such as John Milton's belief that truth always will conquer falsehood "in a free and open encounter."[6] Mill extend Milton's argument when he asserted that the vital truth-seeking function compels even protection of falsehoods, so long as they cause no harm.[7]

### *Self-Government*

Alexander Meiklejohn was the most prominent proponent of the "self-government" justification for freedom of expression, but its roots are traceable directly to James Madison:

A popular Government, without popular information, or the means of acquiring it, is but the Prologue to a Farce or a Tragedy; or perhaps both.

Knowledge will forever govern ignorance. And a people who mean to be their own Governors, must arm themselves with the power which knowledge gives.[8]

Meiklejohn would limit full protection to *political* expression. He tied his argument specifically to the American system of representative democracy.[9]

### Safety Valve

This argument views freedom of expression as a means to mediate between societal stability and the need to allow change. Alexander Bickel called this "domesticated civil disobedience," and this safety-valve idea can be traced to John Locke, John Wilkes, the pamphleteer "Cato," and others who directly influenced the First Amendment's framers.[10]

In *The System of Freedom of Expression*, Thomas I. Emerson does much more than merely articulate these four justifications for First Amendment guarantees. He analyzes application of these theories and builds toward a general theory of freedom of expression. Yet Emerson does not claim that any one of the four strands, or even any composite, is absolutely defensible in terms of logic. According to Emerson, toleration of freedom of expression is inevitably an act of faith and political judgment.[11]

It is often impossible to tell what particular justification a court or commentator is using to argue for protection of freedom of expression. Yet even when a specific strand is hard to isolate, the web of theoretical claims surrounding the First Amendment encompasses precedents and powerful legal arguments. In *Cohen* v. *California*,[12] for example, the United States Supreme Court invalidated a conviction for disturbing the peace when a young man appeared in a hallway outside a Los Angeles courtroom wearing a jacket decorated with the slogan "Fuck the Draft." Justice Harlan, often considered a rather conservative justice, wrote the majority opinion, holding that First Amendment protection extends to expression that "conveys not only ideas capable of relatively precise, detached explication, but otherwise inexpressible emotions as well."[13]

The *Cohen* decision thereby extended the concept of freedom of expression to words written across a young man's jacket, words the justices considered offensive to many in both form and content. Cohen's mode of expression was unconventional, but the Court's decision to protect it satisfied most, if not all, of the four theories justifying freedom of expression.

If it is impossible to provide an entirely coherent theory of freedom of expression to cover all the hard cases, it is also difficult to refute the United States Supreme Court's recent claim that First Amendment values are "transcendent imperatives"[14] in American life. There are few words in American law more eloquent than those of Justice Brandeis, writing about, and surely somewhat romanticizing, the origins of the First Amendment:

Those who won our independence believed that the final end of the State was to make men free to develop their faculties; and that in its government the deliberative forces should prevail over the arbitrary. They valued liberty both as an end and as a means. They believed liberty to be the secret of happiness and courage to be the secret of liberty. They believed that freedom to think as you will and to speak as you think are means indispensable to the discovery and spread of political truth; that without free speech and assembly discussion would be futile; that with them, discussion affords ordinarily adequate protection against the dissemination of noxious doctrine; that the greatest menace to freedom is an inert people; that public discussion is a political duty; and that this should be a fundamental principle of the American government.[15]

Ironically, this powerful rhetoric appeared in a Brandeis opinion, joined by Justice Holmes, in which Brandeis concurred in a decision by the Court to *uphold* the conviction of a young woman for violation of a California Syndicalism Act in spite of her First Amendment claims. Yet Brandeis's words, and the eloquence of his successors on the Court, provide a constitutional gloss on freedom of expression that simultaneously confirms, and creates a part of the American tradition. The faith thus initiated embraces tolerance for critics, dissenters, and iconoclasts; it helps to define a tradition transcending specific cases and events.

## The First Amendment to the United States Constitution

Although any discussion of freedom of the press in the United States begins with the First Amendment to the United States Constitution, it is important to note at the outset that American federalism entails dual legal systems. One is the national or federal system; the other entails 50 states, each with its own court apparatus and its own state constitution and laws. The United States Constitution applies to both systems and prevails if the two collide directly. The United States Supreme Court reviews decisions from both systems. Yet state constitutions contain additional language committing the states to principles of free expression.[16] Moreover, since the 1925 *dictum* in *Gitlow* v. *New York*,[17] state judges, legislatures, and officials may not interpret their state constitutional provisions more narrowly than the United States Constitution's First Amendment, as construed by the United States Supreme Court. However, state constitutions may be interpreted to give broader protection to freedom of expression than the federal First Amendment provides.[18]

The First Amendment remains the most significant legal protection for freedom of expression. Ratified in 1791, four years after the adoption of the federal Constitution, the First Amendment states in part: "Congress shall make no law...abridging the freedom of speech, or of the press...." Since these famous words obviously are not self-defining, several basic issues of construction must be considered.

## Scope of First Amendment Coverage

There was no realistic way for the press to claim federal First Amendment protections until after the Civil War for a variety of reasons. Notions of the autonomy and sovereignty of each individual state, for example, permitted Southern states to exclude antislavery speakers, newspapers, pamphlets, and books from their jurisdictions. The antislavery movement and the Civil War produced martyrs for the cause of freedom of the press, as well as further evidence that war is not a good time for civil liberties.[19] The amendments to the federal Constitution passed in the wake of that war, particularly the Fourteenth Amendment, indicate that earlier concepts of federalism changed radically.[20] Now there was a legitimate basis for the claim that the First Amendment protected freedom of expression from state as well as federal governmental actions.

Until the First World War, however, it was generally assumed that freedom of the press was a guarantee only against prior restraints, that is, censorship by a government official through a licensing scheme or similar preclearance mechanism.[21] Laws and judges punished or prohibited publications considered licentious, libelous, or untrue, since such expression was not believed worthy of constitutional protection. State courts were virtually the only courts available for legal disputes involving the press. Yet state judges and juries gave little attention and even less protection to claims made on behalf of freedom of expression, whether grounded in federal or state constitutional language.[22]

The sobering tale of the numerous successful incidents of suppression of the press during and soon after the First World War told by Zechariah Chafee, Jr.,[23] provides an additional, dramatic indication of how recent a phenomenon it is to find courts invoking the Constitution to protect a "vehement, caustic, and sometimes unpleasantly sharp" press.[24] Most of what we now understand to be the meaning of the First Amendment is derived from twentieth century judicial interpretations of eighteenth century language, articulated by judges peering back through more than a century of silence.

Although the United States Supreme Court has never held that the entire Bill of Rights applies to the states, since its 1925 *dictum* in *Gitlow* v. *New York* the Court consistently has stated that the Fourteenth Amendment requires that First Amendment protections apply to states and state officials.[25] Despite attacks by influential critics and judges[26] on this "incorporation" doctrine, First Amendment protections continue to extend beyond the text's prohibition against laws enacted by Congress. Since the states remain the most frequent, direct source of law and law enforcement for most Americans, the seemingly casual application of federal First Amendment standards to the states in *Gitlow*, ironically, must rank among the most significant legal victories for freedom of expression in the United States.

### First Amendment Coverage: The Definition of "Law Abridging," the Public/Private Distinction, and "Bad Motive"

The First Amendment prohibits any "law...abridging" freedom of speech or the press. This language suggests three unresolved, yet fundamental questions. First, how broadly should the prohibition against any law be construed? Second, should the directive against abridging the press extend to shielding journalists, publishers, and the public from manipulation or limitation by private power? Finally, does the Constitution guard the press against unintentional or indirect governmental actions that may impinge on press freedoms?

#### Protection beyond statutory restraints

In a bureaucratized country such as the United States, the most effective restraints on freedom of expression are often far removed from formal statutes. A plethora of corporate practices, for example, as well as numerous rules and regulations of government agencies have great impact on the press, even when the press does not seem to be the intended target.

It is clear that the protections of the First Amendment extend far beyond statutes. Though never held to afford absolute protection, the First Amendment reaches any action attributable to government entities, including federal, state and local officials, and judicial and administrative agencies as well as legislative bodies.[27]

At the same time, it is also clear that the prohibition on "laws abridging" speech is not absolute. Both statutory and common law regulation of speech by federal and state governments is permitted, so long as it is consistent with the doctrines developed by the Supreme Court.

#### The public/private distinction

Because the federal Constitution generally affords protection only against official action—called "state action" in the term of art used by American lawyers—restrictions imposed on publication or distribution of newspapers by corporations or private universities, for example, are considered beyond the protections of the First Amendment.[28] The United States Supreme Court recently reiterated its belief in the "essential dichotomy" between public and private spheres.[29] Nevertheless, how to discern a principle with which to draw this line remains an intractable problem in American constitutional law. Yet the practical consequences of such line drawing makes the public/private distinction an issue of immense practical importance for First Amendment adjudication, though often it is not addressed in discussions of freedom of expression.

Only in *dicta* has the United States Supreme Court hinted that private communication monopolies might themselves constitute violations of the

First Amendment. In *Associated Press* v. *United States*,[30] Justice Black's opinion for the majority held that the First Amendment provided no defense for publishers on trial for antitrust violations. But Justice Black also wrote:

> Surely a command that the government itself shall not impede the free flow of ideas does not afford nongovernmental combinations a refuge if they impose restraints upon that constitutionally guaranteed freedom.... *Freedom to publish means freedom for all and not for some. Freedom of the press from governmental interference under the first amendment does not sanction repression of the freedom by private interests.*[31]

The idea that freedom of the press might be restrained by private interests, premised on the notion that a truly free and open marketplace of ideas is the essential goal, has not prevailed as a matter of constitutional law.[32] But such concerns do figure frequently in statutory and administrative regulations.[33] Additionally, there is increasing recognition that government itself greatly affects the market of ideas, since government is a major and active producer of expression.[34] Concern about government speech is often combined with growing awareness that control of newspapers and publishing companies today is concentrated in fewer, larger corporate hands.[35] Private constraints on the availability of diversity in publications surely will constitute one of the most significant theoretical and practical problems for freedom of the press in the years ahead.

### No "bad motive" requirement

Determining what government actions abridge freedom of expression also is becoming more difficult today. This problem occurs against a backdrop of scientific and philosophic attacks on the very concept of provable direct causation,[36] and takes place at a time when, in other contexts, the United States Supreme Court increasingly refuses to recognize constitutional violations unless discriminatory governmental motivation is proved.[37]

Nonetheless, to make out a First Amendment claim, it is still not necessary to prove that government officials intentionally abridged freedom of the press, though proof of such motive is relevant.[38] Moreover, if it appears that the government intended to fetter or punish the press, and if this motive seems to be the only explanation for the governmental action under attack, then proof of motive may be enough to establish a violation of the First Amendment.

*Grosjean* v. *American Press*[39] illustrates the way the bad motive of government officials may be held to be sufficient though not necessary. At the behest of Governor Huey Long, the Louisiana legislature enacted a statute providing that all newspapers with circulations of over 20,000 copies had to pay a license tax of 2 percent of their gross receipts. License taxes are customarily upheld by American courts, and judges allow legislatures broad discretion in taxing schemes. In *Grosjean*, however, the tax clearly was adopted to punish the *New Orleans Times-Picayune*, which had been critical of Governor Long and his policies. The United States Supreme Court unanimously held:

> The tax here is bad not because it takes money from the pockets of the appellees.... It is bad because, in the light of its history and of its present setting, it is seen to be a deliberate and calculated device in the guise of a tax to limit the circulation of information to which the public is entitled in virtue of the constitutional guarantees.[40]

Similarly, in the recent decision in *Board of Education, Island Trees* v. *Pico*,[41] a strong suspicion about the motive of the school board in removing selected books from school libraries led the United States Supreme Court to remand the case to the lower court to explore that issue. The board had voted to remove books by Kurt Vonnegut, Bernard Malamud, and others from the school library soon after several members returned from a convention where lists of condemned books were distributed. Although the discretion of school boards often is said to exemplify local control idealized in the American theory of government, Justice Brennan's plurality opinion stressed the possibility that the local school board exercised its broad discretion improperly.

The constitutional right invoked by Justice Brennan in *Island Trees* appears to be the rather new and still vague right to receive information.[42] As the Court in *Island Trees* struggled to resolve conflicting claims of students, experts, and elected school officials, the justices found it difficult to pinpoint who had what right. A majority of the Court indicated, however, that an overt political motive limiting dissemination of books to the public might establish a violation of the First Amendment.

First Amendment claims generally arise in litigation that does not involve the bad motive issue. In the United States, those defending governmental action or laws alleged to infringe freedom of the press usually not only deny that their purpose is suppression, but also allege that any infringement on the press is merely incidental to other legitimate governmental purposes. Claims of legitimate purposes range from aiding the legal process to protecting the privacy or autonomy of individuals to guaranteeing vital aspects of national security.

The tension between such claims and an unfettered press is discussed in more detail below. Yet it is important to recognize that the ideal of a free press in the United States tends to impose a heavy legal burden on those who overtly seek to restrict the press.

### *"Freedom of Speech, or of the Press"*

There are two separate phrases concerning freedom of expression in the First Amendment: one guarantees "Freedom of Speech" and the other freedom "of the Press." Recently, this phrasing provoked vigorous debate about whether the press may legitimately claim protections *beyond* those claimed by ordinary persons. Justice Stewart touched off the dispute in a 1974 speech at the Yale Law School.[43] Suggesting that the press might enjoy special constitutional protections, Justice Stewart seemed to limit such protections to what he alternatively called the "organized press," the "established news media" and the "established press."[44] Several law reviews devoted symposia to the implications of these suggestions; by now, nearly all leading First Amendment experts have had their say on the issue of additional constitutional protections for the press.[45]

Those in favor of added protections for the press point to the vital role the press plays in a democracy, since it provides a check on government activities and abuses, as well as a source of information for the public. This "checking function,"[46] as described by Vincent Blasi, might warrant a constitutional guarantee of special privileges because the press serves as a surrogate or fiduciary for the public. Those opposed to special press privileges claim such an approach permits government officials, courts, or the press itself to define who is and who is not a *bona fide* beneficiary of constitutional privileges. Moreover, Anthony Lewis, for example, suggests that a grant of special privileges to the press inevitably will be accompanied by arguments that the press has unique, reciprocal responsibilities.[47] Therefore, Lewis and others argue, the press actually would find itself less free if it were to receive special constitutional regard. Democracy is not mediaocracy, according to Steven Shiffrin, and citizens associated with the press deserve no greater freedom than other citizens.[48]

The United States Supreme Court thus far has not embraced the argument for special privileges for the press. In fact, in several decisions since 1972 involving claims to reporter's privileges and to a shield against police searches in newsrooms, the Supreme Court rejected the idea that the press should be treated differently from ordinary individuals.[49] In cases arising out of attempts to exclude journalists from courtrooms, a sharply divided Court determined that the press and the public share a right of access to actual trials, though not to pretrial hearings.[50] A majority of the justices did not accept the claim made by a public television station of a press privilege to special access to a jail.[51]

Contrary to Justice Stewart's suggested limitation of press protection to the establishment press, the Court emphatically and repeatedly has held that First Amendment press rights are not limited to established publications. As Justice Black wrote for the majority in *Mills* v. *Alabama*: "The Constitution specifically selected the press, which includes not only newspapers, books, and magazines, but also humble leaflets and circulars, to play an important role in the discussion of public affairs."[52]

Although discussion of the vital role of the press tends to emphasize the role of the press in public affairs, the Supreme Court has made it clear that protection extends to printed matter that merely entertains, since such material is still a vital element of free expression.[53] This approach has drawn a good deal of criticism. Commentators from Alexander Meiklejohn to Herbert Marcuse to Robert Bork attack the concept of a free market-place for *all* kinds of ideas,[54] a concept at the core of many First Amendment precedents. Critics suggest a variety of limitations: some would protect only political speech, variously defined[55]; others would emphasize certain kinds of protected expression but debunk the notion that pluralism offers a sufficient rationale to attempt to protect all communication.[56]

Yet the United States Supreme Court continues to hold that freedom of the press is not limited to political speech. It should be noted, however, that while corporations have been held to have rights to freedom of expression, some expression, such as commercial speech, explicitly is granted less constitutional protection than other forms of expression.[57] Moreover, a few categories of speech, such as obscene publications, are regarded as entirely outside the range of First Amendment guarantees.[58] Other types of expression such as radio and television communications[59] are treated quite differently.

Finally, as a practical matter, it is obvious that influential newspapers such as the *New York Times* and the *Washington Post* enjoy advantages and access to government functions and functionaries not enjoyed by ordinary individuals, or by a journalist working for a struggling under-ground newspaper.

### The Role of the Courts

The commitment to the independence of the American federal judiciary is both a truism and a unique and significant phenomenon. Judicial freedom from outside pressure or control was celebrated at the beginning of the American Republic, perhaps in most famous form by Alexander Hamil-ton: "The complete independence of the courts of justice is peculiarly essential in a limited Constitution."[60] As early as 1803, in *Marbury* v. *Madison*,[61] Chief Justice John Marshall proclaimed that the United States Supreme Court would have the ultimate say in interpreting the Constitu-tion. Marshall's declaration has been reiterated, perhaps even expanded, in recent decisions.[62]

Yet throughout American history, presidents and legislators, as well as members of the public, often have expressed profound disagreement with, and possible resistance to, judicial interpretations of the Constitution. The list of famous critics includes Andrew Jackson, Abraham Lincoln, and Franklin D. Roosevelt.[63] But in the United States, the cult of the robe appears so powerful and the concept of "the rule of law and not of men" so basic that overt challenges to the authority of the judges "to say what the law is" appear doomed.

Congress does have substantial power over the jurisdiction and funding of the federal courts. It also has constitutional authority to impeach federal judges; moreover, judges must rely on the executive branch to enforce their judgments. In many state court systems, there are even greater controls over judges. And, at least to some extent, as "Mr. Dooley" asserted, "th' Supreme Court follows th' iliction returns."[64] At times this propensity has led the Court to less-than-vigorous protection of First Amendment rights, particularly in the face of popular outrage or fear of the consequences of certain expression.[65]

As mentioned earlier, each state has its own judicial system and constitution. Federal judges hold office for life, but many state judges are elected or appointed for only a term of years. This periodic insecurity is said to make state judges less likely to protect unpopular viewpoints. Nevertheless, state judges sometimes discern state constitutional protections for freedom of expression broader than those granted by federal courts, and the number of such decisions currently seems to be increasing.[66]

In *PruneYard Shopping Center* v. *Robins*,[67] for example, the California Supreme Court held that the right to distribute handbills on the property of a privately owned shopping center is protected under the California Constitution. According to a series of recent decisions by the United States Supreme Court, such leafletting is not protected by the First Amendment because there is not sufficient state involvement to provide the requisite state action.[68]

In the *PruneYard* decision, a unanimous United States Supreme Court sustained the power of the California Court to exceed the standards guaranteeing freedom of expression under the federal Constitution; the California Court's interpretation of its state constitution was held not to be in conflict with the United States Constitution.[69] The recent trend toward increased state court protection of freedom of expression, combined with new emphasis on the constitutional role played by government officials other than judges,[70] is in part a move by litigators and judges to counteract restrictive federal interpretations of First Amendment freedoms. To some extent, freedom of expression in the United States seems to exert its own pressure—almost to enjoy a symbolic life of its own—no matter who controls the apparatus of government.

## THE PRESS AND THE GOVERNMENT

### Historical Background

The history of freedom of the press in the United States has been described in numerous scholarly works. Some admirable studies explore specific incidents while others survey the entire historical sweep of American press freedom.[71] It is not possible to summarize all this historical work. But two connected issues—the evolution of the doctrine of seditious libel and the decisions of the United States Supreme Court when it confronted press claims in the wake of the First World War—provide a useful series of snapshots to illustrate the complex continuum of deeds, decisions, and doctrines.

Within a decade of the founding of the American nation, bitter political differences erupted between the Federalists, in power under President John Adams, and the opposition Republicans, led by Jefferson and Madison. This political tension contributed directly to passage of the Alien and Sedition Acts of 1798.[72] Even in the eighteenth century, it was easy for the administration in power to doubt the loyalty of the opposition. The international situation in 1798, which included competing claims on the United States by England and France, heightened this suspicion. In a pattern that would be repeated in the twentieth century, the federal government attempted to restrict and punish public debate under the guise of controlling sedition. The Adams administration made it a crime for anyone to "oppose any measure or measures of the government" or "to impede the operation of any law of the United States."[73] Republicans viewed the Alien and Sedition Acts as a partisan attack. Jefferson and Madison responded with their own highly partisan states' rights declarations in the Virginia and Kentucky Resolutions of 1798.[74]

The Sedition Act served as the basis for several successful prosecutions of Republican newspaper editors.[75] It was allowed to expire when Jefferson succeeded Adams as President. Leonard Levy has demonstrated, however, that President Jefferson did not fully live up to citizen Jefferson's pronouncements in praise of freedom of the press.[76] Several abortive efforts to prosecute Federalist newspapers were begun during Jefferson's presidency, apparently with his knowledge, if not with his active encouragement.

Nevertheless, it has become a commonplace in the United States to regard the Sedition Act of 1798 as a dark and exceptional page in an otherwise progressive tale of the growth of press freedom. In 1964, the United States Supreme Court said that while that Court never had considered the constitutionality of the Sedition Act, "the attack upon its validity has carried the day in the court of history."[77]

Until the Espionage Acts of 1917 and 1918, Congress did not again formally invoke a national security rationale to restrain freedom of expression. Yet national security claims occasionally were used during the Civil War to suppress freedom of the press through military and executive actions.[78] On occasion, presidents following Lincoln also attempted to stifle the press in the years before the First World War.[79] Simultaneously, state officials imposed restrictions on freedom of the press, and even *they* sometimes defended their actions in terms of national security.[80]

As late as 1907, the United States Supreme Court refused to scrutinize a contempt judgment imposed on a newspaper by the Colorado Supreme Court for several articles and a cartoon critical of judicial action.[81] In his opinion for the majority, Justice Holmes simply assumed that a state court could punish any publication "tending toward"[82] interference with its own judgment. Holmes asserted that even if the First Amendment right to freedom of speech conceivably could be applied to the states, it applied only to prior restraints on publication.

The xenophobia surrounding American entry into the First World War produced and sustained a campaign that invoked national security interests against numerous persons and publications suspected of disloyalty. Anti-German hysteria produced hundreds of bizarre prosecutions under federal and state laws.[83] Widespread federal raids and prosecutions aimed at radicals and aliens continued during the "return to normalcy" following the Versailles Peace Conference.[84] The federal law passed in 1917, and amended in 1918, remains in force today.[85]

Moreover, the theoretical structure for most judicial analysis of the First Amendment comes from the First World War era, which produced the first full-fledged United States Supreme Court consideration of freedom of the press defenses against national security arguments. Zechariah Chafee's masterful study details the bitter political context of the period and the development of First Amendment doctrine during a period the United States Supreme Court recently characterized as "not one of the enlightened eras of our history."[86] Several basic themes developed by Chafee and elaborated by other scholars may be summarized briefly.

First, as the justices began to abandon the idea that the First Amendment only afforded protection against prior restraints, they evolved a set of doctrinal categories with which to test governmental arguments that expression could be legitimately suppressed. The categories they developed ranged from the "bad tendency" test—extremely deferential to the government's claim—through *ad hoc* balancing and several varieties of the "clear and present danger" test.

Second, even when Justices Holmes and Brandeis began to advocate closer scrutiny of governmental justifications for the legitimacy of suppression, they still voted to uphold convictions under the Espionage Act of 1917. In the free speech cases decided by the United States Supreme Court in 1919, rather innocent expression was held to threaten the sort of "clear and present danger" Congress had power to punish.[87]

It was not until Justices Holmes and Brandeis considered an appeal involving the amended Espionage Act of 1918 that they dissented. In fact, no freedom of expression claim prevailed in the United States Supreme Court until 1931.[88] In dissent in *Abrams* v. *United States*,[89] however, Justices Holmes and Brandeis began to articulate special concern for freedom of expression, and suggested that speech and press rights should occupy a preferred constitutional position. Thus, the First World War era helped produce the central motif of a special role for freedom of expression in constitutional adjudication.

In his dissent in *Abrams*, Justice Holmes argued that leaflets sent floating over Houston Street in New York City by a group of Russian Jewish immigrants protesting the landing of an American expeditionary force in Vladivostok were not launched with the intent he believed necessary to prove violation of the Espionage Act. Holmes characterized the expression as "the surreptitious publishing of a silly leaflet by an unknown man" and asserted that the defendants, whom he called "poor and puny anonymities," were not enough of a threat to "turn the color of legal litmus paper."[90] Yet the majority of the *Abrams* Court upheld the conviction, accepting the defendants' self-portraits as "rebels" and "revolutionists."[91]

After *Abrams*, it seemed that virtually any attack on an important foreign policy decision might be suppressed. Moreover, Justice Holmes's approach, focusing on the context of allegedly dangerous statements, could be turned against him and Justice Brandeis. This became obvious in *Gitlow* v. *New York*.[92]

By the mid-1920s, Calvin Coolidge was in the White House and no American troops were engaged in battle. Nevertheless, in *Gitlow* the United States Supreme Court upheld the conviction of a New York Socialist for his role in publishing a manifesto of the Left Wing Section of the Socialist Party. In his opinion for the majority, Justice Sanford used just the kind of fire imagery Holmes introduced in *Schenck*. But Sanford's rhetoric—"A single revolutionary spark may kindle a fire that, smoldering for a time, may burst into a sweeping and destructive conflagration"[93]—undermined Holmes's cautions about the need to consider the proximity and degree of danger threatened by the expression.

Justices Holmes and Brandeis again dissented. They argued that a judicial declaration that Gitlow's words constituted an incitement was insufficient. "Every idea is an incitement,"[94] Holmes asserted. Holmes claimed that the only difference between opinion and incitement would be "the speaker's enthusiasm for the result."[95] The test Holmes would apply involved determining if the expression actually did have a "chance of starting a present conflagration."[96] Holmes thereby brought his clear and present danger test somewhat closer to the First Amendment test District Judge Learned Hand proposed during the First World War in the *Masses* case.[97]

While Holmes and Brandeis began to evolve a protective attitude toward First Amendment freedoms, a majority of the Court severely limited protection for freedom of expression. The Court's decision in *Whitney* v. *California*[98] provides a good example. Upholding a conviction under a California law triggered by the assassination of President McKinley, Justice Sanford asserted that it was "not open to question" that a state might punish "utterances inimical to the public welfare, tending to incite crime, disturb the public peace, or endanger the foundations of organized government and threaten its overthrow by unlawful means."[99] Whitney's membership in a party that advocated criminal syndicalism was enough for the Court to sustain her conviction.

The most significant break in the restrictive pattern of First Amendment discussions by the majority of the Court occurred in *Near* v. *Minnesota* in 1931.[100] For the first time, the United States Supreme Court squarely held that newspapers enjoy a strong constitutional presumption in favor of their freedom to publish. *Near* remains important today primarily for the severe limitations it imposed on the use of prior restraints.[101] The majority opinion, written by Chief Justice Hughes, also marks the first clear constitutional triumph for the right to publish controversial material.

After *Near*, and the *Grosjean* decision that soon followed, the United States Supreme Court appeared to have decided that the press should enjoy special constitutional solicitude. But almost unchallenged wartime censorship during the Second World War soon was followed by a harsh and effective crackdown on dissenters during the Cold War period of the late 1940s and early 1950s. Again it seemed that the bold, sometimes eloquent words of earlier cases were fragile protections; judges appeared to share the public's great fear of a Communist menace.[102]

The vulnerability of First Amendment freedoms during times of crisis, even without a war in progress, became painfully obvious in numerous decisions during the Cold War period.[103] *Dennis* v. *United States*,[104] upholding the conviction of Communist Party leaders under the Smith Act,[105] serves as a paradigm for the era. The *Dennis* version of the clear and present danger standard was taken by Chief Justice Vinson from Circuit Judge Learned Hand's lower court opinion in the case.[106] The Vinson-Hand test was "whether the gravity of the 'evil,' discounted by its improbability, justifies such invasion of free speech as is necessary to avoid the danger."[107]

The *Dennis* decision rested on the assumption that the government need not "wait until the putsch is about to be executed."[108] Instead, judicial notice of danger was sufficient. Vinson proclaimed the requisite connection between the "highly organized conspiracy" of the Communist defendants and "the inflammable nature of world conditions, similar uprisings in other countries, and the touch-and-go nature of our relations with countries with whom petitioners were in the very least ideologically attuned."[109]

Concurring in the result, Justice Frankfurter took similar judicial notice of Communist doctrines advocated by the defendants that, he said, were "in the ascendancy in powerful nations who cannot be acquitted of unfriendliness to the institutions of this country."[110] Justice Jackson, who not long before had returned from his duties at the Nazi War Crimes trials, rejected the clear and present danger formula regarding it as beyond the competence of judges to apply. Instead, Jackson concurred because he believed that convictions of "a well-organized, nation-wide conspiracy"[111] should be upheld just as any other conspiracy to violate the laws would be. Justices Black and Douglas dissented with the hope that, as Black put it, "in calmer times, when present pressures, passions and fears subside, this or some later Court will restore the First Amendment liberties to the high preferred place where they belong in a free society."[112]

To summarize, a majority of the justices in *Dennis* agreed that leaders of the American Communist Party were sufficiently well organized and closely enough connected to an international threat to be convicted of knowingly and wilfully advocating and teaching the duty and necessity of overthrowing the government of the United States by force and violence. As restated by Chief Justice Vinson, the clear and present danger formula afforded little constitutional protection to controversial expression. Indeed, the *Dennis* test was not obviously different from the test employed under the old, often condemned seditious libel doctrine. In a multitude of judicial decisions during the 1950s, as well as in the actions of other private and government officials, the Communist menace was thought sufficient justification to impose a variety of limitations on freedom of expression.[113]

Beginning around 1960, the United States Supreme Court became increasingly skeptical of the security dangers government officials invoked as justification for suppression.[114] Although the Warren Court refused to consider the constitutionality of the Vietnam War and strained mightily to uphold a conviction for draft card burning in the face of a First Amendment challenge, the Court began to use a number of intermediate tests and procedural devices to invalidate convictions for various forms of protest.[115]

*Brandenburg* v. *Ohio*[116] symbolizes the great distance travelled in a relatively short time after *Dennis* by the country and the Court. In *Brandenburg*, the Court struck down convictions of members of the Ku Klux Klan under an Ohio Syndicalism Act enacted at the same time as the statute upheld in *Whitney*. The Court explicitly overruled *Whitney*, describing it as "thoroughly discredited by later decisions."[117] The constitutional test enunciated in the *per curiam* opinion in *Brandenburg*—"that the constitutional guarantees of free speech and free press do not permit a state to forbid or proscribe advocacy of the use of force or of law violation except where such advocacy is directed to inciting or producing imminent lawless action and is likely to incite or produce such action"[118]—combined the context and content approaches suggested by Justice Holmes and Judge Hand in the First World War cases and stressed the time element emphasized by Justice Brandeis. However, the *Brandenburg* standard went further in its protection of expression. Though the *Brandenburg* majority relied on a clear and present danger formula, that test was restated to protect expression unless it posed an actual, imminent threat of lawless action.[119]

Yet in the 1970s the United States Supreme Court, under Chief Justice Burger, increasingly rejected claims that government actions produced "chilling effects" on expression.[120] For example, the Court tended to defer to special circumstances and to experts in permitting restrictions on leaflets and petitions to Congress by military personnel. The Court also condoned a variety of special surveillance techniques.[121]

It is possible to say, therefore, that the amount of constitutional protection that will be afforded to freedom of expression remains uncertain. The *Dennis* test provides weak protection for freedom of expression, as demonstrated in case after case during the 1950s. *Dennis* calculates proximity, degree, and necessity within the rubric of the clear and present danger test. Conversely, the *Brandenburg* variation of the clear and present danger test appears to protect expression, on political matters at least,[122] unless it constitutes an incitement to imminent and highly probable lawless action. However, First Amendment doctrines are not static. They may be expanded or constricted by the Court to provide greater or lesser protection for expression depending on the justices' perceptions of the degree of danger the expression poses. The likelihood that the doctrines will be applied constrictively increases when national security is offered by the government as the justification for suppression. The Court emphatically has rejected the notion that the government might readily punish seditious libel. Within the interstices of numerous tests applied in First Amendment decisions, however, it remains likely that, in tense situations, expression will be punished.

## Prior and Other Restraints on the Press

The following discussion of judicial, legislative, and administrative treatment of contemporary freedom of the press issues summarizes recent attempts to grapple with some of the most vexing problems in press law today. It should be emphasized that every category has both a doctrinal and a practical life of its own; the complexity can only be suggested here. Simultaneously, it is worth noting that little doctrinal unity emerges from recent press law—whether lawmaking is done by judicial, legislative, or executive officials.

In the United States, there is no official system of censorship of the print media. There have been informal instances, as in the censorship of military reporting during the First and Second World Wars, but over the past 50 years the thrust of judicial opinions points toward a strong presumption against the validity of governmental attempts to censor the press. Furthermore, dramatic recent instances of effective reporting in the face of government efforts to intimidate or stop papers from publishing helped to embolden journalists.

Publication of the "Pentagon Papers" while the federal government sought to enjoin publication, as well as hard-hitting investigative reporting about the Watergate scandal in the face of the Nixon Administration's attempts to divert, intimidate, or "sandbag" coverage, illustrate this trend. The American press undoubtedly performs an influential role and sometimes serves as a check on government. Justice Hugo Black celebrated that function in his final opinion, concurring in *New York Times* v. *United States*:

> The Government's power to censor the press was abolished so that the press would remain forever free to censure the Government. The press was protected so that it could bare the secrets of government and inform the people.[123]

As strong as the American tradition against censorship may be, however, there is no absolute rule even against prior restraints. Moreover, a number of informal as well as legal devices permit the government great leeway in controlling or manipulating press coverage. These include exploitation of the symbiotic relationship between reporters and government officials, extensive use and abuse of the classification system, and threats to take legal action against reporters and newspapers. Also, the government has been permitted to make employment conditional on an agreement not to disclose information gained through a government job, even when disclosure does not constitute a security risk. Finally, judges exclude a number of categories entirely from the realm of First Amendment protection. Exclusion by definition includes the categories of (1) portrayal of minors in sexual roles, (2) infringement of copyright, (3) obscenity, and (4) defamation. Also, it is a federal crime willfully to disclose several categories of atomic, military, and intelligence information.

### Censorship: The Presumption against Prior Restraints and the Abuse of National Security

Chief Justice Hughes's opinion in *Near* v. *Minnesota*[124] is the leading modern manifestation of a long tradition of special reluctance to allow government to impose prior restraints on publication. Yet while the Court emphasized the need for freedom to publish even "vile" material, it admitted that there are exceptions. No one could question, Chief Justice Hughes wrote, that "a government might prevent actual obstruction to its recruiting service or the publication of the sailing dates of transports or the number and location of troops."[125]

Three important cases during the 1970s turned on whether particular governmental restraints fell within the permissible exceptions to the constitutional rule against prior restraints: the Pentagon Papers case[126]; *United States* v. *The Progressive, Inc.*[127]; and *Nebraska Press Association* v. *Stuart.*[128] The government asserted each time that the situation was analogous to the exceptions suggested in *Near*. However, the Court invalidated the government's action in two of the three cases. The results in these prior restraint cases illuminate the modern scope of the doctrine.[129]

Abhorrence of prior restraints remains strong in the United States, but these cases actually somewhat weakened the prohibitory rule by what the United States Supreme Court left unsaid as well as by what it said. Moreover, the continuation of an injunction against publication of an issue of *The Progressive* for seven months serves to emphasize the obvious loopholes in the doctrine against prior restraint. In fact, a number of scholars recently have questioned the validity of prior restraint analysis altogether.[130] A summary of the three cases indicates why the doctrine against prior restraints is challenged so frequently today.

### The Pentagon Papers

The Pentagon Papers case involved a multivolume, highly classified history of United States involvement in Vietnam. Daniel Ellsberg, a former government employee who wrote parts of the classified study, released the study to a number of major American newspapers over a period of several weeks in the spring of 1971.

The federal government sought injunctions against publication, claiming that prior restraints were justified because publication of articles based on the Pentagon study would cause grave and irreparable injury to the United States, particularly to American diplomatic efforts. The United States Supreme Court considered the issue in an extraordinary session held only two weeks after the government's first attempt to enjoin publication.

In a brief *per curiam* opinion, by a six-to-three vote, the Supreme Court determined that the government failed to meet the "heavy burden of showing justification for the imposition of such a restraint."[131] Each of the nine justices wrote separately to explain his reasons for support or opposition to the outcome. It is therefore difficult to synthesize a rule from the Pentagon Papers case. What seems to emerge from the opinions of the justices in the majority, however, is a strong presumption against any government use of courts to restrain newspapers prior to publication, at least without some plausible statutory basis.[132]

It should be noted that several justices in the majority indicated that they might consider *subsequent* punishment of newspaper officials for violation of the Espionage Act constitutionally acceptable.[133] But they did not consider the mere act of publishing classified information to be criminal, although the fact of its classified status might be relevant to proof of the criminal intent generally required for prosecution. Actually, there are federal laws that prohibit publication of specific kinds of information, such as photographs or drawings of vital military installations, cryptographic systems, or the identities of foreign intelligence agents.[134] There is also a general prohibition, based on the Espionage Acts, against "communication" that takes place with "intent or reason to believe that the information is to be used to the injury of the United States, or to the advantage of any foreign nation."[135] The legal significance of these phrases is unclear, however. There is serious doubt, for example, whether the term "communication" covers publication directed to the public. Further, the very law containing this criminal provision specifically disclaims any congressional intent "to authorize, require or establish military or civilian censorship or in any way to limit or infringe upon freedom of the press or of speech...."[136]

Congress recently enacted a law prohibiting disclosure of the identities of American undercover operatives. Even this statute, called the Intelligence Identities Protection Act of 1982, makes most identification a criminal offense only when exposure occurs "with reason to believe that such activities would impair or impede the foreign intelligence activities of the United States."[137] The constitutionality of this law, passed in reaction to publications by Philip Agee, which he conceded were intended to disclose the identities of CIA agents, has yet to be tested in the courts.[138]

### The Progressive *case: seven months of prior restraint*

Knotty statutory questions concerning alleged atomic and military secrets also complicated the prior restraint issues in *United States* v. *The Progressive, Inc.*[139] The case was not definitely resolved, however, because the federal government withdrew its request for an injunction after the controversial material, allegedly exposing the "H-bomb secret," was widely disseminated by other newspapers. Yet the government did "temporarily" restrain publication of the contested article for seven months. This successful prior restraint is particularly striking when one considers that the government stipulated, early in the litigation, that information on which the article was based was already accessible to the general public and revealed nothing that would be new to "a competent scientist*."[140] Nevertheless, the United States Supreme Court refused to grant an extraordinary writ of mandamus when journalists and *The Progressive* sought to hasten the appellate review process.[141] Even proceedings in the

---

* Compare this position to the German mosaic theory developed in the *Der Speigel* case, Kohl, "Press Law in the Federal Republic of Germany," text accompanying n. 91 *infra*. (Editor's note)

case including judicial opinions, oral arguments, and submission of briefs took place under tight secrecy constraints.

In his decision, based almost entirely on evidence presented in secret, District Court Judge Warren claimed the test he applied was simply a variation of the clear and present danger test. Yet much of Judge Warren's analysis suggested a return to the old "bad tendency" approach, supplemented by explicit balancing of costs and benefits.[142] Given the importance of the alleged threat—the release of the secret of the hydrogen bomb—it was relatively easy for government attorneys to convince the court that preservation of the *status quo* outweighed *The Progressive's* desire to reach the newstands quickly with its story. Subsequent revelations about the general availability of the "secret" information altered public and press perceptions, however, and considerably weakened the government's case.

On appeal, the government responded to these developments by stressing the idea that certain documents are "born classified." This concept would permit the government to treat material as classified from its inception, without ever submitting it to the formal classification system for review. Additionally, the government could reclassify information, even when that material consisted entirely of information already in the public domain, whenever it deemed it sufficiently important to do so.[143]

Since there was no dramatic judicial resolution to bring down the curtain on the *Progressive* case, it is easy to ignore its implications. The federal government succeeded in obtaining and sustaining a prior restraint on publication of a magazine article for seven months. In itself, this is an important first occurrence in the American law of freedom of the press.

*Judicial Prior Censorship:* Nebraska Press Association *v.* Stuart[144]

In *Nebraska Press Association*, Nebraska state judges imposed and upheld an order restraining the press from publishing any facts about a particularly gruesome murder of six family members in a small Nebraska town. The United States Supreme Court unanimously invalidated this "gag order." Chief Justice Burger's opinion, joined by four other justices, noted that "prior restraints on speech and publication are the most serious and least tolerable infringement on First Amendment rights."[145] Yet the legal test the Chief Justice applied involved the balancing of a number of factors, and appeared to invalidate the order only because available alternative methods were untried and because the restraining order could not be entirely effective.[146]

In *Nebraska Press Association*, therefore, a majority of the Court used a weak form of the old clear and present danger test as stated in *Dennis*, and combined it with explicit balancing of policy considerations. Though the Court invalidated the Nebraska gag order, its doctrinal approach appears less protective of freedom of expression than the approach announced in earlier decisions such as *Brandenburg* v. *Ohio* and *Near* v. *Minnesota*. In those cases the Court refused to engage in utilitarian cost-benefit analysis, but relied instead on what in effect was almost a conclusive presumption against prior restraints.[147]

### Summary

Government censorship through prior restraint orders failed in several important recent decisions. Yet even when decisions appear to be victories for freedom of the press, they may contain troublesome developments. The Pentagon Papers decision appears to grant Congress significant leeway in making some types of publication criminal; *Nebraska Press Association* suggests that explicit judicial balancing of policy concerns is appropriate. The ability of the federal government to persuade courts to restrain publication of *The Progressive's* article for more than half a year demonstrates that the prohibition against prior restraints in the United States is far from absolute. Virtually every conflict involving a question of prior restraint may raise questions of the proximity and degree of danger, as articulated in *Dennis*. But symbolic pronouncements and legal precedents still create an unusually strong presumption against imposition of judicial restraints prior to publication.

## Seditious Libel and the Reputation of Public Officials

Writing for a majority that invalidated a large libel judgment imposed on the *New York Times*, Justice Brennan held in *New York Times* v. *Sullivan*[148] that neither criminal nor civil law is constitutionally valid if it inhibits debate on public issues in a manner reminiscent of the seditious libel laws. Until that 1964 decision, legal standards for defining and remedying defamation had been left almost entirely to the states. Historically, little concern was shown for First Amendment values necessarily implicated in the process of adjudicating defamation cases. In the words of the torts scholar Dean William L. Prosser, defamation is defined as:

> that which tends to injure "reputation" in the popular sense; to diminish the esteem, respect, goodwill or confidence in which the plaintiff is held, or to excite adverse, derogatory or unpleasant feelings or opinions against him. It necessarily, however, involves the idea of disgrace.[149]

Defamation was simply assumed to be a category of expression that fell outside the protection of the First Amendment. Legal restrictions and self-imposed restraints inevitably followed the prevailing presumption that there simply was no constitutional protection for defamatory expression.

While truth was a defense to defamation under the law of most states, the burden of proving truth was on defendant newspapers in actions brought against them. Additionally, the common law permitted recovery without proof of any damage to the plaintiff if the plaintiff's claim was based on certain types of published statements considered to be automatically defamatory. These included: erroneous statements that a person had a "loathsome" disease; accusations of serious criminal conduct; and charges of incompetence or unfitness in a professional calling (for example, "public official A is a Communist"; "Dr. B. is a butcher"). This final category allowed public officials who were criticized great leeway in framing their complaints.

The United States Supreme Court transformed the landscape of American defamation law with its *Sullivan* decision. An Alabama state court jury had awarded Sullivan, a Montgomery police official, damages of $500,000. Sullivan's name had not been mentioned in an advertisement seeking support for the civil rights movement, but the advertisement claimed that Montgomery police surrounded and blocked a black college campus, thereby slightly exaggerating the incident.

In his opinion for the majority, Justice Brennan asserted that because the First Amendment contemplates a system of freedom of expression in which "debate on public issues should be uninhibited, robust and wide-open," it is necessary to protect "even some falsehood."[150] If the press were obligated to warrant the truth of all that it prints, Brennan wrote, its vigor would be sapped and public debate limited.

The test announced in *Sullivan* held the press liable for defamatory falsehoods against public officials only if these officials could prove "actual malice." This term of art is much harder to prove than "malice," as malice is commonly understood. Actual malice is defined in *Sullivan* as publication of falsehood "with knowledge that it was false or with reckless disregard of whether it was false or not."[151] Thus the Supreme Court went a long way toward freeing newspapers from the threat of potential defamation actions.

The Supreme Court initially extended the constitutional protections of the *Sullivan* test to defamation suits brought by all "public figures" and to all matters "of public or general interest."[152] In *Gertz* v. *Robert Welch*,[153] however, the Supreme Court under Chief Justice Burger, held that the actual malice standard protected newspapers only against suits brought by a relatively narrow class of public officials and public figures. The *Gertz* decision prohibited assessing presumed and punitive damages against media defendants, absent actual malice. Yet *Gertz* left state and federal courts free to impose any libel test they might wish to adopt, so long as they did not impose liability without fault in suits involving plaintiffs not considered public figures or public officials.

In *Gertz*, and in a number of decisions since, the United States Supreme Court sharply limited the category of public figure protection for newspapers. In decisions involving a socially prominent heiress, a scientist whose federal grant subjected him to Senator Proxmire's "Golden Fleece" award for alleged waste of public money, and a person once convicted of criminal contempt for failure to appear before a grand jury, the Court found the plaintiffs not to be "public figures."[154] The "mere negligence" standard was held to afford sufficient protection for the First Amendment interests of the defendant publications.

The Court also rejected a First Amendment defense in *Herbert* v. *Lando*,[155] in which the plaintiff attempted to prove that CBS television coverage of his role in Vietnam was defamatory. In that case, the plaintiff conceded that he was a public figure and that the actual malice standard applied to him. Therefore, the majority opinion by Justice Powell held that since Hebert was obliged to try to prove actual malice under *Sullivan*, in pretrial discovery he was entitled to inquire as to the mental states and editorial decisions of those involved in putting together the news segment. The Court rejected the journalists' First Amendment argument that this discovery would intrude into their editorial discretion and that it would have a chilling effect on future reporting.

Today, the United States Supreme Court is sharply divided about the reach of the First Amendment in defamation suits. The *Sullivan* decision constitutionalized the issue, but the cases that reach the Court still turn on their own particular facts. Many defamation suits are settled before trial. Those that are litigated usually are decided in state courts and turn on their particular facts and state law. If a jury awards a large sum of damages against a media defendant, the jury's decision is often reversed on appeal.[156] Moreover, when a federal constitutional issue arises, judges and litigants find themselves without clear directions from the Supreme Court. The Supreme Court appears unable to formulate coherent criteria applicable beyond the particulars of each case.[157] The Court clearly has receded from the sweeping declarations in favor of freedom of the press in *Sullivan*. How far the retrenchment goes remains problematic. Undoubtedly, *Sullivan* still provides significant protection for newspapers in their reporting about political as well as other public figures.

Results in defamation cases still may turn on whether plaintiffs are deemed to be either public officials or public figures. If they are not, newspapers are in a rather vulnerable position and can be held liable if the plaintiff is able to prove mere negligence. Though *Sullivan* extended constitutional protection to robust debate involving public persons, no decision has held that First Amendment claims by newspapers automatically prevail over the interests of private individuals in their reputations.

## The Press and the Privacy of the Individual

At the same time that the United States Supreme Court constitutionalized the law of defamation in *New York Times* v. *Sullivan*,[158] it also started to develop the idea of a constitutional right to privacy. Initial recognition of this privacy right in *Griswold* v. *Connecticut*[159] involved state regulation of birth control within the marital relationship. But soon the Court held privacy to be a right entailing constitutional protection for both secrecy and autonomy of the individual.[160]

The simultaneous development of constitutional protection for an "uninhibited, wide-open and robust" system of expression and for the individual's right to make personal decisions heightened the inevitable tension between press and privacy rights. Common law tort remedies for invasion of privacy remained, exacerbating press versus privacy controversies.

Dean William L. Prosser distinguished four types of privacy-related torts:

1. Intrusion on the plaintiff's physical solitude.
2. Publication of private matters violating the ordinary decencies.
3. Putting plaintiff in a false position in the public eye, as by signing his name to a letter attributing to him views that he does not hold.
4. Appropriation of some element of plaintiff's personality for commercial use.[161]

Summarizing the difficulties inherent in the press and privacy rights conflict, Prosser noted that the rights meet in a "head-on collision." The line between privacy and freedom of the press is still neither clear, nor complete.

Thus far, the United States Supreme Court has avoided direct consideration of how to weigh these two values. In cases involving newspaper reports that identified the victim of a brutal rape-murder,[162] and a juvenile offender, despite a state statute barring identification,[163] the Court held that since the information already was available in open court records, states could not bar newspapers from publishing the names. Similarly, the Court held that Massachusetts could not totally exclude the press from state courts trying certain kinds of sex crimes but should weigh the relevant factors on a case-by-case basis.[164]

In recent decisions the Court greatly increased the potency of individual privacy claims. In separate but related areas, judges have begun to broaden the scope of tort claims for invasion of privacy and compensation for publicity.[165] Such claims may prevail against the media in spite of First Amendment defenses. Courts use a balancing test to determine if an individual has a right to suppress his unpleasant past or to share in the commercial exploitation of his glorious present. Rights to convey and receive information protected by the First Amendment are weighed against the individual's interests in his own personality and personal concerns. Results turn on subjective judicial views of what matters are of importance to the public, who is a public figure, and what constitutes commercial exploitation.

## Access to Government Information

The question of ownership and control of government information is near the core of much current controversy over whether there is a constitutional dimension to the public's right to know. The right to know is also connected to debate about whether there is a special press right of access to government functions, documents, and officials beyond that accorded to all persons. At the same time, on both the federal and state levels, a significant number of statutes and regulations passed over the past two decades require that citizens generally be granted access to government records and activities.

The United States Supreme Court appears unable or unwilling to decide whether there is a public right to know and if the press should be afforded special rights to access. Recent disagreements among the justices about access to pretrial hearings and to criminal trials provide good examples of these difficulties. A complicated structure of both official and informal restraints lies beneath the surface of the current debate. Also, comparison with the highly regulated television and radio media—and debate about whether technological innovation now renders extensive regulation of these media unsupportable—hangs over debate about whether, and to what extent, there is a constitutional right to know. At a time when most Americans are said to rely on evening television broadcasts for their sense of the news, and when respected newspapers are rapidly going out of business throughout the country, these issues are of great practical importance.

### Administrative and Statutory Rules

Beginning in the 1960s, Congress and most state legislatures took giant steps in the direction of opening up governmental records and processes to public scrutiny. Yet at least 100 federal statutes contain provisions that either absolutely prohibit disclosure of specified information by government officials or allow them discretion to withhold information.[166] Also, agencies nearly always develop their own regulations prohibiting or limiting disclosure. It is impossible, therefore, to discuss the scope or impact of federal liberalizations and restraints with specificity, or even to begin to analyze parallel provisions and their practical impact in the 50 state governments. Even under the federal Freedom of Information Act (FOIA),[167] many nondisclosure provisions remain. As the United States Supreme Court said about the FOIA in *Federal Aviation Administration* v. *Robertson*, "Congress intended to leave largely undisturbed existing statutes dealing with disclosure of information by specific agencies."[168]

Congress responded to the *Robertson* decision with the Sunshine Act of 1976,[169] relaxing some of the statutory restraints already in force. Ever since, there has been a continuous dialogue of congressional amendments and judicial interpretations addressing the myriad and complex statutory issues under the FOIA.[170]

In *Environmental Protection Agency* v. *Mink*,[171] for example, the United States Supreme Court held that the FOIA exempted an executive branch decision to classify information and thereby to restrict judicial review, even though it was a congresswoman, Representative Patsy T. Mink of Hawaii, joined by 32 other members of Congress, who sought the information and questioned its classification. Even after congressional amendments in response to the *Mink* decision, foreign affairs and defense matters still generally are exempt from the FOIA's reach, as was made clear in several recent decisions.[172] Yet in *Department of the Air Force* v. *Rose*,[173] the Supreme Court rejected the argument by the Air Force Academy that, under the FOIA, summaries of honor code hearings should be exempt from disclosure to student law review editors. The Court stated that the intention of the FOIA was to create "a workable compromise between individual rights and the preservation of public rights to Government information."[174]

Over the past 15 years, thousands of judicial decisions have construed the FOIA. FOIA lawsuits frequently involve complicated factual issues and murky questions of statutory interpretation. Though it is difficult to generalize, it is possible to discern a recent trend making it more difficult for journalists, scholars, and private citizens to obtain information. This tightening is occurring through expanding judicial interpretations of FOIA exemptions and through procedural barriers developed by administrators and judges.[175] Moreover, information made available under the FOIA and under its state counterparts is thought to be available as a matter of legislative discretion, rather than constitutional command. Therefore, Congress and state legislatures are free to tinker with the categories of information they deem suitable for release.

Journalists and scholars still have found invaluable material through freedom of information acts and sunshine laws that open government information and processes to public scrutiny.[176] Yet such laws already bristle with exceptions and political support for further restrictions seems to be increasing. Access to judicial materials generally cannot be obtained under either kind of statute. Additionally, recent executive orders extended the entire federal security classification apparatus so that it includes more information and encompasses more vaguely defined categories of restricted information.[177] Other executive orders, as well as the Intelligence Identities Protection Act of 1982, further illustrate a trend toward limiting expansive earlier interpretations of the public's right to know.[178]

While it is impossible to be sure how a hypothetical case would be resolved if a journalist brought a constitutional challenge to specific restrictions on access to government information, Supreme Court decisions suggest that the Court would not enthusiastically embrace such an affirmative constitutional claim.[179] The only exception seems to be a limited constitutional right of access to traditional government functions, such as criminal trials.[180]

### Censorship by Contract

Americans like to stress that the United States has no Official Secrets Act. But recent judicial decisions, legislation, and executive actions make it clear that the federal government can prevent employees from disclosing almost anything concerning their work and any information they obtain in the course of their employment.

Largely because judicial decisions approving contractual constraints on expression are only a few years old, it remains unclear how far "muzzling by contract" will be allowed to become a precondition for government work. Furthermore, the practical effectiveness of this contractual approach to plugging leaks and stopping whistle blowers remains in serious doubt. In any event, recent actions enforcing agreements restricting expression have important symbolic, as well as practical, ripple effects.

In *Snepp* v. *United States*,[181] the United States Supreme Court held, without waiting for briefs or hearing oral argument, that a judge could constitutionally order a former Central Intelligence Agency employee to obtain prior CIA approval for all his future publications. Moreover, the Court established a constructive trust and ordered Mr. Snepp to pay the government for all past and future profits from his book, *Decent Interval*. The Court ordered this unusual remedy despite the government's concession, at least for purposes of the litigation, that Snepp's critical account of the final days of United States forces in Vietnam contained no classified information.

The Court's brief *per curiam* opinion simply said that Snepp had agreed to submit all publications for prior CIA review and that the government had "a compelling interest in protecting both the secrecy of information important to our national security and the appearance of confidentiality so essential to the effective operation of our foreign intelligence service."[182]

The *Snepp* decision underscored the extent to which the government can limit the ability of employees to express themselves freely or to publish their opinions or accounts of their experiences after they leave government service. The First Amendment was not held to protect employees from waiving present and future freedom to publish, even when information restricted by individual employment contracts is not classified.

Even before *Snepp*, the CIA had succeeded in obtaining judicial sanction of its preclearance authority in several lower court opinions. In *United States* v. *Marchetti*,[183] the Fourth Circuit Court of Appeals enjoined publication of a book by a former CIA agent. In *Knopf* v. *Colby*,[184] the same Court upheld the CIA's contractual preclearance claim when the Knopf publishing house contested deletions ordered by the CIA. Finally, in *Haig* v. *Agee*,[185] the United States Supreme Court rejected the constitutional and statutory claims of a former CIA agent whose passport was revoked because of his acknowledged campaign "to expose CIA officers and agents." In the majority's consideration of Agee's constitutional claims, Chief Justice Burger conceded that the revocation rested at least in part on Agee's speech. Citing the exceptions proclaimed in *Near* v. *Minnesota*, however, Chief Justice Burger argued that "Agee's disclosures, among other things, have the declared purpose of obstructing intelligence operations and the recruiting of intelligence personnel. They clearly are not protected by the Constitution."[186]

These recent decisions involving publications by former CIA agents may not establish doctrine which goes beyond their special facts. But the Court's summary action in *Snepp* and the "whirlwind treatment of Agee's constitutional claims"[187] suggest that today there is more constitutional leeway for officials who seek to restrict "secret" information or attempt to halt or punish publication on grounds of employment contracts. Undoubtedly, judicial willingness to elevate security at the expense of First Amendment claims is somewhat related to legislative enthusiasm for greater statutory restraints and the executive branch's more stringent approach to information leaks.

## Cozy Connections and the Checking Function: Politics and the Press

In recent years, the United States Supreme Court has echoed and expanded the theme developed by Madison and Jefferson that the press should serve as "a formidable censor of the public functionaries, by arraigning them at the tribunal of public opinion."[188]

During the 1970s, there was much evidence of the ability of the press to perform this checking function, and to withstand the pressures and temptations flowing from those in power. The withdrawal of American troops from Vietnam and of Richard Nixon from the presidency are examples of the ability of the press to publish critical articles and opinions despite political pressure. While it is impossible to prove that critical press coverage directly caused these events, there can be little doubt that both occurred in part because of persistent, probing coverage that gradually altered American public opinion. Recent state and local government history also indicates the great, albeit less dramatic, impact of skeptical press coverage on political events.[189]

It would be a mistake to assume that the relationship of journalists and public officials is entirely or even largely adversarial. Hard evidence of cooperation, collaboration, and even complicity between the members of the fourth estate and government officials is often elusive, yet understanding that such relationships exist aids understanding of the role of the press in the United States.

There is no official means for government to manage news. Yet government officials often attempt to control the press subtly, by exploiting their symbiotic relationship with journalists and publishers. They use exchanges of information, background briefings, and grants of special access in informal, but frequently successful, attempts to influence the flow of information. Discussion over cocktails and news "leaks" to favorite reporters are *de rigeur* in what often amounts to a love-hate relationship between officials and journalists.

Most government officials obviously are bound formally not to disclose certain aspects of their work. Just as obviously, such formalities often are honored in the breach. A regular scenario in Washington, D.C., for example, involves the announcement of renewed attempts by high administration officials to discover and plug "leaks." Ambitious politicians and disgruntled civil servants simultaneously compete with one another, and often with the leak-pluggers themselves, to exploit their shared recognition that knowledge is power. Information possessed and selectively shared can be immensely significant in fighting political battles or launching campaigns.

Nearly every politician is a self-styled expert in press relations; many boast privately of their ability to manage the press. A presidential news conference exemplifies the paradox of attempting to control the flow of news in an ostensibly open forum. Journalists learn a great deal from presidential errors and misstatements during such performances, illustrating the clash of motives as well as cooperative impulses of politicians and journalists.

Certainly, the American journalistic tradition may boast accurately about stories dug up by enterprising reporters despite attempts by government officials to manage the news subtly and ingeniously. Yet there also have been famous decisions to withhold or alter stories at the request of high officials. Probably the best-known example is the willingness of *New York Times* editors to water down a page one story on the eve of the Bay of Pigs invasion, following President Kennedy's phone call to urge such restraint. Kennedy said later he regretted his own intervention to forestall press coverage, since his administration would have been embarrassed out of the subsequent fiasco had the *Times* published what it knew.[190] Editors at the *Times* later claimed that their earlier decision to abide by a presidential request influenced their determination to, go ahead with publication of the Pentagon Papers 10 years later.

Well-known examples of compliance with government requests not to publish, however, may overshadow the multitude of subtle decisions that can amount to "responsible" self-censorship. It is difficult to evaluate such decisions and probably impossible to suggest any formal ethical code concerning release of information touching the private lives of public officials or potentially serious breaches of national security. Whether an issue involves the health of a Supreme Court justice or an alleged diplomatic or security secret, the form and scope of publication is believed to be a matter left largely, though not entirely, to the discretion and professional sense of journalists.

## THE PRESS AND THE JUDICIAL PROCESS

### Free Press and Fair Trial

Like other government officials, Supreme Court justices today are concerned about press coverage of their own words and deeds, as well as with legal matters generally. The justices, therefore, may be particularly sensitive about the increasingly common phenomenon of confrontation between reporters and the judicial process. For many years, for example, the United States Supreme Court's decisions precluded photographic or television coverage of trials. When the Court recently relaxed these restrictions, many state courts began experimenting with televised trial coverage.[191] But the United States Supreme Court today remains adamantly opposed to similar coverage of its own oral arguments. The justices also remain extremely secretive about their deliberations.

In a more familiar decision-making role, the justices vehemently disagreed recently about whether state judges may bar the press altogether from pretrial hearings or actual criminal trials. The Court held that the press and the public may be entirely excluded from pretrial hearings, but not from actual trials unless there are findings of serious and specific exigent circumstances. Yet the range of sources and arguments used by the Court reveals how uncertain the Court remains about the effect of First Amendment claims on access to the judiciary.

In *Gannett Co.* v. *DePasquale*,[192] the Court concentrated on the Sixth Amendment right to a public trial. The sharply divided Court upheld a judicial order barring the public and the press from a pretrial hearing concerning suppression of evidence in a murder case. The defendant and the prosecutor joined the trial judge in agreeing that the exclusion was necessary to ensure a fair trial.

Justice Stewart's majority opinion insisted that the Sixth Amendment's guarantee of a public trial was intended to benefit litigants, and not the public, at least as applied to pretrial hearings. He found it unnecessary to determine whether the First Amendment would guarantee the public any access at all. Justice Powell, concurring, found a First Amendment basis for the public access claim, but called for a flexible accommodation of that interest with the interests of the defendant; Powell argued that this approach favored secrecy in *Gannett*. Justice Rehnquist, who also concurred, explicitly rejected Powell's suggestion of judicial balancing. Rehnquist characterized such an approach as the idea that "the first amendment is some sort of 'sunshine law.'"[193]

Justice Blackmun wrote a partial dissent, joined by Justices Brennan, White, and Marshall, in which he attempted to articulate a standard permitting courtroom closure only in exceptional circumstances. Blackmun advocated a strong presumption in favor of open courtrooms, overcome only when a defendant could demonstrate that closure was "strictly and inescapably necessary in order to protect the fair trial guarantee."[194]

A year after the *Gannett* decision, however, the Court held by a seven to one vote in *Richmond Newspapers, Inc.* v. *Virginia* that the actual trial of a criminal case must be open to the public "[a]bsent an overriding interest articulated in findings."[195] Each of the justices in the majority submitted a separate opinion and each proposed his own theory in support of the outcome. Justice Rehnquist was the lone dissenter.

In the opinion announcing the judgment, Chief Justice Burger stressed the long history of open criminal trials in England and the United States. He noted the "nexus between openness, fairness, and the perception of fairness."[196] Several interrelated First Amendment provisions, as well as other constitutional provisions, provided support for the presumption favoring a right for the public and the press to attend trials.[197]

Justice Stevens endorsed the Court's holding, considering the case to be a "watershed" decision because it recognized a constitutional right of access to newsworthy matter. Justice Brennan, joined by Justice Marshall, wrote a lengthy concurrence concerning the idea that the First Amendment plays a structural role to secure and foster the American system of republican self-government. Brennan developed the idea that the public has a First Amendment right to receive information and extended this theme to include access to judicial proceedings, proclaiming that "under our system, judges are not mere umpires, but, in their own sphere, lawmakers—a coordinate branch of *government*."[198] Justice Rehnquist's dissent decried what he termed excessive interference with different ways justice might be administered in the states. He rejected any constitutional basis for the right of access to courts whatsoever.[199]

To summarize, the United States Supreme Court now distinguishes between pretrial hearings, which need not be open to the public or the press, and criminal trials, which must be open to both, absent overriding considerations keyed to the specific context of each case. The emerging pattern continues to reflect sympathy for the predicament faced by the trial judge and sensitivity to the historical and functional importance of open criminal trials. The justices remain divided about whether and to what extent the press has a special or additional constitutional claim of access premised on its role as a surrogate for the public.

## Reporters' Privilege and Legislative Actions to Protect the Press

Jailing newsmen was and remains extremely rare in the United States. It is safe to say that there is no general contempt power to punish journalists for unpleasantries they publish about courts. Moreover, in a number of decisions over the last 40 years, the United States Supreme Court invalidated contempt citations imposed on reporters and newspapers by judges upset by coverage of events in and around their courtrooms.[200] Nevertheless, a contempt citation for disobeying a judicial order may be upheld, even if the underlying order is clearly unconstitutional and actually is held to be so eventually.[201] Additionally, contempt citations against journalists for refusals to disclose their sources have been sustained recently.

In several decisions in the 1970s, the United States Supreme Court seemed to agree with prosecutors and lower courts that journalists should enjoy no special First Amendment defense when compelled to give testimony before grand juries. The Court's sharply divided analysis in *Branzburg* v. *Hayes* and its companion cases,[202] denying a constitutional shield to reporters, has been extended by lower courts to testimony sought by prosecutors and trial judges acting upon discovery requests made by defense attorneys. The best-known example of resistance to an order to disclose involved Myron Farber, a reporter for the *New York Times*, who went to jail rather than comply. Farber investigated a series of mysterious deaths at a New Jersey hospital. After his articles appeared, New Jersey authorities indicted Dr. Mario Jascalevich for murder. The doctor's defense attorneys then sought notes, statements, and other relevant materials possessed by Farber and the *New York Times*.

A New Jersey judge decided to examine the materials himself to determine what should be turned over to the defense. When Farber refused to comply, the judge found him and the *New York Times* to be in contempt. Time was of the essence since the criminal trial was already underway. Two United States Supreme Court justices refused to grant a stay and no other appellate review was available.[203] Farber spent 40 days in jail, and the *New York Times* spent over a million dollars in legal fees and fines. Farber's incarceration ended only when Jascalevich was acquitted. Several years later, both Farber and the *New York Times* were pardoned by New Jersey Governor Brendan Byrne as he left office.

Summarizing *Branzburg, Farber*, and several other recent decisions, Thomas I. Emerson recently stated, "Instead of concern that the press remain 'uninhibited, robust and wide-open,' the Burger Court is satisfied if the press is not subjected to 'official harassment.' "[204] Yet law enforcement personnel and judges still do not casually order journalists to disclose confidential sources or similar information. They know that they are likely to become involved in time-consuming and expensive legal battles, and that many appellate courts require a strong showing of necessity for the information sought and a lack of alternative sources for the same information.

Moreover, as Justice Brennan recently stated *In re Roche*, it now may be that "a majority of the Court recognizes at least some degree of constitutional protection for newsgatherers' confidences."[205] In *Roche*, Brennan initially stayed a civil contempt adjudication against a Massachusetts television journalist, though the contempt citation ultimately was upheld.[206] Attempts to invoke constitutional protections for journalists' confidences continue to be treated on a case-by-case basis, focusing largely on the context and consequences of refusals to cooperate. Among the factors explicitly weighed are (1) the type of legal proceeding involved; (2) the availability of alternative, albeit less convenient, sources for the same information; (3) the importance of the information to the case; and (4) the possibility that harassment by government officials is an element of the inquiry. It is far easier for journalists to resist disclosure in ordinary civil suits, even without a journalist shield law, than it is to resist a judicial order to disclose information sought by a defendant in a murder trial.

It should be emphasized that even when the United States Supreme Court decides that a journalist does not enjoy special constitutional protection against an order to reveal confidential sources, or that a newspaper does not have special protection from searches, as in *Zurcher v. Stanford Daily*,[207] the Court's decision does not preclude legislation extending these protections to journalists. A significant trend in recent press law has been for state legislatures and Congress to respond to United States Supreme Court decisions that reject First Amendment claims by enacting new protections for journalists.

Over half the states now have passed some form of special law to provide journalists with a legal shield against inquiries of government officials or grand juries concerning confidential sources.[208] Additionally, the United States Department of Justice promulgated internal guidelines recognizing the sensitive nature of inquiries aimed at journalists and seeking to limit overzealous law enforcement.[209] Congress itself responded to the *Zurcher* decision with the Privacy Act of 1980,[210] prohibiting police searches of newsrooms for evidence concerning criminal activity of third parties, unless the police invoke special procedures or are able to satisfy requirements more stringent than those generally required for a search. Although press representatives testified unsuccessfully against this special treatment for newsrooms,[211] the statute, as enacted, is an unusual example of federal legislation singling out those engaged in "public communication" for protection not afforded to everybody else.

State shield laws vary greatly in the degree of protection they give the press. Most are phrased in nearly absolute terms; others provide qualified protection by establishing only a presumptive press privilege that can be overcome if a substantial reason to do so can be demonstrated.[212] These statutes, and the Department of Justice guidelines, also differ greatly as to who qualifies as a protected journalist and how strong and in what form a showing must be made to overcome the journalist's privilege.

## Summary

Recent legislation that purports to favor the press, as well as laws aimed at publications thought to interfere egregiously with national security, should be considered against the backdrop of current controversy over whether journalists should enjoy special, privileged status beyond what is enjoyed by all citizens. The historic importance attributed to freedom of the press and the traditions and real power of the press in the United States assure, at a minimum, that explicit legal restrictions on the press could not be imposed easily, and would generate publicity and debate. Today, the press generally is able to publicize its objections to legal restrictions and to enjoy a receptive audience, perhaps particularly among those in government, since political futures are thought to depend on popular support.

## PRIVATE ARRANGEMENTS AFFECTING THE ROLE OF THE PRESS IN SOCIETY

### Introduction

A basic tension in American law pits emphasis on individualism against a view of the press as a vital surrogate, functioning on behalf of individuals. In fact, the press is sometimes championed as the only institution able to speak for those who lack the means to express themselves.[213] Probably the most obvious example of the conflict between individuals and the press as an institution occurs in the area of defamation law.

In a mass media culture, however, where corporate and governmental institutions affect and even control much of everyday life, there is often a kind of paternalism in defenses of freedom of the press. Yet the self-fulfillment of the solitary individual through free expression seems increasingly romantic and unreal. In fact, some consider the press a part of the problem and not a part of the solution to today's widespread anomie.

The clash of privacy and the press in defamation suits already has been treated in some detail.[214] We now turn to several further manifestations of the conflict between a right to report or to know and a right to assert oneself as an individual or not to be known at all.

## Individual Access to the Media

A fundamental premise of First Amendment theory is that newspapers should be free to decide for themselves how they wish to influence the public and the government. This approach generally leads to denial of requests by individuals to access to the print media, and to rejection of attempts to force newspapers to print corrections or replies to editorials or news coverage.

In *Mills* v. *Alabama*,[215] the United States Supreme Court invalidated a state ban on publishing election-day views about election issues. The statute involved an outright ban on election-day expression, and made no attempt to equalize political access. The Court stressed the autonomy of the press, even if editorials published on election day might skew election results. Jerome Barron used *Mills* to develop the idea that the press has an affirmative obligation to provide access to its pages, an argument he premised on the idea that the free marketplace of ideas is essentially a romantic and anachronistic notion in an era of communications monopolies.[216]

In *Miami Herald Publishing Co.* v. *Tornillo*,[217] however, the Court rejected the claim that a newspaper is obliged to grant space to persons wishing to respond to its coverage or editorial positions on public issues. Chief Justice Burger's majority opinion stated, "A responsible press is an undoubtedly desirable goal, but press responsibility is not mandated by the Constitution and like many other virtues it cannot be legislated."[218] An affirmative right of access, Chief Justice Burger wrote, "fails to clear the barriers of the First Amendment because of its intrusion into the function of editors."[219] The Supreme Court has adopted a very different approach to access to television and radio,[220] however, and has allowed some regulation of newspaper advertising.[221]

## Self-Regulation and Press Pass Denials

In the United States, the existence of press councils is entirely voluntary. Enforcement of ethical rules or standards of reporting is rare. On a national level, the only significant press council is the National News Council, established in 1973. Its importance is still in doubt.

Perhaps the most obvious example of private decisions that directly affect and regulate news coverage is the determination of who should get press passes. Deciding which journalists and news organizations will receive the limited space available in the congressional press gallery or at presidential news conferences obviously determines how news is covered. These scarce resources often are allocated by press associations or by informal understandings between press and government officials. Yet there have been relatively few judicial decisions dealing with the issuance of press passes, and none by the United States Supreme Court.

A few generalizations emerge from the lower court opinions, however. It is generally thought to be unconstitutional for government officials to exclude particular reporters or particular newspapers from local and state press conferences or from access to police records otherwise available to the press.[222] On the federal level, several decisions indicate that press galleries in Congress and the White House may not be closed to particular periodicals or to specific reporters unless regular procedures and clear-cut standards are followed.[223] But the District of Columbia Court of Appeals determined, in a case involving *Consumer Reports*, the magazine of the Consumers Union, that exclusion of a publication from the congressional gallery by a private press association should not be reviewed judicially.[224] Congress was held to have delegated enough authority to the private press association to justify the defendant's claim that Congress made an unreviewable, discretionary decision.

It is clear that basic questions concerning limited access to public facilities and events remain unresolved. The general judicial approach has been to invalidate exclusion of particular correspondents and publications if the exclusion appears to be arbitrary or based on personal animosity. Both Congress and the Executive have been given the opportunity, however, to demonstrate their reasons for exclusion, for example, exclusion of lobbyists who seek access to legislators under the guise of being journalists, or the protection of the president's physical security. Moreover, private press association exclusion has not been litigated often, and may be unreachable either because there is insufficient government involvement to constitute the state action required for most constitutional claims or, paradoxically, as implicating so much discretionary involvement by government that the decision is beyond the proper scope of judicial review. Public officials also remain free to use their discretion to favor particular journalists with exclusive interviews, news tips, and off-the-record briefings.

## Internal Monitoring

A final restraint on journalistic decisions and excesses is the phenomenon of internal monitoring, a trend that has grown markedly during the last decade. Many of the largest newspapers in the country have hired "house critics" or "ombudsmen," and they sometimes publish their findings and criticisms of internal practices. A number of major papers also have introduced *op-ed pages*, columns written by non-staff members. Corrections or retractions are now more openly displayed. Finally, vigorous letters to the editor columns appear in many American newspapers and there are at least a dozen journalism reviews that cover and comment on news coverage.

## CONCLUSION

This essay stressed that many basic questions about the press in the United States are not resolved, and some are still to be addressed. It emphasized the gap or chasm between the bold commitment to a robust and free press and the somewhat drearier reality of newspaper life today. While there is no typical newspaper, there is a growing trend toward single-newspaper communities. The publisher is often an absentee owner of a chain of newspapers. Reporters and editors frequently enjoy special, cozy relationships with those who are powerful or well-connected. At times, there is a significant gap between the demands of courageous journalism and the limited way in which the law actually protects reporters and editors.

Yet it would be a gross error to assume that the American press is not unusually, perhaps uniquely, forceful and untrammeled. With good reason, journalists in the United States are celebrated for outspoken reporting and critical commentary about those in power. The American press enjoys a glorious tradition, full of important stories unearthed and told effectively despite repeated efforts to stifle independent, iconoclastic journalism.

The most important aspect of press law in America is that the law affords great leeway to journalists. A basic cultural continuity proclaims independence of thought and spirit. This helps give the press breathing space and the opportunity to build. A history of nearly total freedom of the press may be largely myth; nevertheless, the dream of a fearless and free press is dreamed by many Americans much of the time. In the United States, that dream helps determine law and daily life for the press.

## NOTES

1.   *See, e.g., Kovacs* v. *Cooper*, 336 U.S. 77 (1949); *DeJonge* v. *Oregon*, 299 U.S. 353 (1937).

2.   Holmes, "John Marshall: Remarks on a One-Hundredth Anniversary," in *James Bradley Thayer, Oliver Wendell Holmes, and Felix Frankfurter on John Marshall* 133 (M. Howe ed. 1967).

3. Unpublished letter from Kurt Vonnegut to Judge Jon O. Newman, Second Circuit Court of Appeals (Feb. 15, 1982) (quoted with Mr. Vonnegut's consent).

4. *See, e.g.*, T. Emerson, *The System of Freedom of Expression* (1970); Emerson, "Toward a General Theory of the First Amendment," 72 Yale L.J. 877 (1963); Emerson, "Legal Foundations of the Right to Know," 1976 Wash. U.L.Q. 1.

5. *Abrams* v. *United States*, 250 U.S. 616, 630 (1919) (Holmes, J., dissenting).

6. Milton elaborated this theme in his famous attack on prior censorship in *Areopagitica, A Speech for the Liberty of Unlicensed Printing, To the Parliament of England* (1644).

7. J. Mill, "Of the Liberty of Thought and Discussion," in *On Liberty* 15 (AHM Publishing 1947).

8. Letter from James Madison to W.T. Barry (Aug. 4, 1822) in 9 *Writings of James Madison* 203 (G. Hunt ed. 1910), *quoted in Branzburg* v. *Hayes*, 408 U.S. 665, 723 (1972) (Douglas, J., dissenting).

9. For an idea of Meiklejohn's changing notions of what is properly considered political expression, *compare* A. Meiklejohn, *Free Speech and Its Relation to Self Government* 66 (1948) *with* Meiklejohn, "The First Amendment is an Absolute," 1961 Sup. Ct. Rev. 245.

10. A. Bickel, *The Morality of Consent* 57–58 (1975). *See generally* P. Maier, *From Resistance to Revolution* (1972).

11. T. Emerson, *The System of Freedom of Expression* 6–8 (1970).

12. 403 U.S. 15 (1971).

13. *Id.* at 26.

14. *Board of Education, Island Trees* v. *Pico*, 102 S. Ct. 2799, 2807 (1982) (Brennan, J., plurality opinion).

15. *Whitney* v. *California*, 274 U.S. 357, 375 (1927) (Brandeis and Holmes, JJ., concurring).

16. *See, e.g.*, "Developments in the Law—The Interpretation of State Constitutional Rights," 95 Harv. L. Rev. 1324 (1982); Linde, "Courts and Censorship," 66 Minn. L. Rev. 171 (1981).

17. 268 U.S. 652 (1925).

18. *See, e.g.*, Linde, "Courts and Censorship," 66 Minn. L. Rev. 171, 202–206 (1981); *Alderwood Associates* v. *Washington Environmental Council*, 96 Wash. 2d 230, 635 P.2d 108 (1981) (en banc); *Freedman* v. *New Jersey State Police*, 135 N.J. Super. 297, 343 A.2d 148 (1975).

19. For examples of southern suppression of the press, *see* L. Filler, *The Crusade Against Slavery*, 1830–1860 (1960); J. Lofton, *The Press as Guardian of the First Amendment* (1980). For restraints on the press during the Civil War, see J. Randall, *Constitutional Problems Under Lincoln* (Rev. ed. 1951).

20. *See, e.g.*, *Patsy* v. *Board of Regents, State of Florida*, 457 U.S. 496, 502–507 (1982); *Mitchum* v. *Foster*, 407 U.S. 225, 242 (1972); Soifer, "Protecting Civil Rights: A Critique of Raoul Berger's History," 54 N.Y.U. L. Rev. 651 (1979).

21. *See, e.g.*, *Patterson* v. *State of Colorado ex rel. Att'y General*, 205 U.S. 454 (1907).

22. *See, e.g.*, Rabban, "The First Amendment in its Forgotten Years," 90 Yale L.J. 514 (1981); Anderson, "The Formative Period of First Amendment

Theory," 24 Am. J. Legal Hist. 56 (1980).

23. Z. Chafee, Jr., *Free Speech in the United States* 36–195 (1941 ed.).

24. *New York Times Co. v. Sullivan*, 376 U.S. 274, 290 (1964).

25. 268 U.S. 652, 666 (1925).

26. *See, e.g.*, Fairman, "Does the Fourteenth Amendment Incorporate the Bill of Rights? The Original Understanding," 2 Stan. L. Rev. 5 (1949); *First National Bank v. Bellotti*, 435 U.S. 765, 822 (1978) (Rehnquist, J., dissenting); Bork, "Neutral Principles and Some First Amendment Problems," 47 Ind. L. J. 1 (1971).

27. *See, e.g.*, *Lamont v. Postmaster General*, 381 U.S. 301 (1965); *New York Times Co. v. Sullivan*, 376 U.S. 254 (1964); *Supreme Court of Virginia v. Consumers Union*, 446 U.S. 719 (1980).

28. *See, e.g.*, *Hudgens v. National Labor Relations Board*, 424 U.S. 507 (1976); *Lloyd Corp. v. Tanner*, 407 U.S. 551 (1972).

29. *Jackson v. Metropolitan Edison*, 419 U.S. 345, 349 (1974). The United States is probably unique in the extent of the legal efforts made to preserve the separation of the public and private spheres. In constitutional law, the attempt to maintain mutually exclusive categories—with dramatically different results depending on which category a particular case is said to fit—already had produced "a conceptual disaster area" by the late 1960s. *See* Black, "Foreword, 'State Action,' Equal Protection, and California's Proposition 14," 81 Harv. L. Rev. 69, 95 (1967). Nevertheless, both the desire to compartmentalize and the range of the conceptual disaster expanded significantly in recent years. *See, e.g., Flagg Bros., Inc. v. Brooks*, 436 U.S. 149 (1978); *Rendell-Baker v. Kohn*, 102 S.Ct. 2764 (1982).

30. 326 U.S. 1 (1945).

31. *Id.* at 20 (emphasis added).

32. For a good recent summary and critical analysis of decisions involving claims for what he terms the "enhancement theory" of the First Amendment, see Powe, "Mass Speech and the Newer First Amendment," 1982 Sup. Ct. Rev. 243.

33. *See, e.g.*, Newspaper Preservation Act, 15 U.S.C. §1801 (1976) (exempting newspapers from antitrust laws); *FCC v. NCCB*, 436 U.S. 775 (1978) (upholding Federal Communications Commission restriction on co-ownership of newspaper and broadcast media).

34. *See, e.g.*, Shiffrin, "Government Speech," 27 U.C.L.A. L. Rev. 565 (1980); M. Yudof, *When Government Speaks: Law, Politics and Government Expression in America* (1982).

35. *See, e.g.*, B. Bagdikian, *The Media Monopoly* (1983); Lange, "The Role of the Access Doctrine in the Regulation of the Mass Media: A Critical Review and Assessment", 52 N.C. L. Rev. 1 (1973); Barron, "Access to the Press—A New First Amendment Right," 80 Harv. L. Rev. 1641 (1967). *See also Miami Herald Publishing Co. v. Tornillo*, 418 U.S. 241, 249–250 (1974) (Burger, C.J.): "Newspapers have become big business and there are far fewer of them to serve a larger literate population. Chains of newspapers, national newspapers, national wire and news services, and one-newspaper towns, are the dominant features of a press that has become noncompetitive and enormously powerful and influential in its capacity to manipulate popular opinion and change the course of events. . . ."; Twentieth Century Fund Task Force Report for a National News Council, *A Free and Responsive Press* (1973); N. Rosse, B.M. Owen, J. Dertouzos, "Trends in the Daily Newspaper Industry 1923–1973," *Editor & Publisher International Yearbook*

1978 (once dominated by family-owned businesses, the newspaper industry is increasingly a creature of conglomerates).

36. *See, e.g.*, H. Hart and A. Honore, *Causation in the Law* (1959); W. Prosser, *Handbook of the Law of Torts* §§ 41, 42 (4th ed. 1971); Malone, "Ruminations on Cause-in-Fact," 9 Stan. L. Rev. 60 (1956).

37. For example, claims of racial or sexual discrimination in voting and employment will not be sustained unless plaintiffs are able to provide proof of a "bad" intent or motive that triggered the challenged actions. *See, e.g., Personnel Administrator* v. *Feeney*, 442 U.S. 256 (1979); *City of Mobile* v. *Bolden*, 446 U.S. 55 (1980); *General Building Contractor's Ass'n, Inc.* v. *Pennsylvania*, 102 S. Ct. 3141 (1982); Soifer, "Complacency and Constitutional Law," 41 Ohio St. L. J. 383 (1981). *But see Rogers* v. *Lodge*, 102 S. Ct. 3272 (1982) (totality of circumstances considered to assess bad motives in race discrimination in voting).

38. *See, e.g., Board of Education, Island Trees* v. *Pico*, 102 S.Ct. 2799 (1982); *Mt. Healthy School District* v. *Doyle*, 429 U.S. 274 (1977).

39. 297 U.S. 233 (1936).

40. *Id.* at 250.

41. 102 S.Ct. 2799 (1982). *See also Minneapolis Star and Tribune Co.* v. *Minnesota Comm'r of Revenue*, 103 S.Ct. 1365 (1983) (differential tax treatment of press use tax not justifiable absent special conditions and therefore invalid as undue burden on freedom of press).

For a discussion of the distinction between government action that is intended to have a direct impact on expression and action that is not aimed at the communicative aspect of expression but which has incidental impact on expression, *see* Ely, "Flag Desecration: A Case Study in the Roles of Categorization and Balancing in First Amendment Analysis," 88 Harv. L. Rev. 1482 (1975). *See also* L. Tribe, *American Constitutional Law* 580–608 (1978).

42. A right to know or to receive information has been the subject of extensive scholarly comment. *See, e.g.*, O'Brien, "The First Amendment and the Public's 'Right to Know,' " 7 Hastings Const. L.Q. 579 and citations at 580–81 & n.4; Emerson, "Legal Foundations of the Right to Know," 1976 Wash. U.L.Q. 1. The development and current state of the doctrine through judicial decisions remain quite murky, however.

43. *Reprinted in* Stewart, "Or of the Press," 26 Hastings L.J. 631 (1975). A useful explanation of the process and ideas involved in drafting, adopting, and ratifying the Press Clause of the First Amendment may be found in Anderson, "The Origins of the Press Clause," 30 U.C.L.A. L. Rev. 455 (1983). Anderson argues that freedom of the press was the primary concern, with freedom of speech a secondary matter. Anderson also maintains that those who passed and ratified the Press Clause already had begun to develop a theory of a vital, special role for the press within their democratic experiment in government.

44. *Id.* at 632.

45. *See, e.g.*, 34 U. of Miami L. Rev. 785 *et. seq.* (1980); 7 Hofstra L. Rev. 559 *et. seq.* (1979).

46. Blasi, "The Checking Value in First Amendment Theory," 1977 A.B.F. Res. J. 521.

47. Lewis, "A Preferred Position for Journalism?" 7 Hofstra L. Rev. 595 (1979).

48.   Shiffrin, "Defamatory Non-Media Speech and First Amendment Methodology," 25 U.C.L.A. L. Rev. 915, 923 (1978). *See also* Van Alstyne, "The Hazards to the Press of Claiming a 'Preferred Position,'" 28 Hastings L. J. 761 (1977); Lange, "The Speech and Press Clauses," 23 U.C.L.A. L. Rev. 77 (1975).

49.   *Branzburg* v. *Hayes*, 408 U.S. 665 (1972) (Branzburg was a staff reporter for the *Courier-Journal*, daily newspaper in Louisville, Kentucky. The companion cases, *In re Pappas* and *United States* v. *Caldwell* involved, respectively, a newsman-photographer working for a New Bedford, Massachusetts television station and a *New York Times* reporter). *See also Zurcher* v. *Stanford Daily*, 436 U.S. 547 (1978), discussed *infra*, text accompanying notes 207–211.

50.   *See infra*, text accompanying notes 192–199.

51.   *Houchins* v. *KQED*, 438 U.S. 1 (1978) (4–3 decision, Marshall and Blackmun, JJ., took no part). The television station argued that it should have access because the jail was otherwise open only on a limited basis for occasional visits by the public. *Compare First National Bank of Boston* v. *Bellotti*, 435 U.S. 765, 800 (1978) (Burger, C.J., concurring) (Press Clause only "complementary to and a natural extension of speech clause liberty") *with* Anderson, *supra* note 43 at 487. ("Epistemologically, at least, the press clause was primary and the speech clause secondary").

52.   384 U.S. 214, 219 (1966).

53.   *See, e.g., Erznoznik* v. *City of Jacksonville*, 422 U.S. 205 (1975); *Jenkins* v. *Georgia*, 418 U.S. 153 (1974); *Time, Inc.* v. *Hill*, 385 U.S. 374, 388 (1967).

54.   A Meiklejohn, *Political Freedom: The Constitutional Powers of the People* (1965); Marcuse, "Repressive Tolerance," in R. Wolff, B. Moore, Jr., and H. Marcuse, A *Critique Of Pure Tolerance* 81 (1965); Bork, "Neutral Principles and Some First Amendment Problems," 47 Ind. L.J. 1 (1971).

55.   *Id.*

56.   *See generally* M. Shapiro, *Freedom of Speech: The Supreme Court and Judicial Review* (1966).

57.   In *First National Bank of Boston* v. *Bellotti*, 435 U.S. 765 (1978), the majority specifically reserved the question of whether corporations have the same First Amendment rights of advocacy as natural persons. Nonetheless, the Court insisted that corporations and recipients of their speech share a First Amendment right sufficiently strong to override a state's attempt to control corporate spending on referendum issues not materially affecting the corporation's business. Chief Justice Burger, concurring, stressed that to hold otherwise would be to grant the "institutional press" unacceptable special privileges and status, *id.* at 801.

For recent opinions about commercial speech, *see, e.g., Hoffman Estates* v. *Flipside, Hoffman Estates, Inc.*, 455 U.S. 489 (1982); *Central Hudson Gas & Electric Corp.* v. *Public Service Comm'n*, 447 U.S. 557 (1980); *Pittsburgh Press Co.* v. *Pittsburgh Comm'n on Human Rights*, 413 U.S. 376 (1973).

58.   *See, e.g., Smith* v. *United States*, 431 U.S. 291 (1977); *Paris Adult Theatre I* v. *Slaton*, 413 U.S. 49 (1973); *Miller* v. *California*, 413 U.S. 15 (1973) (emphasis on discretion of each community to define obscenity standards).

59.   *See, e.g., Red Lion Broadcasting Co.* v. *Federal Communications Comm'n*, 395 U.S. 367 (1969); *Columbia Broadcasting System* v. *Democratic National Committee*, 412 U.S. 94 (1973); Powe, *supra* note 32; Van Alstyne, "The Möbius Strip of the First Amendment: Perspectives on *Red Lion*," 29 S.C. L. Rev.

539 (1978); R. Cass, *Revolution in the Wasteland: Value and Diversity in Television* (1981); F. Friendly, *The Good Guys, the Bad Guys and the First Amendment: Free Speech vs. Fairness in Broadcasting* (1977).

60.   *The Federalist* No. 78, at 466 (A. Hamilton) (C. Rossiter ed. 1961).

61.   5 U.S. (1 Cranch) 137 (1803).

62.   *See, e.g., United States* v. *Nixon*, 418 U.S. 683 (1974); *Cooper* v. *Aaron*, 358 U.S. 1 (1958).

63.   *See* Jackson, "Veto Message, July 10, 1832" II *Messages and Papers of the Presidents* 576, 581–583 (Richardson ed. 1896) ("mere precedent is a dangerous source of authority"); Lincoln, "First Inaugural Address, March 4, 1861," VI *Messages and Papers of the Presidents* 5, 9–10 (Richardson ed. 1897) ("if the policy of the Government upon vital questions affecting the whole people is to be irrevocably fixed by decisions of the Supreme Court. . . the people will have ceased to be their own rulers"); Roosevelt, "Proposed Speech on the Gold Clause Cases, Feb. 1935," 1 *F.D.R.—His Personal Leters, 1928-1945*, 459–460 (Elliott Roosevelt ed. 1950) (quoting Lincoln with approval and adding that Supreme Court decisions cannot be allowed to "imperil the economic and political security of this nation.")

64.   F. Dunne, "The Supreme Court Decisions" in *Mr. Dooley At His Best* 77 (E. Ellis ed. 1938).

65.   *See, e.g.*, L. Levy, *Freedom of Speech and Press: Legacy of Supression in Early American History* (1963); L. Levy, *Jefferson and Civil Liberties: The Darker Side* (1963); M. Shapiro, *Freedom of Speech: The Supreme Court and Judicial Review* (1966); J. Smith, *Freedom's Fetters: The Alien and Sedition Laws and American Civil Liberties* (1956); J. Lofton, *The Press as Guardian of the First Amendment* (1980).

66.   *See* "Developments in the Law—The Interpretation of State Constitutional Rights," 95 Harv. L., Rev. 1324, 1409 (1982).

67.   447 U.S. 74 (1980).

68.   *See, e.g., Hudgens* v. *NLRB*, 424 U.S. 507 (1976); *Lloyd Corp.* v. *Tanner*, 407 U.S. 551 (1972) (overruling *Amalgamated Food Employees, Local 590* v. *Logan Valley Plaza, Inc.*, 391 U.S. 308 (1968)).

69.   447 U.S. 74 (1980).

70.   *See, e.g.*, P. Brest and S. Levison, *Processes of Constitutional Decision-making: Cases and Materials* 887–1016 (2nd ed. 1983); Linde, "Courts and Censorship," 66 Minn. L. Rev. 171 (1981).

71.   *See, e.g.*, F. Friendly, *The Good Guys, the Bad Guys and the First Amendment: Free Speech vs. Fairness in Broadcasting* (1977); S. Unger, *The Papers and the Papers* (1972); N. Hentoff, *The First Freedom: The Tumultuous History of Free Speech in America* (1980); M. Franklin, *Mass Media Law* 8–10 (1977); Anderson, "The Origins of the Press Clause," 30 U.C.L.A. L. Rev. 455 (1983); Levy and other sources cited *supra* note 65; Chafee, *supra* note 23; J. Alexander, *A Brief Narrative of the Case and Trial of John Peter Zenger* (S. Katz ed., 2d ed. 1972); F. Friendly, *Minnesota Rag: The Dramatic Story of the Landmark Supreme Court Case that Gave New Meaning to Freedom of the Press* (1981).

72.   *See generally* R. Ellis, *The Jeffersonian Crisis* (1974); L. Levy, *Jefferson and Civil Liberties: The Darker Side* (1963); J. Miller, *The Federalist Era, 1789-1801*, 228–277 (1960).

73.    Sedition Act, 1 Stat. 596 (1798).

74.    *See generally* R. Ellis, *The Jeffersonian Crisis* 144–148 (1974); Koch and Annon, "The Virginia and Kentucky Resolutions: An Episode in Jefferson's Defense of Civil Liberties," 1948 Wm. & Mary Q. 147–176.

75.    *United States* v. *Lyon*, Wharton's St. Tr. 333 (1798); *United States* v. *Haswell*, Wharton's St. Tr. 684 (1800); *United States* v. *Cooper*, Wharton's St. Tr. 659 (1800); *United States* v. *Callender*, Wharton's St. Tr. 688 (1800). *See* Berns, "Freedom of the Press and the Alien and Sedition Laws: A Reappraisal," 1970 Sup. Ct. Rev. 109.

76.    *See* L. Levy, *Freedom of Speech and Press: Legacy of Supression in Early American History* (1963); L. Levy, *Jefferson and Civil Liberties: The Darker Side* (1963). *But see* D. Malone, *Jefferson the President: First Term, 1801–1805* (1970). For a social history of newspapers, and an analysis of the relatively recent rise of the ideology of objectivity, *see* M. Schudson, *Discovering the News* (1978).

77.    *New York Times Co.* v. *Sullivan*, 376 U.S. 254, 274 (1964).

78.    *See, e.g.*, J. Randall, *Constitutional Problems under Lincoln* (rev. ed. 1951); C. Rossiter, *American Dictatorship* (1948).

79.    *See, e.g.*, N. Hentoff, *The First Freedom: The Tumultuous History of Free Speech in America* (1980); H. Nelson and D. Teeter, *Law of Mass Communication* 33–35 (1969). For example, President Theodore Roosevelt sent a special message to Congress suggesting that Joseph Pulitzer should be prosecuted, since several of Pulitzer's newspapers vociferously opposed the purchase of the Panama-Canal.

80.    *See supra* note 23.

81.    *Patterson* v. *State of Colorado ex rel. Attorney General*, 205 U.S. 454 (1907).

82.    *Id.* at 463.

83.    *See generally* Z. Chafee, Jr., *Free Speech in the United States* (1941 ed.). *See also* Gunther, "Learned Hand and the Origins of Modern First Amendment Doctrine: Some Fragments of History," 27 Stan. L. Rev. 719, 770 (1970).

84.    Chafee, *supra* note 83 at 204–215; J. Higham, *Strangers in the Land* (1963). *See also* cases collected in W. Preston, *Aliens and Dissenters: Federal Suppression of Radicals, 1903–1933* (1963); Cover, "The Left, the Right and the First Amendment: 1918–1928," 40 Md. L. Rev. 349 (1981). *Cf. Goldman* v. *United States*, 254 U.S. 474 (1918) (Holmes, J.) (upholding conviction of Emma Goldman and Alexander Berkman for conspiracy to induce refusal to register for the draft; trial judge instructed jury that constitutional free speech guarantee was not relevant to the case).

85.    Espionage Act of June 15, 1917, ch. 30, 40 Stat 217, now codified as 18 U.S.C. § 2388.

86.    *Katzenbach* v. *Morgan*, 384 U.S. 641, 654 n.14 (1966).

87.    *Schenck* v. *United States*, 249 U.S. 47 (1919); *Frohwerk* v. *United States*, 249 U.S. 204 (1919); *Debs* v. *United States*, 249 U.S. 211 (1919). The clear and present danger test was announced by Justice Holmes in *Schenck*, 249 U.S. 47, 52 (1919). It accompanied his famous statement that while the First Amendment does not protect "a man in falsely shouting fire in a theatre and causing a panic," the government must show "whether the words are used in circumstances and are of such a nature as to create a clear and present danger that they will bring about the

substantive evils that Congress has a right to prevent." For a general discussion, *see* Rogat, "Mr. Justice Holmes: A Dissenting Opinion," 15 Stan. L. Rev. 254 (1963). For an elegant posthumous updating of Rogat's work, *see* Rogat and O'Fallon, "Mr. Justice Holmes: A Dissenting Opinion, Part II," (unpublished manuscript, University of Oregon School of Law). *See also* Ragan, "Justice Oliver Wendell Holmes, Jr., Zechariah Chafee, Jr., and the Clear and Present Danger Test for Free Speech: The First Year, 1919," 58 J. Am. Hist. 24, 29–31 (1971); Green, "Liberty Under the Fourteenth Amendment," 27 Wash. U.L.Q. 49 (1942); Hall, "The Substantive Law of Crimes, 1887–1936," 50 Harv. L. Rev. 616 (1937).

88.   The clearest indication of the sea-change in judicial interpretations of the first amendment was in *Near* v. *Minnesota*, 283 U.S. 697 (1931). *See generally* F. Friendly, *Minnesota Rag: The Dramatic Story of the Landmark Supreme Court Case That Gave New Meaning to Freedom of the Press* (1981); Symposium, "*Near* v. *Minnesota*, 50th Anniversary," 66 Minn. L. Rev. 1 (1981). However, one month earlier in *Stromberg* v. *California*, 283 U.S. 359 (1931), the Supreme Court held unconstitutional a state law banning display of a red flag. It could be argued that the decision in *Fiske* v. *Kansas*, 274 U.S. 380 (1927), was the initial victory for a First Amendment claim in the U.S. Supreme Court, yet Justice Sanford's unanimous opinion invalidating the application of Kansas' criminal syndicalist legislation rested primarily on the arbitrariness of the particular convictions at issue, and the majority held that they violated the due process clause of the Fourteenth Amendment.

89.   250 U.S. 616, 624 (1919) (Holmes, J., dissenting).

90.   *Id.* at 629.

91.   *Id.* at 624.

92.   268 U.S. 652 (1925).

93.   *Id.* at 669.

94.   *Id.* at 673.

95.   *Id.*

96.   *Id.*

97.   *Masses Publishing Co.* v. *Patten*, 244 F. 535 (S.D.N.Y.), *rev'd*, 246 F. 24 (2d Cir. 1917). Judge Hand had denied the postmaster of New York authority to continue to refuse to mail copies of *The Masses*, "a monthly revolutionary journal." The postmaster argued that the magazine could be banned under the Espionage Act of 1917 because its criticism of the war effort tended to cause insubordination and resistance to the draft among the troops and populace. Judge Hand conceded that "words are not only the keys to persuasion, but the triggers of action." Yet he determined that it was necessary for the government to show that expression actually urged upon others that it was their duty or in their interest to resist the law. Otherwise, the government could not prohibit expression; the words were constitutionally protected as mere agitation, and not "direct incitement to violent resistance." *See generally* Gunther, *supra* note 83.

98.   274 U.S. 357 (1927).

99.   *Id.* at 371. Within a few months California Governor C.C. Young pardoned Anita Whitney, who was a Wellesley College graduate and the niece of former Supreme Court Justice Stephen J. Field. Governor Young, relying heavily on the opinion by Brandeis, made his own determination that criminal syndicalism did not constitute a clear and present danger. Z. Chafee, Jr., *Free Speech in the United States* 352–354 (1941 ed.).

100.   283 U.S. 697 (1931).

101.   *See, e.g.*, Blasi, "Toward a Theory of Prior Restraint: The Central Linkage," 66 Minn. L. Rev. 11 (1981); F. Friendly, *Minnesota Rag: The Dramatic Story of the Landmark Supreme Court Case That Gave New Meaning to Freedom of the Press* (1981).

102.   *See, e.g.*, S. Kutler, *The American Inquisition* (1982); V. Navasky, *Naming Names* (1982); D. Caute, *The Great Fear* (1978).

103.   *See* cases collected in N. Dorsen, P. Bender, B. Neuborne, *Political and Civil Rights in the United States* 101–182, 194–279 (4th ed. 1976).

104.   341 U.S. 494 (1951).

105.   54 Stat. 671, 18 U.S.C. §11 (1940).

106.   341 U.S. 494, 510 (1951), quoting 183 F.2d 201, 212 (2d Cir. 1950). The times, the perceived threat, and Judge Learned Hand's own views seemingly changed from Hand's opinion in the *Masses* case. *See* notes 83 and 97, *supra*.

107.   *Id.*

108.   *Id.* at 509 (until putsch comes to shove, as it were) (Vinson, C.J., plurality opinion).

109.   *Id.* at 511.

110.   *Id.* at 547.

111.   *Id.* at 568. For an interesting link between perceptions of Europe and the cases involving the First Amendment in the United States, *see* Cover, "The Origins of Judicial Activism in the Protection of Minorities," 91 Yale L.J. 1287 (1982).

112.   Dennis at 581.

113.   *See, e.g.*, *Barenblatt* v. *United States*, 360 U.S. 109 (1959); *Uphaus* v. *Wyman*, 360 U.S. 72 (1959); *American Communications Ass'n* v. *Douds*, 339 U.S. 382 (1950) and sources cited *supra* at notes 102–103. *But see Yates* v. *United States*, 354 U.S. 298 (1957).

114.   *See, e.g.*, further developments in *Communist Party* v. *Subversive Activities Control Board*, 367 U.S. 1 (1961), discussed in Dorsen et al., *supra* note 103, at 134–135. *See also Scales* v. *United States*, 367 U.S. 203 (1961); *Noto* v. *United States*, 367 U.S. 290 (1961); *United States* v. *Robel*, 389 U.S. 258 (1967). *But see Flemming* v. *Nestor*, 363 U.S. 603 (1960).

115.   For the Warren Court's refusal to consider the constitutionality of the Vietnam War, *see, e.g.*, *Mora* v. *McNamara*, 389 U.S. 934 (1967); *Sainoff* v. *Schultz*, 409 U.S. 929 (1972); *Atlee* v. *Richardson*, 411 U.S. 911 (1973). For the decision upholding the draft card burning conviction, *see O'Brien* v. *United States*, 391 U.S. 367 (1968), discussed and defended in Ely, "Flag Desecration: A Case Study in the Roles of Categorization and Balancing in First Amendment Analysis," 88 Harv. L. Rev. 1482 (1975). For a clear summary of the procedural approaches and intermediate tests developed by the Warren Court, *see* Dorsen et al., *supra* note 103 at 51–59.

116.   395 U.S. 444 (1969).

117.   *Id.* at 447.

118.   *Id.*

119.   *See generally* Linde, " 'Clear and Present Danger' Reexamined: Dissonance in the *Brandenburg* Concerto," 22 Stan. L. Rev. 1163 (1970).

120.   *See, e.g., Laird* v. *Tatum*, 408 U.S. 1 (1972); *Brown* v. *Glines*, 444 U.S. 348 (1980). *But see Landmark Communications, Inc.* v. *Virginia*, 435 U.S. 829

(1978). The Court invalidated a criminal conviction and fine imposed on a newspaper, the *Virginia Pilot*, for reporting accurately that a judge was under investigation by a judicial conduct commission. Chief Justice Burger's opinion for the majority stressed that the subject of the publication "lies near the core of the First Amendment." *Id.* at 838. Rejecting both what he termed the categorical approach and "mechanical application" of the clear and present danger test, *id.* at 842, Burger proclaimed the responsibility of judges to go beyond deference to legislative judgments. He found Virginia's criminal sanction for reporting confidential information to be an unconstitutional restraint on First Amendment rights.

121.   In *Brown*, the Court upheld the requirement that servicemen obtain permission from their commanding officers before circulating petitions to Congress or posting any printed or written material within any Air Force installation. For the use of military personnel to conduct surveillance, *see Laird* v. *Tatum*, 408 U.S. 1 (1972). For the use of informers without obtaining a warrant, *see Hoffa* v. *United States*, 385 U.S. 293 (1966). For the use of telephone records, *see Smith* v. *Maryland*, 442 U.S. 735 (1979) (installation of pen register to record numbers dialed from home phone held not to be a search under Fourth Amendment, since no expectation of privacy concerning numbers dialed). For the use of bank records, *see California Bankers* v. *Schultz*, 416 U.S. 21 (1974). *But see United States* v. *United States District Court*, 407 U.S. 297 (1972) (rejecting claim of inherent Executive power to authorize electronic surveillance in internal security matters without prior judicial approval); *Kissinger* v. *Halperin*, 424 F. Supp. 838 (D.D.C. 1976), 434 F. Supp. 1193 (D.D.C. 1977), 606 F.2d 1192 (D.C. Cir. 1979) *aff'd* 452 U.S. 713 (per curiam), *reh. denied* 453 U.S. 928 (1981) (allowing lower court decision to stand). Judge J. Skelly Wright wrote for the D.C. Circuit: "The First Amendment buttresses the individual's protection against indiscriminate or unreasonable wiretapping. Such surveillance invades the citizen's constitutionally protected right to free private discussion and must inevitably chill public speech. Either result is intolerable." 606 F.2d 1192, 1199 (D.C. Cir. 1979).

122.   *See* Greenawalt, "Speech and Crime", 1980 A.B.F. Res. J. 645.

123.   403 U.S. 713, 717 (1971) (Black, J., concurring).

124.   283 U.S. 697 (1931).

125.   *Id.* at 716. Chief Justice Hughes went on to list two other exceptions stating, "On similar grounds, the primary requirements of decency may be enforced against obscene publications. The security of the community life may be protected against incitements to acts of violence and the overthrow by force of orderly government." *Id.*

126.   *New York Times* v. *United States*, 403 U.S. 713 (1971).

127.   467 F. Supp. 990 (W.D. Wisc.), *appeal dismissed*, 610 F.2d 819 (7th Cir. 1979).

128.   427 U.S. 539 (1976).

129.   In addition to the prior restraint cases discussed in the text, *see also Bantam Books, Inc.* v. *Sullivan*, 372 U.S. 58, 70 (1963); *Organization for a Better Austin* v. *Keefe*, 402 U.S. 415, 419 (1971); *Southeastern Promotions Ltd.* v. *Conrad*, 420 U.S. 546 (1975).

130.   *See, e.g.*, Barnett, "The Puzzle of Prior Restraint," 29 Stan. L. Rev. 539 (1977); Jeffries, "Rethinking Prior Restraint," First Annual Seminar: The First Amendment and National Security, Center for Law and National Security, January

8–11, 1982. *But see* Blasi, "Toward a Theory of Prior Restraint: The Central Linkage," 66 Minn. L. Rev. 11 (1981).

131. *New York Times* v. *United States*, 403 U.S. 713, 714 (1971), quoting *Organization for a Better Austin* v. *Keefe*, 402 U.S. 415, 419 (1971).

132. The six Justices in the majority in this important prior restraint case divided as follows:

a. Justices Black and Douglas argued that the government did not, under any circumstances, have the power to "make laws enjoining publication of current news and abridging freedom of the press in the name of 'national security.'" 403 U.S. 713, 718.

b. Justice Brennan basically agreed with Black and Douglas, but he added reservations that were based on—but even more limited than—the famous *Near* exception. *Id.* at 726–727. Brennan argued that the government may obtain a prior restraint *only* during wartime or its equivalent and *only* on a showing that publication would "inevitably, directly and immediately," *id.*, cause an occurrence akin to imperiling the safety of a transport already at sea.

c. Justices Stewart and White argued that a prior restraint could be justified only when the government could show "direct, immediate, and irreparable damage to our Nation or its people." *Id.* at 730.

d. Justice Marshall premised his agreement with the majority on the absence of a basis for the Executive branch to invoke the jurisdiction of the courts in its attempt to halt publication of national security information. *Id.* at 741. (Marshall therefore did not reach the First Amendment issue.)

e. The three dissenters, Justices Harlan and Blackmun and Chief Justice Burger, believed that courts should give only limited review to an Executive determination that disclosure would "irreparably impair" national security, and that the timing of Supreme Court review was unduly precipitous. *Id.* at 748–752 (Burger, C.J., dissenting); 752–759 (Harlan, J., dissenting); 759–763 (Blackmun, J., dissenting).

133. *Id.* at 721 (Douglas, J., concurring); *id.* at 733 (White and Stewart, JJ., concurring).

134. *See generally* Edgar & Schmidt, "The Espionage Statutes and Publication of Defense Information," 73 Colum. L. Rev. 929 (1973).

135. 50 U.S.C. §798 (1976).

136. *Id.*

137. Intelligence Identities Protection Act of 1982, 96 Stat 122.

138. *See, e.g.,* S. Rep. No. 97–201, 97th Cong., 2d Sess. 7 (1981).

139. 467 F. Supp. 990 (W.D. Wisc.), *appeal dismissed*, 610 F.2d 819 (7th Cir. 1979). In March, 1979, the United States government sought and was granted an injunction barring *The Progressive* from publishing an article written by Howard Morland entitled "The H-Bomb Secret: How We Got It, Why We're Telling It." The government claimed inherent authority and authority under the Atomic Energy Act of 1954, 42 U.S.C. §§2011–2296. District Judge Robert W. Warren issued a preliminary injunction restraining publication; he also continued a protective order governing the speech and conduct of Morland, *The Progressive*'s editors, and their lawyers. In addition to basic arguments concerning prior restraint, the government differed with the defendants over the meaning of many provisions of the Atomic Energy Act. For example, the magazine claimed that the

government had not shown that the information "will be utilized" to injure the United States or to aid a foreign country. They also claimed they had no "reason to believe" that the information would be so used. They stressed the widespread availability of the information at issue, as well as the low level of classification for those parts the government claimed were still classified. The defendants also argued that the Atomic Energy Act actually diminished rather than enlarged whatever inherent constitutional power to stop publication the government might claim. Finally, the defendants claimed that even if the government could demonstrate some violation of the Atomic Energy Act, the act itself could not survive First Amendment scrutiny. It should be disclosed that the author of this chapter worked on this case for the American Civil Liberties Union, helping to represent Erwin Knoll and Sam Day, Jr., editors of *The Progressive*, on appeal.

140.   *See* Morton Mintz, *Washington Post* A–1, June 9, 1979.

141.   *Moreland* v. *Sprecher*, 443 U.S. 709 (1979) (writ of mandamus denied).

142.   467 F. Supp. 990, 992–993 (W.D. Wisc. 1979).

143.   For a discussion of this and other issues raised by the case, *see* Cheh, "The *Progressive* Case and the Atomic Energy Act: Waking to the Dangers of Government Information Controls," 48 G.W.L. Rev. 163 (1980); Note, "A Journalist's View of the *Progressive* Case: A Look at the Press, Prior Restraint, and the First Amendment from the Pentagon Papers to the Future," 41 Ohio St. L.J. 1165 (1980); Comment, *"United States* v. *Progressive, Inc.:* The National Security and Free Speech Conflict," 22 Wm. & Mary L. Rev. 141 (1980). *See also* Knoll, "National Security: The Ultimate Threat to the First Amendment," 66 Minn. L. Rev. 161 (1981).

144.   427 U.S. 539 (1976).

145.   *Id.* at 559.

146.   *Id.* at 563–567. Burger's opinion relied on a weak form of the clear and present danger test, invoking the approach used in *Dennis* v. *United States* (1951). The remaining justices argued for a test they believed to be more protective of freedom of the press. Justice Brennan, joined by Justices Stewart and Marshall, insisted that a prior restraint could never be upheld simply because it was necessary to guarantee a fair trial. Justice Stevens wrote separately and basically agreed with Brennan, though on a somewhat more limited basis. *See also Landmark Communications, Inc.* v. *Virginia*, 435 U.S. 829 (1978), discussed *supra* note 120.

147.   395 U.S. 444, 447 (1968); 283 U.S. 697, 713 (1930).

148.   376 U.S. 274 (1964).

149.   W. Prosser, *Handbook of the Law of Torts* § 111 at 37 (4th ed. 1971).

150.   376 U.S. 254, 270 (1964).

151.   *Id.* at 280.

152.   *Rosenbloom* v. *Metromedia*, 403 U.S. 29 (1971). For a good summary of early cases following *Sullivan* such as *Rosenbloom*, *Curtis Publishing Co.* v. *Butts*, 388 U.S. 130 (1967), and *Associated Press* v. *Walker*, 388 U.S. 130 (1967), *see* G. Gunther, *Constitutional Law: Cases and Materials* 1336–1338 (10th ed. 1980).

153.   418 U.S. 323 (1974).

154.   *See Time, Inc.* v. *Firestone*, 424 U.S. 448 (1976) (erroneous report of Palm Beach heiress's grounds for divorce libelous, since she had not voluntarily assumed the role of public figure); *Hutchinson* v. *Proxmire*, 443 U.S. 111 (1979) (scientist whose research on monkey behavior was federally financed not a public

figure, so Senator's charge of wasteful government expenditure could be defamatory); *Wolston* v. *Reader's Digest Ass'n, Inc.*, 443 U.S. 157 (1979) (plaintiff in public eye briefly in 1958 for failure to appear before a grand jury investigating espionage not a public figure in terms of a libel suit premised on 1974 book). One judge said, soon after *Gertz*, "Defining public figures is much like trying to nail a jellyfish to the wall." *Rosanova* v. *Playboy Enterprises, Inc.*, 411 F. Supp. 440, 443 (S.D. Ga. 1976) (Lawrence, C.J.), *aff'd* 580 F. 2d 859 (5th Cir. 1978).

155.  441 U.S. 153 (1979).

156.  For an interesting empirical study, *see* Franklin, "Suing Media for Libel: A Litigation Study," 1981 A.B.F. Res. J. 795. *See also* Lewis, *"New York Times v. Sullivan* Reconsidered: Time to Return to "'The Central Meaning of the First Amendment,'" 83 Colum. L.R. 603 (1983).

157.  For an ambitious attempt to clarify the area, *see* R. Sack, *Libel, Slander and Related Problems* (1980).

158.  376 U.S. 254 (1964).

159.  381 U.S. 479 (1965).

160.  *See, e.g.*, *Roe* v. *Wade*, 410 U.S. 113 (1973); *Eisenstadt* v. *Baird*, 405 U.S. 438 (1972); *Planned Parenthood of Missouri* v. *Danforth*, 428 U.S. 52 (1976).

161.  W. Prosser, *Handbook of the Law of Torts* 844 (3d ed. 1964).

162.  *Cox Broadcasting Co.* v. *Cohn*, 402 U.S. 469 (1975).

163.  *Smith* v. *Daily Mail Publishing Co.*, 443 U.S. 97 (1980).

164.  *Globe Newspaper Co.* v. *Superior Court*, 102 S.Ct. 2613 (1982).

165.  *See* Dorsen et al., *supra* note 103 at 526–42; Beytagh, "Privacy and a Free Press: A Contemporary Conflict in Values," 20 N.Y.L.F. 453, 482 (1975); Nimmer, "The Right to Speak from *Times* to *Time*: First Amendment Theory Applied to Libel and Misapplied to Privacy," 56 Calif. L. Rev. 935 (1968); Treece, "Commercial Exploitation of Names, Likenesses, and Personal Histories," 51 Tex. L. Rev. 637 (1973); Nimmer, "The Right of Publicity," 19 Law & Contemp. Probs. 203 (1954); Warren and Brandeis, "The Right to Privacy," 4 Harv. L. Rev. 193 (1890).

166.  *See* Rourke, "The United States," in I. Galnoor, ed., *Government Secrecy in Democracies* 117 (1977). *See also* Lively, "Government Housekeeping Authority: Bureaucratic Privileges Without a Bureaucratic Privilege," 16 Harv. C.R.—C.L. L. Rev. 494 (1981).

167.  5 U.S.C. § 552 (1976 and Supp. III 1979), 80 Stat. 150 (1966). For a comparative survey and discussion, *see* A. Mathews, *The Darker Reaches of Government: Access to Information about Public Administration in the United States, Great Britain and South Africa* (1978).

168.  422 U.S. 255, 269 (1975).

169.  Government in the Sunshine Act, 90 Stat. 1241 (1976) (codified in scattered sections of 5 U.S.C. and 39 U.S.C.).

170.  For an early summary of the most important requirements and most significant exemptions of the Freedom of Information Act *see* Clark, "Holding Government Accountable: The Amended Freedom of Information Act," 84 Yale L.J. 741 (1975). The Duke Law Journal publishes a useful annual review of Freedom of Information Act developments. For a practical guide to federal statutes granting access to government information, *see* Cox, "A Walk Through Section 552 of the Administrative Procedure Act; the Freedom of Information Act; the Privacy

Act; and the Government in the Sunshine Act," 46 U. Cin. L. Rev. 969 (1977).

171.    410 U.S. 73 (1973). The information being withheld related to a planned nuclear test on Amchitka Island, Alaska. The documents sought were classified "secret" or "top secret," and the agency defended its refusal to divulge information on the basis of the state secrets and interagency memoranda exemptions in the FOIA.

172.    *See, e.g., Weinberger* v. *Catholic Action of Hawaii*, 454 U.S. 139 (1981); *Baldridge* v. *Shapiro*, 445 U.S. 345 (1982); *United States Department of State* v. *Washington Post Co.*, 456 U.S. 595 (1982); *Federal Bureau of Investigation* v. *Abramson*, 456 U.S. 615 (1982).

173.    425 U.S. 352 (1976).

174.    *Id.* at 381, adopting the opinion below at 495 F.2d 261, 269 (2d Cir. 1974).

175.    *See, e.g.*, decisions cited in Lively, *supra* note 166; Kennedy, "Foreword: Is the Pendulum Swinging Away from Freedom of Information?" 16 Harv. C.R.—C.L. L. Rev. 311 (1981).

176.    *See, e.g.*, Kutler, *supra* note 102 at vii (significant amount of information derived from FOIA materials); series of articles in *Des Moines Register* in August, 1982, documenting extensive campus surveillance during 1960s and 1970s, based on information obtained by reporters through FOIA.

177.    *See, e.g.*, "The Secret About Secrets," N.Y. Times, Apr. 24, 1983, at E20, col. 1; Maitland, "Needless Federal Secrecy is Charged," N.Y. Times, Apr. 25, 1983, at B12, col. 4; "Will Iron Bars Plug the Leaks?" N.Y. Times, Apr. 24, 1983.

178.    *See, e.g.*, Exec. Order No. 12333 and 12334 (Dec. 4, 1981) (detailing means of obtaining, reviewing and keeping secret United States intelligence activities); Exec. Order No. 12356 (April 2, 1982) (security classification tightened); Intelligence Identities Protection Act, 96 Stat. 122 (1982). *See generally* M. Halperin & D. Hoffman, *Top Secret National Security and the Right to Know* (1977). For a different point of view, the *Intelligence Report*, a monthly publication by the ABA Standing Committee on Law and National Security, is quite useful.

179.    There has been considerable discussion in the scholarly journals concerning the sources and limitations of a constitutional right to know. *See, e.g.*, Emerson, "The Affirmative Side of the First Amendment," 15 Ga. L. Rev. 795 (1981); BeVier, "An Informed Public, An Informing Press: The Search for a Constitutional Principle," 68 Calif. L. Rev. 482 (1980); O'Brien, "The First Amendment and the Public's 'Right to Know,'" 7 Hastings Const. L.Q. 579 (1980); Baker, "Scope of the First Amendment Freedom of Speech," 25 U.C.L.A. L. Rev. 964 (1978). For an interesting comparative study, *see* A. Mathews, *The Darker Reaches of Government: Access to Information about Public Administration in the United States, Britain and South Africa* (1978).

180.    *See infra* section on the press and the judicial process.

181.    444 U.S. 507 (1980) (per curiam).

182.    *Id.* at 509 n.3. For a discussion of *Snepp, see* Medow, "The First Amendment and the Secrecy State: *Snepp* v. *United States,*" 130 U. Pa. L. Rev. 775 (1982). For examples of critical press commentary on the *Snepp* decision, *see* Lewis, "Why Uncle Sam Ought to Sue Henry Kissinger for $5 Million," Des Moines Reg., June 10, 1980; "The Court Uses a Hatchet," Boston Globe, Feb. 25,

1980; Lewis, "Disorder in the Court," N.Y. Times, Feb. 25, 1980.

183.   466 F.2d 1309 (4th Cir.), *cert. denied*, 409 U.S. 1063 (1972).

184.   509 F.2d 1362 (4th Cir.), *cert. denied*, 421 U.S. 992, *reh. denied*, 442 U.S. 1049 (1975).

185.   453 U.S. 280 (1981).

186.   *Id*. at 308–309.

187.   *Id*. at 320 n.10 (Brennan with Marshall, JJ., dissenting).

188.   L. Levy, ed., *Freedom of the Press from Zenger to Jefferson: Early American Libertarian Theories* 341–342 (1966). For an illuminating discussion of Jefferson and Madison on the subject, *see* Blasi, "The Checking Value in First Amendment Theory." 1977 A.B. F. Res. J. 521.

189.   For a vivid description of the interplay among press, government officials and the public, *see, e.g.*, D. Halberstam, *The Powers That Be* (1979); G. Talese, *The Kingdom and the Power* (1978). Judicial decisions concerning publication of the Pentagon Papers are treated in detail in S. Unger, *The Papers and the Papers* (1972). Recognition of good journalism, and its impact on state and local government affairs, may be readily found in issues of the *Columbia Journalism Review*.

190.   For a thorough discussion of the Bay of Pigs incident and its repercussions, *see* G. Talese, *The Kingdom and the Power* 4–7, 116, 474 (1978).

191.   Among the restrictive holdings were *Sheppard* v. *Maxwell*, 384 U.S. 333 (1966); *Estes* v. *Texas*, 381 U.S. 532 (1965). Florida was the first state to permit courtroom camera coverage in a decision in April 1979, *In re Petition of Post Newsweek Stations*, 370 So. Rep. 2d 764 (Fla. S.Ct. 1979).

192.   443 U.S. 368 (1979).

193.   *Id*. at 405 (Rehnquist, J., concurring).

194.   *Id*. at 440 (Blackmun, J., concurring and dissenting with Brennan, White, and Marshall, JJ.).

195.   *Richmond Newspapers* v. *Virginia*, 448 U.S. 555 (1980).

196.   *Id*. at 570.

197.   *Id*. at 575–576.

198.   *Id*. at 595 (Brennan and Marshall, JJ., concurring) (emphasis in original).

199.   *Id*. at 605–606.

200.   In recent decisions, the U.S. Supreme Court consistently has held contempt citations invalid in cases involving criticism of judges. In *Bridges* v. *California*, 314 U.S. 252 (1941), the Court invalidated orders against Harry Bridges and the *Los Angeles Times* for a telegram and editorials concerning a criminal sentence. *See also Pennekamp* v. *Florida*, 328 U.S. 331 (1946) (invalid contempt for criticism of judge for dismissing indictments); *Craig* v. *Harney*, 331 U.S. 376 (1947) (invalid contempt for criticism concerning refusal to accept to jury verdict). In *Wood* v. *Georgia*, 370 U.S. 375 (1962), the Court invalidated a contempt order against an elected sheriff for expressing his personal views about a matter before a grand jury. *Cf. United States* v. *Grace*, 103 S. Ct. 1702 (1983) (invalidating statute that prohibited display of any banner or flag in or around the Supreme Court building on First Amendment grounds).

201.   *See, e.g.*, *Angelico* v. *Louisiana*, 593 F.2d 585 (5th Cir. 1979); *Times-Picayune Publishing Corp.* v. *Schulingkamp*, 419 U.S. 1301 (1974); *Walker* v.

*Birmingham*, 388 U.S. 307 (1967); *United States v. Dickinson*, 465 F.2d 496 (1972) *on remand*, 349 F. Supp. 227 (E.D. La. 1972), *aff'd*, 476 F.2d 373 (5th Cir.), *cert. denied*, 414 U.S. 979 (1973).

202.    408 U.S. 665 (1972); *see supra* note 49.

203.    *New York Times Co. v. Jascalevich*, 439 U.S. 1301 (1978). *See also In re Farber*, 78 N.J. 259, 394 A.2d 330, *cert. denied*, 439 U.S. 997 (1978).

204.    Emerson, "First Amendment Doctrine and the Burger Court," 68 Calif. L. Rev. 422 (1980).

205.    448 U.S. 1312, 1316 (1980) (Justice Brennan, acting in his capacity as a single circuit justice, considering an application for a stay of a lower court order during the summer when the full Court was not in session). The Supreme Judicial Court of Massachusetts affirmed the order holding Roche in contempt, 381 Mass. 624, 411 N.E. 2d 466 (1980).

206.    There still have been relatively few journalists held in contempt and incarcerated. In addition to Farber, the most notorious example occurred in 1971, when William Farr, a reporter for the *Los Angeles Herald-Examiner*, spent forty-six days in jail for contempt because he refused to divulge how he obtained a copy of a deposition taken in connection with the Charles Manson murder trial. Cases in which reporters are ordered to produce information are reported regularly in *Media Law Reporter* and in *News Media and the Law*.

207.    436 U.S. 547 (1978). Justice White's plurality opinion rejected the claim by the *Stanford Daily*, a college newspaper, that the First Amendment should be given consideration in applying Fourth Amendment criteria to the search of a newspaper office.

208.    *See* J. Gora, *The Rights of Reporters* 243–248 (1974).

209.    Regulations promulgated by the Justice Department under the Privacy Protection Act of 1980, 42 U.S.C. §2000aa, 94 Stat. 1879 (1980).

210.    42 U.S.C. §2000aa, 94 Stat. 1879 (1980).

211.    Privacy Protection Act, S. Rep. No. 96–874, 96th Cong., 2d Sess. 8 (1980).

212.    A summary of state shield laws as of 1974 may be found in J. Gora, *The Rights of Reporters* 243–248 (1974). More recent developments are discussed in Eckhardt and McKey, "Reporter's Privilege: An Update," 12 Conn. L. Rev. 435 (1980). Most of the state statutes provide nearly complete protection against the compelled disclosure of news sources; *see, e.g.*, Md. Ann. Code, Art. 35 §2 (1957); Ann. Cal. Codes, Evid. Code §1070. Other states provide qualified immunity, meaning that the privilege is presumed unless the person or institution seeking information is able to show a substantial reason for disclosure; *see, e.g.*, La. Stat. Ann. Rev. Stat. 45: 1451–1454; Minn. Stat. Ann. §§595.021–595.025. The statutes also vary as to who is eligible for protection. Some simply list "editor or reporter"; others include only reporters, *e.g.*, Ariz. Rev. Stat. Ann. § 12–2237; and some cover all members of a newsgathering organization, *e.g.*, Ann. Cal. Code, Evid. Code § 1070.

213.    The complicated and sometimes paradoxical relationship of individual autonomy claims to the vital institutional role of the press is evident, for example, in a comparison of the work of two leading contemporary first amendment theorists. Vincent Blasi, in "The Checking Value in First Amendment Theory," 1977 A.B.F. Res. J. 521, presents an impressive argument for protecting the

press precisely because of its role as a vital check on government. In "Press Rights and Government Power to Structure the Press," 34 U. Miami L. Rev. 819 (1980), C. Edwin Baker attempts to distinguish offensive and defensive press claims. Moreover, Baker, who is a powerful advocate for individual self-fulfillment as the primary value realized in freedom of expression, suggests that it would be good to distinguish among publishers, journalists, and the public in wrestling with freedom of the press claims. *See also* Chevigny, "Philosophy of Language and Free Expression," 55 N.Y.U. L. Rev. 157 (1980). For a good overall recent survey, *see* M. Franklin, *Cases and Materials on Mass Media Law* 1–73 (1982).

    214. *See supra* section on the press and the government.

    215. 384 U.S. 444 (1966).

    216. Barron, "Access to the Press—A New First Amendment Right," 80 Harv. L. Rev. 1641 (1967).

    217. 418 U.S. 241 (1974). Professor Barron argued the case for Tormills.

    218. *Id.* at 256.

    219. *Id.* at 258.

    220. *See, e.g.,* F. Friendly, *The Good Guys, the Bad Guys and the First Amendment: Free Speech and Fairness in Broadcasting* (1972); R. Cass, *Revolution in the Wasteland: Value and Diversity in Television* (1981).

    221. *Pittsburgh Press Co.* v. *Pittsburgh Comm'n on Human Relations*, 413 U.S. 376 (1973); Baker, "Commercial Speech: A Problem in the Theory of Freedom," 62 Iowa L. Rev. 1 (1976).

    222. *See, e.g., Borreca* v. *Fasi*, 369 F. Supp. 906 (D. Haw. 1974); *Lewis* v. *Baxley*, 368 F. Supp. 768 (M.D. Ala. 1973); *Quad-City Community News Service, Inc.* v. *Jebena*, 334 F. Supp. 8 (S.D. Iowa 1971).

    223. *See, e.g., Sherrill* v. *Knight*, 569 F.2d. 124 (D.C. Cir. 1977) (Secret Service ordered to establish formal system of procedural protections before denying "bona fide journalist" a White House press pass); *Consumers Union of United States, Inc.* v. *Periodical Corresp. Ass'n*, 365 F. Supp. 18 (1973), *rev'd* 515 F.2d 1341 (D.C. Cir. 1975). For a vivid description of who gets to attend presidential press conferences, and what goes on among the journalists assigned to the White House, see von Hoffman, "The White House News Hole," *The New Republic*, Sept. 6, 1982, at 19. *See also Ludtke* v. *Kuhn*, 461 F. Supp. 86 (S.D.N.Y. 1978) (New York Yankees baseball team could not exclude female reporters from locker rooms since there were less restrictive ways to protect players' privacy.)

    224. 515 F.2d 1341 (D.C. Cir. 1975). (Nonjusticable question also barred by Speech and Debate Clause immunity.)

# PART 2

## The Continental Approach

# Three

# Press Law in France

**Roger Errera**

## INTRODUCTION

The law that laid the foundation of liberty of the press in France was passed
on July 29, 1881, several years after the Republicans came into power. It
was part of a series of laws enacted between 1881 and 1901 establishing the
legal basis of civil liberties.[1] These included the law of 1881 on freedom of
assembly, the law of 1884 on the freedom to unionize, the law of 1901 on
freedom of association, and the law of 1905 on the separation of church
and state. Passage of the law establishing freedom of the press marked the
end of a struggle between several governments and the press since the
beginning of the century. Freedom of the press had been limited by various
legal devices employed by the executive branch of government: prior
restraint and censorship, security payments (which required deposit of a
fee prior to publication of a newspaper), the law of seal (imposing an
indirect tax which burdened the paper and consequently raised its price),
and above all, the institution of legal suits against the editors of a
newspaper and journalists working under them. It was not clear whether
these legal proceedings were to take place in the *cour d'assises*, which held
trials with a jury, or in the *tribunal correctionnel*, without a jury. The issue
was debated for several generations.

This chapter will not describe in detail the history of the press in
France during the nineteenth century.[2] The deliberations that preceded the
law of 1881 show that it was prepared with great care, and that those
responsible for the law remembered past battles for liberty. Since 1876,

This chapter is a revised and expanded version of a paper presented at a conference on civil
liberties in France and in the United States, held in Paris in 1979 under the auspices of the
Sterling Currier Fund and of the Columbia University Center for the Study of Human Rights.

legislative proposals which would liberalize the restrictive press law surfaced. In 1880, one of the famous leaders of the press, Emile de Girardin,[3] presided over a special committee that conducted a comprehensive study of the proposals.

The law of 1881 is much more than a "law on the freedom of the press." It does not merely repeal the restrictive laws of the past, but is a veritable press code. The spirit and substance of the law may be summarized in the following manner.

The law applies not only to newspapers and journals appearing on a regular basis but to the entire range of printed expression, and its resources: the printer, the bookshop, bill posting, news vendors, and sales. Freedom is the basic rule applied in all these areas. In addition to regulating the press, the law contains a penal code and a code of criminal procedure. An amendment relating to offenses against public institutions (offenses against persons were set aside for further discussion)—according to which "there are no special offenses of the press," and "[w]hoever uses the press or any other mode of publication will be liable according to general law"—was rejected. The law thus provides narrow definitions of several press offenses.

As the *rapporteur* stated, the law sought to suppress only "acts intended to disturb the social order, destroy collective security, and prejudice private interest."[4] In this spirit, the principal categories of offenses created by the law of 1881 are intended to protect the following:

1. Private individuals, by the law of defamation, insult, and the right of reply.
2. Public order and public morals, by laws against incitement to crime or military disobedience, publication of false rumors disturbing the public peace, and pornography or obscenity (*outrage aux bonnes moeurs*).
3. Public institutions, by laws prohibiting insult of the President, and defamation or insult of governmental administrative bodies.

The substance of the law, and the high quality of the debates in Parliament and in France generally which accompanied its adoption, reveal the values that inspired the law as well as its limitations. The law crowned the conquest of political power (this is the beginning of the Third Republic) with emancipation of the press, freeing the press once and for all from the political and legal restrictions that had kept it restrained. The goal was not merely to repeal oppressive laws, but to repeal laws that were the product of special circumstances:

> In the past fifty years there had been about as many laws of the press as there had been governments; several governments had even passed several laws, new ones correcting the old; all had carefully made the laws conform to their

principles, and had made them subordinate to anything the government deemed essential to its own welfare. It is thus that press codes, almost always drafted according to the turn of events, and as variable as the circumstances, being sometimes liberal and sometimes reactionary, and always adopted to conform to the crisis and fears of the moment, alternated with the time and the circumstances between two opposing philosophies which could not be reconciled: the philosophy of liberty, and the philosophy of oppression.[5]

The press was envisioned as both the instrument and the expression of democracy: It provided the means for all to participate in political debate and safeguarded political pluralism. Thus, throughout the entire Third Republic, the press played an important social and political role. This role asserted itself for the first time during the Dreyfus Affair.[6]

The shortcomings of the 1881 law, emanating from those areas which it failed to address, are evident today but were not as evident to those who were its contemporaries. The law does not regulate the press enterprise, its form, or its financing, nor does it regulate media concentration or labor regulation of media personnel and journalists. Rather, the most classic economic liberalism accompanies political liberalism. This is not surprising.

## The Constitutional Status of the Freedom of the Press

Unlike other constitutions, the French Constitution of 1958 does not contain a declaration of rights and liberties. Thus, at first glance, it is not surprising that there is no express mention of liberty of the press. However, freedom of the press is given recognition equivalent to that accorded a constitutional guarantee:

1.   The Declaration of the Rights of Man and the Citizen of 1789, which has constitutional value and is mentioned in the preamble of the 1958 Constitution, declares (in Article 11):

> The unrestrained communication of thoughts and opinions, being one of the most precious rights of man, every citizen my speak, write, and publish freely, provided he be responsible for any abuse of this liberty in those cases determined by law.

2.   The preamble of the Constitution of 1958 refers to the preamble of the Constitution of 1946. The latter refers to "the fundamental principles recognized by the laws of the Republic." In French law, these principles have a constitutional value by virtue of the decisions of the Constitutional Council.[7] Thus, freedom of expression in general, and freedom of the press in particular, are liberties of constitutional stature. So far, the Constitutional Council has not decided on cases concerning press law.

3.   The French guarantee of freedom of the press is unlike that found in the First Amendment to the United States Constitution. In France, courts do not have the power to invalidate statutes that violate the Constitution. Only the Constitutional Council can do so, and it must review the statute after Parliament adopts it, but *before* it is promulgated. (Laws passed before 1958 are not within the Council's jurisdiction.) Administrative decrees and regulations are reviewed by the Conseil d'Etat and administrative courts. During the Algerian War in particular, administrative decisions were used as a means of limiting freedom of the press.

4.   In addition to the constitutional guarantees, lower civil, criminal, and administrative courts interpret existing law in keeping with the principle of freedom of the press. After 1881, many laws were passed that restricted freedom of the press. The case-law developed in interpreting these laws will be discussed below.

## THE LAW OF THE PRESS

The Law of the Press, passed in 1881, was later expanded and amended several times. The law requires all journals or written publications to conform to certain simple structural regulations. A journal should have an editor. The editor is legally responsible for *everything* published by the journal. Publication (or actually, formation) of a journal is to be preceded by a declaration made before the *Procureur de la Republique*. This declaration must indicate the title of the journal, its publication format, the name and address of the editor, and the mark of the printing office where it is to be printed.

On publication of each edition, a specified number of copies should be deposited with the administrative authorities and the courts. (The law of June 21, 1943, generally regulates this mandatory deposit of all literary works and audiovisual productions).

In 1944, at the beginning of the French liberation, the temporary government enacted the ordinance (in fact, law) of August 26, 1944, which regulated the production and organization of the press. The law represented a reaction against practices that had been denounced before the war, and was inspired by certain ideas emanating from the Resistance. It had several goals.

First, it was designed to simplify newspaper liability. Therefore, it required that the editor of a newspaper should also be the owner or the majority stockholder, or have power of attorney of the journal's corporation. This was a reaction against the former practice of setting up "straw men" to comply with the letter of the law.

As a second goal, the law created ethical standards for press financing:

- The board of directors was to approve all transfers of stock.
- Certain industrial or commercial positions were declared incompatible with editorial obligations.
- Underground advertisement was prohibited.
- Newspapers could not receive foreign funds, except for advertising.
- All newspaper stockholders were to be French.
- Press monopolies were discouraged: one individual could not direct more than one daily paper.

A third goal was to improve the quality of public information about press companies: newspapers were required to publish regularly specified information indicating who was liable, how the newspaper was organized financially, and who owned its assets. Publication of newspapers' accounts was also required.

Notwithstanding its sound aims, the law, which was prepared in great haste and without professional guidance, quickly became obsolete. The necessary regulations which had to follow were never enacted. In any event, after the war the press was more immediately concerned with other matters, in particular with allocation of paper—then a scarce resource—and allocation of the assets of former newspapers. Government instability and public apathy prevented the replacement of this law with another press statute.

For some time, certain trade unions (those of journalists in particular) have periodically requested that the law be enforced. In 1978 Mr. Hersant, owner of a chain of French newspapers, was indicted for violating the 1944 ordinance as a result of a complaint filed against him by several journalist unions and by the Federal Association of Consumers. During the following five years 16 other persons have been indicted in the same case. As of April 1984, the matter has not been resolved. In February 1984 the National Assembly passed a government bill limiting concentration and amending the 1944 legislation.

The following shall be considered below:

- Specific press offenses
- Prohibited publications
- Governmental powers
- Judicial review over governmental measures restraining press freedom

## Specific Press Offenses

One cannot fail to be astounded by the vast quantity of press offenses found in French law (the term "press" being understood to comprise all public expression). This observation applies equally to the law of 1881 in its current form, which is the culmination of numerous reforms adopted in the past century, and to press offenses contained in other statutes.

1.    Chapter four of the 1881 law deals with crimes and offenses committed through the press "or by any other mode of publication." Only Articles 23 to 37 (sections 1 through 4) deal with actual offenses; articles 38 through 41 (section 5) concern prohibited publications and immunities. Several observations are in order here.

    a.    The notion of "incitement to crimes and offenses" is very broad.

        i.    If someone successfully incites the commission of an offense, he is punishable as an accomplice. This is the case even if the *crime* is merely attempted but not actually committed (Article 23).

        ii.    Incitement to commit certain crimes or offenses is punishable in itself, even where the expression lacks effect. These crimes are of several different types, and include incitement to military disobedience, incitement to theft or other felonies (murder, looting, arson, extreme violence, crimes involving explosives, attacks against the national defense, treason, spying, and crimes against the state), and incitement of discrimination or racial hatred or violence (Article 24, last paragraph).

        iii.    Article 24 not only makes incitement criminal, which by definition concerns future crimes, but also concerns the vindication of crimes performed in the past including social crimes (murder, looting, arson, theft, and crimes involving explosives), war crimes, and offenses involving collaboration with the enemy.

    b.    Although it may be considered equitable to prohibit insult (*injure*) ("any excessively offensive expression or words of scorn or abuse containing a charge without a factual basis," Article 29, paragraph 2) or defamation ("an allegation or charge of a *fact* prejudicial to the honor or reputation of the individual to whom the fact is imputed," Article 29 paragraph 1) of private individuals, it might seem surprising to find that the insult or defamation of certain government officials is subject to greater penalties. The privileged officials may be classified into the following four categories:

        i.    Certain foreign dignitaries, including chiefs of state or heads of governments, ministers of foreign affairs (Article 36 prohibiting "grave affront" [*offense*]), ambassadors, and diplomats (Article 37 prohibiting "outrage").

        ii.    The President of the Republic (Article 26 prohibiting "grave affront").

    iii. All ministers, civil servants, members of Parliament, and citizens entrusted with an official duty or public commission (Articles 31 and 33 regulating insult and defamation), provided that the defamatory remarks concern a duty for which special protection is required.

    iv. The entire administration and all public entities: The courts, the armed forces, public officials, and public administrations are protected against insult and defamation (Articles 30 through 33).

2. Although the law of 1881 was initially planned as a comprehensive statute encompassing all press offenses and regulating all proceedings and governmental measures concerning expression, the century following its enactment witnessed passage of additional statutes proscribing certain press behavior. It would be impractical to list these press offenses here. It suffices to note that the tax code, the public health code, and the penal code all contain limitations on the press.

One example illustrates the breadth and variety of press offenses recognized in modern French law, namely, offenses relating to the armed forces. Four statutes refer to such offenses:

    a. The law of 1881 punishes incitement to military disobedience (Article 25).

    b. The National Service Code extends Article 25 to any person doing national service (Article 132). Article 50 of this code, which regulates conscientious objectors, forbade "propaganda, of any form, exclusively intended to incite others to seek to evade the obligation of military service." It was abrogated in 1983. Articles 129 through 131 punish incitement to insubordination, regardless of whether it is followed by any action.

    c. The Penal Code imposes heavy penalties (5 to 10 years of imprisonment) on "anyone who during peace time knowingly participates in a scheme to demoralize the army with intent to harm the national defense" (Article 84).

    d. The Military Justice Code penalizes incitement to assist in military desertion, regardless of whether any action results (Article 394).

## Prohibited Publications

French law specifically proscribes certain publications. An exhaustive list is not provided here, but the proscriptions may be classified according to the general interest that the law seeks to protect:

1. Confidential information and related matters (although Article 11 of the Code of Criminal Procedure concerning the secrecy of *instruction*

does not apply to the press): It is prohibited to publish indictments or any other records of criminal proceedings before they have been read in public (law of 1881, Article 38, paragraph 1).

2.   Privileged judicial or administrative information: Publication of "any information pertaining to operations or decisions of the Judicial Council (*Conseil supérieur de la Magistrature*) (Article 38, paragraph 2) is prohibited. Under this law, such information can be published only if communicated by the council president or vice-president.

The court may prohibit reporting of any civil trial (Article 39, paragraph 3).

3.   It appears that certain laws were intended to limit or eradicate press sensationalism. Thus, unless the investigating magistrate so authorizes, publication of any illustration replicating the circumstances of a felony or of a crime perpetrated against an individual is prohibited (Article 38, paragraph 3). Publication of any declaration or document including recommendations (excluding official reports) concerning the execution of a criminal condemned to death, is also prohibited (Article 15, paragraph 3 of the Criminal Code). Thus, in 1973, a court in Paris fined the editors and journalists of three newspapers, *L'Express, Paris-Match*, and *Spécial-Dernière*, for having reported on the execution of two criminals.[8]

4.   The law also assumes that certain types of litigation require confidentiality, either to shelter the content of the proceedings or the identities of the parties involved. Regarding the former, it is prohibited to publish information about an action for defamation when the charge relates to an individual's private life, concerns actions more than 10 years old, or involves illegal acts that were pardoned or fell under the statute of limitations. Reports on proceedings concerning legitimacy, divorce, judicial separation, marriage annulments, and abortions are also prohibited (Article 39, paragraph 1). Publication of juvenile court proceedings is also prohibited (Article 14 of the ordinance of February 2, 1945, on juvenile delinquents). As to the identity of the parties involved, publication of any written material or illustration revealing the identity of a minor is prohibited in cases in which a minor has run away from home or from the institution entrusted with his welfare, committed suicide, or committed a felony or an offense (unless publication is otherwise requested by the family, the prefect, the public prosecutor, the investigating magistrate, or a judge of a juvenile court (Article 39, second and third edition of the law of 1881).

Publication of any information concerning the origins of an adopted person is also prohibited unless the person has been dead for 30 years (Article 39, *quater*).

5.   The law protects interests related to national security. Clauses in several laws, necessarily vague, prohibit the following:

a. Disclosure by any person entrusted with information, or any other person, of information or documents to any unauthorized person or the public "where national defense requires secrecy or where knowledge of the information can lead to disclosure of a secret of national defense" (Articles 75, section 2 and 73, section 3 of the Penal Code).

b. Disclosure to any unauthorized person or the public of "military information which has not been made public by the competent authority, where the disclosure necessarily tends to harm the national defense" (Article 78 of the Penal Code).

c. Communication or publication of information relating to measures which have been taken to discover and arrest perpetrators and accomplices of acts of treason, espionage, and other acts against the national defense, or concerning prosecutions, investigations, or court hearings on such matters (Article 79, section 6 of the Penal Code).

d. Utilization of public opinion polls by persons eager to "predict" future political development has provoked an attempt to "insulate" the period immediately preceding an election. Thus, during the week preceding an election and throughout the election process, publication, broadcasting, or comment on any such poll directly related to an election or referendum is prohibited (law of July 19, 1977, Article 2).

## Governmental Powers

The government's power to enforce the criminal law related to the press is vested in the public prosecutor, who is subject to the authority of the Minister of Justice. In addition, certain laws confer the power to prohibit all or part of a publication as well as to seize publications.

1.    The decree of May 6, 1939, which is still enforced and currently incorporated into the law of 1881 (Article 14), authorizes the Minister of the Interior to prohibit completely publication of any book or magazine that is not French, or is written in a foreign language. Once a prohibition is declared, the administration is authorized to seize the prohibited works. Sale or reproduction of such a publication constitutes an offense.

2.    The law of July 16, 1949 (modified in 1958 and 1967), authorizes the Minister of the Interior to take the following measures in cases concerning sale or distribution of any publications (including books) that "present a danger to youth by virtue of their licentious or pornographic character, or emphasis upon crime or violence":

a.    Prohibition of sale to minors.

b.    Prohibition of public displays or billboards.

c.   Prohibition of newspaper advertisements or handbills directed to potential buyers, or radio or television advertisements.

The minister can enforce all or part of these measures. A decision to prohibit a work must be made within the year following publication or the mandatory deposit. Violation of a prohibition order is punishable, and seizure of such material is authorized. If, within a year three works published by the same publisher were subjected to two of the aforementioned prohibitions, the publisher is required to deposit all similar works with the Ministry of Justice, and wait three months before he begins selling them. This procedure must be followed for five years.

3.   Article 702 of the Code of Criminal Procedure permits seizure where necessary to avoid disclosure of a secret relating to national security: "To insure against disclosure of a secret of national defense the administration may take preventive measures, whereby any writing, printed material, or other instrument of disclosure may be seized."

### Evolution of French Press Law

Given this formidable mass of law delimiting freedom of expression, one may wonder how the French law on freedom of expression evolved. The laws were enacted piecemeal. As indicated earlier, the law of 1881, remarkable and rather advanced for its time, was frequently amended. Moreover, as time passed, other laws increasingly contained clauses concerning the press. Under what circumstances? Most laws originated in periods of political and social crisis in France. Thus, the law of December 12, 1893 prohibiting incitement to certain crimes was a response to the wave of anarchist attacks that swept over France at the end of the nineteenth century. In 1939, the belated decision to combat "subversive propaganda introduced into France by the foreign press and rectify the deficiencies of prior legislation to achieve public order and promote the national defense" (official statement preceding the decree of May 6, 1939) prompted creation of the governmental power to censor all foreign publications. In 1949, Parliament regulated children's literature and publications creating a moral danger for children, in response to criticism which, justly or not, was provoked by the appearance of American comics and by a perception of a purported link between juvenile delinquency and the content of certain children's magazines. The practices of those conducting opinion polls and their clients engendered a political reaction which was transformed into the law of July 19, 1977.

A more recent example concerns two criminals. One had been convicted for numerous armed assaults and murders; the other had been convicted for a bank robbery that had been pulled off in rather dramatic circumstances. The two escaped from prison, under circumstances that were equally spectacular. Subsequently each published in France, under his own name, an account of his adventures. One of these books was made into a film. The Minister of Justice then introduced a bill to Parliament providing for the compulsory forfeiture, by means of a judicial determination, of any profit realized from the account of a crime by a criminal, his accomplice, or any other person (such as a publisher or a movie producer). Confiscated profits were to be placed in a special account that would primarily serve to compensate victims of the crimes. After indictment, but before conviction, the funds at issue would be temporarily attached until a judicial decision was rendered. Anyone diverting the funds was subject to heavy fines. In support of the bill, the Minister of Justice argued that it was scandalous to permit convicted criminals to make such tremendous profits from self-aggrandizing accounts of their crimes. The same goes for their publishers, the minister maintained. The minister asserted further that existing law did not prevent such scandalous behavior. What law was referred to? Four statutes may be cited.

1.    Under Article 31 of the Penal Code, no person convicted of a crime may collect "any money, funds, or any other share of his income" while imprisoned (Article 29). Nonetheless, the funds may be managed by the convict's guardian. Thus, the convict may assume control of the funds at the end of his term, and until that time, the guardian can make use of them for others.

2.    The above mentioned law of July 16, 1949, permits the Minister of the Interior to restrain distribution of any written material which, by virtue of its emphasis on crime or violence, presents a danger to youth. Clearly though, those measures do not affect publication profits.

3.    Article 430 of the Code of Criminal Procedure provides that the Minister of Justice must authorize the transmission of any writing by prisoners if it is designed for publication. However, since search procedures of visitors to prisons are not rigorous one may bypass this requirement by smuggling out the written work.

4.    Article 24 of the 1881 law clearly authorizes punishment of any person vindicating a crime. If the individual is convicted, an order may be issued authorizing seizure of the *apologie* and destruction of all copies intended for sale. However, Article 24 is limited to the *apologie* of particular crimes (the most serious); moreover, like other criminal law, this clause is narrowly construed. Thus, the account of a crime is frequently not classified as an *apologie*.[9]

When the bill was debated in the Senate, the Minister of Justice indicated that this state of the law accounted for the failure to proceed against two works, one of which was *The Death Instinct*, by a convict named J. Mesrine. Proceedings had not been instituted because the Ministry of Justice had determined that there was little chance of obtaining a conviction, and that a dismissal in such circumstances was undesirable.[10] Those opposed to the bill observed that it overlooked two fundamental principles of French law. First, the requirement of a nexus between the penalty imposed and the individual punished. In this case, the law would punish a publisher or a movie producer though neither had committed a crime. Second, the requirement that one charged with a crime be presumed innocent until proven guilty was violated in this case, by the provision permitting temporary confiscation of profits after indictment but before conviction. Several senators also noted that it would be difficult to identify precisely those funds in a publisher's account attributable to a particular work. They warned that such intrusion into a publisher's financial affairs would deter publications. Such an effect would directly chill freedom of expression. In the midst of this debate, the Minister of Justice cited examples of criminal schemes inspired by books or movies that recounted a crime.[11] The Senate adopted the bill. However, in the meantime, one of the criminals died and the government abandoned the bill.

The bill suggested a problem concerning the relationship between the law—particularly criminal law—and morality. In the words of the Minister of Justice, "from the point of public morals, it is disturbing that commercial exploitation of a criminal account should be a source of profit for an editor or film producer."[12] The question is whether this feeling of moral outrage (which is not necessarily identical toward the author of the story and the publisher) should be translated into law. A devil's advocate would argue that restricting application of the bill to serious offenses (*crimes*) would permit drug dealers, pushers, and authors of (very immoral) *délits* quietly to collect profit from accounts of their crimes. However, one may question the ultimate purpose of confiscating the profits. No one will deny that the goal of compensating the victims is admirable and should be given priority. However, once the victims are provided for, further confiscation operates as a fine, or even implies that the state and the publisher responsible for the works form a partnership. (Under a separate but theoretically related branch of law, the government imposes a supplementary tax on pornographic films.) As of this writing there has been little public discussion of the relationship between law and morality.[13] Certainly, forbidding anyone from profiting from the account of crimes, other than those enumerated in existing law, constitutes an innovation worthy of consideration. It also constitutes a legal precedent, or the start of a legal development.

### Problems of Enforcement

A second question concerns enforcement of the press statutes. To what extent does the government avail itself of this impressive arsenal of law? The answer is that the laws are applied, although inconsistently; enforcement varies in accordance with the times and political bent of the government, and of newspapers journalists, and publishers. It is thus inaccurate to think either that the statutes are mechanically enforced on a regular basis  or that they are never enforced. During two periods of crisis, which differed in nature and duration, namely, that of the Algerian War and that which succeeded the events of May 1968, the government invoked these laws against the dissenting press.

1.   During the Algerian War,[14] these measures were either administrative—consisting of newspaper seizures or prohibitions, and banishment of journalists from Algeria—or judicial—consisting of proceedings instituted against editors, journalists, managers, and authors. The grounds of such suits included participation in a conspiracy to demoralize the Army with the intent of harming the national defense, incitement to military disobedience, disclosure of national security secrets, incitement to crimes against the state, publication of works by Algerian nationalists or support of their cause, or publication of information on torture.[15]

2.   After May 1968, measures were directed against leftist press and publications. The measures included seizures, prohibitions against foreign publications, and prosecution of leaflet distributors. This last point deserves amplification. In Paris, a number of police orders restrict or prohibit distribution of pamphlets in certain areas, on the grounds that public order or traffic concerns so require. Even a cursory reading of these regulations discloses rules that are surprising and even picturesque. For example, the ordinance of March 18, 1936, prohibits distribution of leaflets from an airplane. The list of places where distribution of journals and other printed matter is prohibited includes slaughter houses, the stock exchange (ordinances of June 27, 1914, and January 14, 1934), and public markets (ordinance of November 8, 1948). A 50-year-old ordinance forbids anyone to sell or distribute writings or other printed matter or designs "tending to disturb the public order in front of entrances to barracks, churches, and factories" (ordinance of February, 5, 1929).

It is common knowledge that these regulations are not generally enforced, but are applied selectively. Thus, they can serve, as they have in the past, as a basis for stopping and searching distributors of political tracts[16] or certain newspapers.[17]

Other key measures utilized include prohibitions against insult and defamation of the police or of a foreign chief of state, and the *apologie*.

Certain publishers (such as Francois Maspero) and certain daily papers such as *Libération* were quite frequently subjected to judicial proceedings and administrative measures. One cannot help but wonder about the real motives for these actions: Were they a neutral effort to enforce the law, or, given the costs and expenses involved, were they used to interfere with or even totally suppress certain newspapers or publishing houses? Careful consideration of the facts suggests that the second hypothesis is quite plausible.

The circumstances surrounding F. Maspero, a left-wing publisher, provide a significant illustration of this point. During and subsequent to the Algerian War and the events of May 1968, Maspero published and distributed many books and periodicals. The following measures were taken against him and his firm (the list is not complete):

    a. Administrative measures: prohibition of foreign periodicals and other foreign works.[18] When these prohibitions were violated, the administration proceeded to confiscate works and institute criminal proceedings against the publisher. Books were also confiscated.

    b. Criminal proceedings. Among the key charges were:

        i. Insult to the police.

        ii. Offensive language against a foreign chief of state.

        iii. Attacks upon national integrity.

        iv. Incitement to military insubordination or desertion.

        v. Reorganization of a banned association for having offered for sale, in 1970, several editions of a leftist proletariat journal, *La Cause du Peuple*; the government, invoking the 1936 law, had banned this movement.[19]

This governmental policy, clearly directed at one person, was targeted at the financial situation of Maspero. The plan was to make the cost and expenses resulting from these measures so heavy as to either force him to modify his line or go bankrupt. Maspero was unsuccessful in challenging the administrative measures in court. Also, he was frequently fined. However, he neither modified his position nor went bankrupt.

French law authorizes the government to initiate criminal proceedings. In each case, the Public Prosecutor, who is subject to the authority of the Minister of Justice, evaluates the totality of circumstances to determine whether proceedings may appropriately be commenced. That the law should authorize the government to subject a publisher, *whoever he is*, to so many criminal proceedings in addition to the above-mentioned administrative measures is highly abnormal, and poses a threat to freedom of expression.

Currently, the French law on freedom of the press and other written matter, the product of the once disordered and now systematic accumulation of statutes and powers, accords the executive potentially dangerous control over expression. The hundredth anniversary of the 1881 press statute should provide, in the next years, an occasion to abolish the outmoded and antilibertarian tendencies which have subsequently developed in the press law of France.

## Judicial Review over Measures Limiting Freedom of the Press

Under the French judicial system, administrative courts and the Conseil d'Etat have the power to annul administrative measures limiting press freedom. Is this power exercised in a manner adequately protective of freedom of expression? This question shall be considered, keeping in mind that freedom of expression, like other liberties, is not absolute, and may conflict with other interests and liberties.

The administrative judge rules on the decision *after* the administrative action has been challenged through a *recours pour excès de pouvoir*. This slow process, which affects matters on appeal (to the Conseil d'Etat) as well as those cases heard before the administrative judge, is especially regrettable when fundamental liberties are at stake. It is particularly burdensome where freedom of the press is concerned, since time is a vital factor here. Of course, the Conseil d'Etat may order a stay of execution of a challenged decision or regulation. However, this power is invoked sparingly; it is actually considered a privilege exercisable only when two conditions are met: implementation of the challenged measure will cause irreparable injury to the plaintiff, and the grounds of annulment are sufficiently substantial to justify its repeal. In a recent case concerning prohibition by the Minister of the Interior of a foreign work (*Prisons d'Afrique* by J.P. Alata, published by Le Seuil, 1976), the Conseil d'Etat refused to order a stay of execution.[20]

The scope of judicial review will be discussed as applied in three different areas, which include (1) measures relating to foreign publications, (2) measures concerning publications that constitute a danger to young persons, and (3) seizures.

### Measures Relating to Foreign Publications

The relevant statute is the *décret-loi* of May 6, 1939,[21] now incorporated into Article 14 of the 1881 law: "Circulation, distribution, or sale of journals or other written material, published regularly or irregularly, which is written in a foreign language, can be prohibited by a decision of the Minister of the Interior. This prohibition may also be enforced against journals or other written material from a foreign country not written in French, regardless of where they are printed." Four questions must be considered here: (1) What are the legal purposes of such a prohibition? (2) What is a foreign publication? (3) What is the scope of judicial authority over such probitions? (4) What role do the international agreements signed and ratified by France play in such matters?

### The legal purposes of prohibition

The executive order of May 6, 1939, passed in accordance with the law of March 18, 1939, granting the government special powers, was preceeded by a report to the President of the Republic denoting the objective sought: "To eliminate effectively subversive propaganda brought into the country via the foreign press...so that public order and the national defense can be maintained."[22] The date of the statute, which authorized the government to take "measures necessary for the country's defense," clearly indicates that it was originally intended only to shield the country from publications threatening national security. Nevertheless, during the past 20 years, courts gradually have broadened the scope of the statute.

Originally, the Paris Administrative Court[23] and the Paris Court of Appeals (the latter was trying a publisher who had violated a prohibition)[24] had thought that the Minister of the Interior could invoke the law only to safeguard public order or national defense, but not to protect "good morals," which would authorize the regulation of pornographic publications.

This jurisprudence proved ephemeral; shortly thereafter the Conseil d'Etat upheld a ban of *Sexus*, by Henry Miller, on the grounds that "the theme of the novel was contrary to good morals" and therefore could be prohibited pursuant to the 1939 statute.[25] This jurisprudence has since been confirmed.[26]

The Conseil d'Etat has issued other judgments establishing that a foreign publication may be banned for reasons concerning public order. One such decree was issued against the French edition of a Cuban review, *Tricontinental* (also banned in the original)[27] and one against *La Tour de garde* ("The Watchtower"), a periodical of Jehovah's Witnesses.[28]

Can the Minister of the Interior ban a foreign publication on some other grounds, for example, to avoid compromising French diplomatic relations with another country? This was essentially the grounds for a number of prohibitions, including that against the book by Alata[29] and that against several African writers.[30] In 1973 the Conseil d'Etat upheld the legality of a ban justified on the grounds that "serious allegations contained in the work . . . threatened to discredit administrative and academic authorities, and thus to harm the international reputation of the French university."[31]

In 1980, reversing a decision of the Paris administrative court the Conseil d'Etat decided that foreign policy considerations were a valid legal ground for the banning of a foreign publication.[32]

By extending the scope of the 1939 law to the uncertain realm of "good morals," courts have exceeded the statute's original intent. Including foreign relations within the scope of the law is bad judicial policy.

*What is a foreign publication?*

Several criteria currently serve to define the term "foreign publication":

- Works in a foreign language, regardless of where they were printed.
- Printing or publication abroad.[33] Maintaining this jurisprudence in its

totality may deter the ever-increasing French practice to publish abroad.

• The foreign nationality of the author, even if the work is translated into French[34] or if the book is published in France and written in French.[35]

The notion of foreign origin poses tricky problems of evaluation when intellectual matters are concerned. The statement of the purposes of the 1939 *décret-loi* declares: "publication...is a complex procedure which includes elements of both a material nature (printing, distribution) and of an intellectual nature (management, editing)." It has thus been intended to permit prohibition of publications edited in France and written in French, if it can be reasonably determined that the publications are of foreign origin. The Conseil d'Etat had occasion to rule on this point, though it should be noted that the case before it had been too clear-cut: the French edition of the Cuban journal *Tricontinental* carried the same title and the same format as the Cuban edition, and was limited to the translation, into French, of articles that had been published in the Cuban edition, whose distribution was prohibited in France. Though the French edition was published in France by a French publisher, it was held that the edition constituted a foreign publication.[36]

*Scope of judicial review*

Given the very broad scope of the law, the fact that it applies to books as well as periodicals, and the fact that the measures of prohibition, being police measures, were not preceded by any adversary procedure until 1979, the question of the scope of judicial control assumes particular importance.

The French administrative judge does not exercise the same extensive control over prohibitions against foreign publications that he does over measures restraining the French press. This is so regardless of whether the measure is of a general nature[37] or concerns publications dangerous to youth,[38] although one might expect otherwise, since a fundamental liberty—freedom of expression—is at issue. Why? The reason is twofold. First, the "legislator has entrusted special powers to police authority without stipulating conditions on their use."[39] The second reason concerns the sphere involved. Until now, administrative courts have not wished to exercise strict control over measures involving foreigners.[40] Thus, until 1973, decisions of the Conseil D'Etat dismissing suits challenging prohibitions of a foreign publication declared that when a publication was prohibited on the grounds of public order or good morals and the danger was recognized, the court will not hear arguments regarding the degree of gravity of such a danger. In 1973, the Conseil d'Etat took one step toward greater supervision by verifying the existence of a "gross error of judgment" committed by the minister,[41] which means, in the words of the *Commissaire du Gouvernement*, an error "both obvious and serious." In this instance, he proposed to repeal the prohibition against *Tricontinental*, but the Conseil d'Etat affirmed the validity of the prohibition. In the past few years, the Conseil d'Etat has used the notion of "gross error of judgment" in its review of decisions concerning deportation of aliens.

### The role of international agreements signed and ratified by France

A proposal for a directive, under the Treaty of Rome, was adopted by the Commission in 1964,[42] but the Council of Ministers has not decided on this matter. The proposal requested member states to repeal restrictions concerning the press on freedom of establishment and freedom to render services. This directive would directly affect regulations concerning foreign publications. In a case involving the ban of a newspaper published in Belgium, the Paris Administrative Court considered the compatibility of French regulations with the Treaty of Rome. The court held that the ban did not conflict with the Treaty of Rome because the articles of the treaty on free circulation of merchandise (Article 30), freedom of commercial establishment (Article 52), and the freedom to render services were subject to exceptions for reasons of public order or security.[43] Commentators have thought that Article 36 of the Treaty of Rome, which authorizes restrictions on importation "justified by reasons concerning public morality, public order, and public security," necessarily permits administrative courts to exercise greater discretion over the validity of such bans.[44]

The European Convention on the Rights of Man declares in Article 10:

1. Everyone has the right to freedom of expression. This right shall include freedom to hold opinions and to receive and impart information and ideas without interference by public authority and regardless of frontiers. This article shall not prevent States from requiring the licensing of broadcasting, television or cinema enterprises.
2. The exercise of these freedoms, since it carries with it duties and responsibilities, may be subject to such formalities, conditions, restrictions, or penalties as are prescribed by law and are necessary in a democratic society in the interests of national security, territorial integrity or public safety, for prevention of disorder or crime, for the protection of health or morals, for the protection of the reputation or rights of others, for preventing the disclosure of information received in confidence or for maintaining the authority and impartiality of the judiciary.[45]

Clearly, the language of Article 10 contemplates a number of legal restraints on freedom of expression. The Conseil d'Etat has not yet had the opportunity to rule on its compatibility with French regulations concerning foreign publications.

The United Nations covenant on civil and political rights, which France has signed and ratified, permits, in Article 19, section 3, restraint of the liberty to acquire information provided that such a restriction is authorized by law, and is necessary for the protection of national security, public order, public health, or public morals.

Clearly, enforcement of the *décret-loi* of May 6, 1939 poses a number of legal problems. It should also be emphasized that a prohibition may apply to two sorts of publications: first, publications relating to the flourishing international trade in pornography[46]; and second, books or periodicals of a political character, as has been indicated by examples cited above. However, the "glorious" era of prohibition, which involved books by Nabokov and Miller, deemed licentious in that time, has ended. In conclusion, taking into account particularly those cases in which courts on appeal belatedly intervened to strike down an administrative prohibition for being *ultra vires*, and considering the fact that a stay of execution was not ordered, it is regrettable that publishers did not systematically take advantage of the legal remedies available in the administrative court.

### Measures Concerning Publications Presenting a Danger to Youth

The law of July 16, 1949, modified in 1958 and 1967, has two purposes: First, it ensures the "morality" of publications intended principally for children and adolescents (many adults read them). Under the law, these publications may not "contain any illustration, narrative, news, heading, or insert, favorably presenting gangsterism, lying, theft, laziness, coward-ice, hatred, debauchery, or any act classified as a felony or as a crime, or tending to demoralize children or youth, or inspiring or supporting ethnic prejudice. These publications may not contain any advertisement or announcement of publications tending to demoralize children or youth" (Article 2). Violation of these rules can result in fines or imprisonment.

Second, the law authorizes the Minister of the Interior to take the following measures, without preliminary proceedings, against such publications:

> [Prohibiting] any offer, gift, or sale to minors of a publication presenting a danger to youth because of its licentious or pornographic character, or on account of references to crime or violence...[and prohibiting anyone] to devise, in support of these publications, any advertising in the form of a prospectus, announcement or insert published in journals, or circulars addressed to potential buyers, or broadcasts over radio or television.

As was discussed previously, the law automatically requires a publisher who has been subject to a specified number of these measures during 12 consecutive months, to make a preliminary deposit of all "similar" publications. Moreover, a prohibition against the sale of one edition of a journal relieves agents and distributors from the obligation to distribute any editions. Two prohibitions effectively end any distribution. Publications that have been subject to two prohibitions are subject to an increased VAT rate.

A commission composed of civil servants, educators, and representatives of the public and press, under the jurisdiction of the Minister of Justice, is empowered to advise the Minister of the Interior of which publications are likely to pose a danger to youth. However, the Minister of the Interior remains free to make a final judgment.

Since I have elsewhere examined the cluster of problems engendered by these measures,[47] I will limit myself here to a few observations.

1.   These measures have served as the basis for very broad, albeit often incoherent or even contradictory, government action.[48] Today, one finds that measures abrogating prior decisions[49] coexist with new decisions concerning other types of publications.[50] Possibly, this is a sign of what the military refers to as instability of the front.

Sometimes, consensus of opinion leads the Minister of the Interior to take measures against a newspaper. A recent example of this concerned the weekly *Detective*, which specializes in accounts of crime, rape, and other such news items, all abundantly illustrated on the cover of and inside the journal, and on billboard advertisements. It was indisputable that the journal was coarse and vulgar—and well known as such for a long time. The commission, mobilized by numerous protests emanating notably from feminist groups, proposed to the Minister of the Interior that action be taken against the journal. This was done, by an *arreté* issued on December 1, 1978, which prohibited sale of the journal to minors. Public display of the journal and billboard advertising were also prohibited. At this time, it was disclosed that *Detective*, like many other journals, received financial aid from the state. The ultimate irony, which was not publicly noted, was that Mr. André Beyler, the editor of *Detective*, was a member of the commission concerning publications presenting a danger to youth.[51]

2.   What is the extent of judicial review over such measures? As an adjunct to its power to repeal a measure on appeal, the Conseil d'Etat can review the factual findings. It can determine whether the journal or book banned from distribution presents a danger to youth by virtue of its licentious or pornographic character, or on account of its emphasis on crime or violence. However, it does *not* determine whether the danger was sufficiently grave to justify the measure.[52] Thus, the Conseil d'Etat repealed, as an error of law (*erreur de droit*), a measure taken because "the general spirit of the book, its lack of morality, and its vulgar and inept style" had rendered it inadvisable reading for youth.[53]

## Seizure of Publications

Seizure of a publication, book, or newspaper is one of the most serious measures available. Seizure entails or is actually intended to suppress a work. For the press, seizure is definitively harmful. It is thus important to clarify the circumstances in which French law permits seizure.

### The legal basis of seizure

There are two types of seizure.

*Administrative seizure:*  Some statutes authorize administrative seizure in unusual circumstances, e.g., the law of August 9, 1849, concerning a state of siege,[54] the law of April 3, 1955, concerning the state of emergency[55], or Article 16 of the Constitution.[56] Seizure may be authorized by special laws, such as Article 702 of the Code of Criminal Procedure, which allows seizure when deemed necessary to avoid disclosure of a secret pertaining to national defense, or by general laws such as the *décret-loi* of May 6, 1939, which authorizes seizure of foreign journals.

*Seizure ordered by the judiciary:*  There are five instances of judicial seizure.

- In cases involving proceedings for certain press offenses, the investigating magistrate may order seizure of some copies of a publication (though the entire edition may not be seized).
- Under Article 290 of the Criminal Code, the *"officiers de police judiciaire"* may seize, prior to proceedings, any written object the character of which is so contrary to good morals that it creates an *immediate* danger to public morality. In addition to this power of seizure, judicial police are also authorized to pull down, tear up, or cover billboards. This power is inapplicable, however, where a book is subject to the deposit requirement, and which states the names of the author and printer.
- In cases concerning violation of the law of 1949 on publications presenting a danger to youth, the judicial police can seize any publication illegally displayed, and destroy any pertinent advertisements.
- Under Article 66 of the law of March 2, 1957, on literary and artistic property, the judicial police and the investigating magistrate may seize any illegal reproduction of a protected work.
- Under Article 9 of the Civil Code, which concerns protection of privacy, a judge may order seizure in order to prevent an invasion of privacy even before a matter has been finally decided or an order for damages for reparation of prejudice has been issued. In emergencies,

such measures can be enforced more quickly through a special proceeding (known as *référé*).

### The scope of review by the Conseil d'Etat and administrative courts

Full review is exercised over administrative seizures concerning freedom of
the press. As in other cases in which the Conseil d'Etat and administrative
courts have jurisdiction over a dispute involving a fundamental liberty,
they will consider whether the circumstances were such that the competent
administrative authority was required to take the challenged measure to
maintain public order.

This jurisprudence has been applied to seizures,[57] as well as to other
measures such as prohibitions on distribution which a mayor or prefect has
enforced in certain areas or against particular newspapers.[58]

During the Algerian War, prefects used the powers conferred on them
by Article 30 of the Code of Criminal Procedure (formerly Article 10 of the
preceding code) to order seizure of newspapers. This article (briefly repealed by Parliament during 1933–1935, then reenacted), has aroused
criticism; it authorizes the prefect (and in Paris, the police commissioner)
to take "any action" necessary to "verify" felonies and crimes against the
security of the state and to bring the violators before the competent
tribunal. Actually, when the prefects employed these powers to seize a
journal, they *in fact* did so purely and simply to prevent distribution, and
not only to prevent harm to state security. In conformity with classical
jurisprudence, the Conseil d'Etat reestablished the true nature of the
measure (which was administrative, not judicial), and annulled what
amounted to an act which was procedurally *ultra vires*.[59]

Clarification is in order here. During the Algerian War numerous
journals were seized, in Paris as well as in Algeria. Nonetheless, few of
these seizures were appealed. Certainly, the fact that the cases would be
decided only after the fact, and frequently after considerable delay,
provides some explanation for why they were not appealed. Unfortunately, French administrative law contains no procedure for expedited review
of such matters which by nature are pressing. While an expeditious ruling
on a "hot" matter has its disadvantages, it is essential if one wishes to
provide substantive rather than mere formal justice. Law is not intended to
provide pleasure to a select few jurists who will weigh the analytical value
of decisions, but is meant to resolve, without unreasonable delay, concrete
disputes brought before the courts.

## LEGAL PROTECTION OF PUBLIC OFFICIALS

Under French law all public officials, in the broad sense of the term (civil,
military, judicial, and all others participating in general government

administration), enjoy special legal protection. This protection is composed of several different elements.

1. The general statute on civil servants (*statut gènéral de la fonction publique*) (ordinance of February 4, 1959) declares:

> [O]fficials have the right, in accordance with rules determined by the penal code and other special laws, to be protected from any threats, insults, abuse, or defamation of which they are the object. The State...should protect officials from threats and attacks of any sort made against them in the course of performing their duties, and, if necessary, provide a remedy for any resulting damage. [Article 12]

When the government deems that protection of an official is necessary, it may select the means to do so, such as instituting judicial proceedings, making a public statement, or taking individual measures concerning the official.

2. Under Article 12 of the law of 1881, a public official acting in official capacity has a special right of reply whereby he may correct any newspaper report of his official performance that he deems inaccurate. The newspaper must publish this correction immediately.

3. The law of 1881 also imposes a special penalty on anyone who defames a public official acting in his official capacity (Article 31), or defames or insults an administrative or elective body (Articles 30 and 33).

Thus, the French legal system in effect accords public officials protection in addition to that available for private individuals. This dual system is justified on the grounds that officials deserve to be well protected from attacks on account of the burdens their public duties impose on them. In fact, officials and administrative bodies invoke these clauses only occasionally. The right of reply is employed fairly frequently; since there is a general right of reply, the right of officials to reply may seem to be a minor or useless addition to the law of the press. This is not so, however, and it is a useful prerogative, sparingly used. The provisions on defamation of public institutions are intrinsically more problematic. They were occasionally invoked against leftist journals that had criticized the armed forces in a manner declared defamatory. (The problem of the relation between the press and the courts will be considered later.)

## THE RIGHT OF ACCESS TO OFFICIAL DOCUMENTS

Since 1978, everyone in France has a right of access to official documents, in accordance with conditions prescribed by law. This section will trace the origins of this legal reform—the previous state of the law, criticisms levied against the status quo, and the transitional stage of reform reflected by the 1977 law; it will then discuss the substance of the 1978 law.

## The Origins of Reform

Since 1973, reform of the law governing public access to official documents has been considered by several studies. The earlier studies were undertaken by a commission whose very name suggests its broad and thankless task: the Commission on Coordination of Official Documents (created by the decree of July 13, 1971).[60] The commission, composed exclusively of officials, and subject to the Prime Minister's authority, was to study "how to improve the work of documenting government administration efficiently and fruitfully and to supervise coordination of publication and distribution of official documents." The commission did a remarkable work.[61] Three of its reports, those of 1973, 1974, and 1975, analyze the problem of public access to official documents and make proposals for reform. One can use information in these reports, as well as that found in other studies,[62] to sum up the state of the law before the reforms of 1977 and 1978.

### The State of the Law Before the Reforms

1.   There was no general law providing for disclosure of official documents, and no right to be informed. The administration was not obliged to disclose documents or reveal the basis of its decisions except when such an obligation was imposed by a statute. The power to withhold information was complemented by Article 10 of the ordinance of February 4, 1959, which subjected officials to a duty of silence.[63] Furthermore, the Penal Code imposes severe sanctions on disclosure of secrets pertaining to national security (see particularly Articles 75 and 76).

This principle has numerous exceptions which are classifiable into three categories.

   a.   General statutes. Two examples illustrate this point. The first involves access to public archives: the decree of November 19, 1970, on communications to the public concerning national and regional archives, and the law of January 3, 1979, concerning public and private archives. The second involves access to certain documents pertaining to municipal administration, which has long been permitted. Article 37 of the Revolutionary Law of the Seventh of Messidor, second year declares: "Any citizen may examine [municipal] records, on pre-established days and times; records will be available for examination in official premises, in accordance with necessary surveillance measures"; this law does not apply to records of current matters but to archives only. Article 58 of the municipal law of April 5, 1884, created a right of access which benefits local residents.[64]

   b.   Statutes requiring the administration to make documents pertaining to certain administrative decisions are available to persons affected by the decisions.[65]

c.  In some instances access is granted to records of which the administration is sole trustee, e.g., official records relating to births, deaths, marriages, etc., police records, land surveys, tax records, etc.

2.  A discussion of the rights of members of Parliament is useful here, as these rights have a direct impact on the degree to which Parliament may control executive action. In some areas all members of Parliament have access to certain official documents. For example, the ordinance of January 2, 1959, the principal law on government finance, specifies those documents which must be submitted with an appropriations bill (Article 32). Many laws also require the government to report to Parliament annually on their enforcement and development.[66] Other laws give rights of access to particular representatives, such as budget committee *rapporteurs*. Finally, the ordinance of November 17, 1958, which was modified in 1960, 1963, and 1977, vests some access powers in parliamentary investigatory and supervisory committees.[67] Aside from these statutory privileges, members of Parliament do not possess any special prerogatives of access.

3.  In practice, this state of affairs proved most unsatisfactory. There was no general right to information and secrecy remained the rule.

The jurisprudence of the Conseil d'Etat, so bold and liberal in other realms, proved rather reserved here. The administration was not required to provide interested parties with the reasons underlying its decisions, unless expressly required to do so by statute. The reserve of the Conseil d'Etat in this area may either be understood as reflecting judicial self-restraint, or as reflecting the Conseil d'Etat's insensitivity to the importance of the right of access.[68]

### Criticism of the Status Quo

The situation on access to administrative documents was increasingly criticized. This led to the idea of dedicating an entire statute to the right of access. The second report of the Commission on Coordination of Administrative Documents, published in 1974, vigorously criticized administrative secrecy. The commission observed that administrative secrecy had an uncertain legal basis, and stressed that the ends which it served were dubious and its effects open to challenge. The commission further observed that secrecy did not ensure administrative independence or efficiency as was generally asserted. Secrecy could not constitute a system. Moreover, information is not a "neutral" good; rather, information plays an active role in the strategy of an interest group dealing with the state. The report noted that secrecy engenders suspicion and reinforces inequality, since certain interest groups actually do have access to information.

The report recommended that the right to access be recognized on several grounds. It would provide the administration better protection from itself, equalize administrative prerogatives, and improve supervision.

At a time when the State was imposing an increasing number of disclosure obligations on private persons (businesses, associations, and individuals) either for its own purposes (census reports, investigations, and opinion polls) or for the benefit of others (stockholders and consumers), it was inconsistent for the administration to refuse to recognize its own duty to inform. In conclusion, the report insisted that if habits and attitudes were to change, the right to know should be recognized by statute, due to psychological and political as well as legal reasons: "In reality, the administration will open its records only if the legislator expressly requires it to do so."[69]

In 1976, Prime Minister Barre declared in the Assembly:

> Administrative secrecy is necessary, for it protects the interests of state security, and thereby protects the citizen's rights. However, it must not serve as an alibi, or mask the true basis for government decisions. It is thus fitting to enlighten the nation on state decisions. A precise system regulating administrative secrecy, and a method of informing the nation on primary collective decisions shall be worked out.[70]

### The Stage of Transition: The Decree of 1977

The government preferred to act by decree. The decree of February 11, 1977,[71] established a commission entrusted with improving public access to state administrative documents.[72]

It took only several months to prove that the decree was inadequate, and practically impossible to apply. The commission itself indicated this in its first report.[73] It stated that it was impossible to establish a list of communicable documents, in view of their number, diversity, and the difficulty of precise classification. Such a system could engender only incomplete lists, difficult to interpret and restrictive in meaning, which would generate numerous disputes and thus undermine the purpose of the decree. The commission then acted, with a mixture of boldness and common sense which can only be approved, in a manner *inverse* to that contemplated by the decree. It drew up a list of all the documents which could *not* be communicated. In other words, a principle was established whereby it was assumed that everything could be disclosed unless indicated to the contrary.[74]

The second object of interest in the report is found in its analysis of executive reaction to the decree. The report noted that the distinction between communication and publication was frequently misunderstood: "For a number of administrations, the 'publishable' is equated with the 'accessible' so there is *a priori* no question of providing access on request to that which was not deemed expedient for publication."[75] This confusion, real or contrived, reveals the state of mind of the administration on this problem.[76]

The report, in its analysis of ministerial responses, notes that they "almost uniformly tend to be restrictive, and lacking in a willingness to give access to documents other than those already available...."[77] What accounts for this attitude? The administration invokes protection of individuals (which quite logically can lead only to eradication of communication with third parties), protection of superior state interests, and above all, administrative necessity. As is written in the report:

> Too often, refusals to provide access seem inspired by an instinctive and all inclusive mistrust of the constituents, who are *a priori* considered to be exclusively concerned with defending their own interests to the detriment of the public interest, and by the unexpressed belief that any change in the traditional practice is unacceptable and would complicate administrative action without providing a corresponding benefit.[78]

Under these circumstances, the government could either leave the decree of 1977 in force, notwithstanding the criticisms, or, submit a bill to Parliament recognizing a right to know. Neither route was taken and the definitive reform introduced in 1978 was the result of Parliamentary initiative.

## The Reform of 1978

The law of July 17, 1978,[79] originated in a bill introduced shortly after the 1978 elections, which contained various measures intended to improve relations between the public and the administration.[80] Parliament made several amendments to the original bill. The result is known as the first title (Articles 1 through 13) of the law of July 17, 1978, entitled: "On liberty of access to administrative documents." The law may be summarized as follows:

1.   All those subject to French jurisdiction (French and foreign, groups and individuals) have a right of access to all general official documents.

2.   Official documents are "all files, reports, studies, accounts, official reports, statistics, directives, instructions, circulars, notes and responses of ministers which interpret positive law or describe administrative procedures, opinions, with the exception of opinions (*avis*) of the Conseil d'Etat and administrative courts, proposals and decisions on written procedures, audiovisual records, and all mechanized information unrelated to specific individuals" (Article 1, paragraph 2).

3.   The law applies to documents of the state, *départements*, and municipalities, and documents of public corporations and organizations (including those governed by private law) entrusted with administering a public service.

4. All persons have the right of access to documents containing information on matters concerning their interests and opposed to them.[81]

5. There are eight types of situations where access may be denied (Article 6).

   a. secret deliberations of the government or authorities within the executive's jurisdiction;

   b. secrets of national defense and foreign affairs;

   c. currency and government credit, and state and public security;

   d. matters *sub judice* including preliminary procedures unless otherwise permitted by the competent authority;

   e. matters of individual privacy including employment and medical records;

   f. commercial and industrial trade secrets;

   g. matters concerning investigation of customs or tax violations, conducted by the competent authority; and

   h. any secret generally protected by law.

To enforce these exceptions, all documents inaccessible to the public by virtue of their special nature, are enumerated on lists by a ministerial order, issued after the commission on access to administrative documents has issued an opinion on the matter.

6. In 1979, the law was further clarified: it excluded cases involving access to a particular file. Where an individual demands access to his *own* file, the administration *cannot* decline on the ground that individual privacy, confidential employment or medical records, or trade secrets are involved.[82]

7. A person denied access to documents must be notified by a written decision setting forth the reasons therefore. Lack of response within two months constitutes a denial. In the case of a denial, the interested party may request the opinion of the Commission on Access to Official Documents.[83] This opinion must be delivered within a month. It is then submitted to the administration, who has two months to inform the commission of the final action taken. Until the interested party receives notice that the competent authority has reported to the commission, he may not appeal denial of his demand of access.

8. The law anticipates regular publication of two types of documents: first, "directives, instructions, circulars, and ministerial remarks and responses comprising an interpretation of positive law or a description of administrative procedures," and second, "announcements concerning administrative documents." This last phrase refers to the lists of excluded documents.

9. Finally, various other clauses of the law should be mentioned: rights of access are subject to laws on literary and artistic property. Exercise of the right of access does not authorize a beneficiary of the right or a third party to reproduce, distribute, or commercially exploit a

document.[84] The requirement that official documents be deposited at the public archives does not impede the right of access. It was designed to frustrate any administrative attempt legally to elude application of the law.

The membership of the commission on access was altered by the decree of December 6, 1978,[85] to conform to the broadened scope of the law. The new commission has 10 members.[86] The government must provide the commission with access to documents and useful information, and must cooperate with it in any way necessary.[87]

## Conclusions Regarding Access

Two observations may serve as conclusions.

1.   Concerning access to official documents, France may be said to occupy a position halfway between the United States and Britain. The French law of July 17, 1978, differs from the United States Freedom of Information Act, yet unlike Britain, France has abandoned the *status quo ante*. The report of the Commission on Coordination of Official Documents triggered a major and timely reform. The French report was thus more fruitful than the report of the British Franks commission (1972) or the 1978 White Book.[88] No judicial matter interrupted the French bill for reform, whereas England has recently witnessed several fairly spectacular affairs: that concerning the publication of Richard Crossman's memoirs[89] and the suit initiated against Campell, Aubrey, and Berry over the incident of the famous "Colonel B."[90] Originally, each country's government—conservative in France, socialist in Britain—had been indifferent to the problem of access to government information, and probably hostile toward reform. The fact that this attitude was overcome in France—in two stages, and fairly rapidly—was due to the work of the commission which had discretely introduced acceptable propositions for reform. Moreover, the intermediate stage brought about by the decree of 1977 had probably enabled a previously hesitant administration to be more accepting of reform. The rest has been achieved by Parliament, with government consent. This acquiescence may be attributed to the fact that the government had recognized that it was too late to oppose reform or scheme against it. Much can be learned from this.

2.   The second observation concerns enforcement of the reform. Obviously, it is too early to present a balanced evaluation sheet. However, an analysis of recent developments discloses the following points. The reform was passed at a time when the public was, or at least appeared to be, fairly indifferent. Apparently, this state of affairs has changed. Members of Parliament have cited the 1978 law in reference to administrative reports raising controversial issues: government financial aid to

industry[91] or the project for reform of war pension regulations.[92] Recently, during a National Assembly debate, Mr. Alain Richard, a member, charged the administration with bad faith in providing access to requested documents. He listed the following as among those documents that had been withheld:

> Opinions of the superior council of gas and electricity regarding installation of certain industrial enterprises; opinions of the superior council on classified construction, where construction had involved a number of nuisances; the Gruson report on primary nuclear waste, which had been requested by the President of the Republic; monthly measures executed by the central office on protection against atomic radiation.

Richard also requested that the administrative courts and the Conseil d'Etat be given the power to compel the administration, by means of an injunction, to provide access to documents where it was under a duty to do so. He thought, and rightly so, that only the injunctive power could make the administration comply with the right of access and that such means would not be disproportionate to the ends sought.[93]

How the law shall be utilized, will depend on the attitude of the community, including associations, firms, and unions, as well as scholars, researchers, and other individuals involved in the communication network. Will France, like other countries, witness use of this law by associations for the defense of consumer rights? Will private enterprise use the law to serve its own ends? It is too early even to begin responding to such questions.

However, by way of conclusion, two parting observations can be made. Considering the entrenched tradition of secrecy in French administration, a certain minimum of time is required before the behavior and attitudes of individuals and institutions change. Given this reality, it is fortunate that the reform occurred in two steps. It can even be said, that the fact that the law is still quite unknown facilitates necessary administrative changes. Finally, the reform closely corresponds to the real aspirations and needs which had been increasingly expressed in French society. The defendant undergoing criminal proceedings, the party to a civil suit, the wage-earner in an enterprise, the stockholder of a corporation, the consumer of products and services—all had been aware of their right to be informed and their right of access to certain documents.[94] Also, that abstract and omnipresent personnage—the constituent—may now be added to the list. This is clearly a sign of administrative progress and democratic growth.

Clearly, one can only give a provisional evaluation of the reform. The two first reports of the Commission on Access to Administrative Documents[95] indicate that the new right has been fairly broadly asserted by the people toward all levels of government. Individuals, associations, and unions are now much more aware of the existence of the new right of access to government information. They have been able to put it to ever greater use. The Commission is playing a major role in educating the Administration and reducing its reticence with regard to the new legislation. The press has not often utilized the law, probably because of the belief, sound or not, that there are more efficient means to obtain official information, and also because of the delays.

## THE PRESS AND THE ROLE OF THE JUDICIARY

The problems posed by the relationship between the press and the judiciary must be viewed in the light of the particular circumstances prevailing in France. In the United States, the meaning of the guarantees of "free press and fair trial" have been continously debated by the public, press professionals, and legal scholars. The technique of "gag orders," as well as the question of the right of access to judicial proceedings and its relation to constitutional principles, received considerable judicial attention.[96]

There is no French counterpart to the common law which permits courts to issue decrees for contempt of court. From this perspective, France thus indisputedly has more respect for press rights.

The principal laws bearing on the relations of the press and the courts are described below.

Several statutes protect the judge's person; these include Article 31 of the press law (defamation), Articles 222 through 224 of the Penal Code (committing a grave affront against a judge), Article 228 of the Penal Code (attempting to harm a judge), the statutory duty of protection imposed on the Minister of Justice, and the right of reply.

Other statutes protect the court as an institution, such as that prohibiting insult or defamation (Articles 30 and 33 of the Law of the Press) or that against demonstrations. Article 227 of the Penal Code imposes fines and imprisonment on "whoever publishes, before a definitive judgment is rendered, any commentary tending to influence witness testimony, a decision to investigate, or a judgment."

Article 226 of the Penal Code imposes fines or imprisonment on "whoever seeks by public acts, words, or writings, to discredit a judicial act or decision, under circumstances likely to harm judicial authority or independence."

Article 226 has been recently invoked against *Le Monde*. In November 1980, investigative proceedings were instituted against the editor and the author of five articles that *Le Monde* had published between 1977 and 1980. Each article had discussed the judicial process and had referred to decisions rendered by specific courts, in particular the Court of State Security, a court of political jurisdiction that has been criticized by jurists since its creation in 1963, and which was finally suppressed in 1981. Article 226 had previously been invoked against other newspapers, but the intensity of the investigations, the newspaper's character, and declarations by the Minister of Justice, Mr. Peyrefitte, combined to create a national affair of the matter and provoked criticism of laws whose vague language threatened liberty. In 1981, however, a law of amnesty was passed, which pardoned, *inter alia*, those who had violated the Law of the Press, and consequently mooted the proceedings.

Another case which is relevant in this context concerns film censorship. In France, a film can be shown only if the Minister of Culture so authorizes (by *visa*), pursuant to a recommendation by a commission composed of public officials, members of the film industry, and others.[97] The case in point revolved around a film about a pending criminal trial in which two lovers were accused of having murdered their respective spouses. Mr. Cousty and his mistress, Mrs. Balaire, were accused and convicted of the murders of Mrs. Cousty and Mr. Balaire. Mr. Cousty was sentenced to death by the Haute Vienne criminal court in June 1972, and Mrs. Balaire was sentenced to 10 years of imprisonment. On appeal, Mr. Cousty's case was remanded and he was eventually sentenced to perpetual solitary confinement. In 1972, before the second trial, Mr. Chabrol, a screenwriter, made this bloody affair into a film entitled *The Bloody Wedding*.[98] It portrayed the crimes and offered a theory explaining why they had been committed. The Minister of Culture issued a *visa* for the film, effective only *after* termination of the criminal trial. The film director and distributor challenged the decision. In the Conseil d'Etat, the *Commissaire du Gouvernment* argued: "It goes without saying that a number of general interests, for which the government is responsible, have a stake in the smooth operation of the courts, and that impediments to this operation are generally injurious to the public order." It pointed out that the courts and judicial proceedings, as well as the police, had always been a source of interest to the film industry, now more than ever. The Conseil d'Etat affirmed the minister's decision.[99] It held that "[w]hen, in light of its specific reference to a criminal trial in process, or to parties involved in the trial, a film shown to the public seriously risks disturbing the calm needed by the court to evaluate the facts elicited by the trial before it, the minister is entitled to take any measures necessary to protect the rights and fundamental interests of the parties." The Conseil d'Etat also said that "[i]f the film had been open to public viewing during the weeks preceding the trial, it is possible that the interpretation of the behavior of the principal characters, and in particular of the premeditation, would have tended to prejudice the rights of the accused."

Two problems exist here. First, was it likely that the court—which means here the nine jurors and three judges—would be influenced by such a film? As of 1941, judges and jurors have deliberated together after the public session has ended. Contrary to the practice in other countries, they are not segregated when the trial lasts longer than a day. It is one thing to protect the court, and another thing to protect the accused. It seems to me that liberty also requires the weak to be shielded from the strong. In this case, protecting the accused was of greater priority, and should have been preferred to certain admittedly extreme forms of freedom of expression. The accused is accorded a presumption of innocence, but his fate hangs in the balance. Against him stand the indictment, representatives of the victims, and very often public opinion. Thus, anything capable of prejudicing the accused's position or hampering his defense must be avoided or excluded. In this case, the film could have had such a prejudicial effect.

## Journalists and Professional Secrecy

French journalists do not enjoy a privilege of professional secrecy. Journalists called as witnesses before a court may not remain silent, especially concerning their news sources. Journalists' unions would, of course, like recognition of such a right, but there is no reason to think that the government or Parliament are disposed to grant it.[100]

## THE RIGHTS OF INDIVIDUALS AND GROUPS

The three issues that will be considered here are (1) defamation, (2) invasions of privacy, and (3) group libel.

## Defamation

The term "defamation" has been defined previously.[101] In reality, does French law sufficiently protect defamation victims? A comprehensive response to this question would entail detailed examination of the relevant case law, which is beyond the scope of this essay. However, several observations should be made. Procedurally the defamation law requires defamation suits to be handled with dexterity and delicacy. For this reason, many actions are unsuccessful.

Courts appear rather vigilant in this domain, whether the matter concerns the elements of a cause of action for defamation, the award of damages, or fines. This is true regardless of whether the matter involves public figures (politicians, stars, etc.), other individuals, or associations, as the following examples indicate.

In 1966, a journal published an article asserting that well-known individuals comprising the regular clientele of a particular Manhattan store specializing in the sale of leather objects were devoted to certain acts of depravity. The store owner and two companies obtained a judgment for damages against the journal.[102]

### Protection for Individuals

All persons are protected under the law of defamation, regardless of their status. In 1975, editors of four newspapers, (*Le Parisien Libéré, L'Aurore, France-Soir, Paris-Match*) were fined for having falsely imputed that Mesrine, a convicted criminal, had committed certain crimes. The editors asserted in their defense that the plaintiff's honor could not be harmed, "because he had already lost all the esteem of his fellow citizens." The court correctly rejected such a singular argument, the danger of which is clear: "neither the plaintiff's personal views nor public opinion of the criminal are of consequence, for the law protects all individuals."[103] In 1977, this jurisprudence was affirmed in another case concerning an article in *France-Soir* alleging that Willoquet had planned to kidnap the son of the President of the Republic and keep him hostage to obtain release of his (Willoquet's) wife. The editor of the journal was fined.[104]

### Protection for Surviving Relatives

Sometimes a publication of the circumstances of a crime constitutes a defamation of the criminal's surviving relatives. In 1953, a journal published an illustrated story in several editions which described a crime committed 32 years earlier. In order to marry his mistress, a man had attempted to kill his wife, and made it appear as though she had committed suicide. He was convicted. His wife and son had been named in the article, and depicted in the illustrations. The Cour de Cassation ruled that they had necessarily been brought into "disrepute" by virtue of the public exposure of a family tragedy which had been forgotten. The court stated:

> This unique reminder of the crime and the surrounding circumstances, which served no legitimate purpose, necessarily caused these persons, in the eyes of a public who had not known them or had forgotten them to assume the images of the ridiculed spouse and murderer's son, and thus caused conscious harm, by a specific slur, if not on their honor, then at least on their reputation.[105]

### Scope of "Defamation"

Two examples illustrate the scope of the theory of defamation. Publically saying to an officer of the military reserve, "Corsicans are not French," constitutes defamation.[106] Affixing a swastika to the wall of a house in 1945, when the Germans surrendered, constituted a defamation in those circumstances, because the act incriminated the residents of the house in respect of their conduct during the occupation.[107]

## Protection of Privacy[108]

Owing to innovative jurisprudence by the courts, French law adequately protects invasions of privacy, at least under circumstances of public exposure. Courts have long affirmed the existence of a true *right* to privacy. One may request a remedy where privacy is violated, without having to prove, as in the case of defamation, that there was error or prejudice. The good faith of the intruder is not relevant. This jurisprudence was codified in the law of July 17, 1970:

> Each person has the right to have his privacy respected. Judges are entitled, independently from the award of damages, to prescribe any measure, such as sequestration, seizure, or any other measure necessary to prevent violation of the *intimacy* of private life. In case of emergency, these measures may be ordered in a *référé*. [new Article 9 of the Civil Code]

These are excellent principles. Liberty requires protection of individual privacy, particularly where it is violated by the press and other media of communication. Nevertheless, the utilization of the law by private individuals and courts have posed several problems.

Both before and after passage of the law of 1970, individuals deeming themselves injured requested expedited relief (a procedure *en référé*), i.e., court order, before a trial, of seizure of a journal or book, restraint of sales, or modification of certain passages. Courts grant such requests fairly easily. Typically, the complainant can obtain relief in these cases which cannot be granted in defamation cases. It is also standard for the complainant to lose interest in the litigation once an order of seizure or a substantial modification of content is obtained. Finally, judicial principles pertaining to invasions of privacy are frequently invoked by public figures who are subject to caustic criticisms related not to their private life but to their *public* life. Nonetheless, courts have granted seizure in such cases, on the grounds that the nature of criticism required immediate action.

For example, in 1975, the vice-president of the Paris court ordered, in an expedited procedure, suppression of a passage in a book concerning a former member of Parliament, his wife, and his son. In that passage, the three were accused of having been agents of the Komintern in France before the war.[109]

In the same year, a weekly ecological publication, *La Gueule ouverte*, published a satirical article, violently criticizing Mr. Leprince-Ringuet, a member of the Academie Française, for his support of nuclear power. Leprince-Ringuet was caricatured on the cover of the journal as standing between two policemen, under the heading: "The crook Leprince-Ringuet before his judges."[110] Several days later, the vice-president of the Paris court allowed Leprince-Ringuet, who failed to appreciate this form of satire, to seize all editions of the journal. The opinion specifically stated:

> [W]ithout having investigated whether the accused publication has treated the private life of Leprince-Ringuet [which was, of course, *the* issue], it is sufficient that the exhibition of his image in a caricature...depicting him in particularly outrageous terms which challenged, with no real basis, his intellectual integrity and scientific knowledge, struck an intolerable blow to his person, which will not be remedied by a future grant of damages. The mental disturbance to which he has been subject is to be all the more condemned since the charges which have been reproduced above may be converted into evidence of a conscious intent to denigrate, constituting even in a polemic, a typical abuse of freedom of the press. An emergency exists in such conditions, which justifies the judge in an expedited procedure to order a seizure to terminate the disturbance.[111]

In reality, the matter concerned defamation, but a trial on defamation would not have authorized seizure, and would have been limited by other procedural rules.[112]

## Group Libel

Group libel concerns a situation in which publication harms a group rather than a particular individual. This suggests the following problem: Is it sufficient to treat such cases as offenses and leave the matter to the discretion of the prosecutor as to whether to initiate proceedings, or should groups satisfying certain express conditions be allowed to sue? There are three instances in which French law allows private groups to initiate litigation:

1.  Gross affronts to public morality.

2.  Apologia of war crimes, punishable by the press law. In 1971, the Cour de Cassation issued a significant decision on this matter. A Mr. Le Pen had put out a record entitled "Men and Events of the 20th Century: the Third Reich," which contained various Nazi hymns and chants. The record jacket presented Nazism in the most "objective" manner possible. Le Pen was convicted for vindicating war crimes. The opinion emphasized "the absence of any reference to the crimes which had marked Hitler's rise to power and the climate of terror in which this ascent was realized." Under such circumstances, the publication as a whole "tended to incite readers to make a value judgment in favor of the

directors of the National Socialist Party who had been adjudged war criminals, and constituted an attempt to provide partial justification for their crimes."

The opinion additionally affirmed the right of an association of concentration camp survivors to join the proceedings: "[H]aving been specially created to conserve the memory of those who had died in concentration camps," the association had "suffered direct and personal harm from the vindication of these war crimes, displacement of these persons having been one of the crimes."[113] This opinion rectified prior jurisprudence that restricted the rights of associations in such matters, particularly in cases concerning associations of the Resistance or camp survivors.[114] One can only approve this legal evolution.

3.   Racism. For several years, France, which in 1971 ratified the 1965 International Convention on Elimination of All Forms of Racial Discrimination, has provided legislation penalizing

- all forms of racial discrimination (Articles 416, 416–1, 187–1 and 187–2 of the Penal Code),[115] and
- "defamation (and insult) of a person or group of persons on the grounds of their origin, or relation or lack of relation to a particular ethnic group, nation, race or religion"[116] or provocation of "discrimination, hatred, or violence towards any person or group of persons on the grounds of their origin, or relation or lack of relation to a particular ethnic group, nation, race, or religion."[117]

The law, passed in 1972, also permits any association which has been certified for at least five years and by its charter is committed to combatting racism, to exercise all rights available to individual plaintiffs in the two preceding instances. Nevertheless, when a violation of these laws is has been directed a person in his individual capacity, the association may be recognized as a party only if it proves that the individual has agreed to such joinder.[118]

The law is a necessity. Its prohibition of racial defamation and provocation to hatred or discrimination have frequently been applied by courts, such as in cases concerning articles directed against foreign workers,[119] or anti-Semitic articles.[120] Three recent decisions should be mentioned here.

In 1978, the publisher responsible for a new edition of *Mein Kampf* (who had limited himself to reproduction of the 1934 French edition) was ordered to withdraw the edition from sale and to insert three additions: extracts from the judgment of Nuremberg, from the law of 1972 against racism, and the decision on the publisher's conviction. The International League against Anti-Semitism, which had instituted the action, received monetary damages.[121]

In 1977, a respectable daily provincial paper, *La République du Centre*, published, together with other advertisements, employment offers accompanied by the qualification "Europeans." An antiracist association filed a complaint for racial discrimination (against the author of the advertisement), for aiding and abetting discrimination (against the local director of the advertising agency), and for provocation to racial discrimination (against the editor of the paper). In a judgment rendered November 6, 1978, the Orléans court sentenced the editor and the local director to a suspended fine. The author of the ad was sentenced to a fine.[122] In 1983 the editor of the daily *Libération*, was convicted for having published a violent anti-Semitic reader's letter.[123]

## ECONOMIC AND FINANCIAL PERSPECTIVES

It is beyond the scope of this essay to consider economic and financial problems of the press. These have already been given comprehensive attention,[124] particularly concerning state aid, which is of great significance in France.[125] In addition, problems relating to those in the employ of the press or related enterprises cannot be discussed, although they should be; these involve the role of writers' associations,[126] recruitment, the training and sociology of journalists,[127] and finally, the impact of new printing techniques on the role of journalists.[128] In France, as elsewhere, the press has rapidly developed into a concentrated industry, which has so far not been subjected to direct government intervention (except to favor or disrupt a particular operation). Organizations dedicated to upholding antitrust laws (the Antitrust Commission) did not enter the press domain.

## NOTES

1.   For a reappraisal of the idea of a "golden age of liberty in this context," *see* J.P. Machelon, *La République Contre les libertés? Les restrictions aux libertés publiques de 1879 à 1914*, Presses de la Fondation nationale des sciences politiques, Paris, 1978.

2.   *Cf. Histoire génerale de la presse française*, edited by C. Bellanger, J. Godechot, and F. Terrou, 5 vols., Presses universitaires de France, Paris, 1969–1976: I. *Des origines à 1814*; II. *De 1815 à 1871*; III. *De 1871 à 1940*; IV. *De 1940 à 1958*; V. *De 1958 à 1975*.

3.   On Emile de Giradin, *see* T. Zeldin, *France, 1848–1945*, Vol. 2, *Intellect and Pride*, Oxford, The Clarendon Press, pp. 494–497 (1977).

4.   Lisbonne Report, Chambre des Députés, cited in *Recueil Sirey*, 1881, Part 4, p. 66.

5.   *Ibid.*, Pelletan Report, Sénat.

6.   P. Miquel, *l'Affaire Dreyfus*, Presses universitaires de France, Paris, 1964,

and P. Vidal-Naquet's introduction, "Dreyfus dans l'Affaire et dans l'histoire," in Alfred Dreyfus, *Cinq anneés de ma vie (1894–1899)*, F. Maspero, Paris, 1982.

    7.  For information on the Constitutional Council and judicial review over the constitutionality of laws in France, *see particularly*, L. Favoreu and L. Philip, *Les grandes décisions du Conseil Constitutionnel*," Second ed., Sirey, Paris, 1979; "Le Conseil Constitutionnel," in *Pouvoirs*, 13, 1980; *Textes et documents sur la pratique institutionnelle de la Vème République*, edited by D. Maus; *La Documentation française and CNRS*, Paris, 2nd ed., 1982. On the French legal system generally, *see* A.T. von Mehren and J.R. Gordley, *The Civil Law System*, 2nd ed., Little, Brown, Boston (1977). For further commentary, *see* J. Beardsley, "The Constitutional Council and Constitutional Liberties in France," 20 *American Journal of Comparative Law* 431 (1972) and "Constitutional Review in France," *The Supreme Court Review* 189 (1975); B. Nicholas, "Fundamental Rights and Judicial Review in France," 82 *Public Law* 155 (1978).

    8.  *See Le Monde*, January 5 and 26, 1973, and February 23, 1973. The death penalty was abolished in 1981.

    9.  *See e.g., Journal officiel*, Sénat, session of April 26, 1979, p. 103.

> In both cases... there was a crime, an account of the crime, and a confession of the crime, but there was no apologia of the crime. In neither case, either that of the 39 crimes acknowledged by Mesrine, or that of the aggravated theft committed by Spaggiari, was there glorification of the crime. Consequently, it could not be maintained that either work constituted an "apologie."

In 1978, the editor of *Paris-Match* was indicted for vindication of a crime, for having published (in the August 9th edition) an interview with Mesrine, who was a fugitive at the time. He is now dead. See *infra* n.10 and text accompanying n.10.

    10.  The Minister of Justice gave the following details on one of the books:

> A fugitive criminal wrote a work in which he acknowledged his crime. This is not a political crime. The French publisher had acquired his rights from a Swiss national, editor of a publishing house, who had himself acquired them from a foreign corporation whose sole shareholder was a Lichtenstein company. This company, through a foreign lawyer and a foreign accountant, had been in contact with a French-speaking person of an indeterminate profession who had represented the fugitive criminal. Thus, it follows that the company in question was formed for the sole purpose of exploiting the profit rights to be derived from an account of crime. On another occasion, this company transferred the film rights of the story to the Swiss publishing house and then reconveyed them to a French production company which produced the movie in less than a month in order to disttibute it before the crime related in the film had been adjudicated, although the accused was still a fugitive.

*Ibid.*, p. 1019.

    11.  *Rapport de la commission des lois*, presented by Mr. Tailhades, No. 261, Sénat, supplement to the minutes of the April 4, 1979 session and debates; April 12 and 26, 1979 sessions, *Journal officiel*, Sénat, pp. 753–767, and 1010–1028.

    12.  *Ibid.*, p. 1019.

    13.  *See generally* L. Blom–Cooper and G. Drewry, eds., *Law and Morality, A Reader*, Duckworth, London, 1976; P.M.S. Hacker and J. Raz, eds., *Law,*

*Morality and Society, Essays in Honor of H.L.A. Hart*, Oxford University Press, Oxford, 1977.

14.    The basic work on this period remains that of A. Heymann, *Les Libertés publiques et la guerre d'Algérie*, Librairie générale de droit et de jurisprudence, Paris, 1972.

15.    *See* the two books by P. Vidal-Naquet: *La raison d'Etat. Textes publiés par le comité Maurice Audin*, éditions de Minuit, 1962; *La torture dans la République, ibid.*, 1972, 2nd ed, Maspero, 1975.

16.    Cf. *Le Monde*, June 21, 1972; J. Robert, "Colportage et vente à la criée", *ibid.*, July 14, 1973.

17.    On *La Cause du peuple* and the newspaper of the Action Committee for Prisoners (C.A.P.), *see Le Monde*, July 17 and 24, 1973; February 15, 1974.

18.    For periodicals *see Mundo Obrero* and *Tricontinental*. Among books, *see* C. Kamitatu, *La grande mystification du Congo-Kinshasa*, Maspero, 1971; M. Beti, *Main basse sur le Cameroun*, Maspero, 1972; J. Chomé, *L'ascension de Mobutu*, Maspero (1974).

19.    *See* P. Viansson-Ponte's article, "La liberté et la loi. Six inculpations en une semaine," *Le Monde*, March 14, 1972, and the letters by M. Maspero published in *Le Monde* on April 12 and October 24, 1973, as well as his article entitled "Vive la Censure!," *Ibid.*, February 6, 1974.

20.    *Alata et autres* April 28, 1978, *Rec.*, p. 193. (The banning took place in October 1976.)

21.    *Journal officiel*, May 7, 1939, p. 353.

22.    *Supra* n. 21.

23.    Administrative Court of Paris, January 14, 1958, *Société Olympia Press, Gaz. Pal.*, 1958, p. 236; D.1978, Som., 80.

24.    Paris Court of Appeals, Feb. 5, 1958, *Baudet, J.C.P.* 1959. III. 63 note P., Mimin, D.1958. 468.

25.    *Société "les Editions de la terre de feu"*, February 19, 1958, *Rec.*, p. 114.

26.    *Société Olympia Press*, Dec. 17, 1958, D.1959, 175, concl. Braibant and, for the criminal, Cass. crim., *Van Vuuren*, Feb. 18, 1959, D.1959. 263.

27.    Société anonyme *Librairie F. Maspero*, Nov. 2, 1973, *Rec.*, p. 611, *J.C.P.* 1974. 17642, concl. Braibant, note R. Drago; *Rec. Dalloz-Sirey*, 1974, 432, note Pellet; *Gaz. Pal.*, 1974, 100, note Pacteau; *A.J.D.A.*, 1974, II, 604, note Franc and Boyon., p. 577.

28.    *Joudoux et Riaux*, June 4, 1954, Rec., p. 346; *A.J.D.A.*, 1954, 360, note Pinto. By a decision of Nov. 26, 1974 (*Journal officiel*, Dec. 1, 1974) the Dec. 19, 1952 decision banning this periodical was repealed.

29.    The book described tortures suffered by the author after his arrest in Guinea. Answering a deputy's question, the Minister of the Interior declared that publication of the book must be prohibited "given its sharp criticism of a foreign government [the regime of Sékou Touré of Guinea]." It was likely to compromise diplomatic relations which had just been established between France and that government. *Journal officiel*, National Assembly, Feb. 12, 1977, answer to question n. 3356. By administrative order of June 19, 1975, (*Journal officiel*, June 12), the periodical *Guineé Perspectives nouvelles*, the voice of the Opposition in Guinea, was banned in France. According to *Le Monde*, June 25, 1975, this measure "was a

condition imposed by M. Sékou Touré for resuming of diplomatic relations with France."

30.   E.g., C. Kamitatu (Zairean national), *La grande mystification du Congo-Kinshasa*, Maspero, 1971; Beti, *Main Basse sur le Cameroun*, Maspero, 1974; J. Chome (a Belgian lawyer) *L'ascension du Mobutu*, Maspero, 1974.

31.   *Monus*, July 18, 1973, *Rec*. p. 527.

32.   Paris Administrative Court, July 5, 1978, *Société anonyme Librairie Maspero, A.J.D.A.*, 1979, 50, note Julien-Laferriere. The case concerns J. Chomé's book *L'ascension de Mobutu*, Maspero, 1974. The judgment was reversed by the Conseil d'Etat: January 30, 1980, *Ministre de l'Intérieur* v. *S.A. Librairie F. Maspero, rec*. p. 53. *A.J.D.A.*, 1980, 242.

33.   *Joudoux et Riaux, supra* n. 28; *Monus, supra* n.31.

34.   *Société "Les éditions de la Terre de Feu"*, Feb. 19, 1958, *Rec*. p. 114.

35.   *Société anonyme Librairie Maspero, A.J.D.A.*, 1979, 50, *supra* n.32 Conseil d'Etat, January 30, 1980, *supra*, n.32. *But see also* July 9, 1982, *Ministre de l'Intérieur C. Société Les éditions du Seuil et autres*: the banning of Alata's book was finally annulled, on the grounds that the book, written in French and printed in France, had not been written under foreign influence or inspiration, although Alata had lost the French nationality when he wrote it. The wisdom of the Conseil d'Etat's decision can be questioned: one can only approve of the annulment of the banning of the book. But are the courts really in a position of stating that a book has been written under "foreign" influence or with the help of "foreign documentation"?

36.   *Société anonyme Librarie F. Maspero*, Nov. 2 1973, *supra*, n.27.

37.   *Cf.*, for the seizure of a book, *Ministre de l'interieur c. Fabre-Luce*, Dec. 20, 1967, *rec.*, p. 511; for the prohibition of a periodical, *Société nouvell d'imprimerie, d'édition et de publication*, Nov. 23, 1951, *rec.*, p. 553; R.D.P., 1951 1098, concl. Letourneur; for the local ban of a newspaper, *Association Enbata*, Jan. 10, 1968, *rec.*, p. 28.

38.   *Société Olympia Press*, May 8, 1961, *rec.*, p. 625.

39.   Braibant, *concl. cit.* concerning the decision of Nov. 2, 1973.

40.   For the dissolution of a foreign association, *Association franco-russe dite Rousky Dom*, Apr. 22, 1955, *rec.*, p. 202.

41.   *Société anonyme Librairie F. Maspero*, Nov. 2, 1973, *supra*, n.27.

42.   Directive Proposal III/COM (64) 182, of July 1, 1964.

43.   Administrative Court of Paris, Mar. 16, 1971, *Garot et société du journal Le Point, rec.*, p. 840; *Revue trimestrielle de droit européen*, 1972, 465, note J.L. Bonnefoy.

44.   Cf. *A.J.D.A.* 1974, 582.

45.   I. Brownlie, ed., *Basic Documents on Human Rights*, 343 (1971).

46.   *See, e.g., Journal officiel*, Nov. 25, 1970, p. 10821. Article 290 of the Penal Code permits *officiers de police judiciaire* to seize at the border, before any legal proceedings, all written or pictorial publications which are "contrary to good morals." The International Convention for Suppression of Circulation of Obscene Publications of Sept. 12, 1923, ratified by France and promulgated by the decree of March 12, 1940, obliges the states to define offenses and to coordinate international schemes to enforce the convention. As a commentator said of this provision in

1965, "Sexual modesty is a virtue difficult to define and the concept of modesty seems singularly in flux today." *Juris-classeur de droit international*, fasc. 406: Repressive Conventions in International Law, no. 16.

47.    R. Errera, *Les libertés à l'abandon*, Editions du Seuil, 3d revised edition, 1975, pp. 42–77.

48.    *Ibid.* pp. 63–64.

49.    *Journal officiel*, Oct. 11, 1975, arrêté of Oct. 1, 1975.

50.    *See*, for journals publishing sexual classified advertisements, *Journal officiel*, Nov. 29, 1975, and Dec. 14, 1975; for homosexual publications, *ibid.*, Jan. 30–31, 1978 and March 11, 1978.

51.    Arrêté of the Minister of Justice, Mar. 26, 1977; *Journal officiel*, Apr. 1, 1977, p. 1809. Over 40 years ago, *Detective* had been the object of a local prohibition which had been affirmed by the Conseil d'Etat: *Société des publications Zed*, Jan. 29, 1937.

52.    *Cf.* Dec. 5, 1956, *Thibault, rec.*, p. 463; D. 1957. 20 Concl. Mosset; Nov. 8, 1961, *Societe Olympia Press, rec.*, p. 264. Concl. Braibant; Feb. 4, 1970, *Société Daily Girl Press, rec.*, p. 1132.

53.    Jan. 3, 1958, *Société, Les éditions du Fleuve noir, rec*, p. 5; D.1958. 570, note Rouyer-Hameray. *See also* May 9, 1980, *Veyrir, rec.*, p. 221.

54.    The military authorities have the right...4) to prohibit any publication...deemed likely to incite or perpetuate disorder. [Article 9]

55.    The decree declaring or law prolonging a state of emergency may by express disposition...2) empower [the Minister of the Interior and the Prefect] to take all measures necessary to assure control of the press or any other publications. [Article II]

56.    Art. 16 authorizes the President of the Republic to seize emergency powers. *Cf.* Apr. 22, 1966, *Société Union africaine de presse, rec.*, p. 276; *J.C.P.* 1966, 14805, conc. Galmot, note Drago.

57.    Tribunal des Conflits, *Action Française*, Apr. 8, 1935, *rec.*, p. 1226; *R.D.P.* 1936. 310, concl. Josse (concerning the seizure of all copies of the newspaper *Action Française*; D.1935. 3.25, note Waline.

58.    Nov. 30, 1928, *Pénicaud*, S. 1929.3.1.; Jan. 28, 1938, *Dauvergne*, S.1938.3.47; Jan. 29, 1937, *Société des publications Zed.*, *supra* n. 51; *Isaac*, June 17, 1938, *rec.*, p. 547; and more recently, Feb. 3, 1978, *C.F.D.T. et C.G.T.*, *rec.*, p. 47 for prohibition, by decree, of distribution of printed matter to passengers of vehicles traveling on public roads. The legality of the prohibition was upheld.

59.    *S.A.R.L. le Monde et Société Frampar et Société France edition et publications* June 24, 1960, *rec.*, p. 412; D. 1960. 744, note Robert; S.1960. 348, note Debbasch; J.C.P. 1960, 11, 11743, note Gour; R.D.P. 1960, 815, concl. Heumann. *See also Rodes*, Dec. 1, 1965, *rec.*, p. 1006.

60.    *Journal officiel*, July 16, p. 7004.

61.    The reports were published in *Administration et documentation*, La Documentation française, Paris, 1973; *La coordination documentaire; L'accès du public aux documents administratrifs, id.*, 1979.

62.    *See*, among others: M. Herbiet, "Le secret dans l'administration," *Annales de la faculté de droit de Liège*, 1975, Nos. 1 and 2, pp. 53–204; J.C. Boulard, "Rapport sur le secret et l'administration française," in *Le secret professionel*, Dalloz, Paris, 1975, pp. 659–689; English ed: *Administrative Secrecy*

*in Developed Countries*, edited by Donald C. Rowat, Macmillan, London, 1978; "Liberté d'information et communication aux administrés des documents publics dans la théorie et la pratique françaises. Situation actuelle et projets de reforme," *Rapport présénté par M. Louis Fougère, Conseil de l'Europe, Colloque sur la liberté d'information et l'obligation pour les pouvoirs publics de communiquer les informations*, Strasbourg, 1976; P. Dibout, "Pour un droit à la communication des documents administratifs," *Revue Administrative*, Sept.-Oct. 1976, pp. 493–510. *See* Y. Manor, "France," in *Government Secrecy in Democracies*, I. Galnoor, ed., Harper, New York, 1977.

63.   This article declared:

> In addition to any duty contained in the penal code on matters of professional secrets (see article 378 of the penal code), an official is bound by a duty of professional discretion relevant to any fact or information which he has learned in the course of performance or on account of his duties. Any deviation from the regulation on records and governmental documents, or any communication to a third party made contrary to these regulations is categorically prohibited. Except in cases expressly determined by current regulations, an official is bound by this duty of confidentiality and cannot be released from the prohibition set forth in the preceding sentence unless the minister supervising him so authorizes.

> 64.   Any resident or taxpayer has the right to examine in place, or copy in whole or in part, the official minutes of the municipal council, and the budgets, accounts, and municipal ordinances of the municipality. An individual assumes liability for any records published.

This statute, which has remained intact for the past 95 years, is still valid (Article L. 121–19 of the Communal Code). Decisions of the Conseil d'Etat clarified the scope of the right.

65.   This applies particularly to laws permitting investigation prior to a decision, i.e., cases of expropriation, edicts, or urban organization or planning which involve a taking. These laws contemplate a certain degree of publicity when commencement of the procedure is announced, and require that certain documents be available to the public, and that interested individuals be given an opportunity to present their views. In other cases, a right of access to particular records is recognized pursuant to the right of defense as is the case in disciplinary proceedings, where an official is accorded the right to review his file.

66.   As there are many laws of this sort, it is impossible to list them here.

67.   Investigatory commissions are formed to gather fundamental data on specified *facts*. Supervisory committees study administrative, financial, or technical management of governmental organizations or public enterprises. Members of these committees, and all those who participate in or are present during their work, are required to maintain secrecy. Not until the law of July 19, 1977, were the powers of commission reporters sufficiently defined regarding rights of access to documents and information. One principle is decreed: "*Rapporteurs* must be furnished any information likely to facilitate their task. They are empowered to examine all governmental documents." Exceptions concern documents of a confidential nature pertaining to national defense, foreign affairs, or the internal or

external security of the state, and matters concerning the principle of separation of powers (Article 6 of the ordinance of November 17, 1958, pertaining to the operation of parliamentary assemblies, modified by the law of July 19, 1977). Thus, in 1973, the Senate Supervisory Committee on Wiretapping was met with a claim based on the exception for secrets pertaining to national defense, which effectively paralyzed its work (*See*, on this matter, R. Errera, *Les Libertés à l'àbandon*, 3rd revised edition, Editions du Seuil, Paris, 1975, pp. 205 et seq.)

68.  *See* G. Isaac, *La procédure administrative non contentieuse*, Librarie générale de droit et de jurisprudence, Paris, 1968.

69.  Commission de Coordination de la Documentation Administrative, *La coordination documentaire, L'accès du public aux documents administratifs, op. cit.*, Annex II, p. 56.

In 1975, the mediator's annual report proposed the same reform: statutory creation of a right to information. *Rapport annuel du médiateur*, La Documentation française, 1975, Paris, p. 89. A year later, the Central Planning Office issued a report containing express proposals: Commissariat du Plan, *Rapport de la Commission de la vie sociale, VIIIème Plan*, 1976. At the same time, two bills were simultaneously submitted to the National Assembly. No. 2455, National Assembly, *Proposition de loi établissant la liberté d'accès des citoyens aux documents et informations detenus par l'adminstration*, introduced by the Socialist Party; No. 2463, National Assembly, *Proposition de loi relative à l'accès des citoyens aux documents administratifs*, introduced by the Communist Party.

70.  *Journal officiel*, National Assembly, Oct. 5, 1976, p. 6325.

71.  *Journal officiel*, Feb. 12, 1977.

72.  If municipal and provincial administrations had been included, a statute would have been necessary, by virtue of Article 34 of the Constitution. The commission had the power to classify documents, and to decide which documents could be transmitted on demand; to issue recommendations where access was denied and to advise the administration regarding application of the legal system on communication of documents. The commission's annual report was to be published.

73.  Commission chargée de favoriser la communication au public des administratifs, *Premier rapport au Premier ministre*, La Documentation française, 1978, Paris.

74.  The commission also determined that a distinction between documents and categories of documents served no purpose:

> The problem is to...admit that in principle, all documents should be accessible, with the exception of those enumerated on registered lists. This involves recognizing that the public has a *right* of access to all administrative documents, with the exception of those, limited in number, of which free access would harm the general welfare, or rights of particular parties.

*Ibid.*, pp. 11–12 (emphasis supplied).

75.  *Ibid.*, p. 13.

76.  The same may be said of its tendency to take refuge in those statutes providing for secrecy, in particular Article 10 of the ordinance of February 4, 1959.

77.  *Ibid.*, p. 14.

78.  *Ibid.*, p. 16.

79. *Journal officiel*, July 18, 1978.

80. No. 9, National Assembly, *Proposition de loi portant diverses measures d'amélioration des relations entre l'administration et le public*. The bill, was composed of rather disparate elements and contained no measure on access to official documents. It was debated several months after adoption of the law of January 6, 1978, on computers, government files, and privacy, which gave interested parties the right to contest the accuracy of information contained in their government files.

81. If the matter concerns information contained in the individual's government file, the law of January 6, 1978, applies. If an individual so requests, his own observations on the matter may be attached to the document.

82. However, medical information may only be transmitted to the person via a physician of his own choosing who acts as an intermediary. *See* Conseil d'Etat, January 22, 1982, *Administration generale de l'Assistance publique à Paris*, J.C.P. 1983. 19943 note Rapp. *rec.*, p. 33. Parliament adopted this amendment in the course of a debate on the reasoning of administrative decisions. This shows the link which members of parliament and probably the public perceived between the two problems. In either case, the citizen's right to be informed prevails.

83. The law confirms and defines this task of the commission, which is now charged with "insuring respect for freedom of access to administrative documents."

84. Article 10 of the ordinance of February 4, 1959, was amended to conform to the new law. The new law is coordinated with Article L 121–19 of the Communal Code.

85. *Journal officiel*, Dec. 7, 1978. For a list of commission members, see the decree of Mar. 30, 1979, *Journal officiel*, Mar. 31.

86. One representative of a municipal council or of a general council, designated by a joint decision of the President of the Senate and the President of the National Assembly, one representative of the Prime Minister, the Director-General of the Archives of France, one member of Parliament, a senator, a university professor, and the Director of French Documentation.

87. The decree of December 6, 1978 abrogated the decree of February 2, 1977.

88. *Reform of Section 2 of the Official Secrets Act, 1911, House of Commons, Paper 7285*. HMSO, London, 1978.

89. Problems posed by publication of former ministers' memoirs are, of course, different, but studying the two together may be instructive. The solutions elicited by these two situations suggest the same essential tendencies. *See Report of the Committee of Privy Counselors on Ministerial Memoirs*. HMSO, London, 1976.

90. *See, generally*, Supperstone, "Press Law in the United Kingdom," (*this volume*).

91. A deputy asked the Prime Minister under which classification of noncommunicable documents, as defined by Article 6 of the law of July 17, 1978, did the report of the Inspection des finances on state financial aid to industry, belong. Access to this report had been denied to a Parliament member by the government. (Question no. 16371, National Assembly, *Journal officiel*, May 19, 1979). Answering to another question, the Prime Minister specified that publication of administrative orders, contemplated by Article 6 of the law, which provides for exceptions to the principle of communication, is not a prerequisite to application of that Article.

(Answer to question no. 12019, National Assembly, *Journal officiel*, Apr. 25, 1979).

92.    *See* the Senate debate on this matter, *Journal officiel*, Sénat, May 17, 1979, p. 1266 *et seq.*

93.    Associations dedicated to protection of the urban or ecological environment will probably use the law to improve the quality of their information, as well as the strength of their actions.

94.    *See, L'information en droit privé*, edited by Yvon Loussouarn and Paul Lagarde, Librairie générale de droit et de jurisprudence, Paris, 1978.

95.    Commission d' accès aux documents administratif, *L'Accès aux documents administratifs. Premier rapport d'activité*, 1979–1980, La Documentation française, Paris, 1981. *See also* the second report, 1982.

96.    Among the numerous commentaries on this matter, *see especially* Anthony Lewis, "A Preferred Position for Journalism?" 7 *Hofstra L. Rev.* 595 (1979); Ronald Dworkin, "Is the Press Losing the First Amendment?," *The New York Review of Books*, p. 49, Dec. 4, 1980.

97.    The grounds of the decision are specified. The minister can also forbid those under 13 or 18 years of age from viewing a film and can also prohibit exportation (decree of January 18, 1961).

98.    Chabrol had even wanted to shoot the film in the town where the events took place, but the residents prevented this.

99.    *Chabrol et autres*, Conseil d'Etat, June 8, 1979, *Rec.*, p. 271, A.J.D.A., 1079, p. 24 and 44; concl. Bacquet in *Revue de droit public*, 1980, p. 222.

100.    On this question *see* E. Derieux, "Secret professionnel du journaliste," *La Croix*, December 16, 1981.

101.    *See* text *supra.*

102.    The editor was excluded from the action on procedural grounds. *Braunschweig c/Société des éditions Planète*, T.G.I., Paris, Apr. 16, 1968, D. 1969.19 note; J.C.P. 1969 11 15841, note Chavanne.

103.    T.G.I. Paris, Nov. 10, 1975; *see Le Monde*, Nov. 12.

104.    *Le Monde*, Jan. 16–17, 1977.

105.    Cass. Crim., March 10, 1955, *J.C.P.*, 1955, 11 8845, note Chavanne.

106.    Cass. Crim., Dec. 8, 1966, *Barriere, J.C.P.*, 1967, 11 15008.

107.    Cass. Crim., Feb. 23, 1950, Bouithier, D. 1951, 217, note Minin.

108.    *Cf.* R. Errera, "The Protection of Private Life in French Law: Recent Developments,"· *The Human Rights Review*, Autumn 1977, p. 151.

109.    *Le Monde*, March 26, 1975.

110.    *La Gueule ouverte*, no. 41, Feb. 1975.

111.    *Le Monde*, Feb. 26, 1975.

112.    In the following edition, the journal again portrayed Leprince-Ringuet on its cover, standing between two policemen under the heading: "Conclusion of the Leprince-Ringuet trial. The prosecutor demands the death penalty." *La Gueule ouverte*, no. 42.26, Feb. 1975.

113.    Cass. Crim., Jan. 14, 1971, *Le Pen et autres, J.C.P.*, 1972, 11 17001, note Blin; D.1971, 103; *Revue de science criminelle*, 1977, pp. 35–57.

114.    Cass. Crim., Feb. 11, 1954, *J.C.P.*, *Revue de science criminelle*, 1954.367 (the Bardèche case).

115.  *See* J.P. Brill, "La lutte contre la discrimination raciale dans le cadre de l'article 416 du code penal," *Revue de science criminelle*, 1977, pp. 35–57.

116.  Article 32, paragraph 2, of the law of 1881, as amended by the law of July 1, 1972.

117.  Article 24, last paragraph, law of 1881, as amended.

118.  Article 48–1, law of 1881, as amended.

119.  Paris Court of Appeals, July 17, 1974, D.1975. 468, note Foulon-Piganiol.

120.  This was the case in 1973, of the *Bulletin URSS*, published in Paris by the Soviety Embassy information office, which had published an article recapitulating an anti-Semitic text of the czarist period concerning the "Elders of Zion." More recently, *Aspects de la France* was convicted for having published an anti-Semitic article at Charlie Chaplin's death (*see Le Monde*, Mar. 2 and 30, 1979). In 1978, M. Iffrig, the editor of a journal for Alsacian autonomy was convicted twice for having published anti-Semitic articles which provoked racial hatred. *See Le Monde*, July 5, 1978; July 12, 1978; Oct. 21, 1978; Dec. 6, 1978 and Dec. 21–22, 1978.

121.  T.G.I., Paris, July 12, 1978, *L.I.C.A.*, *Comité d'action de la Résistance c/Nouvelles editions latines, Nouvelles Galéries et société lorraine de magasins moderns*. *Cf. Le Monde*, July 15, 1978 and the answer of the Minister of Justice to a deputy's question, *Journal officiel*, National Assembly, Sept. 9, 1978, question no. 344.

122.  *See Le Monde*, November 11, 1978.

123.  *See Le Monde*, June 7 and 8 and July 6, 1983.

124.  *See* Conseil economique et social, *Rapport sur la qestion des entreprises de presse*, presented by M. Vedel, *Journal Officiel*, Avis et rapports du Conseil economique, August 7, 1979; "Le pluralisme dans la presse écrite: conditions et enjeu," *La Croix*, Dec. 8 and 9, 1978.

125.  For a general study of the situation in Europe, *cf.* Anthony Smith, *Subsidies and the Press in Europe*, P.E.P., London, 1977; for an earlier evaluation, *see Rapport du groupe de travail sur les aides publiques aux entreprises de presse*, presented to the Prime Minister by M. Serisé in *Cahiers de la press française*, no. 92, Sept. 1972, pp. 3–56. *See also*, F. Devevey, "L'aide de l'Etat," *Cahiers Français*, no. 178, Oct.–Dec. 1976, pp. 43–45. State aid to the press is the subject of annual discussion in Parliament during the budget debates. *See*, by way of example, in 1979, *Avis de la commission des affaires culturelles du Sénat sur le projet de loi de finances pour 1979*, vol. X, Information-Presse, presented by M. Caillavet, Sénat, no. 75, supplement to minutes of the Nov. 21, 1978 session. *Cf. also* G. Dumont, "Les aides publiques à la presse, *Administration*, Dec. 1978.

126.  *Rapport sur les problèmes posés par les sociétés de rédacteurs*, presented by M. Lindon, La Documentation Française, 1970; French Federation of Journalists' Societies and the University of Caen Center of Study and Documentation on Information, *Pour un statut de la presse. Le droit des citoyens à l'information...*, Caen, 1976, Two senators introduced a bill on the press in 1979: Sénat, No. 269, supplement to minutes for the Apr. 10, 1979 session, proposition by MM. Caillavet and Thyraud. *See also* D. Périer-Daville, *La liberté de la presse n'est pas a vendre*, Editions du Seuil, 1978. *Le Monde* is the only newspaper where

the "société des redacteurs" has a central roĺe. *See* the Lindon report, *op. cit.* and also, on this newspaper: M. Legris, *"Le Monde" tel qu'il est*, Plon, 1976; P. Simonnot, *"Le Monde" et le pouvoir*, Les Presses d'aujourd'hui, 1977; J.N. Jeanneney and J. Julliard, *Le Monde de Beuve-Mery ou le métier d'Alceste*, Editions du Seuil, 1979.

127.    Cf. J.G. Senders and P. Ferdj, *Les journalistes, Etude statistique et sociologique de la profession.* Dossiers du C.E.R.E.Q., La Documentation française, Paris, 1974.

128.    For a general overview of the French press, cf. P. Albert, *La presse française*, La Documentation française, Paris, 1979.

# Four

## Press Law in the
## Federal Republic of Germany

## GENERAL FRAMEWORK

### The Jurisprudence of Freedom of the Press

For many centuries the history of freedom of the press in Germany was one of censorship and suppression of mass distribution of free thought. German press history can be divided into roughly four periods.

1.  Around 1450, Johannes Gensfleisch, called Gutenberg, invented the printer's press in the city of Mainz; in 1486, the Bishop, who was also the sovereign of Mainz, introduced prepublication review for all printed material.[1] This was a world dominated by religion, in which both the publications[2] causing the church response and the opposition fighting for freedom of thought[3] were provoked by ideas that today may be considered purely matters of faith. The Renaissance and the Reformation made educated individuals aware of their identity and their right to an independent spiritual search. Since the legitimacy of the secular rulers rested on religion's (ultimately God's) authority, any unorthodox view of baptism, communion, and similar issues also constituted, at least indirectly, a threat to the throne. It is hardly surprising that all secular rulers soon introduced universal censorship on the diets (*Reichstag*) of Worms (1524) and Speyer (1529). Nevertheless, it would be a modernistic falsehood to insinuate purely political motives. The main thrust was to safeguard "true faith." Until the late eighteenth century censorship and the ensuing unsuccessful struggle for freedom of expression remained primarily a religious matter.

2.  A second period began in the late eighteenth and early nineteenth centuries. Although universal censorship remained the law of the land, the theoretical justification for free expression changed dramatically. The Enlightenment created a new perspective of world order. The monarch's

185

power still was traced to "God's grace," but "natural" law bound him to respect the newly perceived boundaries between state and society, and to recognize the private individual as the basic social unit. He could interfere with society only to the extent required by state interests, and his actions were expected to rest on reason, not sheer will. Since the private individuals were as capable of reason as the monarch, his actions thus were subjected to their critical appraisal. Freedom of speech and freedom of the press now became political issues. The periodical press was transformed into an institution whose main aim was to provide space not only for reporting but also for the exchange of individual arguments. The political aspects were furthered by foreign thought and practice. Under predominantly French and American influences, the quest for freedom of the press was a fight for the individual human right of cultural and political expression. At the same time, the struggle had a collective element insofar as "reason" and *communis opinio* could be discovered by public discussion. Radical social changes helped these ideas gain momentum. With the advent of industrialization, the last remnants of the medieval feudal order broke down. Factory owners—a new proud group whose role was as yet undefined—appeared on the scene. Unwilling to await graciously the favors a monarch might grant, they insisted on their *rights* (so long as they could not obtain *privileges*).

In most German states legislation corresponding to the new theoretical development failed to follow. On the contrary, most rulers fortified censorship with additional barriers. These included requiring editors to obtain a permit, which was granted or refused arbitrarily; to put up bail; and to pay a special stamp tax. That criminal law was used as a weapon against heretical views is hardly worth mentioning. The 1848 revolution seemed to sweep away these oppressive measures. Article 143 of the 1848 Reichs Constitution gave every German the right to free expression. It further provided that

> the freedom of the press may by no means and under no circumstances be curtailed, suspended or abolished by preventive measures, namely censorship, permits, bail, impositions by the state, regulations of printers, or booktrade, postal restrictions or other hindrances to free traffic.

Within months, however, as the liberal revolution collapsed, all the petty hindrances that had proved so effective were reintroduced. Yet, it should not be overlooked that at least one major step was successful: censorship remained abolished until Hitler rose to power.

Some observers consider the introduction of the Reichspressgesetz of May 7, 1874,[4] as another major step toward freedom of the press. In drastic contrast to the 1848 Constitution, which concentrated on the rights of the individual, section 1 of the act stated, "The freedom of the press is subject only to those limitations which are provided for or allowed by present law." Indeed, the new press law did mean progress since it abolished most governmental restraints. The press flourished in the new atmosphere of freedom, but these conditions did not last long. In 1878, important parts of the Reichspressgesetz were suspended and all publications promoting "the dangerous aims of the Social Democrats" were forbidden. However, nonsocialist papers were not affected by these measures. Their prosperity was enhanced greatly by new technical and economical developments such as the introduction of the rotating press and the advent of an organized advertising market. This was a turning point in the history of the press. Publishers, authors, and political organizations that wanted to participate in the marketplace of public discussion were joined by the entrepreneur—the businessman who wished to earn a good return on his investment. His purpose was not to promote discussion and further "reason," but "to gain the widest circulation possible by pleasing everybody,"[5] mainly his actual and potential advertising clients. In this ever-growing field, the publisher became a domineering figure; the employed and economically dependent writer was perceived as a provider of services rather than as an independent thinker.

Legal doctrine, however, hardly recognized this dramatic change, and theoretical justifications for freedom of the press remained basically unchanged,[6] even after a democratic system of government was instituted following the First World War. Most legal scholars echoed the justifications for free speech which developed during the Enlightenment. Thus, freedom of individual expression and its contribution to public discussion of cultural and political affairs constituted the basic rationale of Article 118 of the Weimar Constitution of August 8, 1919, roughly fashioned after the 1848 Constitution.

Marked changes in the structure of the press continued during the era of the Weimar Republic (1919–1933). Press concentration intensified[7] and big industrial companies became involved in the publishing markets. Alfred Hugenberg established the first press empire with a multitude of papers, most of them "dedicated" to "sensations," all of them promoting the ideas of the right-wing Deutschnationale Volkspartei (DNVP). Although Hugenberg never gained the market share that Hearst won in the United States, he may have surpassed Hearst in political importance by laying the ideological basis for Hitler's eventual ascendance to power. Political opponents, journalists, and many intellectuals were well aware of the discrepancies between the reality of press coverage and the theoretical concepts favoring press freedom. Nevertheless, mainstream legal scholarship remained widely unchanged.[8] It should also be noted that under the Weimar Constitution the guarantee of press freedom was mainly a guideline to the legislature in regulating matters pertaining to the press. But a publisher could not ask for its enforcement in court if he felt that his individual rights were violated.

3.   Reality and ideology corresponded perfectly under Nazi rule (1933–1945). Freedom of the press was suspended a few weeks after Hitler's rise to power on February 28, 1933, and all socialist and communist papers were expropriated. All other papers were quieted by the infamous Reichskulturkammergesetz of September 22, 1933.[9] Under this act, only members of the *Kammer*[10] ("chamber") were allowed to publish. An author, journalist, or publisher had to be "reliable" to become or remain a member. In addition, the Schriftleitergesetz of October 4, 1933,[11] authorized the Propaganda Minister to ban any journalist "for reasons of the public good." A journalist was "free" to perform his duty to the public by promoting the ideas and programs of Nazi ideology. The press was perverted into a docile servant of the Führer.

4.   Following a short standstill after the Second World War, the Western Allies attempted slowly to rebuild a democratic press by, at their discretion, granting publishing licenses to antifascist individuals and political parties. The Federal Constitution of 1949 (Basic Law) ended this transition period with a strong commitment to a free and uninhibited press. Section one of Article 5 provides:

> Everybody has the right to freely express and distribute his opinion by means of word, letter, and picture and to inform himself through all generally accessible sources. The freedom of the press and the freedom of reporting by means of radio and film are guaranteed. No censorship can be established.[12]

Theories abound as to the exact meaning and rationale of Article 5. Because they cannot be dealt with adequately in a short survey, the following remarks are limited to observations that either reflect the consensus view or were presented by the Federal Constitutional Court.[13]

The guarantee of freedom of the press is a reaction to Nazi oppression of free thought. The constitutional text suggests an attempt both to revitalize the liberal tradition of the 1848 Constitution and to take into account the historical experiences.

Freedom of the press, like freedom of speech, is an individual right to self-expression. At the same time, it has a collective aspect: it is "the basis of a free, democratic order,"[14] an essential element of a democratic state.[15] In the words of the Federal Constitutional Court:

> Especially a free periodical political press is indispensable for modern democracy. If the citizen is called upon to make political decisions, he must be fully informed; he has to know and weigh controversial opinions which others have formed. The press promotes this permanent discussion, comments on information, gives orientations, and critically sums up the constantly newly formed opinions and demands of society and different groups, makes them the object of public discussion and brings them to the attention of government and parliament, so that they have a measuring stick for their actions.[16]

In short, the press is "medium" and "actor" in the process of forming public opinion.[17] While the Federal Constitutional Court has always emphasized the close connection between freedom of the press and democracy, it has also pointed out that the freedom applies as well to other areas, including entertainment.[18] Furthermore, by recognizing and investigating new issues in all areas, or by providing a fresh look at old issues, the press promotes the reception processes vital for social change.[19] Thus, the individualistic aspect, important as it is, is not sufficient, and the state must recognize and promote the social value of press freedom.

## The Legal Guarantee of the Press—Some Technical Details

Article 5 of the Constitution provides for freedom of the press as an individual right and as "an institution." Thus, it is not limited to the purely individualistic justifications of freedom of speech. Moreover, in contrast to earlier constitutions, this provision is no mere governmental guideline. Rather, every person can rely on it in court against state interference. Indeed, not even a statute passed by the two-thirds majority generally required for changes of the Constitution can reverse article 5;[20] only a revolutionary act suspending or abolishing the Constitution as a whole can repeal it. All branches of government, including the courts, must respect both aspects of Article 5. Thus, the social value of the press or its institutional guarantee must be taken into account by the courts even in litigation between two private parties.

There are two similar guarantees below the constitutional level. Practically meaningless are provisions guaranteeing press freedom found in the press laws of the 11 West German states.[21] More relevant is the European Human Rights Convention of November 4, 1950, which by the Law of August 7, 1952, is part of the German legal system. While the convention does not mention the press expressly, its Article 10 provides for freedom of speech and freedom of information regardless of national boundaries. Although not exceeding Article 5 in content, this provision permits review by the European Court in Strassburg.

## The Role of the Courts

Warned by prior experiences, especially during the Weimar Republic, Article 1, section 3 of the Constitution provides explicitly that the basic rights (*Grundrechte*), including press freedom, are binding on the legislative, executive, and *judicial* branches of government. Article 19, section 4 of the Constitution complements this provision by guaranteeing judicial protection against violation of these rights. The main guardian of the basic rights is the Federal Constitutional Court. But contrary to a common misconception both at home and mainly abroad, it is not the only one. *All* courts are legally bound to disregard preconstitutional statutes, i.e., laws passed before May 23, 1949, if they violate Article 5 of the Constitution.[22] Although all courts also have the duty to review the constitutionality of postconstitutional laws, they cannot declare such statutes invalid. When a decision depends on the question of a statute's validity and the court thinks the statute violates basic rights, it must stay proceedings and present the constitutional question to the Federal Constitutional Court.[23] Only the Federal Constitutional Court can declare the law as invalid, and its decision has a binding force not only with respect to the particular case but generally.[24] Moreover, if a citizen believes a court has violated his basic rights, he can appeal ultimately to the Federal Constitutional Court.[25]

In numerous decisions the Federal Constitutional Court has developed important details of the individual and institutional aspects of press freedom. Just a few can be elaborated here. Significantly, "all preparatory activities, especially the collection of information,"[26] as well as the act of publishing, are protected. Therefore, not only the publisher and the journalist can rely on the constitutional guarantees; under certain conditions, even a bookkeeper called upon to testify as to payments made to certain informants may invoke the Constitution.[27] Despite the omission of the word "everybody" from the second sentence of Article 5,[28] it is generally agreed that both Germans and foreigners enjoy this freedom, as well as every domestic[29] legal entity,[30] except the state and its subdivisions.

The freedom applies to all products of the printing press, regardless of content.[31] The quality of the product may be relevant, however, when press freedom conflicts with other "basic rights."[32] According to the theory advanced by the Federal Constitutional Court, the conflicting interests must be balanced, and the balancing process may involve "the ways and means of reporting."[33] The most common conflict arises between Article 5 and Articles 1 and 2. These latter articles guarantee what in German doctrine is commonly called "rights of personality" (*allgemeines Persön-lichkeitsrecht*). If one dares to attempt a translation, its main features might be called "the right not to be defamed and the right to privacy." Two cases illustrate typical situations underlying this normative conflict.

In the *Soraya* case, a journal specializing in reports on high society and aristocracy published a fictitious interview with the ex-wife of the then-Iranian emperor in which the princess allegedly commented in detail on her marriage. After the ordinary courts had granted damages for mental pain and suffering, the publisher appealed unsuccessfully to the Federal Constitutional Court claiming, *inter alia*, that those judgments violated Article 5. The Federal Constitutional Court made perfectly clear that the guarantee did not include the right to invade another's privacy and put that person in a false light by publishing falsehoods.[34] The individual's interests plainly were to be rated higher than the interest of the journal.

The *Lebach* case, which involved television but is also applicable to the press, was more complicated. A public television company wanted to present a fairly well researched documentary play about a spectacular crime that had aroused considerable public interest several years earlier. The play presented a theory for the felons' underlying motives. One of the convicted criminals, a minor figure in the crime who was close to release and who with the help of his friends and parents had made promising preparations for reintegration into society, successfully enjoined the play's presentation. Carefully taking into account the special effectiveness of this medium, the particular form of presentation, and its nationwide reach, the Federal Constitutional Court held that the potential destruction of the plaintiff's opportunity to lead an integrated life, which would result from broadcast of the play, outweighed the freedom of the broadcaster.[35] The media, it was clearly pointed out, not only had rights; they carried a heavy responsibility to the public, especially toward the weak members of society. Despite the *Lebach* case, the courts have frequently pointed out that prominent persons who are in the public limelight—whether because they hold public office or whether, like show-business personalities, they seek media attention—are entitled to much less sensitivity. Strong, harsh criticism is allowed if necessary. In factual reporting, the press has to follow decent journalistic standards of care; but truth is not required.[36]

Press freedom also encompasses advertising.[37] When petitioned by a publisher from an area close to the Swiss border, the Federal Constitutional Court invalidated a statute prohibiting German papers from printing advertisements for foreign employment since "ads are news, too."[38] While there is a consensus approving the extension of constitutional protection to advertising, it is also contended that the court should have grounded its decision on the "institutional" aspect of the guarantee. If, as the court has pointed out frequently, the press is run by private individuals or companies as business ventures,[39] then the present system cannot survive without advertising income. If a government were indiscriminately permitted to limit particular kinds of paid advertisements without proving a compelling public interest,[40] it could silence the vast majority of newspapers, magazines, and journals.

As the *Lebach* and *Soraya* cases demonstrate, the guarantee is not restricted to the state-citizen relationship. To be sure, this relationship was historically of major concern and should continue to be of concern, since historical situations might recur. Moreover, it would violate the constitutional guarantee if the state tried "directly or indirectly to control or steer the press as a whole and parts of it."[41] But it is equally important to recognize that, contrary to nineteenth century liberal beliefs, individual freedom under modern conditions by no means guarantees a process of free and uninhibited discussion. The state should implement this freedom in two different ways.

First, the judiciary must acknowledge the "institutional aspect" of the constitutional guarantee whenever it encounters private interests that might be detrimental to a free process of communication and public debate. The *Blinkfüer* case illustrates this aspect.[42] During the Cold War between East and West, the Springer group, one of Germany's most powerful publishers, suggested to all distributors that they not sell the magazine *Blinkfüer* which, after the Berlin wall was erected, displayed lack of patriotism by publishing East German radio programs. The group indicated that retailers who continued offering *Blinkfüer* to the public might have to stop selling Springer products. The Federal Constitutional Court maintained that Springer as well as *Blinkfüer* were entitled to their opinions and that a call for a boycott was absolutely legal if used as a means to further public discussion. But the Court also held that it was unconstitutional for a private person or legal entity to use its economic power to silence another voice.

The *advertising pamphlet* cases present another example of the "institutional" aspect of the guarantee.[43] Everyone is free to distribute papers fully financed by ads. The Federal Supreme Court held, however, that such publications, which by including an editorial section pretend to appear as substitutes for regular papers, actually inhibit public discourse. Since these publications violated the underlying philosophy of Article 5, they were considered illegal under section 1 of the Unfair Competition Act (*Gesetz gegen den unlauteren Wettbewerb*).

The second way by which the state implements the constitutional guarantee is through legislation. In the famous *Spiegel* case,[44] the Federal Constitutional Court recognized that the judiciary was not alone in safeguarding a free process of communication. The legislative branch "might be called upon to counteract dangers that might arise for a free press system by the evolution of press monopolies."[45] Although media concentration has constantly increased and many suggestions for legal reform have been proposed,[46] very little successful activity can be reported. Lawmakers, always close to reelection, have hardly ever dared to engage in a fight with the press. The only success in battling further concentration is the Law of June 28, 1976, which modified section 23 of the Gesetz gegen Wettbewerbsbeschränkungen (GWB).[47] Although generally mergers are controlled only when, among other conditions, the annual turnover of the companies involved exceeds 500,000,000 DM, mergers in the press sector are controlled at the 25,000,000 DM level. Thus, for all practical purposes, the antitrust authorities can forbid all press mergers when they would be harmful to competition in the relevant markets. Some mergers have been prevented in recent years; however, it remains to be

seen whether this sole instrument to battle monopolies and close oligopo-
lies will suffice. Doubts are frequently voiced.[48]

Although censorship and indirect suppression such as special press
taxes were effectively abolished, freedom of the press is not unlimited.
Article 5, section 2 of the Constitution states expressly that "these
guarantees are subject to the commonly applicable laws, to the legal
provisions protecting minors and to the right not to be defamed and
slandered." The basic intention of this clause is obvious: the press has no
special status before the law.[49] Despite its obvious import, the phrase
"commonly applicable laws" remains enigmatic. In a Solomonic formula,
the Federal Constitutional Court held that the "commonly applicable
laws" should be viewed and interpreted in a manner such that the basic
values guaranteed by the Constitution are not violated.[50] Therefore, in
interpreting all statutes, each court must consider the constitutional
guarantee as the primary guideline of interpretation. If—and only if—the
laws accordingly interpreted do not violate the basic value judgments of
Article 5, section 1, sentence 2, they are constitutional. Clearly, this
approach requires a highly sophisticated judicial process and makes it
harder for attorneys to predict the results of litigation.

## THE PRESS AND THE STATE, PARTICULARLY
## THE EXECUTIVE BRANCH

The Basic Law expressly forbids the state to control the press.[51] Nevertheless, there are a multitude of legislative and especially administrative
regulations of the press. Some are motivated by an intention to provide a
legal framework for a free press, others—more important in this context—
by a wish to suppress discussion.

### The Press Laws

Both scholarly and judicial opinion agree that the press laws of the 11
states constitute just a legal framework to ensure press freedom. This view
might be explained historically. Press laws have existed for more than 100
years[52] and have been understood as enhancing rather than stifling
freedom. Under Article 75, section 12 of the Constitution, the power to
legislate the details of press matters passed from the central government to
the states. Since then, all states have enacted new press laws which, while
varying in detail, basically follow the same pattern. Because Hamburg is
the publishing center of the country, its press law of January 29, 1965,[53]
serves as the most relevant example.

Paragraphs 1 through 3 of the press law explicate the freedoms guaranteed by Article 5 of the Constitution.[54] Paragraph 4 provides for a right of information.[55] Paragraph 5 prohibits the publication of indictments and similar official documents in criminal proceedings prior to their formal introduction into the proceedings.[56] Since the publication of such documents constitutes a crime according to section 353 of the Criminal Code, this paragraph is at best unnecessary. At first glance, paragraph 6 seems to be potentially dangerous because it proclaims a duty to investigate the veracity of all news using all reasonable care due under the circumstances.[57] But a closer look, as well as actual practice, show that any such fear is unjustified, for the press law provides no sanction for its violation. The paragraph is invoked in defamation cases, e.g., when a journal publishes false rumors stemming from doubtful sources without any prior effort at verification. Clearly, the courts would construe the same standard of care even if paragraph 6 did not exist. Paragraph 7 defines the kind of publications encompassed within the law.[58]

Paragraph 8 provides that periodicals must publish in every issue the name of the printer and publisher and the name and address of the "responsible editors" (*verantwortliche Redakteure*).[59] No qualifications are specified for printers or publishers, but the responsible editor must reside in West Germany, including Berlin (West), must not be disqualified from seeking or voting for public office,[60] and must be at least 21 years of age and possess full legal capacity.[61] To act as responsible editor without these qualifications or to employ such a person constitutes a criminal offense punishable by a fine or imprisonment[62]; it is a misdemeanor not to publish this *impressum*. The historical intention of these rules is obvious. They were included in the Reichspressgesetz as a warning not to print ideas "dangerous" to the administration or to libel the majesties. During the Bismarck years the grim joke was told that the responsible editor should be called the "sitting editor," since he was liable to sit in jail. Today, as contemporary "majesties" are not protected from vigorous criticism and biting public attack,[63] this threat certainly has diminished. Yet the basic aim remains not to allow the press to evade civil or criminal sanctions by not naming the author of a damaging article. The criminal aspect is best illustrated by paragraph 19: it first pronounces what is self-evident in light of Article 5, section 2 of the Constitution, that all crimes committed by way of a printed product are punishable according to the (mostly federal) criminal law. The section states further, "If a crime has been committed by means of a printed work...the responsible editor [will be held criminally liable]...if he has willfully or negligently failed in his duty to keep the publication free from offending matter."[64] To my knowledge, no noteworthy cases involving this section were reported in Hamburg or elsewhere, nor have serious criticisms been directed at this feature of the press law.

Paragraph 10 requires the publisher to indicate what part of the periodical has been paid for.[65] This duty applies equally or even more so to parts of the publication written by the editorial staff which, though not paid for explicitly, are either demanded by an advertiser to accompany a paid commercial or offered by the publisher as a free service.[66] Whoever pretends falsely that he is presenting his own ideas for public discussion violates the basic rationale underlying Article 5. Consequently, no one has ever challenged the validity of paragraph 10. Although violations of this paragraph are not totally uncommon, prosecutions[67] are rare. Paragraph 11 provides for a right of reply.[68] Paragraphs 12 through 18 and 22 contain rules regulating confiscation of press products and the right of the press to refuse to present evidence. These provisions are now obsolete because of federal legislation.[69] The remaining paragraphs regulate the statute of limitations and technical questions.

In sum, the press laws of the states impose certain obligations on the press that are not unduly cumbersome in daily business. They establish certain rules that theoretically might infringe on the free exchange of ideas, but in practice have not resulted in suppression, and other rules that obviously further the constitutional guarantee. On the whole, the state press laws reflect nineteenth and early twentieth century ideas and by no means address the most pressing problems of today. For many German observers, the legislative and executive branches are not the main potential enemies of a free discourse on political and nonpolitical ideas. Rather, economic power and press concentration present the primary real threats. Most attempts to attack these problems on the only adequate (i.e., federal)[70] level have failed. Nearly all governments of the last 13 years have promised a new *Presserechtsrahmengesetz* ("federal guidelines").[71] Yet in the face of strong concerted opposition by the publishers, which no ruling party apparently dared to offend, they have failed to fulfill their promises.

## Internal and External Security and the Press

Despite the reservation mentioned above, the relationship between press and government, particularly the executive branch, is one of tension. The executive branch, attempting to fulfill its duties efficiently, necessarily tends to identify its policies with the interest of the state and to classify sensitive documents "top secret" rather liberally. On the other hand, it is precisely the duty of the press to disturb, to investigate, and to criticize. Thus, it is hardly surprising that the press community tends to draw the lines of the public's right to know and the press's right to inform wider than do the administrators. While there is general agreement that within certain limits national security requires secrecy and that certain constitutionally based principles are not open to attack, it is impossible to agree on exactly where to draw the line. Except in rare, obvious cases, the value judgment of whether a security interest is genuine or illegitimate will always remain uncertain. If the secret decision of a government to develop nuclear weapons is disclosed, strategic advantages for an actual or potential enemy are apparent; for some portions of the population, however, it will not be clear that this decision should be made without public debate. The following discussion will survey briefly the legal attempts to minimize these uncertainties and describe actual practices that are potentially dangerous to a free discourse of ideas.

### The Legal Framework

During the Cold War, penal legislation in a perfectionistic manner tried to suppress any thought remotely linked to Communism. Although the Law of June 25, 1968,[72] relaxed considerably the criminal sanctions applicable to the press, an unprecedented wave of terrorist activities by the Red Army Faction (*Rote Armee Fraktion*) caused a dangerous revival of illiberal ideas. The federal government, pressed to act by public outrage but uncertain as to the most effective strategy, introduced, among other measures, the infamous section 88a of the Criminal Code[73] to combat the ideological foundations of this and comparable groups. It provided, *inter alia*, that anyone who distributed a publication advocating certain serious crimes, including murder, robbery, and arson, was criminally responsible. This section was violated even if the publisher-distributor did not advocate himself or approve of the intentions expressed in the publication, although subsection 3 of section 86 might have sheltered publication of works by Shakespeare, Marx and possibly even Bakunin. That section provided that no crime was committed if the distributor's intention was to enlighten the citizenry,[74] to fight anticonstitutional activities, to further the arts or sciences, or to report on current affairs, history, or "similar aims." The vague wording indicates the drafters' guilty conscience. At the same time, its vagueness increased the risks for authors and publishers to distribute unorthodox ideas and, consequently, could limit public information and discussion. Fortunately, the same political forces that introduced section 88a proved wise enough to abolish it recently.[75]

In spite of the doubts expressed above, the present legal framework of criminal restrictions relevant to the press is rather liberal. The law can be divided into three groups.

### a.   The protection of certain constitutional values

As a reaction to Hitler's attack on Germany's neighbors, Article 26 was inserted in the Basic Law, stating that a war of aggression is unconstitutional and that all "acts suited and intended to prepare such a war" should be punished. Sections 80 and 80a of the Criminal Code complement this constitutional provision. The former provides for a life sentence for anyone actually preparing such a war; the latter for a five-year prison term for publicly advocating such a war. While its intent is laudable, section 80a certainly might inhibit the free exchange of ideas in defense matters. Should it be illegal to discuss the possible benefits of a first strike on foreign territory when attack seems imminent? Or would such a proposition fall outside the realm of section 80a? Both questions, fortunately, have not yet had to be answered.

### b.   The protection of internal security

Any society based on democratic conflict and consensus will inevitably attempt to prevent destruction of its system and combat the use of force or threats of force to influence vital decisions. Sections 81 and 82 of the Criminal Code provide a minimum sentence of 10 years imprisonment for anyone using or threatening to use force to destroy the existence of the Federal Republic, a state of the Federation, or their constitutional systems. These norms have attracted very little interest in judicial practice and legal scholarship. It could be argued, however, that a broad interpretation of the terms "threat" or "force" could yield serious restrictions on freedom of speech and freedom of the press. It remains uncertain how the courts will decide the issue. In view of Article 5, section 2 of the Basic Law and the theories developed by the Federal Constitutional Court as to its meaning,[76] this author does not foresee serious dangers.

Sections 86 and 86a of the Criminal Code touch on freedom of expression and freedom of the press by prohibiting, *inter alia*, the distribution of propaganda for unconstitutional parties, or by organizations that support unconstitutional parties, and the use of symbols of unconstitutional organizations. Both sections were passed as reactions to the Nazi era and were intended to prohibit the display of the swastika, SS crossbones or uniforms, or similar Nazi symbols. The intention was honorable: freedom should not be used to destroy freedom. Most observers agree that both provisions are constitutional because they incorporate the doctrines developed by the Federal Constitutional Court. A criminal court applying these provisions cannot determine a party's constitutionality; the sanctions can be applied only if the Federal Constitutional Court has positively determined the party's unconstitutionality.[77] Moreover, to fall within the statute's scope, the propaganda must attempt to undermine the constitutional system or peace among nations.[78] Thus, the statute allows use of the symbols and old propaganda in artistic and scientific works or when their use is intended to enlighten the public or to discourage unconstitutional activities. More importantly for the press, there is no prohibition on the use of such symbols in reports on current or historical ideas or—and here lies a great opportunity for the judiciary to further the rationale underlying Article 5 of the Basic Law—for "similar aims."[79]

Sections 105 and 106 aim to secure internal security by providing severe sanctions for attempting by force or threat of force to influence the decisions of the President, executive branch, legislature, or courts. Until recently[80] these provisions were generally held to be theoretically important, as a signal to possible anticonstitutional forces, but practically without relevance. From a comparative perspective, section 89 appears like a fairly normal balance between freedom of expression and the interest in survival. It prohibits planned attempts to undermine the willingness of members of the armed forces or the police force to defend the security of the Republic or its constitutional system. Such attempts are punishable only if the security or existence of the Federal Republic, its constitutional system, or fundamental constitutional principles[81] are intentionally undermined.

### c.   The protection of external security

The laws governing the protection of external security correspond to those in most other Western democracies. Espionage and treason are punishable by stiff prison sentences.[82] Contrary to a legislative tradition that took for granted the meaning of words or considered it wiser to leave the definitional task to the courts, this law is remarkable in the precision with which the legal terms are defined. For example, section 93 of the Criminal Code does not allow either the administration or the courts to determine what constitutes a "state secret." A governmental opinion that certain factual information, to which there is limited accessibility, must be kept secret to protect external security, is insufficient to punish a person who publicizes this information. Criminal sanctions apply only when a court agrees that those facts *had* to be secret, that the publication actually caused a detriment to external security, and that the detrimental effects were severe. Although many of the uncertainties expressed above remain, it is reassuring to know that a classification of "top secret" alone cannot prohibit public discussion of important issues. At the least, an independent judiciary must agree with the administration. The remaining stifling effects on public discourse cannot be neglected, but so far no convincing proposals to balance better the conflicting interests have been made.

At first glance, the Federal Republic can take special pride in section 93, subsection 2, which states that secrets involving anticonstitutional activities cannot be considered state secrets. Yet, whoever reveals an "illegal" state secret to a foreign power or agent remains criminally liable.[83] Some pride may remain. Although the general publication of a "legitimate state secret" is punishable by imprisonment of at least one year,[84] a journalist or publisher who reports on an "illegal" state secret[85] cannot be punished. Despite the uncertainties, the potential dangers for the press are further limited in perhaps the most important cases—those in which the government and courts disagree with the press on the legality of the secret. Publication of a genuine secret by one who, however erroneously, considers it illegal, is not a crime if, *inter alia*, the person acted with the intention to fight the supposed illegal activity, or if his act "according to the circumstances is an adequate means to reach this aim."[86] Adequacy, however, "as a rule,"[87] can be presumed only if prior to disclosure the publisher contacted a member of Parliament and asked him or her to counteract the presumably illegal activities. Inadequate as this "adequacy rule" might be, it constitutes at least an attempt to open an alley to democratic control of potentially dangerous and possibly illegal government decisions. One might decry—or applaud—the fact that the publication of genuine state secrets is still a serious crime. Yet in West German history it remains a considerable advance that sections 94 and 95 distinguish between the spy and traitor who furthers the interest of foreign powers and the journalist who does not share these intentions.

### d.   "Prior restraint and censorship"

For observers from common law jurisdictions it might be briefly mentioned that neither in conflicts between the press and the state nor between the press and the individual has a theory of "prior restraint" developed. If a publication violates private rights or the criminal law, it can be forbidden,[88] and if the publication is already on the market, it can be confiscated by court order.[89] The general impression in German legal opinion is that "prior restraint" is a nonissue and that it is certainly better to avoid harm than to compensate it afterwards. As might be suspected, this agreement is based on the fact that only the independent judiciary, not the administration, can suppress publications. Executive measures to suppress publications would plainly violate the constitutional guarantee[90] against censorship.

In contrast to most countries, no administrative censorship may be established in Germany even in times of extreme internal or external crises. Although certain legal limitations for those crises have been discussed, they were not enacted into law because the Press Council promised to establish professional rules serving this purpose,[91] but so far no such rules have been developed. Had the Press Council established such rules, they certainly would not bind the admittedly few nonmember publications. Because member publications have shown considerable disrespect for Press Council rulings in the past, one might doubt their effectiveness even where members are concerned.

### Legal Practice: Scandals and Possible Dangers

Criminal sanctions may have had both a chilling and a positive effect on freedom of the press. Because most of the criminal provisions discussed above remain untested in actual proceedings, their effect on a democratic system of government is speculative. Some scandals have occurred, however, raising questions about the adequacy of the relevant criminal rules and their interpretation by the administration.

## The Spiegel Affair

The major scandal involving the government and the press was the famous (infamous) *Spiegel* affair. In October 1962, the magazine *Der Spiegel* published a cover story revealing detailed military information about the NATO maneuver "Fallex Sixty-Two." Fallex Sixty-Two was a military exercise designed to simulate a war between the Soviet Union and Western Europe. The *Der Spiegel* article implied that NATO forces, including the West German armed forces, were not adequately prepared to counter an Eastern attack. Many citizens, including the staff of the general prosecutor's office, were amazed and surprised by these discoveries. In response to the article's publication, federal and Hamburg state police raided and searched the *Der Spiegel* offices for several weeks, confiscating large amounts of editorial materials, and jailing several editors. In addition, the then-defense minister Strauss arranged the illegal arrest of *Der Spiegel* journalists who were then abroad. All state officials, except the defense minister, acted legally.

The publisher of *Der Spiegel* filed a complaint with the Federal Constitutional Court. By a four-to-four split decision, the Court[92] issued an unusually long and intensive opinion, in which it held that neither the actions taken—including the raids, confiscations, and intrusions into editorial secrecy—nor the laws on which those actions were based were unconstitutional. A thorough analysis of the decision would reveal that the dissent advanced better arguments for the unconstitutionality of at least some acts and that the lower court judge, who permitted the raids and confiscations, misinterpreted the law by not considering the constitutional guarantee of freedom of the press.[93] For purposes of the present discussion, it is more important to focus on the political and legal consequences of the affair.

Public outrage at the *Spiegel* affair was strong enough to topple a coalition and to force the defense minister to resign.[94] It was influential enough to effect a total revision of the criminal law of treason. And it was the major force leading to the amendments, which limit press risks by providing clear definitions and by distinguishing between the spy, who sells information to foreign powers, and the journalist, who publishes information to promote public discussion.[95]

The *Spiegel* affair affected not only politics and criminal statutes. Criminal law doctrine changed considerably. Prior to the *Spiegel* event, criminal court decisions and legal writing[96] accepted the so-called "mosaic theory." The theory was also upheld by the majority in the *Spiegel* case itself. According to this theory, a person who collects scattered facts, each of which separately is not secret but once unified constitutes a state secret, can be found guilty of treason for publishing the organized material. Because the primary duty of the press is to collect information from all accessible sources, to interpret this information, and to incorporate seemingly irrelevant pieces into a new picture, the mosaic theory presented a grave threat to reporting on military matters. The mosaic theory is not dead, but since the *Spiegel* case no court has applied it, nor has any serious writer supported its use against press publications.

In view of the developments on the political, statutory, and doctrinal levels, it seems that nothing in the history of the Federal Repulic of Germany has enhanced the classic individualistic aspect of freedom of the press more than the attack on the press engendered by the *Spiegel* affair.

## The Frankfurt Airport Case

Until recently, the criminal provisions prohibiting the use of force or threat of force to influence decisions by the constitutionally competent organs[97] were considered practically irrelevant. But a shift may be occurring with the *Frankfurt Airport* case. For many years the government planned to expand the Frankfurt airport. The proposed expansion involved destroying a large forest area and increasing the number of cities exposed to noise from aircraft. These plans, discussed in public and in many court battles[98] for over 10 years, met with bitter opposition by a majority of local citizens and by the new "green" (ecological) movement. For a long time demonstrations took place daily; whole batallions of the police force were, and still are, stationed at the construction site to repel the generally passive, but occasionally violent, resistance. When a new government decision concerning the airport extension was at hand, a mass rally was held in the state capital in which one of the main speakers demanded an antiextension decision from the government by noon the next day. Otherwise, he said, "we'll all take a walk to the airport tomorrow afternoon." The next day thousands of demonstrators approached the airport, rendering it practically inaccessible to passengers and blocking interstate highways for several hours. Viewing the speaker's statement as an illegal threat to use force against the government, the federal prosecutor instituted criminal proceedings against the speaker pursuant to section 105 of the Criminal Code. Although the trial will focus primarily on freedom of speech in the strictest sense—freedom of the spoken word—it also will be of considerable importance to the press, since section 105 does not distinguish between spoken and printed words. It would be futile to forecast the outcome of the trial. Yet, the court will have to consider the value judgment of the constitutional guarantee of freedom of expression, to interpret the phrase "threat of force" (can it be "force" to approach places that are generally freely accessible if thereby the access of others is necessarily hindered?), and to consider very carefully whether the call for a walk implied an intention for illegal actions such as the blocking of highways.

## The Reputation of State and Public Officials

German criminal law contains several provisions that might remind a foreign observer of the infamous doctrine of seditious libel. Section 90 of the Criminal Code prohibits defamation of the federal President by publicly spoken word or print; section 90a protects the Federal Republic and its symbols; and section 90b protects the state and federal legislatures, governments, and constitutional courts and its members against similar public attacks.

In practice, however, sections 90a and 90b have been, and probably will remain, totally unimportant. Although section 90a has been applied several times against persons stealing or destroying flags, no president or other member of government has ever permitted[99] prosecution, and rightly so. If, according to Article 5 of the Basic Law,[100] vigorous, harsh criticism of public officials is an acceptable and necessary part of a democracy, then it is rather difficult to imagine a prosecution under these provisions, which, it should be emphasized, must be interpreted in light of Article 5.[101] One may fantasize only a situation in which publicly spoken or printed avalanches of profanities are launched at the President without any express or implied factual references; in such a case prosecution may ensue. But such developments seem practically remote. The applicability of section 90b is further limited by the requirement that the speaker must "intentionally further activities directed against the existence of the Federal Republic and her basic constitutional rules."[102]

It is hardly surprising that, with few exceptions, litigation concerning the reputation of public figures, whether officials or others, if pursued at all, takes place before the civil rather than the criminal law court.[103] Theoretically, sections 90a and 90b afford more protection to official reputation. Yet in light of Article 5 of the Basic Law actual practice presents a totally different picture. For example, a member of Parliament will rarely succeed under section 90b because of the requirement that the defamer intended to defame the Republic and its basic values. If the member of Parliament attempted to proceed under the regular criminal rules of defamation,[104] he would receive even less protection than a private citizen. Section 193 of the Criminal Code provides that no defamation exists if critical statements are made in the interest of "justified reasons." Today, there is common agreement among courts and scholars that critical supervision of public officials by the press constitutes such a reason.

Although section 90b remained practically irrelevant, for a while it seemed as if section 90a might inhibit underground or alternative newspapers. After the Red Army Faction murdered a prominent judge, an anonymous writer, using the pen name "Mescalero" published an article about the crime in a student paper in the university town of Göttingen. His exact comments remained unknown to the public for a while. After a few days, the whole country learned of one phrase from the article—that the author could not suppress "a secret feeling of happiness" about this murder. Public outrage and legal reaction followed instantly. It may indeed have been in extremely bad taste to express publicly happiness about a murder. The Göttingen courts, however, did not limit their judgments to matters of taste; they confiscated the paper and convicted the responsible editors pursuant to section 90a. Other student papers and individuals who reprinted the Mescalero article faced similar charges. In an attempt to provide the public with more complete information, approximately 30 professors republished the entire Mescalero article. Of those prosecuted some were acquitted and some convicted; others faced disciplinary measures by their employers.[105] After the initial hysteria subsided, most cases involving the reprints ended with acquittals. Because freedom of the press is not intended to guarantee the press *enterprise* as such, but to promote public discussion, it is particularly important not to stifle the spontaneous, unorthodox opinions that are unrepresented in the traditional press.

In conclusion, two points should be emphasized:

1. Despite the hardships suffered by those involved, the scandals and other attacks by the administration on the press led frequently to a public reaction resulting both in a liberalization of the criminal law and in greater press freedom.
2. Sections 90a and 105 of the Criminal Code may, under certain interpretations, stifle free expression.

## Access to Governmental Information

Any democratic government is aware of the crucial role played by the press in forming public opinion. Thus, as a rule governments employ special agencies or officials to provide information to the press. In addition to the official public relations agents, there are the "generally well informed and reliable sources"—government officials or party functionaries close to government—who occasionally leak information to journalists about secret developments, trends, or plans. Given the reality of the electoral process, such information will rarely be lacking. But if the press were limited to this information alone—as it unfortunately seems to be at the local level—it would serve merely as a conduit for government propaganda, and would not fulfill its primary function in a democratic society. Consequently, for the press to perform its role effectively, it must gain access to information that the government would not voluntarily disclose. One might argue that in a democracy all important discussions are held in parliament, whose sessions are open to the public.[106] Such a view would, at best, be naive. It is apparent that in a modern parliamentary democracy many issues have been resolved prior to reaching parliament.

Under German law, the government has no duty to supply any information on its own initiative.[107] Rather, the journalist must actively seek out information. Once the journalist requests information from the government and its agencies, the government has a constitutional duty to reply. The duty to reply is based on the constitutional guarantee of freedom of the press, which is not limited to the final product, and which encompasses the complete process of producing a newspaper or magazine, "beginning with the stage of researching and gaining information and ending with distribution."[108]

The duty to reply has never been seriously tested in the high courts; in particular, the Federal Constitutional Court has not had an opportunity to draw its exact limits. It should be noted that a German journalist confronts higher barriers in gaining access to information than do journalists in countries with freedom of information acts. With few exceptions,[109] files are government business; no outsider may have access to them. Yet, having established the duty to reply, it is obvious that the information contained in government files, or even that which is not filed, is not automatically government property. Scholars generally agree that the state press laws adequately establish the borderline between the "right to know" and the government's interest—not always motivated by self-interest—to classify certain matters.

As mentioned above, the Hamburg statute is representative of the various state press laws. Section 1 of paragraph 4[110] provides that the government has a general duty to answer and lists the reasons justifying a refusal to answer. Under section 2, the government need not answer when (1) criminal, civil, or disciplinary court proceedings might be prejudiced by publication; (2) norms concerning secrecy might be violated; or (3) a compelling public or private interest might be damaged by the disclosure. It is evident that especially clauses (2) and (3) are worded in vague language.[111] At the same time, most practitioners consider paragraph 4 of any state press law as bearing little practical relevance.[112]

If the press and government disagree on whether the requested information should remain undisclosed under section 2, the publisher can seek judicial resolution of the matter. Because of the time factor involved, rarely will a publisher take this approach. Even if the journalist or publisher ultimately wins, hardly anything is gained. "News" of yesterday or yesteryear is, with few exceptions, as uninteresting and unmarketable as stale bread. This is true, even if once victorious in his court battle the journalist claims compensation for the damages incurred by the illegal refusal. Theoretically, such a claim is permitted pursuant to section 839 of the Civil Code[113] and Article 34 of the Constitution. For such a claim to succeed, however, the causal connection between the illegal refusal and the pecuniary loss suffered by the publication would have to be shown. Since any commercial publication contains dozens of articles, it seems impossible to prove that the omitted article would have increased, or prevented, a decrease in sales. Thus, the apparent lack of journalistic resort to the judicial process seems rather justified.

Yet, paragraph 4 of the state press laws is not totally inoperative. In exceptional cases it proves instrumental. For example, there were rumors that members of the big-business community had illegally contributed indirectly to the treasuries of most political parties. Although direct contributions would not have relieved the contributors' tax burdens, contributions to certain clubs and foundations, whose sole purpose was to forward the money to party coffers, were tax exempt—so long as the true aims of the intermediary remained secret. When the state of Northrhine-Westphalia prosecuted some of the contributors for tax evasion, the press could not obtain certain information because the tax laws[114] provided for secrecy. The appellate court of Münster reversed the denial of access. Based on the constitutional right to know and the rule that all generally applicable laws, even tax laws, must be interpreted in light of Article 5 of the Basic Law, the court balanced the interests involved and decided that in a political scandal, in which economically powerful groups could exert an illegal influence on public opinion, the interest in secrecy would have to defer to press freedom.[115]

In general, however, journalists must rely on government leaks and "deep throats" to gain inside information. For this aspect of investigative journalism, two different sets of norms are relevant: (1) rules attempting to inhibit potential informants from disclosing facts to the press, and (2) laws protecting the journalist from forced disclosure of sources.

1.    Among the first set of rules, section 353b and 353c of the Criminal Code play a major role. Any civil servant who discloses a secret, or transfers a document classified as secret, can be punished with a heavy prison sentence. Because the term "secret" is by no means as well defined as the term "state secret,"[116] the dangers for potential informants are obvious. Moreover, the civil service laws of the federation and states impose an obligation of secrecy regarding the information a civil servant receives through his job. Disclosure can lead to fines, reduction in salary, and ultimately, to firing. Those measures seem to be rather effective at

least on the federal and state level; on the local level, gossip can hardly ever be avoided. Nevertheless, even above the local level, secrets are not totally inaccessible to the press. Occasionally, informants are willing to take risks. In addition, Parliament members who are not civil servants are not subject to either the above-described criminal provisions or the civil service laws. As members of parties supporting the government, they have access to many of these "petty secrets." Since they are interested in maintaining a good working relationship with the press, they frequently provide journalists with information.

2.    Informants must rely on press secrecy of their identities. The willingness of civil servants to disclose information would be limited were their identities discoverable in proceedings brought against journalists receiving the information. To avoid such a dilemma, the journalist, as well as everyone involved "in the preparation, making, or distribution of periodicals or radio-broadcasts," has a testimonial privilege regarding "the person of the author or the informant," so long as the information concerns the "editorial"[117] part of the publication.[118] Interpreting an earlier version of the statutory provision that established the privilege, which is still relevant, the Federal Constitutional Court held that not all information received or known to the press was protected by the privilege. For example, a bookkeeper employed by a magazine was held not to be within the realm of the privilege when that magazine was suspected of having bribed prison guards to gain access to a certain prisoner.[119] In that case, the state's interest in punishing severe civil service offenses was considered more important than editorial secrecy.[120]

Two recent cases further illustrate the limits of the privilege. In these cases, the information was not received by the press through informants. Rather, a television company and a newspaper, respectively, covered violent demonstrations. The prosecutors in each case requested access to the films and photographs. The Federal Constitutional Court held that because no informants were involved, the privilege did not apply and the refusals of the paper and radio station were unjustified. Nor, the Court held, was freedom of the press thereby unconstitutionally limited.[121] Some doubts must be expressed. For a police officer raiding the editorial offices of a newspaper it would, at best, be rather difficult to distinguish carefully between leaks and information gathered independently.[122] Furthermore, the ability of the press to cover possibly illegal activities might be severely restricted if, for example, demonstration participants fear that press coverage will contribute to their criminal prosecution. The rocks unfortunately now thrown against police officers might be used against the press. The possible detrimental effects for freedom of the press are, in this writer's opinion, obvious. On an international scale, German law seems somewhat underdeveloped in this respect.

## THE PRESS AND THE JUDICIAL PROCESS

One of the major tenets of classical liberalism is public scrutiny of court proceedings. In a system dedicated to the rule of law, judicial proceedings—not the deliberations of the judges[123]—must take place openly to allow control and criticism in the interest of the accused and of society. While this principle is still widely shared,[124] its justification has changed considerably. It is generally accepted that the original assumptions of direct control are rather illusory. Few people have the time or interest to personally attend and critically survey court sessions. Except for a few sensational cases, every criminal court judge can report on his regular "customers," mainly retired persons. Open court today can contribute to democratic control only if qualified journalists, as representatives of the people, attend and critically report on court sessions, or, at the least, voice their disapproval,[125] thereby providing the sovereign with the information necessary for reform. The same is true regarding civil cases.[126] In exceptional cases the coverage is extensive, informative, and comprehensible, but ordinary civil cases are sometimes even inaccessible to the professional observers, since oral argument may be sparse and the attorneys often merely refer the court to their briefs which are not open to public inspection.

Despite these reservations, it is *communis opinio* that under the present law[127] all court proceedings are open to the public,[128] and thereby open to the press. Consequently, journalists do not face significant problems in gaining access to at least those cases that attract the most interest, that is, criminal proceedings.

There are, however, three primary, and a few minor, barriers to press coverage of court proceedings. These limits are based on concepts having little similarity to the English concept of contempt of court. Only the minor barriers seem to rely on contempt theories. For example, section 169, subsection 2 of the Gerichtsverfassungsgesetz (GVerfG) prohibits radio, television, or movie broadcasts of proceedings on the grounds coverage might inhibit the independent decisions of members of the court, defense, and prosecution. Whether broadcasting can indeed have this effect is a question better suited for a psychologist to answer. A lawyer can merely point out that there exists a certain taboo, which must be explained by experts in other disciplines.

The major barriers rest on a totally different concept, namely, that the person accused or the issues raised, not the court, require protection from public disclosure. By law, the public is excluded from proceedings in which publicity is considered harmful either to one of the parties or to the state. These include family-law proceedings, such as divorce and child custody, and juvenile criminal proceedings which are closed because the legislature does not wish to increase the parties' suffering by opening the sessions to the public.[129] Parallel reasons exclude the public from most proceedings that deal with a person's legal incompetence or confinement to a psychiatric institution.[130] Clearly, similar provisions in dictatorships are frequently abused against political opponents, but in contemporary Germany, the trust in the integrity of the judiciary is so great that abuses are hardly feared. The consequences of exposing highly intimate and unpleasant details about one's life are regarded as more dangerous. After one's personal life is subjected to public scrutiny, including those deviations from "normal" behavior that all individuals share to some degree, it is extremely difficult to resume a "normal" life, even if the judicial result is ultimately favorable. Since the *Lebach* decision of the Federal Constitutional Court,[131] criticism of these provisions has vanished.

Section 172 of the GVerfG permits a court to exclude the public from proceedings for a variety of reasons. In treason cases, it is obvious that state secrets should not be discussed in an open forum. In rape cases, a victim might be inhibited from speaking freely if he or she had to testify before the public and be faced with publicity. Other reasons include the difficulty children might have in testifying before large audiences, or the potential sanctions awaiting witnesses who disclose legitimate trade secrets. To avoid these difficulties, the public may be excluded by court order.[132] The press is necessarily excluded from all cases in which the proceedings are not open to the public by law. But whenever a court has discretion to exclude the public by court order, the press is not automatically excluded. Courts must take into account Article 5, section 2 of the Constitution and the theories developed in that context.[133] Thus, the Court must determine whether the purposes served by closure require merely a limitation on the number of spectators or whether the purposes would be served only by closing the hearing to everybody. For example, if a child needs an intimate atmosphere in order to be willing to testify, the court can reduce the number of spectators and permit a few reporters to attend rather than close the hearing to all members of the public. Even in cases concerning national security, the court may allow journalists to attend. If, however, they publicize the information, they can be punished under section 353d(1) of the Criminal Code. In other cases, the court may order that journalists admitted to nonpublic proceedings remain silent about the facts discussed,[134] or face criminal sanctions.[135]

Arguably, these criminal provisions render press admission to nonpublic proceedings a farce. Critics should note, however, that while disclosure of facts revealed in the *in camera* proceedings is illegal, other facts, including reports on the behavior of the officials involved, may be legally disclosed and permit greater control than would total exclusion. A journalist might also add that there is no better leak than the journalist himself; at least scandalous facts would soon be presented to the general public.

While there is no empirical evidence, it seems that the press has been admitted rather frequently to nonpublic court sessions. Overreaction by a few judges against reporters has been met with public disapproval and immediately corrected by the Constitutional Court.[136] The growth of a few alternative newspapers might change this attitude considerably. The general admission of the press was based on an implicit sense of cooperation between the court and professional journalists and on the expectation that journalists will honor the court's wish that certain information remain undisclosed. Such cooperation can hardly be expected from the alternative press, whose members consider themselves not journalists but ordinary citizens voicing their opinions, impressions, and reactions. The *Brokdorf* case[137] illustrates the problem:

After a mass rally against a new nuclear plant, serious clashes between demonstrators and the police developed which left dozens of people badly wounded. During the first trial of a demonstrator accused of violence against certain policemen, sympathizers of the defendants severely disturbed proceedings. The court excluded the public—in accordance with section 177 GVerfG. It allowed, however, the presence of journalists whose credentials were established by a "press-ID." This ID is issued by the press unions. Three observers of the "alternative" press, who, of course, did not carry such IDs, sought an injunction from the Constitutional Court. The justice on duty, obviously unable to determine whether the applicants were journalists, took a most unusual step. He did not prepare a decision of the court, but wrote a letter stating that he, personally, had serious doubts whether the press could be limited to people identified by IDs issued by private institutions. The local court, also making legal history, accepted this "private" hint, and immediately overturned the earlier decision by admitting the three applicants. The next day, dozens of people, including at least some who were rightfully excluded, presented credentials issued by alternative papers and were admitted. As a result, the audience in the nonpublic session on the following days was more or less identical to members of the public who had been excluded the preceding day.[138]

Since the traditional justification of freedom of the press is the protection of unorthodox views, unpleasant to the mainstream and critical of established institutions, it would be a perversion to offer them less protection. It seems unprincipled to grant more privileges to the established press, than to the "new" press. If, however, the alternative press does not distinguish between journalists and others, the liberal attitude toward the press as a whole might vanish. If that happens, both the professional journalist and the alternative reporter might find themselves outside the courtroom. The trick used by the new press, amusing and charming as it might seem at first glance, might in the end result in the public remaining less informed about certain court proceedings.

## THE PRESS AND SOCIETY, ESPECIALLY THE INDIVIDUAL

At the end of the nineteenth century, the protection of reputation was, at least for the ruling classes, mostly an extralegal affair. The clearing in the middle of the forest where the duel would be fought—not the courtroom—served as a forum to resolve conflicts of honor. The original version of the Criminal Code of 1870 recognized this practice by distinguishing between, on the one hand, battery, manslaughter, and murder, and on the other, the duel.[139] During the Weimar Republic and the early years of the Federal Republic, the main instruments protecting reputation, even for the "better" classes, were the defamation sections of the Criminal Code.[140] Civil courts were rarely approached. Section 823, subsection 2 of the Bürgerliches Gesetzbuch (BGB), which provides for damages whenever a law intended to protect a person is violated, theoretically opened the doors to civil litigation, but since monetary loss had to be proved, this rule remained largely inoperative. A slightly more important, but not prominent, role was played by section 824 of the BGB, providing for damages for the intentional publication of false factual statements detrimental to the business or professional interests of the individual.

During the last 20 years, the criminal courts have rarely been used in conflicts between members of society and the press. The battles now are overwhelmingly fought in civil court. This change was caused not by a modification of statutory law but by a radically new attitude of the civil courts. They "discovered" a "right of personality,"[141] which includes a right not to be defamed and a right to privacy. Even more important, despite the fact that section 253 of the BGB expressly allows damages for nonmonetary losses only when authorized by a statutory provision,[142] and despite the fact that governmental attempts to introduce such provisions for violations of the "right of personality"[143] had failed in Parliament, the Federal Supreme Court "found" that damages for pain and suffering were permitted in "personality right" cases. The Federal Constitutional Court rejected the challenge that the Federal Supreme Court had overstepped the limit set by the constitutional separation of powers, and affirmed the Supreme Court's holding.[144] While questions still remain concerning the adequacy of the theoretical foundation for this decision,[145] its result is seldom questioned.

An individual faced with unpleasant press reports may (1) use his right of reply under the state press laws whenever factual statements were made[146]; (2) suppress the report if he hears about it before publication, or at least prevent its reprint, under section 823(1) and section 1004 of the Civil Code, whenever his "personality right" has been violated; (3) seek damages if publication has led to financial losses; and (4) seek compensation for pain and suffering whenever his "personality right" has been gravely and/or recklessly[147] violated. A person whose business interests have been attacked might also rely on the "right to the enterprise."[148] According to this rather vague concept, which originally was developed for conflicts not involving the press,[149] all acts immediately affecting a business venture may be illegal and may provide grounds for suppressing the publication or seeking damages for financial losses.

The questions raised by these two newly developed "rights" cannot be discussed adequately within the scope of this essay. For our purposes, it is sufficient to point out that relief is not granted whenever the personality or the enterprise is harmed by publication. Rather, the court must weigh the interests involved. Thus, a reporter who criticizes a person or a product is not presumed to act illegally; he is liable if, and only if, his and the public's interests do not override the interests of the person or business venture attacked.[150] Since no scales have been or could be constructed that objectively and precisely weigh those interests, some uncertainty remains. The uncertainty is, however, limited by the case law, which has produced certain clear categories and guidelines for the most frequent clashes, including the following:

- Whenever a person's name or picture is used for advertising without permission, the person's personality right overrides the advertiser's interests, entitling that person to damages for nonmonetary losses.[151]
- In principle, there is a consensus among courts and scholars that a person has a "right to be left alone"—that there simply must be some areas of a person's private behavior that should not be discussed in public. This principle applies, for example, to conversations in the home or on the telephone, as well as to sexual behavior. But there are circumstances when the legitimate interests of the public and mass media might override the interests of the individual. An illegally tape recorded telephone conversation, which discusses burning political questions, and which the press receives, is not banned from publication.[152] A publisher, well known for championing in his papers the fight against vice, may not complain when critics report his participation in orgies.[153] An employee who witnesses a violation of the law at his workplace generally first must seek internal redress by appealing to the workers' council or employer. However, when an investigating journalist researching the methods of a boulevard paper gained employment under a pretext, he was free to publish his findings and opinions, with the exception of a few intimate conversations among colleagues, without first seeking internal redress.[154] An artisan's family, which had never before attracted public attention, received damages for an article reporting their minor child's elopment to Scotland with a friend, despite the "human interest" of the story.[155]
- There is general agreement among lawyers and within the press council[156] that reports of court proceedings concerning juveniles or

minor offenders may not identify the defendant or convicted criminal. Thus, unlike American newspapers, the German press does not report the names of individuals involved in offences such as motor vehicle violations, trespass, or minor theft. Indeed, courts could prevent publication were German reporters to imitate the foreign press. If, however, a public official were involved, publication would be permitted.

- It is generally considered legitimate to identify the personalities involved in cases of major crimes, *e.g.*, murder, arson, kidnapping, and treason. As the *Lebach* case[157] demonstrates, however, this right is not unlimited. The more a publication might inhibit the socialization process of a convicted felon, the less it is entitled to identify the principals involved. Yet, if a prominent citizen, for example, the president, the board chairman of a big company, or a famous author, had committed the same crimes, their involvement could be openly discussed.

- In feuds between politicians or politically or otherwise strongly opposed papers, public discussion must remain uninhibited. The limits are reached when a paper or politician engages in *böswillige Schmähkritik*[158]—a term nearly impossible to translate accurately but meaning "malicious mudslinging." The more "mud" thrown at the speaker, the freer his counterattacks can be.

- When statements of fact are made, the subject of the publication is in a better position: he or she can use the rather ineffective[159] right of reply or can prohibit either the initial publication or repetition of a false statement. Prohibiting the publication is effective, since in "clear" cases the court will issue a temporary injunction against the paper.[160] If the violation of the personality right was grave and/or grossly negligent, the victim can seek damages for nonmonetary losses.[161]

- In business matters, the courts for quite a while were inclined to establish taboo zones. In order not to violate "the right of the enterprise,"[162] criticism of a business venture or product had to be "objective," and had to be published in the least damaging form. This doctrine would have led to a strange imbalance in public discussion since the business man was not bound to objectivity and could manipulate public relations to promote his product. Guided by the Federal Constitutional Court,[163] the Federal Supreme Court finally reversed its attitude. Presently opinions about companies, products, or services violate the law only if the critic intended to harm the company without adequate cause and did so in a ruthless form.[164] Consequently, a consumer group or journal which tests products may judge the product "bad" or "mediocre," so long as neutrality and objective testing methods are maintained. The Federal Supreme Court avoided the role of a National-Super-Testing Institute, with the attendant risk of thereby eliminating all consumer protection activity. It does not decide the correctness of the conclusions, so long as the testing methods were fair[165]

These few examples illustrate both the certainty that has emerged from the case law and the uncertainties that remain. No reasonably cautious editor or publisher would dare to publish fictitious interviews, illustrate an article about a scandal with the pictures of persons not involved in the scandal, or falsely attribute a statement to an individual. The damages generally awarded in these cases are too high[166] to run such a risk; unfavorable publicity following the judgment might be a further deterrent. Attempts by this author to ascertain whether liability insurance might not alleviate these generally presumed deterrents brought an unexpected result. Two of the largest publishing houses reported they had never heard of the possibility and that their papers were not covered by such insurance; the third one responded that, of course, it carried such insurance.[167] But even in this third case, it may be that an insurance company indirectly helps maintain some deterrent element by adjusting its rates to reflect the potential damage awards.

Most likely, a journalist or attorney looking for certainty in the law would be even more distressed by other uncertainties of present German law. In many borderline situations it seems impossible to forecast a decision for two reasons. First, as has been shown, most decisions rely on a sliding scale. The more a person has previously been in the public limelight, the greater the possible scandal; and the greater the political importance of the current issue, the more the press is entitled to invade otherwise closed areas. Second, on its face, the distinction between fact and opinion seems clear and reasonable. In practice,[168] however, the distinction blurs because almost every statement contains elements that both recount and interpret an event. The many court battles in which lower and higher courts disagreed strongly over the correct categorization of a statement illustrates the imprecision of the distinction.[169] The tendency of the higher courts in doubtful cases to characterize a statement as "opinion," thereby enlarging the area of free public discussion, preserves some certainty.

## PRIVATE ARRANGEMENTS WHICH AFFECT THE ROLE OF THE PRESS IN SOCIETY

### Individual and Group Access to the Press

Because newspapers are privately owned, the owner, or frequently the editor-in-chief, decides what to print. Despite the possibility that as a result certain issues might be censured or treated in a false light, individual access to the press has never been seriously considered. With the exception of the right of reply (*Gegendarstellungsanspruch*), it is generally agreed that unlimited individual access to the press would prove chaotic. Reasonable limits have yet to be discovered.

## The Right of Reply[170]

The right of reply, first introduced by the Reichspressgesetz of 1874, is now found in nearly uniform language in the state press laws and in the rules governing most radio stations.[171] The underlying legislative rationale has never been to protect the democratic process and public opinion but to safeguard individuals against false press reports. The protection afforded, however, is rather limited. The press must print a reply if, and only if, they published *factual* statements about a person and the reply is limited to correcting these facts. Furthermore, although the legislature intended to give citizens a simple operational tool,[172] the details of the right of reply are highly complicated. Without much exaggeration it can be said that a citizen's demand for a reply, made without the help of an experienced press lawyer, will prove futile. Even if all formalistic details are observed and a paper prints the reply, the effects are rather limited since the editor may add a so-called "tail" informing the readers that he was legally required to print the reply regardless of its veracity, and that he maintains his original position.

## Group Rights

Group rights are of greater concern than individual rights. It is assumed that problems worthy of public discourse are, as a rule, taken up not by a single person but by more or less organized groups. Group access to and influence on the media continues to be a major topic in "radio law" and, to a much lesser extent, in press law. Several proposals to counteract the publisher's monopoly have been submitted. For example, it has been suggested that the state establish and finance press foundations controlled by representatives of the "relevant groups" in society,[173] or that monopoly papers introduce a "pluralistic page"[174] which would regularly publish the opinions of these groups. None of these proposals has been implemented.

There has been a broader discussion of the *internal* freedom of the press. A strong faction of the legal and journalistic community argues that in an era of ever-increasing concentration, the press's vital role in a democratic society can best be secured by guaranteeing journalists basic independence. Once freed from a publisher's daily interference, the individual journalist's professional standards would best ensure a high level of quality reporting. Further, this freedom would allow journalists to discuss freely the problems they consider of public importance, in the manner they feel suitable.[175] An array of different organizational measures was suggested to ensure journalistic freedom, including (1) the journalists' right to veto the appointment or dismissal of the editor-in-chief who would be in charge of all other journalistic hiring and firing, but only with majority approval of the journalists; (2) a measure prohibiting the owner from interfering in the daily editorial decision making and limiting him to formulating the paper's basic policy. In the event of a change in policy, the journalists could stop working but continue to receive their regular income for up to one year.

These and similar proposals were in vogue in the late 1960s and 1970s. Yet, although the federal government's message to Parliament in 1976 promised to implement such a policy, and although the Ministry of the Interior prepared several drafts of a code ensuring the "internal freedom of the press," the proposals have since drawn little attention. The government's message to Parliament in 1980 referred the problem to the "autonomous decision" of the "social partners" (*Sozialpartner*—a German euphemism for both unions and employers), to be binding on all newspaper owners and unions before the government takes action. Practically speaking, a regulation of internal freedom has been thereby postponed indefinitely, since without the threat of legal measures there is no valid reason for owners to voluntarily relinquish any of their power. Once again, the old rule that it is impossible to pass any legislation against massive opposition by the press has proven correct. It should be mentioned, however, that some owners have formed private agreements with their journalists that fulfill some of these proposals.[176]

## Concentration in the Press Markets

Most counties in the Federal Republic are served by only one daily newspaper.[177] The largest cities in the country, West Berlin and Hamburg, offer several daily newspapers, although most are owned by the same publisher, the Springer group. The choice in Sunday papers is between *Bild am Sonntag* and *Welt am Sonntag*, both Springer papers holding 97.8 percent of the market.[178] The magazine market shows a similar development. The four largest publishing groups occupy a 62.9 percent share of the market.[179] Except for two alternative newspapers begun by the Young Left, which are failing economically, new papers have not appeared. New magazines keep appearing and in large numbers but are mostly geared toward special interests such as sports, electronics, fashions, and sex.

This concentration has been of prime concern in a country whose basic rationale for protecting freedom of the press is the press's role in forming public political opinion.[180] The magnitude of this concern is illustrated by the abundance of legal literature on the subject and by the fact that the federal legislature received reports on this problem from two expert commissions.[181] Indeed, one of the main demands of the 1968 student revolt was to "socialize Springer," and today several hundred of the most well-known writers and intellectuals refuse to cooperate with Springer in any way. The name "Springer" has become a symbol for concentration problems in general. Less noticed than the activities of this publisher, but equally notable, are other developments. A publisher in Northrhine-Westphalia obtained a near monopoly in the Ruhr area by using extremely aggressive tactics in a manner comparable to early Rockefeller tactics. In areas where he could not buy up independent papers, he undercut their prices in both the buyer and advertising markets, while raising the prices in the cities he had already monopolized.[182]

It is impossible to give even a partial report of the proposals to counteract this situation. In addition to the suggestions mentioned above,[183] it can be pointed out that there have been attempts to use the Law Against Unfair Competition. While not useless in defending against a few aggressive tactics by the market leaders, it has basically failed as an instrument against concentration. The only concrete reform that emerged from the concentration discussion was a change in the Cartel Law. By a law of June 28, 1976, a stringent merger control has been instituted for all large and medium-sized publishing houses.[184] A merger can be forbidden by the Federal Cartel Agency (*Bundeskartellamt*) whenever a strengthening of one of the partner's dominant position will result. Only in exceptional cases, which have not yet occurred, can the Federal Minister of Economy grant special permission to merge. It would be false to set hopes too high for this Cartel Law reform. It is true, however, that it has been used several times to fend off the further external growth of mainly the Springer and the Bertelsmann groups. While these groups can no longer buy, or gain a significant influence over, other papers, the problems of internal growth and of economies of scale remain. New newspapers are not to be expected on the market; the barriers to new competition seem insurmountable. The concentration process, at least in the newspaper market, will most likely continue unless the government intervenes. Although government subsidies have been discussed frequently and once actually provided,[185] it seems highly unlikely that a government subsidy plan will be introduced. Besides empty coffers, the main reason for the reluctance of the state is the possibility that such subsidies would be unconstitutional.[186] Generally, it is feared that government money would soon bring about state influence and control.

## Self-Control of the Press

In 1956 the two largest publishing organizations and the two relevant journalist unions joined in instituting a self-control organ modeled on the

British Press Council. The Deutscher Presserat, founded as a private association, consists of twenty individual members, divided equally between delegates of the publishers and the unions. Its proclaimed aims are to recognize and eliminate grievances, to investigate complaints about specific publications and if necessary to reprimand the newspaper or magazine, to establish guidelines for ethical standards, to ensure free access to news sources, to counteract dangers to free information and the process of forming public opinion, which monopolization has brought, and to submit proposals to the legislature.[187] Members of the Presserat are independent of the delegating organizations. Up to five "lay men" can be, but in practice are not, appointed to participate in the council's decision making.

The Presserat has developed a remarkable Code of Ethics (*Publizistische Grundsätze—Pressekodex*), supplemented by Guidelines for Editorial Work (*Richtlinien für die redaktionelle Arbeit*), which delineate in detail professional standards for a wide variety of issues, ranging from letters to the editor, drug problems, and race relations, to court reporting and medical topics. Undoubtedly, the Presserat has played an important advisory role to the government and legislatures on many regulatory proposals concering the press. One of the highlights of its advisory role was the successful fight against attempts to introduce constitutional limitations on press freedom in times of war or internal states of emergency. The Presserat promised to guard state secrets during these situations by means of self-control. Furthermore, a special committee of the Presserat, led by a prominent judge, has handled numerous individual complaints about press reports. The legislature has even recognized the importance of the Presserat by supplying a part of the funds necessary to guarantee the independence of the committee.

Nevertheless, the authority of the Presserat has been substantially weakened in recent years. Its basic assumption—that journalists, whether publisher-owners or employees, were motivated by the same spirit—has proven increasingly unrealistic. Publishers complain bitterly that the unions do not assign independent persons possessing wisdom, experience and repute, but rather functionaries who attempt to pursue union interests. Journalists point out that publishing has long lost its dedication to public enlightenment and, in many cases, is merely another business. They have been particularly enraged by the fact that precisely those publishing houses that were the targets of the code and guidelines have steadfastly refused to publish the Presserat's reprimands. The unions currently threaten to leave the organization.

Everyone, including the unions and the government, would regret to see the Presserat disappear. Government intervention is unwelcome by all concerned. Adequate solutions to the present crisis or proposals for reorganization are, however, not in sight.

## CONCLUSION

In the strictest, most traditional sense, a wide range of controversies exist in German press law today. Although many of these issues are important enough to demand further deliberation, they do not play a major role in current discussions. A consensus exists that the relationship of the state to the press and of the press to the individual is adequately served by the present process of free discussion. Seemingly hopeless attempts to battle further concentration directly, or indirectly by establishing more freedom for employed journalists, attract considerably more attention. Yet today, the focus is on the electronic media, and on questions such as should the electronic media, now operated publicly, but independently of the state, be opened to private enterprise; if so, under what conditions should such an opening be permissible; will cross-ownership of print and electronic media diminish the free exchange of differing points of view; or will the exclusion of print media owners from radio and television result in the demise of the traditional press because of the potential loss of advertising income; and what effects will commercial television have on family life, on children, and eventually on society as a whole?

These are the questions most frequently discussed in Germany today. Within a few years, it will be impossible to contribute a paper to an overview only of press law. Mass media law will be the topic.

## NOTES*

1.  The Bishop's actions preceded by one year the papal bull *Inter Multiplices*, which made *censura praevia* (censorship prior to publication) obligatory for all Roman Catholic bishops. That this was a reaction to the powers of the printing press can hardly be disputed; until this time even the notorious Inquisition was satisfied with *censura repressiva* (censorship after publication). *See generally* F. Schneider, *Pressefreiheit und politische Öffentlichkeit* (1966); D. Stammler, *Die Presse als soziale und verfassungsrechtliche Institution* (1971).

2.  Mainly books and flyers were published. Periodicals were not yet in existence.

3.  The term *Pressefreiheit* ("freedom of the press") was still unknown.

4.  Reichspressgesetz, 1874 Reichsgesetzblatt [RGB1] 65.

5.  M. Löffler and R. Ricker, *Handbuch des Presserechts* 24 (1978).

6.  Only a few, mainly socialist, authors were critical. *See, e.g.,* Lassalle, *Die Feste, die Presse und der Frankfurter Abgeordnetentag*, in 3 *Gesammelte Reden und Schriften* 333, 360–368 (1919).

7.  For details *see* O. Groth, 3 *Die Zeitung* 105 (1928–1930).

8.  *See, e.g.,* the discussion of the 4th Congress of the Association of Constitutional Law Teachers (*Vereinigung Deutscher Staatsrechtslehrer* [VDStRL]) in 4 *Veröffentlichungen* (VDStRL ed. 1924).

*Unless otherwise indicated, translations are by the author.

9.  1933 RGB1 I 661.
10.  The *Kammer* was a fascist version of a writers, artists, and actors union.
O. Hale, *The Captive Press in the Third Reich* (1964).
11.  1933 RGB1 I 713.
12.  Grundgesetz [GG] art. 5, §1.
13.  The Federal Constitutional Court (*Bundesverfassungsgericht*) stands at the apex of West Germany's judicial system. It deals exclusively with constitutional disputes. Beneath the Constitutional Court are the Federal Supreme Courts—the highest federal courts of appeals. Because the legal system is divided into specialized jurisdictions, such as ordinary civil and criminal matters, labor, finance, etc., there is a Federal Supeme Court for each jurisdictional area. All other courts are state courts, which are also divided into specialized jurisdictions. D. Kommers, *Judicial Politics in West Germany* (1976).
14.  10 Bundesverfassungsgerichts [BVerfG] 121 (1959) (*Freiheitlich-demokratische Grundordnung*).
15.  20 BVerfG 162, 174 (1966).
16.  *Id.*
17.  *See, e.g.,* 35 BVerfG 202, 222 (1973); 12 BVerfG 113, 125 (1961); 12 BVerfG 205, 260 (1961).
18.  35 BVerfG 202, 223–24 (1973).
19.  Some observers find this concept rather naive because it clings to the traditional liberal conception of the press as voluntarily and/or more or less mechanically serving enlightenment ideas. For example, Luhmann considers it unrealistic to assume that citizens act rationally; he points out that the mass media reduce the complexity of the world, thereby absorbing potential social conflict and raising the acceptance level of the public. N. Luhmann, *Legitimation durch Verfahren* 126 (1969). Other authors argue that commercial interests and enlightenment ideas—at least under the complex conditions of modern mass media production—cannot be reconciled, and that consequently the periodical press should be turned over to organizations independent of state *and* individual business interests. *See, e.g.,* D. Stammler, *supra* note 1, at 337, 349.
20.  GG art. 19, §2.
21.  *See infra* text, at note 54.
22.  2 BVerfG 124, 128 ff. (1953).
23.  GG art. 100, §1.
24.  Law of March 12, 1952 concerning the Federal Constitutional Court, Bundesverfassungsgerichtsgesetz [BVerfGG] §31 (1952).
25.  *Id.* §90.
26.  50 BVerfG 234 (1979).
27.  As to the limits in these cases *see* 25 BVerfG 296, 305 (1969).
28.  *See supra* text accompanying note 12.
29.  Doubts are expressed about foreign legal entities in 21 BVerfG 208 (1967).
30.  21 BVerfG 271 (1967).
31.  *E.g.,* 35 BVerfG 202 (1973); 34 BVerfG 269 (1973); 25 BVerfG 296 (1969).
32.  34 BVerfG 269, 283 (1973).
33.  50 BVerfG 234, 240 (1979); 34 BVerfG 269, 283 (1973).

34.   34 BVerfG 269 (1973).

35.   35 BVerfG 202 (1973); for a detailed description and analysis *see* W. Hoffman-Riem, H. Kohl, F. Kübler and K. Lüscher, *Medienwirkung und Medienverantwortung* (1975).

36.   The decent journalistic standard of care is not followed if, for example, a journalist falsely attributes statements to a person who has not made them. Everyone is permitted, however, to present his interpretation of another's statements if that "interpretation" is not totally ludicrous.

37.   21 BVerfG 271 (1967).

38.   *Id.*

39.   20 BVerfG 162, 174 (1966).

40.   The government carries this burden in light of art. 5, §2 of the Constitution (for details *see infra* p. 193). It is undisputed that restrictions founded on a legitimate public interest, mainly the protection of minors, are permissible.

41.   12 BVerfG 260 (1961).

42.   25 BVerfG 256 (1969).

43.   The Federal Supreme Court (*Bundesgerichtshof* [BGH]), *see supra* note 13, decided these cases. *E.g.*, Neue Juristische Wochenschrift [NJW] 1971, 2025 (BGH 1971); 51 Bundesgerichtshof in Zivilsachen [BGHZ] 263 (1968); 19 BGHZ 392 (1956).

44.   20 BVerfG 162 (1966); *see* further discussion *infra* at §II.B.2(a).

45.   *Id.* at 176.

46.   *See infra* p. 215.

47.   "Act Against Competition Restrictions."

48.   Mainly, they point out that the law came too late in the process of concentration.

49.   For example, the constitutional guarantee will not bar income tax laws, criminal charges for theft, defamation laws, laws prohibiting the distribution of publications glorifying violence or pornography to children, or the laws of copyright.

50.   This formula was first expressed in a judgment concerning art. 5, §1, sentence 1 of the Constitution, *see* 7 BVerfG, 198, 208, 209 (1958), but has been transferred since to art. 5, §2, sentence 2. *see* 20 BVerfG 176 (1966).

51.   *See supra* notes 12 & 44 and accompanying text.

52.   *See supra* note 4 and accompanying text.

53.   1965 Gesetzes-und Verordnungsblatt der Freien und Hansestadt Hamburg [HGVB1] 15. The Hamburg Press Law is translated and reprinted in U. Schwartz, *Press Law For Our Times* 103-105 (1966).

54.                              Paragraph 1
                           Freedom of the Press

(1)   The press is free. It exists to serve free and democratic institutions.

(2)   The freedom of the press is subject only to those limitations allowed by the Constitution and the provisions of this law.

(3)   Special measures of any kind which encroach upon press freedom are forbidden.

(4)   Professional organizations of the press with compulsory membership and a professional court with statutory powers are not permissible.

(5)   The press is also subject to laws which apply to everyone.

### Paragraph 2
### Freedom of Establishment

Press activity, including the establishment of a publishing house or other works of the press industry, requires no permission.

### Paragraph 3
### Social Function of the Press

The press fulfills a social function especially by collecting and distributing news, expressing its opinion, criticizing or in other ways contributing to the creation of opinion or helping education.

55.                           Paragraph 4
### Right to Information

(1)   It is the duty of officials to give information to representatives of the press and broadcasting which will enable them to fulfill their social function.

(2)   Information may be refused if
    1.   it could encroach upon or damage the proper carrying out of a legal process, trial, imposition of fine or disciplining which has not yet been completed.
    2.   regulations on secrecy or official discretion prevent it or
    3.   a paramount public interest or private interest worthy of protection would be injured by giving information.

(3)   General regulations forbidding an authority to give information to the press are not permissible.

(4)   The publisher of a periodical printed work may require the authorities to supply him with official communications no later than his competitors.

*See* further discussion *infra* at p. 204.

56.                           Paragraph 5
### Publication of Official Documents

The press and broadcasting companies may not publish charge sheets or other official documents concerned in a criminal trial or imposition of a fine before they have been mentioned in open court or the case has been closed.

57.                           Paragraph 6
### The Press's Duty to Take Care

The press must check the accuracy, content and source of all news prior to publication with all the care appropriate to the circumstances. This does not affect the obligation to keep printed works free of offending content (Paragraph 19).

58.                           Paragraph 7
### Printed Works

(1)   Printed works within the meaning of this law are all writings, spoken sound recordings, pictorial representations with and without writing and music with text or commentary which are produced by printing presses or other means of duplication suitable for mass production and intended for distribution.

(2)   Printed works include also the duplicated communications with which news agencies, press correspondents, matrix services and other enterprises supply the press by word, picture or other means. Similarly regarded as printed works are the communications delivered by an editorial subsidiary, irrespective of the technical form in which they are delivered, and news reels.

(3)   Not subject to the provisions of this law are
1.   official printed works provided that they contain official communications exclusively,
2.   printed works which only serve the purpose of business and traffic, domestic and social life such as forms, price lists, advertising matter, family announcements, trading reports, annual reports and directors's reports and similar publications, voting forms.

(4)   Periodical printed works are newspapers, magazines and other publications appearing at permanent if irregular intervals of not more than six months.

59.                         Paragraph 8
                            Imprint

(1)   In every printed work appearing in the Hanse Free State of Hamburg, the name or firm and address of the printer and publisher must be given; in the case of works personally published by the author, the author or the publisher must be named.

(2)   Periodical printed works must also give the name and address of the responsible editor. If several persons are responsible editors, the imprint must contain the required details of each of them. The section or range of subjects for which each is responsible is to be shown. A responsible person must be named for the advertising section: the appropriate regulations concerning the responsible editor apply to him.

(3)   Newspapers and subsidiary newspapers which regularly take over important sections already prepared elsewhere must name in the imprint the editor responsible for the part taken over and the publisher of the other printing works.

60.   This disqualification can only be pronounced by a criminal court for very severe crimes (*cf.* the Code of Criminal Law, Strafgesetzbuch [StGB] §§45, 108c, 358) or by the Constitutional Court pursuant to §39 of the BVerfGG (a practically unimportant norm).

61.                         Paragraph 9
            Personal Qualifications of the Responsible Editor

(1)   A person may act or be employed as responsible editor only if he
1.   is permanently a resident within the area covered by the Constitution (Grundgesetz),
2.   is in full possession of civil rights and has not been disqualified from public office by a court,
3.   has completed his 21st year,
4.   is under no legal disqualification from conducting business.

(2)   The requirements of Section 1, Clauses 3 and 4 do not apply to printed works produced by young people for young people.

(3)   Upon application being made, the responsible authority may in special cases waive the application of Section 1, Clause 1.

62.                                                Paragraph 20
                               Punishable Offences Against the Press Law
Punishment of up to one year's imprisonment or money fine will be imposed on persons deliberately
   1.  publishing official documents contrary to Paragraph 5
   2.  engaging in the capacity of publisher, a person as responsible editor who does not meet the requirements of Paragraph 9
   3.  signing as responsible editor although not fulfilling the requirements of Paragraph 9
   4.  in the capacity of responsible editor or publisher—in the case of author-publisher as author or publisher—breaking the rules on the imprint (Paragraph 8) in a work containing offending matter
   5.  contrary to the ban in Paragraph 15, distributing or reproducing a work subject to a seizure order.

63.   *See infra* at p. 202.

64.                                                Paragraph 19
                                    Criminal Law Responsibility
(1)   The responsibility for criminal action committed by means of a printed work is decided by the general criminal law.
(2)   If a crime is committed by means of a printed work, provided that there is no liability as criminal or accomplice under Section 1 for this crime, punishment of up to one year's imprisonment or money fine may be imposed on
   1.  the responsible editor in the case of periodical printed works if he has deliberately or negligently failed in his duty to keep the publication free from offending matter,
   2.  the publisher in the case of other publications, if he has deliberately or negligently failed in his supervisory duty and the commission of the crime therefore became possible.

65.                                                Paragraph 10
                               Identification of Paid Publications
If the publisher of a periodical printed work has received, requested or been promised payment for the publication of an item, he must clearly indicate this publication with the word "advertisement," if it is not already generally recognizable as an advertisement because of its arrangement and form.

66.   *See, e.g.,* M. Löffler and R. Ricker, *supra* note 5, at 75.
67.   According to the Hamburg Pressegesetz §21–1(2) they are misdemeanors.
68.   For details *see infra* p. 214.
69.   *Cf.* 36 BVerfG 193 (1973); 36 BVerfG 314 (1974); 38 BVerfG 103 (1974) in which the Constitutional Court held that the right to refuse to give evidence was a procedural rule, and thereby a federal, not a state, matter. For details of the federal legislation *see infra* at 117.

70. The Federation possesses legislative power to regulate the general conditions of the press. *See* GG art. 75, no. 2.

71. For the most important draft *see Vorentwurf eines Gesetzes über die allgemeinen Rechtsverhältnisse der Presse*, Recht der Arbeit 1974 [R&A] 303.

72. 1968 Bundesgesetzblatt [BGBl] I 741.

73. Law of April 22, 1976, 1976 BGBl I 1056.

74. *Staatsbürgerliche Aufklärung.*

75. Law of Aug. 7, 1981, 1981 BGBl I 808.

76. *See supra* text accompanying notes 49–50.

77. StGB §§86–1(1), 86a–1.

78. *Id.* §86–2.

79. *Id.*

80. *See infra* text accompanying notes 97–98.

81. Since §92 clearly defines these principles, the judiciary has little elbow room for construing it in an authoritative spirit. Included are the right of the people to vote, the right to form an opposition, the guarantee for a democratic change of power, the independence of the judiciary.

82. StGB §§93–101a. For details see explanations to §§93–101a in the commentaries, *e.g.,* A. Schönke and H. Schröder, *Kommentar zum StGB,* 830–858 (1982).

83. StGB §97a.

84. *Id.* §94–1(2).

85. *Cf. id.* §93–2.

86. *Id.* §97b.

87. Id. §97b–1 (sent. 2).

88. For an example in the private sector see the *Lebach*-dispute described *supra* at text accompanying note 35.

89. For details *see, e.g.,* B. Rieder, *Die Zensurbegriffe des Art. 118, Abs. 2 der WRV und des Art. 5, Abs. 1, Satz 3 des GG* (1970). Nonprinted works can be confiscated by order of the public prosecutor or the police.

90. *See supra* text accompanying note 12.

91. Code of Criminal Procedure, Strafprozessordnung [StPO] §111n.

92. 20 BVerfG 162 (1966).

93. *Cf.* text accompanying and following note 50.

94. In addition to his abuse of power in this case, the defense minister, Franz Josef Strauss, lied to Parliament about his involvement in the affair. It should be mentioned that public memory is short, or forgiving: the same politician is today the leader of an influential party and Prime Minister of a state.

95. *See supra* text accompanying notes 82–87.

96. *See, e.g.,* 15 Bundesgerichtshof in Strafsachen [BGHSt] 17 (1960).

97. *See supra* text accompanying notes 80–81.

98. The airport company or the government consistently won all court proceedings.

99. No proceedings can be instituted without the permission of the defamed organizations or members. *See* §§90–4, 90b–2 StGB.

100. *See supra* text accompanying note 35–36.

101. *See supra* text accompanying notes 49–50.

102. These "basic rules," well defined by §92–1 of the StGB include

representative democracy, the right to form an opposition, the rule of law, and the independence of the judiciary.

103.   *See* Kübler, in *Die Haftung der Massenmedien, insbesondere der Presse bei Eingriffen in persönliche oder gewerbliche Rechtspositionen* 130 (1972).

104.   StGB §§185–200.

105.   For a detailed report *see* T. Blanke et. al., *Der Oldenburger Buback-Prozess* (1979); U. Mückenberger, *Kritische Justiz* 312 (1979); J. Seifert, *Kritische Justiz* 416 (1981).

106.   Public sessions are mandated by GG art. 42,  1 and corresponding provisions in the state constitutions.

107.   20 BVerfG 162, 176 (1966); 12 BVerfG 205, 260 (1961); 10 BVerfG 118, 121 (1966).

108.   20 BVerfG 162, 176 (1966).

109.   For example, anyone may inspect the trade registry (*Handelsregister*) and everybody having a legitimate interest may inspect the real property title registry; these are both regulated by the courts and established for members of the public interested in trading with a company or in buying property.

110.   For the text of section 4 *see supra* note 55.

111.   For such an attempt *see, e.g.,* R. Gross, *Presserecht* 151–156 (1982).

112.   *E.g.,* Struve, in *Medienrecht* 18, 21 (Schiwy and Schütz, ed., 1977).

113.   Bürgerliches Gesetzbuch [BGB] §839.

114.   *See* Abgabenordnung §30.

115.   Archiv für Presserecht [AfP] 1980, 285 (Oberlandsgericht [OLG] Hamm 1980).

116.   StGB §93 and *supra* at note 73.

117.   This term is used in order to exclude the privilege with regard to advertisements.

118.   StPO §53, no. 5.

119.   25 BVerfG 296 (1969).

120.   *Id.* at 306.

121.   AfP 1981, 342 (BVerfG 1981).

122.   Gerhardt, *note* to BVerfG AfP 1981, 342.

123.   Whenever the term "judge" is used it applies equally to professional and lay members of the bench since their duties are identical. Both must decide on matters of fact and law.

124.   A recent discussion, held during the most influential lawyers' convention—the meeting of the Deutsche Juristentag—in Nürnberg in September 1982, led to a nearly unanimous rejection of a suggestion to close criminal courts to the public. *See* 2 *Verhandlungen des 53. Deutschen Juristentags* K162 (1982).

125.   For this approach *see, e.g.,* J. Scherer, *Gerichtsöffentlichkeit als Medienöffentlichkeit* (1981).

126.   This, however, does not mean that the court is open, since only members of the press are admitted. AfP 1970, 66 (BGH 1969).

127.   Rules of Court, Gerichtsverfassungsgesetz [GVerfG] §169.

128.   *See, e.g.,* those concerning the airport extension in Frankfurt, discussed *supra* at text accompanying note 98.

129.   GVerfG §170; Jugendgerichtsgesetz (JGG) §48.

130.   GVerfG §§171, 171(a).

131.  *See supra* note 35 and accompanying text.

132.  This exclusion order is subject to appellate judicial review.

133.  *See supra* note 50 and accompanying text.

134.  GVerfG §174–3.

135.  StGB §353d(2).

136.  In the most spectacular case, a Cologne judge severely criticized by a local alternative paper, excluded a reporter from open session so that the paper could not continue its practice of "untrue" and "defamatory reporting" about the judge. 50 BVerfG 236, 243 (1979). The Federal Constitutional Court gave the judge a proper lesson on the constitutional guarantee of freedom of the press.

137.  The case is as yet unreported. The following description is based on press reports and information received from justices of the Federal Constitutional Court.

138.  Because of an insufficient number of reliable sources, I do not wish to imply that this is a completely accurate description. For the purposes of this discussion, it seems sufficient to note that the facts reported are based on second-hand information, that they are not unlikely, and that if they did not actually occur in this case, they may occur in the future.

139.  R. Höinghaus, *Das neue Strafgesetzbuch für den Norddeutschen Bund* 44 (1870). The sanctions for dueling provided for shorter terms of detention and, more importantly, for honorable detention—*custodia honestas*—in special institutions with fewer restrictions on personal liberty.

140.  StGB §§185–200.

141.  The leading case was the *Schacht-Brief* decision. 13 BGHZ 334 (1954).

142.  In statutory law damages are authorized only in cases where the physical integrity, liberty, or sexual self-determination of an individual has been violated. BGB §§847, 1300.

143.  *Cf. Regierungsentwurf eines Gesetzes zur Neuordnung des zivilrecht-lichen Persönlichkeitsschutzes* of Aug. 18, 1959, BT-Drucksache III 1237; *Reform-entwurf eines Gesetzes zur Änderung und Ergänzung schadenersatzrechtlicher Vorschriften.*

144.  *Soraya, Juristenzeitung* [JZ] 1973, 662 (BVerfG 1973). (Kübler's note)

145.  Kohl, in 3 *Alternativkommentar zum BGB [AK-BGB]* §847 nn. 31–40 (1980).

146.  *See infra* §V.A.1.

147.  *E.g.,* NJW 1971, 698 (BGH 1971); *id.* at 1077; 35 BGHZ 363 (1961).

148.  "*Recht am Unternehmen*" or "*Recht am eingerichteten und ausgeübten Gewerbebetrieb.*"

149.  *See* Däubler in *AK-BGB* §823 nn. 32–50.

150.  *Cf supra* text accompanying note 35.

151.  *See Herrenreiter,* 26 BGHZ 349 (1958).

152.  NJW 1979, 647 (BGH 1978).

153.  *See e.g.,* NJW 1964, 1471 (BGH 1964).

154.  AfP 1981, 270 (BGH 1981).

155.  *Monatsschrift für deutsches Recht* [MDR] 1965, 553 (BGH 1965).

156.  *Richtlinien für die redaktionelle Arbeit,* Nos. 28, 30, at 37 (Deutscher Presserat ed. 1980).

157. *See supra* text accompanying note 35.

158. *E.g.,* 12 BVerfG 113 (1961).

159. *See infra* V.A.1.

160. For details *see, e.g.,* K. Wenzel, *Das Recht der Wort- und Bildberichterstattung* (329) (2d ed. 1979).

161. *See supra* note 147 and accompanying text.

162. *See, e.g., Constanze I,* 3 BGHZ 270.

163. *Lüth,* 7 BVerfG 198 (1958); 12 BVerfG 113 (1961).

164. *See Höllenfeuer,* 45 GBHZ 296, 308 (1966).

165. *See* 65 BGHZ 325 (1975) and Assmann and Kübler, *Testhaftung und Testwerbung,* 142 *Zeitschrift für das gesamte Handels- und Wirtschaftsrecht* [ZHR] 413 (1978) for further reference.

166. The damages may extend to nonmonetary loses. In feuds between prominent public figures damages occasionally amount to 100,000 D.M.

167. All responses are on file at the author's office. It might be added that all informants are personally known and are, in press jargon, "generally reliable sources."

168. And, it should be added, in theory.

169. For example, in a recent, as yet unpublished case, the Federal Constitutional Court held that a politician's statement that another party was the " 'NPD' (a neo-fascist party) in a European context" constituted opinion, while the lower courts had assumed it was a factual statement.

170. For a survey on the right of reply in most Western European countries and a report of harmonization efforts by the Council of Europe, *see* M. Löffler, H. Golsong and G. Frank, *Das Gegendarstellungsrecht in Europa* (1974).

171. *See, e.g.,* for the press, §10 in Bavaria, Hesse and (West) Berlin; §11 in all other states. For radio and TV, *e.g.,* §3 of the law concerning the Hessische Rundfunk, §17 of the Bavarian Rundfunkgesetz.

172. The most frequently used practical lawyers' handbook on the topic—W. Seitz, G. Schmidt and A. Schoener, *Der Gegendarstellungsanspruch in Presse, Film, Funk und Fernsehen* (1980)—Comprises more than 260 pages. For recent developments *see* Damm, *Der Gegendarstellungsanspruch in der Entwicklung der neueren Rechtsprechung* in *Presserecht und Pressefreiheit, Festschrift für Martin Löffler* 25 (1980).

173. D. Stammler, *Die Presse als soziale und verfassungsrechtliche Institution* (1971).

174. K.H. Eckhold, *Konzentration und Teilhabe in Pressewesen* (1973) (doctoral thesis) (available at Kiel University).

175. *See, e.g.,* F. Kübler, *Gutachten D zum 49.Deutschen Juristentag* (1972); P. Lerche, *Verfassungsrechtliche Aspekte der inneren Pressefreiheit* (1974); W. Mallmann, *Referat D zum 49.Deutschen Juristentag,* 10 (1972); *contra, e.g.,* W. Weber, *Innere Pressefreiheit als Verfassungsproblem* (1973).

176. For a survey of these agreements and an empirical appraisal of their positive effects *see* U. Branahl and W. Hoffmann-Riem, *Redaktionsstatute in der Bewährung* (1975). Similar attempts in several other European countries are described by H.D. Fischer, R. Molenfeld, I. Petzke and H.-W. Wolter, *Innere Pressefreiheit in Europa* (1975).

177. *See Wettbewerbsprobleme bei der Einführung von privatem Rundfunk und Fernsehen* 13, 14 (Monopolkommission ed. 1981).

178. This percentage is arrived at by disregarding a Sunday edition of dailies in the Stuttgart area that is supplied only to subscribers. Taking this into account, the market share drops to 85.7 percent.

179. Diederichs, *Die Konzerne der Publikumszeitschriften im IV. Quartal 1979* in *Media Perspektiven* 460, 466 (1980).

180. *See supra* text accompanying notes 15–16.

181. *Bericht der Kommission zur Untersuchung der Wettbewerbsgleichheit von Presse, Funk/Fernsehen und Film* of Sept. 25, 1967, BT-Drucksache V 2120 (Michel Report); *Schlußbericht der Kommission zur Untersuchung der Gefährdung der wirtschaftlichen Existenz von Pressunternehmen und der Folgen der Konzentration für die Meinungsbildung in der Bundesrepublik*, BT-Drucksache V 3211.

182. H. Armbruster et al., *Pressefreiheit* (1970); H. Armbruster et al., *Entwurf eines Gesetzes zum Schutz freier Meinungsbildung* (1972).

183. For a detailed description and analysis *see* P. Ulmer, *Schranken zulässigen Wettbewerbs marktbeherrschender Unternehmen*, 23 (1977).

184. *See supra* text accompanying 175.

185. Law of June 28, 1976, 1976 BGBl I 1697.

186. *Cf.* Deutsches Verwaltungsblatt [DVBl.] 1975, 268 (Verwaltungsgericht [VG] Berlin 1974) with DVBl. 1975, 905 (Oberverwaltungsgericht [OVG] Berlin 1975).

187. *E.g.*, Berger, *Die Pressekonzentration in verfassungsrechtlicher Sicht*, AfP 1968, 794; N. Dittrich, *Pressekonzentration und Grundgesetz* 82 (1971); W. Leisner, *Pressegleichheit* 173 (1976); P. Lerche, *Verfassungsrechtliche Fragen zur Pressekonzentration* 103 (1971).

Five

![bar]

# Press Law in Sweden

Håkan Strömberg

## INTRODUCTION

The origins of modern Swedish press law can be traced to the eighteenth century, when Sweden experienced a period of parliamentary sovereignty known as the "Era of Freedom."[1] Prior to this period, Sweden was an absolute monarchy, and press censorship was exercised more or less rigorously.

Between 1718 and 1772 political power shifted. The King was reduced to little more than a marionette and power rested in the Estates of the Kingdom (*Riksens Ständer*).[2] In 1766 the Estates abolished formal censorship, inherited from the old regime, and the first Swedish act concerning the press was adopted. This act was promulgated by the King under the title "His Royal Majesty's Ordinance on the Freedom of Writing and Printing," and was generally referred to as the "Printing Freedom Ordinance."[3] However, the title "Ordinance" somewhat obscured the full purport of the act, for its text explicitly declared it to be an "irrevocable fundamental law."[4]

The newly won freedom of the press symbolized by the 1766 act proved to be short lived. In 1772, the King regained his power, and the press was successively restrained until censorship was eventually restored. However, in 1809, a coup d'etat established a constitutional monarchy. The press thereby regained its freedom, which was explicitly recognized in the Constitution of 1809 and defined as follows:

> Press freedom means the right of every Swedish man to issue publications without any obstacles previously laid by the public power, to be, afterwards, prosecuted for their contents only before a lawful court, and to be punished therefore in no other case than if these contents be contrary to a clear law, given to preserve general peace without restraining general enlightenment.[5]

This formulation, which appears in nearly the same form in the Freedom of the Press Act currently in force,[6] suggests that the prohibition against prior restraints as well as the requirement that subsequent punishment be applied only through the judicial process have long been cornerstones of Swedish press law.

Following the revolution of 1809, the freedom conferred by the new constitution was reinforced by the enactment of the new Freedom of the Press Act in 1810. The Act was revised in 1812 and remained in force until 1949, when it was replaced by the Act currently in force. Like its predecessors, the current Act is a fundamental law. Its legal status is therefore identical to that of any provision contained in the Swedish Constitution.[7]

An important development in the evolution of Swedish press law occurred in 1974, when the Constitution of 1809 was replaced with a modern constitution. Unlike its predecessor, the new constitution guarantees freedom of expression in general.[8] It also contains a more specific provision which incorporates the extant Freedom of the Press Act.[9] What is most significant is that while the new constitution explicitly recognizes that the *general* freedom of expression may be limited for some purposes by ordinary law,[10] it does not discuss the manner in which the more specific freedom of the press may be limited. This implies that the new constitution provides greater protection for the press than it does for expression in general.

The obvious justification for this extra measure of protection afforded the press is that, historically, the purpose of a free press in Sweden has been regarded as primarily political. Thus, the Freedom of the Press Act itself emphasizes that in deciding whether certain types of expression constitute abuse of press freedom, one should bear in mind that freedom of the press constitutes the basis of a free government.[11] Furthermore, as will be seen, criticism of the political system or of those in power is not punishable under the Act.[12]

Although the principal motivation for the Act is political, the Act does more than protect political expression. Its first article broadly defines the purpose of press freedom as the securing of "free interchange of opinions and enlightenment of the public."[13] Thus the Act seeks to guarantee free expression not only in the political sphere but in religious, scientific, literary, cultural, and social realms as well. In fact, publications offering entertainment of a very light or even coarse character also enjoy the protection of the Act. But there is a limit: the Act does not protect the use of the printed word for purely commercial purposes, e.g., advertising.[14]

It is noteworthy that the Act is applicable to all products of the printing press: newspapers and other periodicals, books, pamphlets, leaflets, etc.[15] It applies to text as well as illustrations. Moreover, in 1976, the scope of the Act was broadened to encompass publications reproduced by such techniques as stenciling and photocopying.[16] The Act applies only subsequent to publication. It thus requires that copies have been distributed to bookstores or newsstands, although it is not necessary to show that any copies were sold.[17]

Theoretically, then, the freedom conferred by the Act belongs to ordinary citizens. However, in practice, it remains a privilege for enterprises involved in publishing books or newspapers, since an ordinary citizen has limited access to any means of reproduction or distribution. Moreover, the ordinary citizen has no right to have his thoughts and opinions published and therefore must depend on the goodwill of publishers. The Act does not even give a right of reply to a person who has been attacked in print.[18]

It is therefore evident that the real value of press freedom in Sweden depends on the diversity of publishing enterprises and the competition among them. It is generally acknowledged that diversity is healthy for free expression, and media concentration is therefore becoming an increasingly topical issue. The government has tried to counteract the increasing concentration of media ownership by extending subsidies to selected newspapers and cultural periodicals.[19] However, there is not as of yet any antitrust law applicable to the press, although the need for such a law has been seriously discussed.[20]

As should now be apparent, Swedish press law is essentially a product of legislation. Consequently, the role of the courts in this area has been narrowly confined. Although Swedish courts have assumed the power of judicial review through a gradual evolution over the last half century[21] (this power was formally recognized in the Swedish Constitution in 1979),[22] judicial review plays a very modest role in Swedish legal practice. Indeed, judicial review has never been exercised in the field of press law. Nevertheless, the courts do perform an important function in ordinary litigation involving the press, since they draw the line between lawful and punishable expression and interpret general principles of criminal law in light of the constitutional guarantee of free expression.[23] Juries perform an important function in trials involving the Act. As will be seen, juries are thought by many to undermine the law's consistency.

## PUBLIC ACCESS TO OFFICIAL RECORDS

Since the purpose of a free press is to secure free debate and general knowledge, particularly about public affairs, it is clear that access to public records is of vital importance. The significance of access was recognized as early as 1776, when the Press Act established the right to know and recognized the concomitant duty of the government to release information. Today, the introductory provisions included in the first chapter of the

Freedom of the Press Act explicitly identify the right to publish official records as one element of press freedom which the Act protects.[24] The second chapter of the Act goes one step further, establishing the general rule that *every* Swedish citizen has the right to study official records.[25] While this general rule is, of course, subject to certain qualifications which will be discussed below, it is significant that secrecy is the exception rather than the rule in Sweden.

The right of access established by the Freedom of the Press Act is broad based.[26] It is not limited to information sought for "political purposes" but instead extends to official information sought for private as well as commercial purposes.[27] Ordinarily, a person seeking access to official information is not required to reveal his aim or even his name. Only if the records demanded are considered classified will this information be required, since it may influence a decision of whether to grant access.[28] Thus, in practice, the principle of publication underlying chapter two of the Act accomplishes more than simply securing access for the press to official information.[29]

In order to qualify as an "official" record and thus be brought within the scope of chapter two of the Act, a particular document[30] must satisfy two requirements. First, it must be kept by a public authority, which in this context includes all organs of the state—the Riksdag, the government, the courts, administrative authorities, and all organs of local self-government. Information originating outside the government is classified as official the moment it reaches the public authority. Second, the information has to reach a certain administrative stage before it becomes subject to disclosure. Thus, there is no right of access to documents pertaining to the administrative decision-making process before a definitive decision has been reached, or to documents pertaining to matters which are still under review. These restrictions are designed to protect the integrity of the governmental decision-making process.[31]

A denial of access may ordinarily be challenged in court, and then appealed to a higher court.[32] However, if a minister has made the decision to deny access, there is no resort to the courts. Only the government may consider the propriety of the minister's decision.[33] Decisions of the government, the Riksdag, and some of its organs are not subject to appeal.[34]

On appeal, the issues which are usually raised are whether the record(s) in question is official, and if so, whether the record(s) is properly considered classified. The determination of whether a document is classified depends on the rules contained in the secrecy law. Originally, these rules appeared in the Freedom of the Press Act itself. But in 1937, as these rules became more numerous and complicated, they were transferred to the Secrecy Act, which is an ordinary law. However, it should not be overlooked that the Press Act still determines the legal framework of the secrecy rules in enumerating the legitimate purposes of secrecy and in describing the form of legislation concerning secrecy. The Secrecy Act now in force (*Sekretesslagen*) was enacted in 1980.[35]

According to the Freedom of the Press Act, which is closely tracked by the Secrecy Act, access to official records may be limited only if it is requested with respect to records relating to:

1. national security and foreign affairs;
2. the central financial, monetary, and foreign exchange policy of the state;
3. administrative action concerning inspection, control, or other supervision;
4. the prevention or punishment of crimes;
5. the economic interest of the community;
6. the protection of personal privacy or economic data; or
7. the preservation of an animal or plant species.[36]

As far as the form of secrecy legislation is concerned, the Freedom of the Press Act prescribes that limitations on access to official records must be precisely specified in a special law (e.g., the Secrecy Act) or in another law to which the special law refers. The Riksdag may delegate to the government the power to promulgate specific regulations regarding the applicability of the secrecy rules. However, in practice this power has been delegated only to a modest extent.

It should be noted in passing that the Secrecy Act not only applies to matters concerning access but also imposes a duty of silence on public officials. The Act forbids public officials from disclosing the content of classified records orally, by letter, or in another manner.

The provisions of the Secrecy Act are generally formulated in one of two ways. Either the information is presumptively secret, and may be disclosed only if there is no risk to the protected interest (for example, information about the health or personal affairs of a patient are presumptively secret unless it is evident that disclosure will not harm the patient or members of his family),[37] or the information is presumptively open, and should not be classified unless disclosure may injure the protected interest (for example, information relating to social insurance is presumptively open and may be withheld only upon proof that the individual or member of his family will be harmed by disclosure).[38]

The Secrecy Act is quite comprehensive and complicated, and it is therefore not possible to treat it here in more detail. However, two final points are worth noting. First, with regard to various types of official records, the Secrecy Act prescribes specific maximum periods of secrecy, ranging from 2 to 70 years.[39] Second, and more importantly, the Secrecy Act does not authorize the imposition of secrecy solely to protect authorities from criticism. Secrecy inevitably inhibits a "free debate and comprehensive enlightenment," and accordingly the provisions of the Secrecy Act should be carefully tailored to balance the public's right to know with the government's legitimate secrecy needs.

## STATE CONTROL OF THE PRESS

In Sweden, state control of the press is relatively modest. To the extent that control is exercised at all, it is only to serve two purposes: to facilitate the prosecution of any abuses of press freedom and to prevent foreign influence over periodicals.

The Freedom of the Press Act requires that any matter produced by means of a printing press must be provided with a declaration of origin, stating the name of the printer and the place and year of printing.[40] Thus, at least one person—who can be held responsible for the contents of the publication—must be identified. Other contributors, such as an author or editor of a book, need not identify themselves.

The printer must also preserve a copy of the publication for a year, and on request must provide a copy to the public prosecutor (the Chancellor of Justice).[41] In addition, he should deliver copies to university libraries,[42] but this obligation serves a cultural purpose and is inconsequential as far as press freedom is concerned.

One interesting feature of Swedish press law is that newspapers and periodicals are regulated more extensively than other publications. A newspaper or a periodical is defined as a publication which appears under the same title at least four times a year,[43] and the conception includes daily newspapers as well as weekly, monthly and quarterly journals. The owner (publisher) of a newspaper or a periodical must be a Swedish citizen or corporation or a person domiciled in Sweden, and must obtain a "certificate of edition" prior to publication. In order to obtain such a certificate, the owner must apply to the Patents and Registration Board at which time the editor of the publication must be identified. The editor must be domiciled in Sweden, over 18 years old, and not under guardianship or bankrupt.[44]

The board's discretion to deny a certificate is rather limited. A legitimate denial may be based on only a few grounds, i.e., that the owner or editor does not comply with the conditions outlined above, or that the title of the newspaper or periodical may be confused with that of a previously registered publication. Any denial of an application for a certificate can be appealed to the Patents Appeal Court and finally to the Supreme Administrative Court.[45]

Once a certificate of edition is obtained, newspapers and periodicals are not subject to any special content-based regulation. Although the newspaper or periodical must bear the name of the editor,[46] editorial discretion is quite broad. The editor alone determines the content of the paper and nothing may be published in it against his will. But the editor's legal responsibility is coextensive with this range of discretion, and he alone is responsible for the contents of his publication. This rule stands in vivid contrast to the rule of responsibility that obtains when publications other than newspapers or periodicals are involved, where, it will be recalled, it is the author who ultimately bears legal responsibility, if he has not chosen to be anonymous. Thus the rules of responsibility in the Swedish system to a large extent depend on the form of publication that is chosen. Today, however, the right of anonymity is very seldom exercised by authors of books.

## RULES PROTECTING CONTRIBUTORS TO PUBLICATIONS

Swedish press law endeavors to encourage publication by offering potential contributors certain privileges. Foremost amongst these privileges are freedom from legal responsibility and anonymity. Because the term "contributor" is broadly defined, these privileges extend not only to authors but also to persons who acquire and/or communicate information for the purpose of getting it published.[47] Thus the entire newsgathering process is protected. A notable exception to this rule is the designated editor of a newspaper or periodical, who bears ultimate responsibility for the content of his publication.[48]

This freedom of newsgathering and dissemination is emphasized in the first article of the Act,[49] which declares that any person shall have the right to acquire (by legal means) information for the purpose of publishing it or communicating it for publication, as well as the right to communicate information, for the purpose of publication, to an author, editor, editorial office, or news agency. These rights are protected regardless of whether or not the information in question is ultimately published.

As a general rule, a person involved in the newsgathering process enjoys total freedom from legal responsibility.[50] Contributors to newspapers and periodicals are similarly protected. However, other authors and book editors are treated somewhat differently. If they choose to identify themselves in a publication, they are held responsible for its contents. If, on the other hand, they choose to remain anonymous, they are effectively insulated from any liability.[51]

The total freedom from responsibility enjoyed by contributors to publications is subject to three important and related qualifications. Any contributor who commits either severe crimes against national security (which are specifically enumerated in the Act), an intentional disclosure of properly classified official records, or an intentional breach of an obligation to observe silence imposed by special legislation, will be held legally responsible.[52] The first of these exceptions, related to severe crimes, has very rarely been applied. One such instance was the 1973 IB (Information Bureau) affair, in which a series of articles and a book entitled *IB and the Threat Against Our Security* alleged that the Swedish Secret Service had used criminal methods of investigation. The book's author and two collaborators were sentenced for espionage. (See also *infra* p. 242.) The third exception—denying protection to a contributor who is subjected to a statutory duty of confidentiality—needs further clarification. The denial of protection does not occur whenever a statutory duty of secrecy is applied. It only occurs when the legislature has explicitly decided that the duty to remain silent outweighs the right to speak. These instances are detailed in chapter 16 of the Secrecy Act. An examination of these instances reveals that, with the exception of national security and foreign affairs, a duty of secrecy imposed by law for the purpose of protecting public interests *does not* outweigh the right to publish. However, a statutory duty of secrecy imposed for the protection of private interests does outweigh the right to publish. The latter category includes the duty of attorneys, priests, and physicians to respect the confidentiality of information related to those who seek their advice.[53] Moreover, in these exceptional cases, the contributor or potential contributor who commits any of these three crimes is punishable regardless of whether or not the information revealed is ultimately published. However, the prosecution and trial of any such person must follow the special procedural rules of the Act.[54]

The basic freedom from responsibility enjoyed by contributors to publications is complemented by a generally available right of anonymity. Thus contributors may choose to be sheltered not only from state punishment but also from social pressures.

In the Swedish system, neither an author, an editor of a publication other than a newspaper or a periodical,[55] nor a communicator of news-worthy information has to reveal his name, pseudonym, or signature in any publication.[56] This right of anonymity is protected in three ways. First, in a trial concerning abuse of press freedom, it is forbidden to discuss or otherwise raise the issue of the identity of the author(s) of an article in a newspaper or a periodical or the communicator of information to a publisher. The identity of an author or editor of a publication other than a newspaper or a periodical may be discussed only if the publication bears the name (or a transparent pseudonym or signature) of a real or pretended author or editor, or if such a name has been disclosed by written admission (perhaps delivered to the publisher) or by an admission before the court.[57]

Second, if an author, editor, or communicator has chosen to remain anonymous, all others involved with the publication in question are generally required to keep the contributor's identity secret. This obligation is imposed upon authors, editors, publishers, printers, and news agencies, as well as all their employees. A breach of silence is ordinarily punishable by fine or imprisonment.[58] However, this obligation to protect the identity of a contributor does not apply where the anonymous contributor may be held responsible for a severe crime against national security, intentional disclosure of classified information, or breach of a statutorily imposed obligation of silence.[59]

Third and finally, the right of anonymity is protected by a prohibition against the investigation by public authorities of the identity of an anonymous author, editor, or communicator, unless it is necessary for the prosecution of an explicitly specified crime. An unauthorized investigation is punishable by fines or imprisonment.[60]

## RULES PROTECTING THE PRODUCTION AND DISTRIBUTION OF PUBLICATIONS

The Freedom of the Press Act recognizes the right of every Swedish citizen or corporation to publish by means of a printing press.[61] More specifically, a right to publish newspapers and periodicals follows from the fact that discretion to deny a permit (certificate of edition) is strictly limited. Books are not regulated either by the Act or by other means.

The Act further proclaims the right of every Swedish citizen or corporation to market, send, or distribute publications.[62] This right extends to sales, free dissemination, and lending. It also implies a correlative right to use the mail and other public means of distributing publications.[63] During the Second World War, when Sweden was neutral, the government tried to suppress some extremist publications by forbidding their transport. Today, such a prohibition would be contrary to fundamental law.

Certain restrictions on the government enhance the freedom to publish. First, and most fundamentally, censorship is prohibited: "No scrutiny of a publication previous to printing and no prohibition of printing thereof may occur."[64]

During the Second World War, an amendment to the former Act of 1812 permitted the introduction of censorship by ordinary law. While no ordinary law was in fact ever passed pursuant to this amendment, the possibility of censorship itself left an imprint on Swedish society which many viewed as abhorrent. Thus, when proposing the Act of 1949 now in force, the Minister of Justice declared that "[c]ensorship is unjustifiable in time of peace; [and] in war it may be a real danger for the country and the democratic order."[65] This view is reflected in the Act, which now forbids the establishment of censorship even during wartime. Instead it is probable that the Board of Psychological Defense[66] would in such a situation invite the press to cooperate voluntarily with the government. Voluntary government/press cooperation also existed during the Second World War.

While the ban on censorship of publications is absolute, the Act does permit the imposition of certain other restrictions on the right to publish.[67] First, the Act provides for seizure and confiscation of publications under certain circumstances.[68] Second, the Act allows for reasonable additional regulations governing time, place, and manner of publication or distribution, but not on the basis of a publication's content. Thus the government may restrict distribution in order to prevent the littering of public places or in order to prevent traffic obstruction. But such restrictions must apply equally to all printed matter. Finally, it should not be overlooked that the Act only applies to public authorities. Restrictions imposed by private persons or organizations do not fall within its ambit.

## THE UNIQUE PENAL AND PROCEDURAL ASPECTS OF THE FREEDOM OF THE PRESS ACT

In Sweden, as in other countries, press freedom has its limits, and its abuse is punishable. What is truly distinctive about the Swedish system is that in order to safeguard free speech against unjustified restrictions, special rules of substantive law and criminal procedure have been designed for prosecution of press-related offenses. The domain of applicability of this specialized legal regime is a matter of paramount importance.

The Act provides that "[o]n account of abuse of the freedom of the press or participation therein, nobody may be prosecuted or sentenced to punishment or damages, nor may the publication be confiscated or seized, in other ways or in other cases than this Act provides."[69] This provision has both substantive and procedural implications. The substantive implications are that abuse of press freedom can result in legal sanctions only in the cases enumerated in the catalogue of crimes which is part of the Act,[70] and that only persons responsible for a publication in accordance with the Act may be convicted. A procedural implication is that any trial for one of the enumerated offenses must be conducted according to the rules set forth in the Act. An ordinary criminal action or disciplinary intervention is therefore forbidden.

The Act explicitly restricts the scope of its specialized penal and procedural regime by excluding certain cases. Thus the Act does not apply to commercial advertising for alcohol and tobacco[71] or to the publication of credit information.[72] Both may be regulated by ordinary law. Similarly, the Act provides that responsibility for an abstruse advertisement, containing, for example, hidden defamation, does not lie with the editor, but with the advertiser, who is to be prosecuted in an ordinary trial.[73] Finally, the generally applicable Penal Code governs the offensive distribution of pornographic pictures and distribution of "brutalizing" publications among youths and children,[74] while the distribution of maps and pictures containing information which imperils national security may be regulated by ordinary law.[75]

Beyond these explicit exemptions, the Act's exclusive regime is presumed to be applicable to every use or abuse of press freedom. However, some publications are considered as falling outside the boundaries of the Act and are therefore regulated by ordinary law. As noted earlier, for purely commercial purposes speech does not fall within the ambit of the Act. Therefore, "economic" crimes committed by means of a printed publication, e.g., fraudulent advertising, have been prosecuted in ordinary criminal proceedings.[76] Similarly, an editor of a newspaper who had permitted the publication of "contact advertisements" from prostitutes, was tried for procuring and sentenced in an ordinary trial.[77] In this latter instance, the advertisements were regarded as commercial.[78]

## CATALOGUE OF CRIMES

Criminal abuse of press freedom is regulated by the Act through an exhaustive catalogue of crimes, which is comprised of two main categories: "prohibited expression," i.e., speech which contains a criminal meaning, and "prohibited publication," i.e., the publication of secret information.

Turning to the first category, prohibited expression is punishable only if it is proscribed by both the Act and the Penal Code. Generally, the relevant provisions of the Code parallel the corresponding provisions of the Act. But it is important to note that if the Penal Code were amended so as to become more restrictive, it would not necessarily apply to challenged publications unless the Act were amended as well. As was indicated earlier, such amendment is possible only every third year. On the other hand, if the Penal Code were amended so as to become more permissive, the amendment would immediately become operative.

The catalogue of prohibited expression comprises the following crimes, all of which have counterparts in the Penal Code:

1.  High treason, committed with intent to subject all or part of the nation to the control of a foreign power, or with the intent of bringing about or obstructing, with the assistance of a foreign power, an act by the highest state organs insofar as the act involves danger that the intention shall be carried out, or any attempt, preparation, instigation or conspiracy aimed at such high treason[79];

2.  Instigation of war, provided that danger that the nation shall be involved in war or other hostilities is provoked with foreign assistance[80];

3.  Sedition, committed with the intent of overthrowing the government

by force and violence, or with the intent of bringing about or obstructing an act by the highest state organs, provided that the act involves danger that the intent shall be carried out, or any attempt, preparation, instigation or conspiracy aimed at such sedition[81];

4. Treason, consisting of causing mutiny, disloyalty, or despair in times of war, emergency or occupation, including any attempt, instigation, preparation or conspiracy aimed at such treason[82];
5. The same crime as 4, occasioned by negligence[83];
6. Incitement to criminal acts, to neglect of civil duties, or to disobedience to a public authority[84];
7. Dissemination of rumors endangering national security in times of war or emergency[85];
8. Threats against, or contempt for, a group of people of a particular race, skin color, or national or ethnic origin, or of a particular religious persuasion[86];
9. Defamation[87];
10. Defamation of a deceased person[88];
11. Insult, by use of offensive language directed at an individual[89]; and
12. Pornographic depiction of children.[90]

Since the 1960s some forms of expression which were formerly punishable have been excluded from the catalogue (as well as from the Penal Code). In 1965, provisions proscribing insults aimed at the Riksdag or against foreign heads of state or diplomats were repealed. In 1971, provisions proscribing blasphemy, pornography, and desecration of the national symbols of Sweden or a foreign state were anulled. In 1976, provisions concerning seditious libel, i.e., insult of the King and/or public officers, were abolished, as were the rules prohibiting the spreading of rumors which would be dangerous to the national supply of food stuffs and other necessities or to law and order or which would undermine respect for public authorities or imperil national security in times of relative tranquility.[91]

The net result of this recent wave of liberalization has been to place the King, public officers, foreign heads of state and diplomats on an equal footing with private persons, at least with regard to defamation and insults.[92] Since, in addition, neither criticism of the state and the political system, in general, nor criticism of the Constitution, government, Riksdag, or courts (the notion of contempt of court is unknown in Sweden), in particular, is prohibited, it is evident that presently there is considerable freedom for political expression in Swedish society.

Notwithstanding the recent tendency toward liberalization, there have been some expansions of the catalogue of prohibited expression in modern times. The provision prohibiting group libel of racial, ethnic, national or religious groups was introduced in 1949,[93] and the provision forbidding instigation of a war risk was added in 1965.[94] The provision concerning child pornography was enacted into law in 1979.

It is also conceivable that the category of prohibited expression will be expanded in the forseeable future. Recently, proposals to prohibit coarser forms of pornography and descriptions of violence, as well as sex discrimination, have been made, but they have not yet produced concrete results. It has also been proposed to prohibit general violations of privacy, but it seems probable that this will remain a matter for self-regulation by the press.

In practice, the only type of prohibited expression that is of any real significance is defamation. Recently, almost all trials for press freedom crimes have involved defamation.

A famous defamation case was litigated in the Supreme Court in 1966.[95] A brother of the late Secretary General of the United Nations Dag Hammarskjöld prosecuted the editor of a newspaper which had printed an article alleging that Dag Hammarskjöld had been responsible for the aircraft crash in 1961 at Ndola, where he and his fellow passengers had been killed.* This allegation, which had originated in the American journal *Fact*, appeared in the German periodical *Der Spiegel* and was subsequently repeated in the Swedish paper. Since it proved to be entirely groundless and was reprinted without serious regard for its veracity, the editor was both fined and compelled to pay damages to the brother of the deceased.[96]†

Turning now to the second main category of press freedom crimes, a prohibited publication is also punishable only if it is proscribed by both the Freedom of the Press Act and the Penal Code. However, since the Act does not adequately define the limits of prohibited publication,[97] the exact character of this category has of necessity been determined by the Penal Code and the Secrecy Act, respectively. Essentially, there are three types of prohibited publications:

1.   Publication of facts, the disclosure of which constitutes a crime against national security under the Penal Code, e.g., espionage;

---

* The article asserted that Dag Hammarskjöld had committed suicide by planting a bomb aboard the plane. (Editor's note)

† Nils Ivan Ivarsson, chief editor of the newspaper *Sydvenska Dagbladet* was ordered to pay Dag Hammarskjöld's brother 10,000 crowns (approximately $1800) in damages for an article printed in the newspaper. The editor was also ordered to pay *day fines*—amounts imposed according to the defendant's salary and not publicly disclosed.

Bengt Öste, editor of the weekly magazine *Idun Veckojournalen*, was fined the equivalent of $400 and ordered to pay $3000 in damages to Dag Hammarskjöld's brother for printing a similar article. *New York Times* 14 October 1965, p. 3, col. 2. (Editor's note)

2. Intentional publication of an official record, properly classified pursuant to the Secrecy Act;
3. Intentional breach of an obligation to observe silence in the cases enumerated in the last chapter of the Secrecy Act.[98]

It is highly unusual for a person who is responsible for the contents of a book or newspaper or periodical to be simultaneously subjected to the rules of confidentiality set forth by the Secrecy Act. It is more likely that the person who has supplied the secret information will be prosecuted in accordance with the rules mentioned earlier in this essay.

Trials for prohibited publication are very rare. However, a very famous 1973 case, often referred to as the IB affair,[99] is worth mentioning in this connection. In a series of articles in a periodical and in a book entitled *IB and the Threat Against Our Security,* it was alleged that the Swedish Secret Service had employed patently illegal methods of investigation such as committing burglary on foreign embassies and homes or offices of citizens, wiretapping, conducting operations in Finland, and cooperating with the CIA and Shin-Beth. In the course of exposing these activities, the authors obviously disclosed some national security secrets, such as the existence and organization of the Secrect Service, the existence of cooperation with intelligence services of other countries, the deciphering of foreign codes, and Swedish activities in Finland. No prosecution for prohibited publication was brought against the editor of the periodical, and a prosecution against the author of the book was withdrawn shortly after it was initiated. Instead, the author of the book and two collaborators were prosecuted and convicted in an ordinary espionage trial for acquisition and communication of secret information for purposes of publication. This case proved to be very controversial and eventually led to some amendments of the Freedom of the Press Act, the major significance of which was that an espionage trial for acquisition and/or communication of secret information for purposes of publication must now be conducted in conformity with the Act's special procedural rules.[100]

## RESPONSIBILITY

Generally, the process of publication in any format is a cooperative enterprise. However, a fundamental principle of Swedish press law is to consider one person involved in the process as exclusively responsible for the contents of a particular publication. Usually, that person is the editor of the newspaper or periodical or author of a book. But in certain circumstances, responsibility is shifted to some other party in accordance with a fixed chain of responsibility. Regardless of who in this chain is ultimately determined to be responsible, the law conclusively presumes that that person was aware of the contents of the publication and willfully participated in the process of publishing.[101]

With respect to newspapers and periodicals, the first party in the chain of responsibility is the editor whose name was submitted to the Patents and Registration Board. If no certificate of edition has been obtained or if there is no competent editor or, alternatively, if it can be established that the editor did not have the power to control the contents of the newspaper or the periodical, responsibility shifts to the publisher. If the publisher is not known, responsibility is transferred to the printer. And if the publication does not bear the name of a printer or bears the name of a printer which a distributor knows to be false or fictitious, the distributor is held responsible, unless the identity of the printer can otherwise be determined.[102] What is most striking about this succession of potential liability is that the author of the challenged piece is never considered responsible.

In contrast, with respect to publications which are neither newspapers nor periodicals (books, pamphlets, leaflets, etc.), responsibility is in the first instance borne by the author, provided that the right of anonymity has not been exercised. If the author cannot be held responsible, an editor, to whom responsibility can be transferred, may be located. This is possible in two cases: when the publication is a collection of contributions by several authors or when the publication represents the work of a deceased author. However, it will be recalled that editors of such publications also enjoy the privilege of anonymity. Thus if neither the author nor the editor can be held responsible, responsibility shifts to the publisher. If, however, the identity of the latter is not known, the printer, or as a last resort, the distributor, bear responsibility.[103]

The foregoing rules of responsibility are primarily applicable in criminal proceedings. In principle, they are also important in determining tort liability,[104] but in this respect, responsibility does not fall exclusively on one party. For example, both the publisher of the paper and its editor can be sentenced to damages in one action concerning the same publication. The rationale underlying this rule is that the injured party will be given a better chance of actually recovering damages if several parties are held liable.[105]

## SANCTIONS

Sanctions for a press freedom crime are fines or imprisonment. These provisions are specified not in the Freedom of the Press Act, but in the Penal Code.[106]

The Act, however, does provide for an auxiliary sanction, known as confiscation, which is designed to limit the deleterious effects of the crime. A confiscation decree implies three things:

1. The destruction of all copies of the publication designed for distribution;
2. The distribution of any copies in violation of the decree is a criminal offense; and
3. The technical means used exclusively for the production of the particular publication (e.g., plates or stereotypes, but not a typesetter or printing press) must be rendered inoperative.[107]

In wartime, a further sanction—suspension—is available. Suspension entails a prohibition on the publishing of a particular newspaper or periodical for a period of time fixed by the court, which cannot exceed six months. Suspension presupposes a severe crime against national security, e.g., instigating an insurrection, treason, or espionage, and the coincident imposition of confiscation. It is imposed by the court together with punishment and confiscation.[108]

Claims for damages resulting from the abuse of press freedom must be based on a press freedom crime.[109] An action for damages may be combined with a criminal prosecution, or brought separately, but in either case, it is necessary to establish first that the offense falls under the catalogue of crimes. For example, damages for violation of privacy are recoverable only if the violation of privacy itself is independently punishable.

In practice, damages are awarded only in defamation cases, although there is reason to believe they would also be awarded in cases of insult or breach of secrecy,[110] if such cases were litigated. Usually, the amount of damages is moderate, so that damage awards can hardly be viewed as much of a deterrent.

Finally, one other sanction is worth noting. In a sentence for defamation against a newspaper or a periodical, the court can order that the sentence itself be published in a subsequent issue of the paper.[111]

## PROSECUTION

Most of the offenses enumerated in the catalogue of crimes call for public prosecution. Only one public official—the Chancellor of Justice (*Justitiekanslern*), whose position is comparable to that of an attorney general—has authority to initiate proceedings under the Freedom of the Press Act.[112] Ordinarily, the chancellor must obtain the permission of the government before initiating a prosecution for a press freedom crime.[113] He has unbridled discretion to prosecute only with regard to a few types of crimes—group libel, pornographic depiction of children, breach of secrecy and, in exceptional cases, defamation. However, when the offenses are *other than* press freedom crimes, the chancellor may prosecute without the government's permission. If, for example, an article in a newspaper implies espionage, the chancellor needs permission to prosecute the editor but not to prosecute the person who is the source of the article.

Public prosecution is further confined by the statute of limitations. The statute requires cases to be brought within a relatively short time after the commission of a press freedom crime. Crimes involving newspapers or periodicals must be prosecuted within six months. All others must be prosecuted within a year.[114]

While most press freedom crimes call for public prosecution, the most prevalent crime—defamation—is generally subject only to private prosecution.[115] Consequently, it is private rather than public prosecution that is most common in press related matters in Sweden. Similarly, cases involving offensive language (insult) are not usually litigated by the government. In some cases, however, public prosecution of these offenses is possible. A public prosecution may be instituted for defamation (against anybody) in special cases if required by the public interest, or for insult of a public officer concerning the discharge of his public duties. This method of protecting public officials is not known to have been utilized by the Swedish government. In either case, the injured party should first file a complaint with the public prosecutor.[116] With the permission of the government, a public prosecution may also be initiated for defamation or insult against the King or another member of the royal family or against a foreign head of state or a diplomat.[117]

In addition to defamation and insult cases, private prosecution is also possible where a breach of secrecy results in damage to private interests. Public prosecution of this type of offense is only allowed after information is furnished by the injured party or if required by the public interest.[118]

Finally, if no person can be prosecuted for violation of a press freedom crime, the public prosecutor or private party can ask the court to confiscate the publication. The resulting *ex parte* proceeding is tantamount to a trial without any defendant.[119]

## SEIZURE

In contradistinction to confiscation, which may only be ordered after a judicial determination that a press freedom crime has been committed, the Chancellor of Justice may, under certain circumstances, order seizure. This is an administrative remedy of a temporary nature. When appropriate, the chancellor may order that all copies of a particular publication designed for distribution should be seized by the police. Distribution of more copies thereafter is punishable. The purpose of this measure is twofold: to ensure the execution of a possible sentence of confiscation and to limit temporarily the effects of the alleged crime.

Prior to trial, seizure is possible only if the crime may trigger a public prosecution. Only the chancellor can order seizure,[120] and prosecution must follow within two weeks after the order. If no prosecution is in fact brought during this period, the seizure order automatically expires.[121] In contrast, once a trial has begun, the court decides whether seizure should be ordered and/or whether such an order should be withdrawn.[122]

In time of war or a national security crisis, publications inciting soldiers to disobedience may be seized by the military. The chancellor must be advised of any such action as soon as possible, and he retains discretion to sustain, modify, or reverse the seizure.[123]

Finally, the chancellor or the court may seize a few copies of a publication in order to ensure their availability as evidence in legal proceedings.[124]

## TRIAL PROCEDURES

As was discussed earlier in this essay, special rules of procedure apply to press freedom cases. Grouped in this category are all cases falling within the catalogue of crimes as well as those cases involving prosecution of an individual who is ordinarily exempt from responsibility but who may, under exceptional circumstances, be tried for a crime against national security or for breach of secrecy committed through publication.[125]

Only 28 of the 100 district courts in Sweden have jurisdiction over press freedom cases.[126] The purpose underlying this allocation of jurisdiction is twofold. It ensures the expertise of the tribunals which adjudicate the relatively rare press freedom cases. At the same time, establishment of at least one press freedom court in each of the 24 Swedish provinces retains a measure of local control over these issues.

In a press freedom trial, the court consists of a panel of three or four professional judges and a jury. Jury participation in the proceedings is the most salient feature of a press freedom trial.[127] Juries are something of an exception in the Swedish procedural system. While laymen often participate in judicial proceedings, they usually serve as members of the court.[128]

Juries were introduced in Swedish press freedom cases in 1815, and were patterned after the Anglo-Saxon model (the English word "jury" was adopted by Swedish law). The impetus for this development was the lack of confidence in the professional judiciary. The introduction of juries was designed to secure the influence of the sound judgment of laymen, particularly in cases concerning criticism of the ruling elite.

In a press freedom case, trial by jury can only be waived by mutual consent. If there is no waiver, a jury will be empanelled.[129] The division of labor between the court and the jury follows certain guidelines. As the trial opens, the court decides whether the defendant should be held responsible for the publication. The jury is then asked to decide whether a crime has been committed. At the conclusion of the main hearing, the court submits to the jury in writing the question of whether a crime has been committed. Often the court will break down the question into several questions relating to different parts of the publication or different elements of the crime. The jury is not permitted to apply any section of law not referred to by the prosecutor.

The jury's deliberations take place in private, and the jurors are forbidden to disclose any details of the deliberations or subsequent voting. The question or questions submitted by the court can only be answered "yes" or "no." No reasons or explanations are submitted.

The votes of at least six of the nine jurors are required to convict a defendant.[130] If the jury votes to acquit, that decision is final and cannot be overruled by the trial court or on appeal. If the jury votes to convict, the court undertakes an independent assessment of the evidence. This can result in either acquittal or conviction, but perhaps under a less stringent section of the law than that applied by the jury. In most cases, the court adheres to the jury's conviction verdict. If both the jury and the court find that a crime has been committed, the court will then impose sanctions, without consulting the jury.

An appeal is possible only in case of conviction, or, alternatively, if no jury has participated in the trial. Consequently, very few cases are appealed. This fact, coupled with the inscrutable nature of jury verdicts, weakens the consistency of Swedish press law. Decisions in individual cases are bound to be ad hoc since previous judicial guidelines are rare.

Despite or perhaps because of this lack of precedent, there are some statutory guidelines designed to rectify this situation. The Freedom of the Press Act provides the following instruction to the court and the jury:

> Any person whose duty it is to pass judgment on abuses of the freedom of the press or otherwise to ensure compliance with this Act shall constantly bear in mind that freedom of the press is a foundation of a free society, always pay more attention to illegality in the subject-matter and thought than illegality in the form of expression, to the aim rather than to the manner of presentation, and, in doubtful cases, acquit rather than convict.[131]

This rule of construction indicates that the Act assigns great weight to the freedom of the press in the balance of justice.

In contemporary Swedish society, the original function of the jury as a safeguard against governmental suppression is hardly relevant. Nearly all press cases concern private defamation. The role of the jury in this context is dubious. Some argue that it makes the result of the litigation unforeseeable and that it exacerbates the damage suffered by the defamed (who, in any event, is in a weak position when litigating against a newspaper).

Proponents of the jury system argue that its function is still relevant, at least where public figures are involved.

## PRESS SELF-REGULATION

The Swedish press enjoys broad freedom and the law tolerates much that may be ethically objectionable. It is therefore not surprising that various press organizations have endeavored to develop an ethical code for the press. This form of self-regulation has both constructive and preventive aspects. It not only supplements the Freedom of the Press Act but also serves to preempt any attempts to amend the Act so as to make it more restrictive.

There are currently three press organizations in Sweden. *Publicist Klubben* (the Club of Publicists) is a cultural association of publicists involved with the press, radio, and television. *Svenska Journalist Förbundet* (the Swedish Federation of Journalists) is a labor union comprised of employees of newspapers, news agencies, and radio and television stations. *Svenska Tidningsutgivare-Föreningen* (the Swedish Association of Newspaper Publishers) is an employer's association for newspaper enterprises. These three organizations have banded together to form *Pressens Samarbetsnämnd* (Cooperation Board of the Press).

Together, these three organizations have adopted an *Ethical Code for the Press, Radio and Television*, to which the Swedish Broadcasting Corporation has also acceded. The code includes publishing rules, professional rules, and rules regulating advertising camouflaged in an editorial format. In addition, the Cooperation Board has adopted guiding principles to regulate advertising designed to influence public opinion.

The rules concerning publication are the most interesting part of the code. They deal with the accuracy of news, modification and rebuttal of previously published matters, respect for personal integrity, including the need for caution in publishing names, authenticity of photographs, and impartiality in reporting legal proceedings.

With respect to this last topic, it should be emphasized that the code constitutes the only means of guaranteeing the accurate reporting of trials. There is no concept of contempt of court in Sweden, and other available remedies are ill suited to accomplish this objective. Of course, the general rules of defamation limit the freedom of a reporter. Furthermore, in some exceptional cases involving national security or sex crimes, for example, a trial may be conducted *in camera*, and photographing in the courtroom is altogether forbidden. But otherwise there are no legal restraints on the reporting of trials, nor on the freedom to comment on or criticize trials or sentences. Consequently, self-regulation plays a very important role in this context.

The three main press organizations have also joined together to establish *Pressens Opinionsnämnd* (the Opinion Board of the Press), which serves as a court of honor in cases concerning the enforcement of journalistic ethics in the periodic press. The board consists of five members and a chairman. Each of the three organizations appoints one member and the other two are appointed jointly by an ombudsman of the Riksdag and the chairman of the Bar Association. The five members then appoint the chairman, who should be a judge.

Cases are brought before the Board by a special prosecutor referred to as *Allmänhetens Pressombudsman* (Press Ombudsman of the Public). The press ombudsman is appointed by a committee of three, consisting of an ombudsman of the Riksdag, the chairman of the Bar Association, and the chairman of the Cooperation Board. The press ombudsman is paid by a foundation jointly established for this purpose by the three organizations.

The role of the press ombudsman is to enforce journalistic ethics ("good journalistic custom") in newspapers and periodicals. He may take action on his own initiative or following a complaint by a private party or corporation. If the ombudsman refuses to prosecute a private complaint, the complainant may then submit the case directly to the board, provided that the complainant is in fact the injured party. The board has discretion whether or not to hear any case submitted to it.

The press ombudsman may also directly contact an editor and request that a modification or reply be published. In clear and less severe cases, he may also declare that a violation of journalistic ethics has occurred. After such a declaration, however, the case may be submitted to the board by either the editor or the complainant.

The Opinion Board decides cases by issuing statements of opinion, which determine whether a violation of journalistic ethics has occurred. In reaching these decisions, the board is not formally bound to follow the Ethical Code, although it often does.

The board's decisions may go beyond the Freedom of the Press Act. For example, the board may denounce defamation of enterprises or corporations and, to some extent, general violations of privacy. Thus the board complements the ordinary jurisdiction in press freedom cases, and often serves as an alternative forum.

After the board issues an adverse statement of opinion, the editor of a reprimanded newspaper or periodical is ordered to publish the statement in its entirety, without undue delay, in a clearly visible format. Here again, in the remedial context, the board goes beyond the Act.[132] Similarly, the publisher is ordered to pay an expedition fee, which is used to cover the costs of the board and the ombudsman. But the board does not award any damages to the injured party. Moreover, since there is no legal procedure to enforce the decisions, it follows that the obligation to comply with it is of a moral rather than of a legal character.

## SOME OBSERVATIONS ABOUT THE
## REALITY OF PRESS FREEDOM IN SWEDEN

This essay has essentially dealt with the legal system of Swedish press law. A relatively detailed presentation of this subject seems justified, since Swedish press law is in many respects original, perhaps unique. Against this background, it is now possible to assess the effectiveness of the legal regime.

As was seen in the introduction and reiterated throughout this essay, the main purpose of the Freedom of the Press Act is to secure a wide freedom of expression. Generally, this objective has been realized. The press enjoys a very strong position in Sweden, and there is a free and open climate of debate. Journalists are proud of their profession and often emphasize their sense of social responsibility (although not always with good justification). Politicians of all persuasions agree that freedom of expression is indispensible in a democratic society, and since the Second World War the government has generally respected the freedom of the press. The most serious clash between the government and the press involved the proper procedural posture of the IB affair, discussed above.[133] The ombudsmen of the Riksdag intervene resolutely against attempts by the authorities to restrain press freedom by such means as abridging the right of anonymity or limiting the freedom of expression of public officers. Every proposal to make the press law more restrictive is vigorously opposed by a united press.

This does not, however, mean that each and every part of the regime of legal rules functions properly or functions at all. Many rules in the Act are never applied. Most of the offenses enumerated in the catalogue of crimes are never committed. As indicated earlier, the only press freedom crime of any significance is defamation. A long period of time has elapsed since a national security crime has been the subject of litigation. Moreover, the complicated chain of responsibility is seldom applied; in most cases, the editor of a newspaper or a periodical or the author of a book is prosecuted.

One of the weaker points of the system has already been alluded to: Juries tend to undermine jurisprudential consistency. Beyond this, it should also be noted that persons injured by newspapers often find themselves at a disadvantage. Since trials are long, arduous, and expensive ordeals without any real guarantee of a predictable outcome, potential litigants are discouraged from suing well-funded media defendants.

Finally, self-regulation of the press on the whole functions rather well. Yet the legitimacy of a system whereby transgressions on the part of the press are adjudicated by its own representatives is open to question. Moreover, the inability of the board to award damages is a definite drawback.

## REFORM PLANS

The Swedish legislative machinery is very efficient, and law reforms succeed one another at a relatively rapid pace. Press law is no exception. Its evolution is far from completed.

In 1977, a committee was appointed to draft a comprehensive law regulating freedom of expression in all important mass media. The law is intended to replace the Freedom of the Press Act, but to retain the status of fundamental law. It will regulate freedom of expression not only in printed publications, but also in the electronic media,[134] in motion pictures and recording industries, in dramatic performances, in exhibitions, and in meetings and demonstrations.

To a certain extent, it should be possible for the committee to formulate uniform rules for all mass media. For example, the catalogue of crimes and the procedural rules of the current Freedom of the Press Act could be extended to encompass all kinds of public expression. However, in other respects, a uniform regulation might not be possible or even desirable. Thus, it may not be possible to proclaim a total freedom of establishment as to radio and television due to the limited number of frequencies and channels available. Similarly, it may be necessary to retain film censorship, which is currently the only censorship that is permitted in Sweden. Furthermore, the principles of exclusive responsibility and anonymity of contributors can play no meaningful role in the regulation of meetings and demonstrations and it is questionable whether they should apply to the theater, exhibitions, and direct reporting on radio and television.

The reasonableness of these reform plans has been questioned by some critics. It has been argued that not all mass media communicators are instrumental in molding public opinion, and that some are of predominantly commercial quality. Fears have also been expressed that the protection now afforded the traditional press will be partially sacrificed on the altar of uniformity.

The task confronting the committee is obviously enormous and very complex. The new draft law is expected to be presented at the end of 1983. If the ultimate result is a new Freedom of Expression Act with the status of a fundamental law, it cannot be adopted before 1985.

## NOTES

1.  For the history of Swedish press law see Hilding Eek, *Om tryckfriheten* (Stockholm 1942). For general information on the Swedish system of public law, see Nils Herlitz, *Elements of Nordic Public Law* (Stockholm 1969).

2.  The Swedish Parliament in the eighteenth century was composed of four chambers representing the four estates: nobles, clergy, burghers, and peasants. In

1866, the Parliament was organized into two chambers and named the Riksdag, which previously had denominated a session of the Estates. (The original meaning of the word "Riksdag" was "national day" or "national meeting.") Since 1971, the Riksdag has had only one chamber.

3. The text is published in R.G. Modée, *Utdrag utur alla publique Handlingar,* tome VIII (Stockholm 1774), pp. 7427–7435.

4. The notion of "fundamental law" was introduced in Sweden during the eighteenth century. It came from the philosophy of natural law prevalent at that time. Fundamental law was probably regarded as an expression of the "social compact," which was the foundation of society. In 1766 it was decided that a fundamental law could be amended only by decisions at two sessions of the Estates. There was an interval of some years between the sessions and new elections were held at every session. In 1766, the Constitution, the Parliament Act, and the Freedom of the Press Act were all regarded as fundamental laws. Presently, the only fundamental laws are the Constitution, the Succession to the Throne Act, and the Freedom of the Press Act.

5. Art. 86 of the Constitution of 1809 (last reprinted in SFS 1971:271).

6. *Tryckfrihetsförordning* 5/4 1949 (SFS 1949:105, reprinted 1982:941). It will be referred to as "the Act" or with the Swedish abbreviation "TF." The definition quoted in the text appears in the first paragraph of TF 1:1.

The table of contents of the Press Freedom Act reads as follows:

1. On the freedom of the press
2. On the publication of official documents
3. On the right to anonymity
4. On the production of printed publications
5. On the edition of periodical publications
6. On the distribution of printed publications
7. On press freedom crimes
8. Rules of responsibility
9. On supervision and prosecution
10. On special means of coercion
11. On private claims
12. On the procedure in press freedom trials
13. On publications printed abroad
14. General provisions

7. Thus the Act can be amended only by two identical decisions of the Riksdag (parliament), and general elections must be held between the two decisions. (Ordinarily, elections to the Riksdag are held every third year.) The second decision is made by the Riksdag in its new composition following the election. After the first decision, a minority of the Riksdag (one third of its members) can demand that the decision shall be submitted to the approval of the people by a plebiscite coincident with the election. *See generally* RF 8:15.

8. According to RF 2:1, every citizen shall in relation to the community be guaranteed, *inter alia,* freedom of expression, defined as "the freedom to communicate information and express ideas, opinions and feelings either orally, in writing, in pictorial representations, or in any other way."

9. As to press freedom and the access to public documents, RF 2:1 refers to the Freedom of the Press Act.

10.  The possibility of restricting freedom of expression and certain other freedoms is regulated by comprehensive provisions in RF 2:12 and RF 2:13.

11.  TF 1:4, quoted later in this essay. (p. 247.)

12.  See p. 240, *infra.*

13.  TF 1:1.

14.  These principles are found in the preparatory works of the Act (SOU 1947:60 p. 120, prop. 1948:230 p. 172).

15.  TF chapter 1:

Art. 5. The present Act shall apply to any matter produced by means of a printing press. It shall likewise apply to any publication which has been multicopied by way of mimeographing, photocopying, or any similar technical process, if

1.  there is a valid publishing license for the publication; or
2.  the publication is provided with a notation to the effect that it has been multicopied and, in connection therewith, gives clear indication as to the identity of the person who has multicopied the publication as well as the place where and the year when such multicopying took place.

Any provision of this Act which refers to matter produced by means of a printing press, or to printing, shall be applied, unless otherwise prescribed therein, *mutatis mutandis,* to any other published matter to which the Act is applicable pursuant to the first paragraph, or to the multicopying of such published matter. The term "published matter" includes pictures, even if there is no accompanying text.

16.  Publications of this type are treated differently than publications produced by a conventional printing press. Publications of the latter variety always fall within the ambit of the Act whereas stenciled and photocopied publications do so only if they are provided with a declaration of origin. The decision whether to file a declaration of origin, and thus whether to fall under the legal regime of the Act is left exclusively to the publisher. If a stenciled or photocopied publication is provided with such a declaration, it is treated in exactly the same way as publications produced by a printing press. If not, the publication is subject to ordinary penal and procedural rules. For the purpose of simplicity, the several provisions of the Act use the term "printed publication" not only for publications produced by the printing press but also for such stenciled and photocopied publications which are provided with a declaration of origin. This legal definition of the term is given in the Act itself. *See* TF 1:5.

17.  TF Chapter 1:

Art. 6. Printed matter shall not be considered as such unless it is published. Printed matter shall be deemed to have been published when it has been delivered for sale or for circulation in some other manner; nevertheless, this definition shall not apply to the printed documents of an authority which are not available to the public.

18.  The Act does indirectly protect the interests of the citizen who has been unfairly attacked by the press. *See* TF 1:4, second paragraph:

In determining the sanctions which under the present Act are attendant upon abuses of the freedom of the press, particular attention shall, in the case of statements requiring correction, be given to whether such correction was brought to the notice of the public in an appropriate manner.

19.    Ordinances 20/5 1976 on state support to daily newspapers (SFS 1976:336) and 18/5 1977 on state support to cultural periodicals (SFS 1977:393).

20.    See the committee report *Massmediakoncentration* (SOU 1980:82).

21.    The most important cases on judicial review are NJA 1928 pp. 88, 125; 1934 p. 515; 1948 pp. 188, 458; 1951 p. 39; 1961 p. 253; 1964 p. 471.

22.    RF 11:14 (SFS 1979:933).

23.    These principles were thoroughly discussed by the Supreme Court in the Hammarskjöld case (NJA 1966 p. 565) mentioned later in this essay (*cf.* the text to notes 95–96).

24.    TF 1:1, paragraph 2, provides that every Swedish citizen has the right "in printed publications to express his thoughts and opinions, to publish official documents and to make statements and communicate information on any subject whatsoever."

For a list of the chapters of the Press Act, see *supra*, n. 6.

25.    In fact, foreigners enjoy the same right of access as Swedish nationals. See TF 14:5, paragraph two:

> Except as otherwise provided in this Act or in other laws, foreign nationals shall be treated on a basis of equality with Swedish nationals.

26.    The right of access implies a right to study and copy the record and also to obtain a copy of the record for a fee. *See generally* the following provisions of TF ch. 2, which regulate the forms of access:

> Art. 12. Any official document which may be made available to the public shall be made available, at the place where it is kept, and free of charge, immediately, or as soon as possible, to any person who desires to have access to the document, in such manner that the document can be read, listened to, or otherwise apprehended. A document may also be copied, or reproduced, or used for the purpose of transfer to a sound recording. If a document cannot be made available without such part of it as may not be made available being disclosed, the remaining part of the document shall be made available to the applicant in the form of a transcript or a copy.

> A public authority shall be under no obligation to make a document available at the place where the document is kept, if that would meet with considerable difficulties. Neither shall any such obligation arise in respect of a recording such as referred to in the first paragraph of Article 3, if the applicant can, without any considerable inconvenience, have access to the recording at a public authority located in the neighborhood.

> Art. 13. Any person who wishes to have access to an official document shall likewise be entitled for a fixed fee to obtain a transcript or a copy of the document or of that part of it which may be made available. However, a public authority shall be under no obligation to make a recording for electronic data-processing available in any form other than a transcript. Neither shall there be any obligation to produce copies of maps, drawings, or pictures or of

any other such recording as referred to in the first paragraph of Article 3 that has just been mentioned, if that would meet with difficulties and the document can be made available at the place where it is kept.

27.   While the Act does not explicitly legitimize access sought for private or commercial purposes, it has been applied in this manner. The rationale is that if the individual seeking access had to answer inquisitive questions, a "chilling effect" would result and the purposes of the Act would thereby be undermined.

28.   *E.g.,* if a person demands to study medical records, his chance to gain access is much better if he is a close relative of the patient or a member of the medical profession than if he is a journalist or a scandalmonger.

29.   Access is further facilitated by chapter 15 of the Secrecy Act, which instructs the government to register all public documents. These registers provide the public with the means to study and identify available documents.

30.   Originally, the right to access comprised only written documents but in 1974, it was extended to other kinds of records, such as microfilm and photographic and computer records. *See* TF 2:3, first paragraph:

The term "document" includes any representation in writing, any pictorial representation, and any recording which can be read, listened to, or otherwise apprehended only by means of technical aids. A document shall be considered to be official if it is kept by a public authority, and if, pursuant to Articles 6 or 7, it shall be considered to have been received, or prepared, or drawn up by an authority.

31.   TF 2:7, first paragraph:

A document shall be deemed to have been drawn up by a public authority when it has been dispatched. A document which has not been dispatched shall be deemed to have been drawn up when the matter or case to which it relates has been finally settled by the authority, or, if the document does not relate to a specific matter or case, when it has been finally checked and approved by the authority, or when it has been completed in some other manner.

Editor's note: The language of the Freedom of Information Act applicable in the United States, 5 U.S.C. § 552(a)(2), provides an interesting parallel:

Each agency, in accordance with public rules, shall make available for public inspection and copying:
(A) *final opinions,* including concurring and dissenting opinions, as well as orders, made in the adjudication of cases;
(B) those statements of policy and interpretations *which have been adopted by the agency....* (emphasis supplied)

32.   If a court, in the first instance, refuses access, the appeal is directed to the nearest higher court. If access is refused by an authority other than a court, the appeal is directed to an administrative court of appeal (*Kammarrätt*), whose decision can be brought under the review of the Supreme Administrative Court (*Regeringsrätten*) without any review permit.

33.   The power of a minister is restricted to information kept within his own

ministry. It does not extend to central, regional, or local authorities and decisions of these organs are amenable to the judicial process.

34.   TF 2:15 gives the basic rules of appeal:

> If a public authority other than the Riksdag or the Government has rejected a request that an official document be made available, or if such document has been made available under reservations which restrict the applicant's right to disclose its contents or otherwise to make use of it, the applicant may lodge an appeal against the decision. An appeal against a decision by a member of the Government shall be lodged with the Government, and an appeal against a decision of another authority shall be lodged with a court.

> In the Act referred to in Article 2 it shall be stipulated in detail how an appeal against such decision as referred to in the preceding paragraph shall be lodged. An appeal of this kind shall always be considered and determined promptly. The right to lodge appeals against decisions by the Riksdag agencies is governed by special provisions.

The details are found in SekrL 15:7 and 8.

35.   *Sekretesslag* 20/3 1980 (SFS 1980:100, reprinted 1982:1106), commonly referred to as SekrL.

36.   *See* chapter 2, art. 2, which sets forth these specific limitations.
Editor's Note: Again, the Freedom of Information Act, 5 U.S.C. §552, furnishes an interesting basis for comparison. *See* the exceptions outlined at 5 U.S.C. §522(b)(1)-(9).

37.   *See* SekrL 7:1.

38.   *See* SekrL 7:7.

39.   In the two cases mentioned in the preceding two notes, the maximum time is 70 years. But the secrecy of contractual agreements between an authority and a private individual can last for only two years (SekrL 8:10). Other time limits are 5, 10, 20, 40, and 50 years.

40.   *See* TF 4:2. Publications which have been produced "by way of mimeographing, photocopying or any similar technical process" do not automatically fall within the ambit of the Act. In essence, the printer of any such publication is provided with the choice as to whether or not to come under the Act's umbrella. In order for this type of publication to be governed by the Act, it must be provided with the same declaration of origin that is automatically required of any publication provided by means of a printing press. *See* TF 1:5.

41.   TL art. 4.

42.   Law 8/6 1978 on obligatory copies of publications and sound and picture recordings. (SFS 1978:487).

43.   TF 1:7.

44.   TF 5:2, TL art. 6.

45.   TF 5:5, TL art. 8.

46.   TF 5:11.

47.   The editor of a book containing the contributions of several authors also enjoys these privileges.

48.   See *infra* p. 243.

49.   TF 1:1, paragraphs 3 and 4:

Any person shall likewise have the right, unless otherwise provided in the present Act, to make statements and communicate information on any subject whatsoever for the purpose of publication in print to the author or any person who shall be considered the author of a representation in such publication, to the editor or editorial office, if any, of any publication, or to an enterprise dealing commercially with the forwarding of news or other communication to periodicals.

It shall furthermore be the right of any person, unless otherwise provided in this Act, to procure information on any subject whatsoever for the purpose of its publication in print, or for the purpose of making statements or communicating information in the manner referred to in the preceding paragraph.

50.    This follows from the exclusivity of the rules of responsibility treated later in this essay.

51.    TF 8:5 and 8:6.

52.    TF 7:3:

If a person makes such statement as referred to in the third paragraph of Article 1 of Chapter 1, or if he, without being responsible under the provisions of Chapter 8, contributes as author or other originator, or as editor, to a representation intended for publication in written matter, and if he thereby renders himself guilty of

1)    high treason, sedition, treason, treachery, espionage, grave espionage, or grave unauthorized dealing with secret information, or attempts at such crime, or preparation for or instigation to such crime;

2)    wrongful delivery of an official document which is not available to the public, or making such document available in contravention of a restriction imposed by a public authority when delivering the document, where such act is committed deliberately; or

3)    deliberate disregard of duty to observe secrecy in cases which shall be specified in a special act of law, the provisions of law regarding liability on account of such crime shall apply.

If a person procures information for such purposes as referred to in the fourth paragraph of Article 1 of Chapter 1 and thereby renders himself guilty of a crime such as referred to in sub-paragraph 1 of the first paragraph of the present Article, the provisions of law regarding liability on account of such crime shall apply.

The provisions of law mentioned here are found in BrB ch. 19 resp. BrB 20:3.

53.    Thus, for example, a policeman but not a social worker can in most cases break an obligation to observe silence without risk.

54.    TF 9:2, 12:1.

55.    Broadly defined, text accompanying n. 43, *supra*.

56.    TF 3:1.

57.    TF 3:2.

58.    TF 3:3 and 3:5.

59.    In the latter two cases, the court must first determine whether it is

necessary to hear a witness whose testimony will breach the obligation of silence. *See* TF 3:3.

60. TF 3:4 and 3:5. The preparatory work (the government bill of 1976) indicates that only the crimes enumerated in n. 5 (TF 7:3) and economic crimes committed through publication or abstruse advertisements, e.g., those containing a hidden defamation, fall under this category.

61. The Act contains no corresponding declaration with respect to publications by means of stencil copying or photocopying, but in fact there are no restrictions on the right to own or use equipment for such purposes. It should also be noted that foreigners, in principle, need special permission in order to engage in commercial activities in Sweden. *See* Law 29/11 1968 on the right of foreigners and foreign enterprises to carry on commerce and industry in the kingdom (SFS 1968:555).

62. TF 6:1.

63. TF 6:4.

64. TF 1:2, first paragraph.

65. Prop. 1948:230 p. 104.

66. The Board of Psychological Defense is an independent authority under the supervision of the Ministry of Defense. Most of its members are civilians.

67. A comparison of the language of the two paragraphs of TF 1:2 indicates that only the ban on censorship is absolute.

68. *See infra*, text accompanying notes 119–124.

69. TF 1:3.

70. *See* discussion of the Act's catalogue of crimes, text accompanying notes 79–100, *infra*.

71. *See* TF 1:9 and law 30/11 1978 containing certain provisions on marketing of alcohol and tobacco (SFS 1978:763 and 764).

72. *See* TF 1:9 and law 14/12 1973 on credit information (SFS 1973:1173).

73. TF 7:2.

74. TF 6:2, BrB 16:11 and 12.

75. TF 6:2 and law 22/5 1975 on prohibition against spreading and export of certain maps resp. of aerial and certain other photographs (SFS 1975:370 and 371). However, there are no known instances of prosecution pursuant to those provisions.

76. NJA 1900 p. 528, 1905 p. 364, 1961 p. 715.

77. NJA 1979 p. 602.

78. It is also noteworthy that the Market Court may intervene in order to challenge undue advertising in printed publications. The rule has been established in the preparatory work of the Marketing Act (prop. 1970:57 p. 66 f.) and has been applied by the Market Court in numerous cases. It has also been recognized by the Supreme Court in the cases NJA 1975 p. 589 and 1977 p. 751. See the article by the author of this essay "Tryckfrihet och marknadsföring" [Freedom of the Press and Marketing] in SvJT 1980 pp. 25–39.

79. *See* TF 7:4(1); BrB 19:1 and 19:14.

80. *See* TF 7:4(2); BrB 19:4.

81. *See* TF 7:4(3); BrB 18:1 and 18:7.

82. *See* TF 7:4(4); Brb 22:1 and 22:12.

83. *See* TF 7:4(5); BrB 22:2.

84. *See* TF 7:4(6); BrB 16:5, 21:10.

85. *See* TF 7:4(7); BrB 22:2(a).

86. *See* TF 7:4(8); BrB 16:8.

87. *See* TF 7:4(9); BrB 5:1 and 5:2. *Defamation* is defined as the spreading of dishonoring information about a person.

88. *See* TF 7:4(10); BrB 5:4.

89. *See* TF 7:4(11); BrB 5:3.

90. *See* TF 7:4(12); BrB 16:10(a).

91. But it is still a criminal offense to spread rumors dangerous to the national security during periods of war or emergency.

92. However, different rules of prosecution obtain in suits involving these public figures. *See* text accompanying notes 116–118 *infra*.

93. The group libel provision was added as a reaction to the Holocaust, and was applied in some older cases involving anti-Semitic propaganda. (NJA 1956 p. 48, 1957 p. 352). Prior to 1949, anti-Semitic propaganda expressed in ways other than publication was punished as disorderly conduct. Recently, the provision has been applied to propaganda directed at immigrants. However, in 1978, an effort by the Church of Scientology to invoke the provision failed, when the Supreme Court held that the provision does not permit private prosecution (NJA 1978 p. 3).

94. However, in 1970, a proposal to make war propaganda criminal was rejected, also the 1965 provision has never been invoked.

95. NJA 1966, p. 565.

96. Ch. 5 art. 1 of the Penal Code, applicable in press freedom cases, defines defamation as follows:

Anyone who depicts another as a criminal or as blameworthy in his way of life or else gives information likely to expose the same person to the disdain of others is guilty of defamation and may be fined. The same section provides that a valid defense for defamation would consist of proof that (1) the speaker was under an obligation to speak or that under the circumstances it was justifiable to express this information; and (2) the information was true or the speaker had a reasonable ground to believe in its truth. For an explanation of the practices of private prosecution, see below, n. 115.

97. TF 7:5:

As an unauthorized publication in printed matter shall be considered any such act which is punishable under provisions of law and which involves:

1. publication of information the disclosure of which would according to law constitute an offense against the security of the Realm;

2. deliberate publication of an official document which is not available to the public;

3. disclosure of information, whereby a person who is responsible for the printed matter under the provisions of Chapter 8 deliberately disregards such duty to observe secrecy as is provided for in the special law referred to in sub-paragraph 3 of the third paragraph of Article 3.

98. The provisions concerning punishment of crimes against national security are found in BrB ch. 19, and concerning breaches of secrecy in BrB 20:3.

99.    *IB* is an abbreviation for the Information Bureau of the Swedish Secret Service.

100.    The IB affair is reported in KU 1974:22 pp. 6 ff. and 166 ff., NJA 1975 p. 585 and SvJT 1974 p. 84.

101.    TF 8:12. This is a *praesumptio juris et de jure.* In other words, it is a legal fiction which cannot be refuted.

102.    TF 8:1–4.

103.    TF 8:5–9.

104.    TF 11:1. As a practical matter, tort liability is possible only in cases of defamation, insult, and to a certain extent breach of secrecy.

105.    TF 11:2.

106.    See the citations of the Penal Code made above in connection with the catalogue of crimes. *Supra,* notes 79–90.

107.    TF 6:3, 7:7.

108.    TF 7:8.

109.    TF 11:1.

101.    TF 8:12. This is a *praesumptio juris et de jure.* In other words, it is a legal fiction which cannot be refuted.

111.    TF 7:6.

112.    TF 9:2. The chancellor is the highest ombudsman of the government (not to be confused with the four ombudsmen of the Riksdag). He represents the state before the courts, supervises all public officers, and has the responsibility of prosecuting them for breach of duty. Generally, the prosecution of press freedom crimes comprises a small fraction of his workload.

113.    TF 9:2, TL art. 2.

114.    TF 9:3.

115.    A *private prosecution* is an action by a private plaintiff in which punishment (and perhaps also damages) is sought. Unless only damages are sought, the trial will be conducted in accordance with criminal rules of procedure.

116.    BrB 5:5. Following the private complaint, the public prosecutor decides whether to initiate proceedings by evaluating the likelihood of obtaining a conviction.

117.    BrB 5:5, 18:8.

118.    BrB 20:5.

119.    TF 9:5.

120.    TF 10:2.

121.    TF 10:4.

122.    TF 10:5.

123.    TF 10:11 and 10:12, i.e., following seizure by the military authorities, the chancellor decides whether the publication should be seized or released. If he opts for seizure, prosecution must follow within two weeks. The judicial proceedings which may follow are governed by the Press Act. Thus, even this type of administrative means is ultimately subjected to judicial review.

124.    TF 10:14.

125.    TF 12:1 par. 2.

126.    In principle only one district court in each of the 24 provinces serves as a press freedom court. *See* TF 12:1 par. 1. However, in four provinces, there are two

competent courts, making a total of 28.

127.  TF 12:2.

128.  In the district courts, five or six politically elected laymen take part in criminal cases and certain civil cases concerning family law. The laymen can outvote the judge, if all or all except for one have a different opinion than the judge. Laymen also participate under similar conditions in the courts of appeal.

129.  The jury is empanelled in the following manner: In each province 24 jurors are elected by the provincial assembly. One third of those elected must have served at one time or another as lay members of a district court. Thus, there are two groups of laymen, one of which has had previous legal experience. *See* TF 12:3. Of these 24, only nine will serve as jurors in any particular case. In order to determine which of the 24 will serve on the jury, the court must first eliminate challengeable jurors. Next, each party has a right to exclude three jurors without prior legal experience from the group and one juror with such experience from the group. The court will then select substitutes by lot from among those who remain until six jurors from the group lacking prior legal experience and three from the group with such experience remain. *See* TF 12:10.

130.  TF 12:2.

131.  TF 1:4 par. 1.

132.  The board may also order an editor to publish a modification or reply.

133.  Text accompanying notes 99–100, *supra*.

134.  Radio and TV are currently regulated by two ordinary laws, the Radio Act and the Radio Responsibility Act, both of 1966. To a large extent, these laws are similar to the Freedom of the Press Act.

## ABBREVIATIONS

| | |
|---|---|
| BrB | *Brottsbalk* 21/12 1962 (SFS 1962:700, with several later amendments). [Penal Code.] |
| KU | *Konstitutionsutskottets betänkande.* [Report of the Constitutional Committee of the Riksdag.] |
| NJA | *Nytt juridiskt arkiv.* [New Archives of Law, containing reports from the Supreme Court.] |
| Prop. | *Regeringens proposition.* [Government Bill.] |
| RF | *Regeringsform* 28/2 1974 (SFS 1974:152, reprinted 1982:940). [Constitution.] |
| SekrL | *Sekretesslag* 20/3 1980 (SFS 1980:100, reprinted 1982:1106). [Secrecy Act.] |
| SFS | *Svensk författningssamling.* [Swedish Collection of Statutes and Ordinances.] |
| SOU | *Statens offentliga utredningar.* [Official Reports of the State.] |
| SvJT | *Svensk juristtidning.* [Swedish Law Journal.] |
| TF | *Tryckfrihetsförordning* 5/4 1949 (SFS 1949:105, reprinted 1982:941). [Freedom of the Press Act.] |
| TL | *Lag* 15/12 1977 *med vissa bestämmelser på tryckfrihetsförordningens område* (SFS 1977:1016). [Law containing certain provisions in the domain of the Freedom of the Press Act.] |

# PART 3

# The Nonwestern Approach

# Six

---

# Israel's Press Law

Pnina Lahav

## GENERAL FRAMEWORK

### Jurisprudence

Israel's jurisprudence of free speech is an amalgam of elements from liberal philosophy and from certain schools of authoritarian political theory. To understand this condition, a brief sketch of Israeli history is needed.

Israel gained political sovereignty in 1948. Prior to that date, the then-Palestine was ruled by successive authoritarian regimes—first the Turks, under the Ottoman empire, then the British as a mandatory power. The ideological and political foundations for contemporary Israel were laid in the early twentieth century, when massive Jewish immigration to Palestine resulted in the formation of the Yishuv.[1] The ideology of the Yishuv was Zionism—the liberation of the Jewish people through the establishment of a sovereign Jewish state. Until 1948, the Zionist leadership focused primarily on survival. All energy was directed toward the goal of securing the existence of the Jewish population in Palestine by establishing a state; the content of the future polity was of secondary importance.

As Israel became a reality, it adopted the English model of government. At birth, Israel was branded a parliamentary democracy; its formal institutions borrowed heavily from the Westminster model and its rhetoric revealed identification with Western liberalism.[2]

Four significant dichotomies are discernible in Israel's jurisprudence of free speech. The first dichotomy is between enlightened Zionism and

Special thanks go to U. Benziman, R. Gavison, E. Harnon, R. Loevy, H. Monaghan, and A. Soifer for reading previous drafts and helping the author with comments and criticisms, and to G. Strassberg and Y. Moyal-Levy for their expert assistance.

pre-emancipation Jewish culture. Zionism cherished the values of the Enlightenment, including freedom of expression and criticism.[3] In contrast, pre-emancipation Jewish culture, conditioned by ghetto mentality and rampant anti-Semitism, frowned upon open criticism, as well as political and religious dissent.[4]

The second dichotomy is between British constitutional liberalism and British colonialism. British constitutional liberalism, admired by large parts of the Zionist elite, reflected a triumph over censorship and other authoritarian devices of suppression. British colonialism, in its efforts to maintain a certain minimum of public order amid the growing political violence between Arabs and Jews, established in Palestine an elaborate legal system of political suppression, including censorship.

The third dichotomy is between Anglo-American and Continental (primarily German) liberalism. Anglo-American liberalism, nurtured by the philosophy of John Stuart Mill, reflects the commitment to a free marketplace of ideas as a guarantor of both a free and open thinking process and self-government. It penetrated the Israeli legal culture through the Anglophilic sympathies of the elite, by the incorporation of a large part of the common law into the law of Palestine[5] and, as a concomitant of the previous two factors, by the increased exposure to legal education in English-speaking countries. Yet, Anglo-American liberalism is tied to individualism, which gives the individual a preferred position over the state.[6] In Israeli culture this trend is countered by the continental brand of liberalism, which delegates a far more central role to the state and hence fosters state supervision and regulation of free expression.[7] The continental brand of liberalism was shared by members of Israel's legal elite who were educated in Europe, primarily in Germany, and by Zionism, which emphasised the *state* as the most precious achievement.

Finally, in terms of jurisprudence, Israel's notions of free speech were influenced by the dichotomy between sociological jurisprudence and legal formalism. Legal formalism, strong in England, in late nineteenth century America, and on the Continent, is characterized primarily by the belief in the autonomy of law. Sociological jurisprudence, on the other hand, recognizes the connection between law and politics; it views the law as a reflection of social mores as well as an instrument for shaping them. In Israel, the legal formalists applied the highly authoritarian colonial laws, inherited from the British Mandate, with little articulated regard to the values embedded in them or to their impact on the polity. Members of the school of sociological jurisprudence, however, endeavored to infuse those laws with liberal values.[8]

These four dichotomies coalesce into one fundamental libertarian-authoritarian dialectic. Thus, the Israeli jurisprudence of free speech is characterized by a profound commitment to freedom of expression, nurtured by tenets of enlightened Zionism, British liberal constitutionalism, Anglo-American liberalism, and sociological jurisprudence. It is in constant struggle with a countervailing notion which would subordinate it to other short- and long-term interests and utilitarian concerns. This authoritarian notion is nurtured by the pre-emancipation Jewish tradition, British colonialism, Continental liberalism, and legal formalism.

Three significant factors have further reinforced the authoritarian notion. First, the left-of-center brand of Zionism, predominant in Israeli politics both before and after independence, valued a highly centralized government, capable of bringing about the socialist transformation to which it aspired. It did not value and was not tolerant of political dissent and caustic criticism.[9] Second, national security problems—the fact that from inception Israel was under a threat of destruction by its Arab neighbors and had been denied legitimacy as a sovereign state—produced a climate both suspicious and intolerant of free expression. Third, the Holocaust, precipitated by the fall of the Weimar Republic and the rise of Nazi Germany, deeply traumatized Israelis and shook their confidence in a regime of free expression. The belief that the Weimar's failure to repress Nazi ideology was a central cause of Hitler's rise to power strengthened the authoritarian notions that speech be subordinated to order.

Two cases—*Kol Ha'am*[10] and *Ha'aretz*[11]—exemplify the fundamental libertarian-authoritarian dialectic. In *Kol Ha'am,* Israel's commitment to freedom of speech and of the press was first expressed.[12] There, the High Court of Justice declared the right to freedom of expression to be an integral part of Israeli law.[13] Three justifications for this principle were advanced by the Court. First, the justification from democracy, i.e., that in order to maintain self-government the polity must have a free and uninhibited press. Second, the justification from the commitment to truth, i.e., that the quest for truth can only be guaranteed if a free marketplace of ideas is maintained. Third, the justification from self-fulfillment, i.e., "the interest of every man . . . to nurture and develop his ego to the fullest extent possible; to express his opinion on every subject that he regards as vital to him."[14]

While many cases have followed this libertarian trend, the authoritarian theme also can be detected in opinions that contemplate a much narrower breathing space for freedom of the press. *Ha'aretz* v. *Electric Company* reflects the latter theme.[15] The issue in *Ha'aretz* was whether a bona fide criticism of public officials should be considered as defamatory. In holding that it should, the Court advanced a critique of the liberal justifications for free expression. The first *Kol Ha'am* justification—the justification from democracy—was to be modified in light of the Weimar experience. Observing that "one of the most efficient instruments used by Hitler . . . in order to destroy the Weimar regime was unrestrained defamation of the elite" and that "we have to fear that history will repeat itself," the Court invoked the Weimar experience to justify limitations on press freedom.[16] The court also found the second justification advanced in *Kol Ha'am*—the free marketplace of ideas—unconvincing because it was "romantic" and unrealistic.[17] Although the Court did not address the third *Kol Ha'am* justification—that from self-fulfillment—it did employ another argument from individualism, grounded mostly on syllogistic logic. The Court first posited that the most important right was the right to life. It next posited that the right to life was concommitant to the right to reputation. The Court then reasoned that since the primary duty of the state (the sovereign) is to protect life (reputation), the principle of free expression should be assigned secondary importance.[18]

These cases reflect the two poles of the dialectic. Both the libertarian and the authoritarian themes recognize that the principle of freedom of expression is not absolute and must be balanced against other interests. Their *methods* of balancing differ, however. The libertarian approach emphasizes that freedom of expression is a "superior right" of "decisive importance,"[19] to be restricted through a balancing process only in moments of "supreme urgency."[20] The authoritarian approach declines to assign the right to free expression a preferred position. Its gambit is a horizontal approach where all rights are assigned equal importance. Upon balancing, it finds the "liberty" of expression subordinated to other "rights," such as the "right" of reputation.[21]

The libertarian-authoritarian dialectic in Israeli free speech jurisprudence is thus quite clear. The libertarian approach emphasizes democracy and self-fulfillment (Enlightenment themes), and reflects Anglo-American philosophy and sociological jurisprudence. The authoritarian trend reflects skepticism about Enlightenment philosophy. It combines a Hobbesian preference for a strong state with a pious belief in the autonomy of law. Upon examination, the Court's rhetoric about the autonomy of law reveals disillusionment with liberalism, and sympathy for a strong central government.

### The Constitution

Israel has no written constitution. It does have a series of Basic Laws that regulate constitutional issues, but no Bill of Rights.[22] Thus, an ordinary statute may legally curtail the rights of free expression and free press. Since 1973, a draft Basic Law, the Rights of Man, has been pending before the Knesset. The bill, modeled largely after the Basic Law of the Federal Republic of Germany, recognizes the right to free expression, but does not address separately the issue of a free press.[23] Also, it allows for considerable restrictions:

> 11.   (Freedom of Expression)
> (a) Every person has the right to express his opinions, to publish them, to disseminate and impart them to others as well as to publish, present, and to

distribute information, and scientific, literary, and artistic research; all of the above may be orally, in writing, and by any other means of communication. (b) None of these rights may be limited except by a law whose purpose is to ensure the existence of a democratic rule, to safeguard the defense of the State and the public peace, to safeguard moral values or to prevent desecration of religion, to safeguard the rights of others, or to guarantee proper legal proceedings.[24]

Pending enactment of a Bill of Rights, Israelis enjoy a common law right of free expression and free press. As discussed above, the right to free expression was first articulated in the *Kol Ha'am* case.[25] To justify its incorporation into Israel's legal system, the Court relied on Israel's Declaration of Independence.[26] The Court held that while the Declaration's commitment to human rights is not legally binding, it serves as a device to guide the Court in interpreting statutes. Thus a statute with a potentially restrictive effect should be interpreted to allow maximum breathing space to freedom of expression.[27]

## The Role of the Courts

The Israeli judiciary is divided into three tiers: Magistrate Courts, District Courts and one Supreme Court. The Supreme Court, presently composed of twelve justices, has appellate jurisdiction over cases decided in the lower courts, and original jurisdiction, in its capacity as the High Court of Justice, when it hears petitions directed at the executive branch of the government.[28]

Because the right to free expression is not assigned constitutional status, the issue of judicial review does not present itself. Nonetheless, in their review of executive discretion, the courts, particularly the Supreme Court, do perform a crucial role in shaping the contours of the right to free speech. Israel's legal system is saturated with statutes and regulations inherited from the British Mandatory Regime.[29] As will become evident throughout this essay, their most salient characteristic is the broad discretionary powers given to the executive branch. One example will suffice: pursuant to the Defense (Emergency) Regulations of 1946, the District Commissioner may deny any newspaper a permit to operate and may censor any material *at his own discretion*.[30] The significance of Israel's courts lies in their ability to supervise these discretionary powers. By limiting the discretion, both through a requirement of due process and through review of substantive standards, the courts can strengthen the press and intensify the quality of its liberty. Indeed, in a number of cases the Court has done just that. Still, in other cases, the Court has upheld the totality of the discretionary powers, thereby making press freedom dependent upon the good will of executive officials.

## THE PRESS AND THE GOVERNMENT

### The Press Law

A Press Ordinance enacted in 1933 regulates Israel's press. The statute, modelled after the Cyprus press law, was introduced into Palestine after the Arab pogroms on the Jewish population of Hebron in 1929.[31] The British government, attributing the cause of violence to the inflammatory Arab press, hoped regulation would reduce the political tension. The Press Ordinance contains three basic structural themes: licensing of newspapers; control of content; and sanctions for violations of the preceding two.[32] As violence in Palestine escalated, the British strengthened their control over the press by issuing the Defense (Emergency) Regulations.[33] Since these measures are interrelated and both still obtain in Israel, they shall be reviewed together.

### *Licensing*

The Press Ordinance requires that all newspapers (the definition of which is very broad) and printing presses be licensed.[34] Publication without a license constitutes a criminal offense.[35]

Both publisher and editor must submit declarations, under oath, listing their qualifications. Although anyone can qualify as a publisher, an editor must meet specific requirements: he must be at least twenty-five years old, with at least a high school diploma, be familiar with the language of the paper, and have a clean legal record.[36] Another requirement is the execution of a deposition to guarantee the payment of fines should the newspaper be convicted of having violated the Ordinance.[37]

In addition to the deposit requirement, the Press Ordinance provides three mechanisms to control the editor and publisher. First, a newspaper must submit two copies of each issue to the District Commissioner for content supervision.[38] Second, any change in the information concerning publisher or editor, permanent or temporary replacement of the editor, or temporary travel outside the country should be reported. Failure to do so may result in cancellation of the permit by administrative discretion.[39] Third, the Press Ordinance requires that all publishing permits must be used at frequent intervals and must not lie dormant.[40] The "frequency of publication" requirement, seemingly innocuous on its face, is an interesting control mechanism. Designed to complement the government's power to suspend publication totally, the frequency requirement makes it more difficult for a publisher or editor of a suspended newspaper to activate spare permits during a suspension. Israel's Supreme Court was presented with this issue only once, in 1952. The Ministry of the Interior had cancelled a permit on the typically authoritarian ground "that [a] permit should be granted only to newspapers whose regular appearance prove their seriousness and the public interest in them."[41] The opinion of the Court reflected the nexus between authoritarianism and legal formalism in Israel. The legal explanation for dismissing the petition was the doctrine of the separation of powers—the reluctance of the judiciary to interfere with the broad statutory discretion granted to the government. The opinion contained no reference to press freedom.[42]

With the exception of one other case,[43] the Israeli government has refrained from utilizing aggressively the permit structure; it thus has spared the courts the task of exploring the ordinance's compatibility with a commitment to a free press.[44] Instead, the government has utilized another licensing device—that provided by the Defense (Emergency) Regulations. Under the Press Ordinance, the Minister has no discretion to deny a permit once all requirements have been met (although he does have power to suspend or revoke the license subsequently). In contrast, the Defense (Emergency) Regulations, which require an additional permit, vest the District Commissioner with seemingly unlimited powers to grant, condition, or revoke the license.[45]

The High Court of Justice had several opportunities to review those powers. In 1964, E1-Ard, an Arab nationalist group, was denied a permit to publish a weekly magazine. While expressing sympathy for the principle of free expression, the Court dismissed the petition on the ground that the broad language of the regulation precluded judicial review.[46] Fifteen years later, in the *El-Assaad* case, an Arab publisher was denied a permit to publish a monthly magazine in Jerusalem.[47] The District Commissioner argued that the Arab Commmunist Party—outlawed on the West Bank and affiliated with the Palestine Liberation Organization (P.L.O.)—stood behind the paper, and that the paper would incite readers to acts of subversion and political violence. In a two-to-one decision, the Court ordered the District Commissioner to issue a permit. The immediate result constituted a triumph for the principle of press freedom and attested to the important role Israel's court plays in safeguarding that principle. Furthermore, some of the dicta in the majority opinion indicated a departure from the formalistic stand of the *El-Ard* case. The Court described the permit power as a "'drastic' and draconian [regulation] enacted by a colonial regime, which is incompatible with basic concepts of free expression in a democratic state." The Court also expressed a preference for the policy of subsequent punishment, stating that it is better to allow the paper to speak first, then review its contents, rather than to suppress initially an attempt to publish.[48]

*El-Assaad* was a qualified victory for the press. Its legal reasoning was not related directly to press freedom. The majority opinion held that because the District Commissioner *chose* to disclose the reasons for declining the permit, the Court was free to evaluate the factual evidence allegedly supporting those reasons.[49] A year later, when an Arab academic sought a permit to publish a scientific weekly, the District Commissioner refused, and declined to supply the reasons for his refusal. In a very technical and deferential opinion, the High Court of Justice upheld the authority of the executive branch to deny a permit while hiding behind a veil of silence.[50] The legal reasoning in all three cases illustrates the authoritarian pole of the Enlightenment-authoritarian dialectic in Israeli free speech law. The opinions are mostly formalistic. In contradistinction to the legal reasoning in *Kol Ha'am*, which attempted to probe the sociopolitical meaning of the statutory language, these opinions resort to a mechanical application of the law. Furthermore, in *Kol Ha'am* the Court took pains to provide the Minister of the Interior with substantive criteria, applicable whenever the suspension of newspapers is at issue (e.g., suspension was warranted only when there was a high probability of danger to the public peace). The permit cases refrained from providing any standards, and thus allowed executive discretion to prevail over judicial reason.

### Control of Content

The Press Ordinance allows the government to compel newspapers to publish, free of charge, any official communiques[51] and official denials of factual information previously published by the newspaper.[52] None of these powers has been used by the Israeli government.

### Sanctions

Violation of any of the provisions of the Press Ordinance constitutes a criminal offense, and may, in some cases, result in seizure and forfeiture of published copies.[53] One sanction of particular significance is the power to suspend publications.[54] This sanction is especially dangerous because of the executive branch's discretion to suspend publication without a court order and for long periods of time. A suspension may not only stifle criticism, it may also prove economically detrimental to a newspaper, which may lose considerable advertising income during the suspension.

Prior to Israel's independence, the British heavily used the sanction of suspension. Between 1948 and 1953, Israel's government invoked it occasionally. However, when the Minister of the Interior suspended the communist paper *Kol Ha'am* (the People's Voice) twice within a period of a few months, the High Court of Justice intervened and effectively narrowed executive discretion. In a landmark decision, which also laid the foundations of the Israeli jurisprudence of free speech, the Court held that the Minister of the Interior can suspend a newspaper *only* if there is a high probability that the publication will result in danger to the public peace.

The Court rejected the bad tendency test as incompatible with democratic principles, and established a variation of the clear and present danger test as the proper criterion for legitimate suppression of expression.

Between 1953 and 1967 Israeli newspapers were not suspended. Following the Six Day War, Israeli law was applied to East Jerusalem and Israeli military rule was instituted over the West Bank. As a result, the composition of newspapers changed, and with it the attitude of the Israeli government toward the press. Until 1967, the Israeli press had been relatively homogeneous. The legitimacy of the State of Israel and the essence of Zionism—that the liberation of the Jewish people requires Jewish political sovereignty—were not questioned. Criticism, however intense, was conducted within this ideological framework. The only notable exception was the effort by the Palestinian nationalist movement El-Ard to express itself in print. The movement's newspapers had been suppressed and El-Ard was subsequently outlawed.[55] This homogeneity did not survive the 1967 War. Palestinian newspapers, located in East Jerusalem, identified with Palestinian nationalism and expressed their support for the Palestinian cause as well as their opposition to Israeli policies, oftentimes in vociferous language.[56] In the reaction of Israel's government one could see the dilemma of Israeli liberalism. On the one hand, the government wished to pursue its commitment to the democratic process and press freedom. On the other hand, it faced, for the first time, a coalition of experienced newspapers[57] that viewed itself as an arm of the Palestinian struggle and expressed itself accordingly. After 1967, and for more than a decade, the government preserved the legal taboo on utilizing the suspension powers of section 19 and attempted to control the Arab press either through its military censor or through its powers of suspension by virtue of the Defense (Emergency) Regulations.[58]

In 1981, the taboo was broken when the Minister of the Interior ordered the suspension of the Palestinian daily *El-Fajr*, for a month, by virtue of his powers pursuant to section 19. The suspension order decreed that the articles published in *El-Fajr* constituted praise and encouragement to terrorist actions and thereby endangered the public peace.[59] Both the government and the newspaper relied on the probable danger test of *Kol Ha'am*.[60] The Court rejected the newspaper's argument that there was no causal relation between the articles and the terrorist activities, and held that the circumstances did justify suspension of the newspaper.[61]

Technically, the Court cited approvingly the *Kol Ha'am* decision and even claimed to apply its doctrine. However, the Court merely paid lip service to the justifications for free expression underlying *Kol Ha'am* and failed to follow the elaborate doctrinal guidelines delineated there. The assumption of a causal connection between free expression and the massive disorder on the West Bank was not explicated in a reasoned fashion. Rather, it was intuitively presumed. The decision in *El-Fajr* clearly strengthens the authoritarian trend in the authoritarian-libertarian Israeli dialectic. But it also illustrates the vulnerability of a liberal order to such circumstances. The *El-Fajr* Court was able to ignore the spirit of *Kol Ha'am* because it viewed *El-Fajr* as a weapon in the hands of the Palestine Liberation Organization in its war against the Israeli State, rather than as a vehicle to express dissenting opinion. So did *El-Fajr* perceive itself. Viewed from the perspective of the Arab-Israeli conflict[62] and given the reality of social violence, it is easy to understand (but not necessarily to condone) the reaction of the Israeli Court.

## National Security

As the preceding discussion makes clear, national security concerns were among the central forces that shaped Israel's press law. The concern for security is real and powerful. It stems from centuries of persecution as well as from the more immediate past of systematic genocide of the Jewish people by Nazi Germany. Moreover, the bloody Arab-Israeli wars and the persistent Arab position, at least until 1967, that the only acceptable solution to the Mideast conflict was the liquidation of the Jewish state, have nourished historical Jewish fears and verified them as real and present. These concerns have created an extreme sensitivity to anything that may threaten survival, including speech. This analysis, however, should not be taken to mean that such concerns are never manipulated for partisan or political purposes. As we shall see below, the powers to suppress speech have also been abused for reasons other than national security.

The legal system permitting regulation and suppression of the press is complex. In large part, it was inherited from the authoritarian British regime in pre-independent Israel. It should be emphasized, however, that while the Arab military threat constituted the immediate cause for adopting this system in sovereign Israel, its legitimacy in the eyes of the Israeli elite also stemmed from other authoritarian trends embedded in the Enlightenment-authoritarian dialectic.

### Genuine National Security Interests

#### Censorship

The same dialectic dominates Israeli censorial practices. On the one hand, the courts have borrowed and institutionalized the Anglo-American doctrine against prior restraint.[63] On the other hand, censorship of information bearing on military and other vital issues is operative.

The Defense (Emergency) Regulations provide for a complex system of censorship that grants broad discretion to the censor and prohibits protest against actual censorship (it is a criminal offense to leave blank spaces in a publication, a practice which attracts attention to the fact that the paper was censored).[64] In practice, however, the censorial apparatus rests on an agreement between the military authorities and the Editors' Committee.[65] The latter is a central institution within Israel's political culture. Knowledge of its history, composition, and philosophy is helpful for understanding Israel's press in general, and its censorship in particular. Members of the committee are editors of daily newspapers, an elite group that is part of the Israeli establishment.[66] Prior to independence, the committee cooperated closely with the Yishuv leadership in ensuring that the Hebrew press reflected and advanced the political goals of the Yishuv. The leadership reciprocated by making committee members privy to highly sensitive information that was not for publication.[67] The committee's existence has been both a symptom and a catalyst of the press's self-image as a body committed to less than total criticism of the government, for whom the value of press freedom is secondary to the primacy of the state. Still, it should be emphasized that the committee helped to consolidate the status of Israel's press as a free institution. Over the years it has sensitized both the government and the public to the importance of press freedom and has managed to impede a number of governmental attempts to contract it.[68] Since 1977 it has become much more aggressive in its criticism of the government and in its insistence on preserving the values of Israeli democracy.

The committee's censorship accord with the army aptly reflects its philosphy. The accord states that "[c]ensorship is founded on cooperation between the military authorities and the press"[69] for the purpose of "preventing the publication of security information, which might aid the enemy or damage the defense of the state."[70] Section 4 further emphasizes the limitation on the power of the censor: "Censorship does not apply to political matters, opinions, commentary, assessments or any other matter except for security information."[71] In practice, a list of sensitive topics is distributed to newspapers and they are obliged to submit any item corresponding to the topics for the censor's approval. "Security information" is defined loosely. According to the censor, one purpose of censorship is to thwart the efforts of foreign intelligence to gather accurate information through open and accessible Israeli sources. The military authorities advance this apology when they suppress information that appears innocent and unrelated to security. An example of such information was the number of doughnuts distributed to the armed forces at the northern front during a Hanukkah party. It was asserted that specifying the number of doughnuts ordered (e.g., 500) and the number of doughnuts each soldier would receive (e.g., 2) would enable foreign intelligence to assess the size of the military force.[72] Some censorial actions, however, are unnecessarily and incomprehensibly strict, e.g., when Israeli newspapers are prohibited from repeating news items published abroad (on the ground that such publication confirms their accuracy), or when the political value of the suppressed information is such that one cannot but suspect that more than security considerations guided the censor.[73]

In addition to implementing the censorship accord, the censor also prevents the publication of "secret information" pursuant to section 113(d) of the Penal Code. This section authorizes the government to decree that decisions and deliberations of the Cabinet's Committee for Security Affairs are "secret information." The censor requires that news items under this heading be submitted for prior approval. Although the practice is of dubious legality, the newspapers comply. This arrangement allows the government to hide political information from the public, simply by declaring that a particular item was discussed or decided in the security committee forum.[74]

Violations of the censorship guidelines, as well as complaints by newspapers that the censor has exceeded his authority, are brought before a committee of three, composed of representatives of the military, the Editors' Committee, and the public. The committee's deliberations are informal but secret. As sanctions for violating the censor's guidelines, it may either reprimand the newspaper or impose a fine.[75]

It is not suprising that Israeli military censorship sometimes expands into political censorship. This is not only expected, sociologically, in a system in which censorship has always been operative and legitimate, but also reflects a positive attitude toward censorship as a legitimate device. As can be expected, the use and abuse of censorship is heightened in periods of war. During the 1982 war in Lebanon, the uncooperative and manipulative attitude of the Israeli authorities toward the local and foreign press reached an unprecedented peak and drew considerable criticism.[76]

The peculiar neutralization of the legal system is even more significant. One consequence of the voluntary accord between the press and the military is that the courts are not called upon to interpret the proper contours of the censorial powers. The de facto absence of the option to litigate censorship issues has affected journalistic consciousness in Israel. Because of the rather cozy behind-the-scenes solution to problems, the dilemma of press freedom and democracy versus national security is never sharpened. Since these issues are at the heart of Israeli concerns, their absence from the court's docket prevents the creation of a critical mass of cases that would force judicial crystallization of the meaning of free speech.

Another consequence of the voluntary accord is the creation of a double standard toward the press. The voluntary accord applies only to those papers whose editors are members of the Editors' Committee. The censor may, but is not obliged to, apply the terms of the accord to other papers. Thus, with respect to some of the Hebrew non-dailies, as well as the Arab newspapers of East Jerusalem (legally a part of Israel), the Defense (Emergency) Regulations and not the voluntary accord are operative. These newspapers are much more restricted than Hebrew papers. Consequently, the informal/formal split also corresponds to consensus/ dissenting newspapers. Newspapers that reflect the Israeli consensus receive much more lenient treatment by the censor than newspapers that champion the Palestinian cause. So far none of the Arab newspapers has challenged the discriminatory treatment in court.

*Criminal statutes*

Israel's penal code is replete with provisions prohibiting speech that is likely to impair national security interests. It is a criminal offense to disseminate "defeatist propaganda...at a time of actual fighting,"[77] or to "display identification with or sympathy toward a terrorist organization"[78] in public. Unlike seditious libel, which will be discussed below, these provisions were not inherited from the Mandatory regime. They were enacted by the Israeli Knesset. Thus, they reflect the independent judgment of Israel's legislature that speech, even if totally remote from action, may be extremely dangerous and ought to be punished. The prohibition on speech should be understood in the context of Israeli politics, in which the large Arab minority always has been suspected of sympathizing with Palestinian national aspirations and in which the Jewish majority itself disagrees about the tactics and strategy of security concerns, as the 1982 war in Lebanon demonstrated so well. Under these circumstances, the criminal law can be easily manipulated to foster unanimity of political thought and to suppress criticism and dissent.[79] While these provisions undoubtedly do represent the authoritarian trend in Israeli free speech jurisprudence, and while occasionally there are calls to invoke them, the libertarian trend has so far predominated and these provisions are seldom invoked against the press.[80]

An important part of the criminal law, deserving special mention, is the offense of *aggravated espionage*. Under section 113(a) of the Penal Code, "[a] person who delivers any secret information without being authorized to do so is liable for imprisonment for fifteen years."[81] Thus, a reporter who publishes leaked secret information, or information in violation of hte censorship regulations, is liable for criminal prosecution. Given the heavy prison term that such an offense entails, it is particularly important to point out that a defense asserting improper classification of the information is not likely to be accepted. Therefore, it is highly unlikely that the Pentagon Papers, for example, could have been published in Israel, not only because of the censor's power, but also because of the heavy hand of the criminal law.

At least one case is known in which journalists were prosecuted for aggravated espionage. Two editors of a sensational, small-circulation magazine, *Bul*, were convicted in 1967 for having violated section 113(a). In Israel, details of the trial have been kept secret.[82] According to the *New York Times*, however, *Bul* published an article about the involvement of Israeli intelligence in the abduction of the Moroccan leader Ben-Barka. The two editors were sentenced to one year in prison, but were pardoned after spending a short time in prison. Details of this episode constitute classified information and therefore it is impossible to analyze the merits of the government's position. According to the foreign press, *Bul* was merely reprinting a news item already published in the French magazine *Aux Ecoutes*, and the prosecution was designed to intimidate and suppress the sensational magazine.[83]

Similarly, in August 1980, the *Washington Star* published a story by its Israeli correspondent about an official investigation of violence on the West Bank. The article also disclosed the identity of the head of Israel's Intelligence Agency—a classified item. The entire story was criticized in Israel as false and unfair. The Attorney General declared that the reporter might be prosecuted, not for the content of the story, but for having published classified information. So far there has been no decision to prosecute.[84] These two incidents support the general contention of journalists that section 113 radiates a chilling effect on press freedom in Israel.

*Seditious libel*

Like prior restraint, seditious libel was declared anathema to democratic values and hence to Israeli constitutional law in the celebrated case of *Kol Ha'am*.[85] Like prior restraint, and in the same paradoxical fashion, seditious libel is part of Israel's criminal law. First introduced into Palestine by the British, the Israeli law against seditious libel makes it criminal, *inter alia*, "to bring into hatred or contempt or to excite disaffection against the State or its...authorities" and "to raise discontent or resentment amongst the inhabitants of Israel."[86] Truth is not a defense.[87] The crime of seditious libel has specific implications for the press. Section 23 of the Press Ordinance empowers the courts to order the closure of a newspaper that publishes seditious libel and to prohibit the person convicted from engaging in *any* journalistic activity for a period of up to three years.[88]

Neither of these provisions has ever been invoked in Israel. In the early years of independence, however, the editors of the communist paper *Kol Ha'am* were prosecuted for criminal libel. An article that criticized Israel's Prime Minister, depicting him as a "traitor" and an "enemy of the working class," triggered the prosecution. The District Court found the article libelous and imposed a fine of 50 Il. on each of the editors.[89] The trial and its outcome are usually considered symptomatic of Israeli intolerance of political dissent during the early years of statehood, an attitude that has since been checked by the *Kol Ha'am* decision of 1953 and the strengthening of the libertarian theme.

## The Broad Israeli Conception of National Security and Its Occasional Abuse

The predominant Israeli conception of national security is rather broad. It extends to matters relating to foreign affairs, Israel's position in the international community, the legitimacy of the Zionist enterprise (i.e., Israel's right to exist as a sovereign nation), and the general welfare of the state. This broad conception of national security yields a rather narrow conception of free expression, and tilts the balance toward security at the expense of free speech. The real dangers and persecution that the Jewish people as a collective experienced historically, and the persistent state of war between Israel and its Arab neighbors, have nourished and shaped these conceptions. Thus, suppression of speech, that to American and critical Israeli eyes may look like an abuse of national security, motivated by partisan political considerations, may look perfectly justified to the decision-makers. This view arises not only because of their failure to appreciate the distinction between public and partisan justifications, but also because their conception of national security is so broad.

A good illustration of the scope of the national security conception is the particular justification for censorship, known as the confirmation theory. For years, the Israeli censor has prohibited the publication of information already published by foreign newspapers, on the ground that its publication in Israel would be considered a formal confirmation by the Israeli government. Application of this doctrine results in depriving the Israeli public of information about Israel that is freely available to the international public. The government's use of this doctrine may be interpreted as a cynical attempt to perpetuate domestic ignorance; but it may also reflect a unified, undifferentiated view of the Israeli polity, where the press is not a check on, but an arm of, the government.

The court tacitly sanctioned a broad conception of national security in the case of *Cohen* v. *Minister of Defense.*[90] In 1962, the Army revoked the accreditation of the military correspondent of *Ha-Olam Ha-Zeh*, a weekly magazine combining radical political criticism with sex and gossip.[91] It is worthwhile to examine the Army's argument in some detail, since it reflects the official mode of thinking. The Army conceded that the revocation of accreditation, which meant denial of access to informational activities provided by the Defense Ministry, was targeted against the magazine (not the particular reporter) because the weekly "act[ed] consistently against the educational spirit of the [Israel Defense Forces]."[92] The Army, further, argued that since no law regulated accreditation, it had full discretion to act "as best fits its interests."[93] Therefore, the Army considered itself free to extend its services only to those newspapers which promote its own goals. The discrimination of which the reporter complained was justified because *Ha-Olam Ha-Zeh* sought to show the government in a negative light and to shake soldiers' faith in the Army and its leadership.

The Supreme Court upheld the Army's position unanimously on jurisdictional grounds. To invoke the jurisdiction of the court, it was not enough to show discrimination. One also had to show that one had a legal right that imposed a duty on the military to give accreditation to reporters: "[H]ere it was necessary to prove the reporter's right, not to engage in his profession which no one contends—but to receive from the military authorities that help and that information which they are willing to give, of their free will, to other journalists. No authority [for such right] was cited either from Israeli case law or from elsewhere."[94]

All three opinions in *Cohen* retained the highly legalistic posture of reasoning described above, again illustrating the nexus between legal formalism and the authoritarian trend in Israel's free speech jurisprudence.[95] Doctrinally, the decision was wrong; it ignored the basic canon of constitutionalism that executive discretion must abide by minimal standards of due process.[96] In a broad sense it ignored the doctrine against prior restraint, which at its core emphasizes the impropriety of utilizing administrative measures to curtail speech. The legalistic reasoning also enabled the Court to ignore the reality of press activity, for which some access to governmental information is essential, and to disregard the chilling effect such an action was likely to have on other papers.[97] Most importantly, however, the Court failed to grasp the philosophical dimensions of the issue. The Court legitimized the Army's unlimited discretion in pursuit of its narrow purposes, but ignored the more profound *raison d'être* of the Army. The Army exists to ensure the state not only in form but also in substance. Surely, Israel's commitment to constitutional government is incompatible with the unchecked, manipulative, and formally discriminatory practice of an executive agency that perforce holds a monopoly over information. As is evident in the Court's analysis of the rights of journalists, Israel's commitment to democracy was similarly perceived as irrelevant to resolution of the case. While journalism undoubtedly is a profession, it seems erroneous to perceive it as just another trade. Journalism has important social and political functions. Uninhibited press criticism of those who hold power is vital for democracy. The Court did not address these issues. Its deference to the executive branch illustrates the Court's tendency to allow unchecked executive discretion whenever issues of national security are even remotely implicated.

It is interesting to observe that despite these rather draconian features of the legal system and the rather marginal role played by the judiciary, freedom of the press persists in Israel. Obviously, the adjustment of press freedom and national security is primarily achieved through informal, nonlegal means. In a way, it is a tribute to the resilience of the press and the support of public opinion. Also, it is a sign of the maturity of the political culture and its slow and painful yet increasing identification with libertarian values.[98]

## The Reputation of Public Officials

Israel's defamation law does not distinguish between public officials and ordinary citizens. It considers public officials neither more nor less worthy of protection.[99] It is also fair to say that the Israeli press is as robust, uninhibited, and wide-open in its criticism of public officials as the press in any contemporary democracy. One indication of press performance is the proliferation of libel suits brought by public officials against the press. Although these suits are generally settled out of court, the mere fact that they are filed suggests that the press is far from complacent.

It is interesting to note that in a recent, particularly important decision, the Supreme Court specifically rejected the American approach, which gives public officials less protection in libel suits.[100] In the case of *Ha'aretz* v. *Electric Company*,[101] the director of the electric company, a public utility, sued *Ha'aretz,* one of Israel's major dailies. The suit was triggered by a series of articles criticizing the director for allowing the company to buy him a luxurious car while the country underwent an economic recession, and for having failed to sell the car subsequently, despite his public pledge to do so. The articles argued that although the director stated that he would sell the car, "in fact the Electric Company is not interested in disposing of the car."[102] thus implying duplicity. For this particular statement, *Ha'aretz* was sued. When the case first reached the Supreme Court, a two-to-one decision incorporated the United States Supreme Court rule of *New York Times* v. *Sullivan* and ruled for the newspaper. The opinion echoed the reasoning in *New York Times* v. *Sullivan*—that the democratic character of the state called for a substantial measure of freedom for the press to enable it to exercise an effective check on those who hold power.[103] The Electric Company appealed for a further hearing; in a four-to-one decision, the Court overturned its previous decision.[104] The Court rejected the theory underlying *New York Times* v. *Sullivan* on several grounds, two of which are relevant to press freedom. First, the Court preferred the English approach, which reasons that the extra exposure of public officials to press criticism "would tend to deter sensitive and honorable men from seeking public positions of trust and responsibility and leave them open to others who have no respect for their reputation."[105] Second, the Court invoked German history, observing that the rise of Nazism was facilitated by unrestrained dissemination of defamatory falsehoods about the Weimar political leadership.[106] The Court devoted only one paragraph to the proper role of press freedom in a democracy:

> I do not slight. . . the importance of the role played by a free press in criticizing the authorities and exposing negative public phenomena and bringing them to public knowledge. But I reject the premise that a responsible press cannot fulfill these functions unless it is given the liberty to defame under the pretext of "fair comment."[107]

This approach captures succinctly the authoritarian theme in the libertarian-authoritarian dialectic that characterizes Israeli free speech jurisprudence. The reductionist interpretation of Weimar's history (unchecked criticism brings about the fall of democracy and the rise of fascism) reinforces the identification with the fundamentally aristocratic British distinction between the worthy ("honorable men") and the unworthy ("who have no respect for their reputation").[108] The elitist conception of the polity, in turn, yields the essential characteristic of a free press—responsibility. Press freedom is legitimately limited by the notion of responsibility, not as independently defined but as shaped by the values of the political leadership (the "honorable men").[109]

It is not easy to ascertain whether the *Ha'aretz* decision has had a chilling effect on press performance. The damages imposed on *Ha'aretz* by the Court were symbolic, and could not themselves have a deterrent effect. A casual reading through Israeli newspapers conveys the impression that the press is confident in its role as a watchdog of those in power, and has not assimilated the standards of responsibility preferred by the Court. If this impression is correct, it may indicate that the cleavage between the libertarian and the authoritarian trends in the Israeli conception of free speech is widening.

## The Right to Know and Access to Official Information

Galnoor has succinctly captured the problem of access to official information:

> [T]here is a "secrecy paradox" in Israel. Government affairs are formally very secretive, yet a great deal of confidential information gets into circulation, occasionally concerning sensitive matters of security and foreign relations and quite regularly concerning internal deliberations on domestic issues.[110]

This "paradox" is but another manifestation of the larger phenomenon of conflicting trends in Israel's politico-legal culture.

While Israel long ago repealed its Official Secrets Act (inherited from the British Mandatory Regime), its statutory law reflects a marked preference for governmental monopoly over information. The Penal Code makes it a criminal offense for public servants to deliver "information obtained...by virtue of...office to a person not competent to receive it."[111] The prohibition is not confined to classified information and is not limited to the duration of government service. Nonclassified material can be divulged no sooner than five years after the particular public servant has retired.[112]

Section 28 of Basic Law: The Government strengthens Israeli sympathy for governmental monopoly over information. The Law allows the Cabinet to classify not only information that is "vital to the state" but "any matter which the Government has decided to keep secret."[113] The Archives Law similarly restricts public access to information of historical interest.[114] This system of rules, coupled with ever-present military censorship, enables the government, at least in theory, to control and manipulate information freely. In practice, however, Israel is plagued by leaks from the ministerial level downward, which appear regularly in the press. So far, the criminal law, which ostensibly prohibits this practice, has not been invoked.[115] Access to sensitive materials is also said to be generally available to those who are members of, or connected to, the establishment (loosely defined). The elitist element is apparent here, since access is granted not on an egalitarian basis, but on the basis of social status and connections.[116]

Decisions of the Supreme Court reflect the familiar contradiction: they oscillate between a recognition of the right to know and deference to executive discretion. An illuminating decision from 1962 reflects the Court's efforts to transplant the right to know into Israeli constitutional law. The case—*Ulpaney Hasrata*—began when the Film Censorship Board refused a permit for a newsreel depicting instances of police brutality during a court-ordered evacuation of a Tel-Aviv slum. In a two-to-one decision, the High Court of Justice revoked the board's decision. Two aspects of this case are interesting: the Court's treatment of the right to know and the government's arguments for suppression. The majority declared that the right to know was part of Israel's constitutional law:

> The citizen's right to disseminate and receive information...is intimately related to the right to freedom of expression and is therefore one of those basic rights [which are not statutory] but which stem directly from the democratic and freedom loving character of the state. The Court will be guided by these basic rights when it interprets statutes and supervises administrative agencies and obviously the administrative agency is obliged to act in accordance with these rights.[117]

The classification of the right to know as a basic right empowered the Court to limit the broad statutory discretion of the Film Censorship Board. It reasserted the commitment, voiced nine years earlier in *Kol Ha'am*, to the values of democracy and an open society, and thus strengthened the libertarian strand in Israel's free speech jurisprudence. Like *Kol Ha'am,* the opinion in *Ulpaney Hasrata* reflects the strong influence of American law and sociological jurisprudence.[118] *Ulpaney Hasrata* expanded the theme in *Kol Ha'am* by confirming the status of the right to know as a basic right. The standard imposed on the Film Censorship Board echoes the "probable danger" formula adopted in *Kol Ha'am:*

> The principle of freedom of information is so vital to our regime, that it should obtain also in the area of newsreels, unless there is a decisive reason to deviate therefrom.[119]

The Court's substantive treatment of the board's discretion in this particular case provides a unique insight into the tension between the libertarian and authoritarian social philosophies. The authoritarian mode of thinking, represented by the Film Censorship Board, reflects the peculiar sociohistorical circumstances of Israel. It is worthwhile to cite the board's argument in its entirety:

> [The Director of the Board] claimed that one of the photographs, showing a woman overlooking the scene with frightened eyes, reminds him of the horror scenes where S.S. (Nazi) troops assaulted Jews...the scenes may bring the blood of a primitive audience to a boil, [so that it] identifies emotionally with the "victims." Therefore there is a need to explain to that audience instantly that this is not the entire story but that the policemen were performing their duty, in enforcing a court order against the residents' opposition. Without such an explanation the newsreel might induce sympathy for law breakers, encourage similar actions in the future and also cast a negative and false light on the police.[120]

Two important elements weave through this argument for suppression. The first is the elitism of the Israeli bureaucracy, reflected in the paternalistic tone and in the notion of ethnic and cultural superiority. The bureaucracy of the early 1960s was composed of East European Jews, who not only associated themselves with Western culture, but also carried the despotic heritage of East European bureaucracy. For them, Afro-Asian Jewry was primitive, hot-headed, and uncritical, incapable of understanding that an act which seemed morally reprehensible might also be perfectly legal [hence formally good]. Therefore, "they" should not be permitted to watch a partial representation which is critical of, rather than apologetic for, police behavior. Thus ethnic prejudice toward Afro-Asian Jewry joined East European despotism and collectivist and statist tendencies of Zionist thought to generate elitist authoritarianism.[121]

*Ulpaney Hasrata* emphatically rejected this attitude. The justices explained in some detail the sociology of information and its vital importance for democracy. Doctrinally, the Court substituted the government's elitism with egalitarianism by tying the right to know to the statutory right to vote. Since the right to vote was already vested in the recently arrived ("primitive") immigrants, they should also have the "the right to know. . .from any source willing to supply information."[122]

The second important element in the government's argument for suppression was the Nazi analogy. The board argued that the film scenes were reminiscent of Nazi behavior and that the implicit analogy between the behavior of the Jewish police and of S.S. troops was so horrifying that it called for suppression.[123] The argument is typical of the Israeli apology for suppression. It works in the following fashion: the object of the criticism (e.g., Israeli police brutality) is compared to Nazi behavior, and thus identifies the Jewish state with Nazism. Such criticism is intolerable, either because it offends the sensibilities of the Holocaust survivors (a psychological argument), or because the Jewish state is antithetical to Nazism and hence any comparison between the two is false by definition (a syllogistic argument). This is generally the pattern by which criticisms that Israeli political culture carries some fascist symptoms are dismissed. In the case of *Ulpaney Hasrata,* however, the Court was not prepared to accept the argument and rejected is as "unfit for a discriminating person."[124]

We have dwelled on the *Ulpaney Hasrata* case in some detail because it is such an excellent paradigm for the libertarian-authoritarian dialectic. The right to know, however, has not always prevailed in the Court. In 1973, the Court accepted the principle of governmental monopoly over information in a case involving a retired government employee who had written a book about the 1948 war.[125] The book was cleared by the military censor, yet the Ministry of Justice denied a permit to publish. The Court dismissed the case without consideration of its merits on the ground that as an "owner" of the information the government was free to withold or disclose it as it saw fit.[126]

## THE PRESS AND THE JUDICAL PROCESS

### Free Press and Fair Trial

In a sense, the issue of free press/fair trial provides an acid test for the commitment of a legal system to free expression, for the courts are both a party to and adjudicators of the dispute. Israeli courts, mindful of the difference in position between England and the United States, opted consciously for a middle-ground approach—less rigid than the British, yet not as permissive as the American.

The free press/free trial issue arises in three main areas. First, the Court's Law[127] gives judges broad discretion to close certain trials, or to prohibit the publication of information related to them. Closure is permitted where the case is related to juveniles or where matters of privacy, morality, and national security are involved.[128] The extent to which newspapers actually comply with the provisions regulating closure is hard to ascertain. The issue of the Court's powers in this regard has not been the subject of litigation.

Second, the Penal Code contains a number of provisions designed to protect the reputation of judges, and the integrity of the judicial process. Section 251 prohibits the publication "in bad faith" of "an incorrect report" of judicial proceedings.[129] Section 255 prohibits, *inter alia,* the publication of "any invective against a judge...with a view to bringing the administration of justice into suspicion or contempt."[130] The language of both provisions is rather broad and, in an authoritarian hand, could be used to stifle criticism of the judiciary, as well as speculation about the political implications of judicial or quasi-judicial proceedings. In this area, however, the courts have inclined toward the libertarian trend. In the course of a number of acquittals during the first years of independence, the Court interpreted the Penal Code narrowly, thus deterring future prosecutions.[131] During the same period, the Court also revoked as *ultra vires* the judicial power to punish summarily for contempt of court.[132] Considering the tender age of the Court, these decisions display a high degree of confidence and a willingness to be exposed to criticism.

The third aspect of the free press/fair trial issue relates to the power to punish for contempt of court. Presently, the Court's Law prohibits publication about matters which are *sub judice* "if the publication might influence the trial or its consequences."[133] In contradistinction to the summary procedure,[134] section 41 of the Court's Law provides for ordinary criminal prosecution and requires the consent of the Attorney General. The authoritative interpretation of section 41 is found in *Disenchik* v. *Attorney General.*[135] *Ma'ariv,* a popular evening daily of which Mr. Disenchik was chief editor, published an article concerning an on-going criminal trial. The article implied that although the defendant pled not guilty before the court, he had confessed his guilt outside the courtroom. A unanimous Supreme Court convicted the newspaper of a misdemeanor and imposed a 200 Il. fine.

Again relying heavily on American law,[136] the Court analyzed the conflict of interests that the case presented. Using a balancing of interests approach, the Court held that a publication could be held in contempt of court if it "contained a 'sufficient quantity' of influence on the trial."[137] The Court distinguished this test from the clear and present danger test in that it did not require that the influence on the trial be imminent or probable. The Israeli doctrine of contempt of court required only a reasonable probability that the publication would influence the trial.[138] The major problem with this doctrine is its inherent vagueness. By relaxing the requirement of proximity between the speech and the danger, the court dropped an important criterion for guiding judicial discretion. Thus, while recognizing that the two interests were in conflict, the Court failed to limit judicial discretion to suppress coverage of the administration of justice. Interestingly, this was the first case in which the Court was called upon to interpret section 41. In previous years there was mounting criticism of the Attorney General's refusal to prosecute newspapers for contempt of court. It is quite likely, therefore, that the Court relaxed the probable danger formula, to signal the press that it should exercise more self-restraint, or else....[139]

The *Disenchik* Court advanced two justifications for the "reasonable probability" doctrine: one psychological, the other philosophical. The psychological justification related to the impact that publication may have. A jury is not part of Israel's legal system, and thus one of the major and most prevalent justifications for press restraint is irrelevant in the Israeli context. The psychological argument could then focus either on the judge or on public opinion. The judge-focused explanation is normally the more difficult one for courts, since by admitting that a judge may be influenced by "illegal" information, they also admit the subjectivity of the judicial decision-making process. The *Disenchik* Court was realistic enough to concede that not only witnesses but also judges might be influenced by such publications, albeit against their conscious wishes.[140] Ironically, however, the Court did not see the contradiction between the psychological justification and the doctrine it developed. For the recognition that judges are "only human" means not only that their professional discretion may be prejudiced by illegal evidence, but also that they may be prejudiced against the press in contempt of court proceedings; hence, they might use the elastic standard of reasonable probability to suppress publications they do not like. In other words, judges were not objective enough for one criminal process, but were sufficiently objective for another.

We now turn to the philosophical justification. In defending its doctrine, the Court observed that the justification for free speech that relies on the free marketplace of ideas was irrelevant to the judicial process, in which a rigid system of rules for identifying truth prevailed. The Court dismissed the perhaps more relevant democratic justification—the role of the press as watchdog of the administration of justice—in a curious fashion. It defined criminal trials as falling outside the orbit of the marketplace of ideas and thus it could ignore the question of how the public's need to know about the functioning of the criminal justice machine affects the doctrine of contempt of court.[141] Again, in deciding whether there is a reasonable probability of injustice, there is a crucial difference between a court that sees only the sensational, mob trial aspects of press behavior, and a court that recognizes the public service rendered by press coverage as well. It seems that the *Disenchik* Court erred in failing to take this factor into consideration. In concurring opinions, two justices advised the press to restrict itself to general criticism not related to a particular trial, or to a "dry and accurate account of the proceedings."[142] Both of these observations, coupled by the analysis of the majority opinion, point to a basic misconception of the press as a critic of the courts and to an elitist conception of courts as being above criticism. The first fails to see that abstract criticism, detached from an empirical base, is less persuasive and less credible. The second does not even allow room for a critical role for the press.

Since *Disenchik,* Israel's Attorney General has not used his authority to prosecute newspapers for contempt of court, despite the fact that the news media do sometimes display insensitivity to the rights of the accused.[143] In recent cases, however, the Court has rebuked the press for unrestrained coverage, and has fashioned alternative means to chill coverage short of direct suppression. First, the Court advocated denial of access to state information about criminal trials, so that "news about an ongoing investigation be publicized [only] when the suspect is first brought to court...and the publication be restricted to information disclosed in open court."[144] Second, the Court attempted to chill a litigant's inclination to appeal to public opinion through the press. In *Bourkan* v. *Minister of Treasury,*[145] a former Arab resident of the Jewish Quarter in Jerusalem challenged a regulation that disqualified non-Jews from purchasing renovated apartments in that area. As probably could be expected from the political context of the controversy, the petitioner appealed to local and public opinion through the press. The Court denied the petition due to, *inter alia,* the petitioner's utilization of the press. The Court distinguished between an appeal to the press before a matter is brought to court, which is legitimate, and an appeal after litigation begins, which is illegitimate. Appeal to the press while the matter is *sub judice* is tantamount to contempt of court, and renders the petitioner unworthy of equitable relief.[146]

These recent decisions are interesting since they reflect the Court's sensitivity to the modern sociology of litigation, where both the government and private parties apply techniques of news management in an effort to influence judicial resolution of legal questions or to manipulate the legal dispute for political purposes.[147] It is questionable, however, whether silencing both state and private litigants—thereby lowering public awareness of politically relevant legal issues—constitutes a proper solution or whether such a solution is feasible.

## A Note on Press Coverage of Government Commissions of Inquiry

A commission appointed by the government to investigate a matter of vital public concern enjoys a quasi-judicial status. Its members are protected by the same provisions of the Penal Code and the Court's Law that are designed to protect the integrity of the judicial process and the appearance of justice.[148] As a result, journalistic coverage of these commissions is as limited as coverage of judicial proceedings. This situation provides ground for skirmishes between the press and the government, particuarly when a commission inquires into a "hot" subject. In 1973, following the Yom Kippur war, the government appointed the Agranat Commission to inquire into the events that precipitated the war. The subject matter was, naturally, of great concern to Israelis, and the press was replete with analysis and commentary. Coverage intensified after the commission released an interim report.

The report was very controversial and charges of fiat appeared in the press. Members of the Commission were stung by adverse public opinion, particularly since they considered themselves unable to respond because of their quasi-judicial status.

In its final report the commission rebuked the press for its behavior, and the government for its failure to defend the commission. The report hinted that the criminal law that protects a judge against verbal insults also protects commission members and could be invoked because the press coverage amounted to contempt of court. The commission wanted the press to refrain from including in its commentary any categorical conclusions and any factual descriptions that could imply categorical conclusions. It recommended that the Attorney General drop his lenient policy toward the press and activate the contempt of court provision in order to deter such press coverage. So far the government has not taken steps to implement these recommendations.[149] The 1982–1983 inquiry by the Kahan Commission into charges of Israeli involvement in the massacre of Palestinian refugees in Lebanon was accompanied by intense press coverage, uninterrupted by official measures.

## Reporter's Privilege

Israeli law does not shield reporters who seek to protect their sources. It is even arguable that the courts cannot grant a qualified reporter's privilege. The argument against a judicially created privilege rests on the fact that the law specifically recognizes other professional privileges but is silent about reporters, and that, furthermore, the Knesset has explicitly rejected the journalist's privilege.

Nonetheless, as Israeli journalists frequently engage in investigative reporting, they do occasionally claim a shield. The Supreme Court has not yet ruled on this issue. A number of district court cases indicate a willingness to recognize a qualified privilege.[150] In these cases the courts struck a balance between the need that justice be done and the good faith attempt by the reporter to advance press freedom through the protection of sources. The rule developed was that the court would not compel disclosure unless the information was relevant to the ultimate decision.[151] Still, the issue has not been of central concern either in journalistic or legal circles.

## THE PRESS AND THE INDIVIDUAL

### Defamation

Enactment, in 1965, of the statute against defamation signified a turning point in the history of Israel's press. In the early sixties, the government presented to the Knesset a rather draconian bill against defamation, to replace mandatory law that was based largely on the British common law. During the years of debate that followed, the press displayed remarkable vitality and vigor. It campaigned energetically against the bill, mobilizing public opinion in Israel and in the international community. It established the Press Council, which issued a Code of Ethics and created a mechanism for self-regulation, thus presenting an alternative to formal control.[152] The enacted statute modified substantially the original bill. Given the history of close identification between the press and the Yishuv leadership prior to independence, and its struggle to establish its self-identity since, the 1960s signified the maturation of the press into a separate entity, confident of its social role.[153] Although the statute that emerged is less than a victory for press freedom, it does reflect the fact that the libertarian theme in Israel's political culture and free speech jurisprudence, if mobilized, has enough muscle to contain and curb authoritarianism.

This essay cannot cover the law of defamation in its entirety. It will present those basic components that are particularly pertinent to the press and dwell on a few court decisions that likewise have a special bearing on the press.

*Defamation* is defined as explicit or implicit expression that makes another person the object of contempt or ridicule.[154] The statute regulates both criminal and civil defamation, and in both cases imposes liability on the "person who brought the defamation to the newspaper and thereby caused the publication thereof"—the editor in chief, the immediate editor, the printer, and the seller. In a civil suit the publisher is liable as well.[155]

Special defenses are carved out for the editor, the printer, and the seller.[156] While these provisions are likely to have a chilling effect on the press, it does not seem that they were invoked in order to inhibit the press in any meaningful way.

The law also recognizes group libel but only as a criminal offense.[157] Prosecution requires the consent of the attorney general. It does not seem that the section has been invoked since the law was enacted.

The law recognizes three major defenses for the publication of defamatory material: (1) if the publication reflects official information of various kinds, such as information which originated in a cabinet meeting or in judicial proceedings[158]; (2) if the publication reflects the truth and "was of public interest"[159]; and (3) if the matter was published in good faith.[160] The formulation of the second defense is particularly interesting, since it reduces the traditional common law defense of truth from the status of a sufficient component to that of a necessary but insufficient one, by imposing the additional requirement that the matter be of public interest. Humane and educational motives lie behind this formulation. It recognizes that the publication of true facts may cause substantial pain to an individual. It recognizes that faction within the news media (commonly called the sensational media or yellow journalism) which lives off people's hunger for information about the rich and famous, and therefore has an interest in fostering this hunger. The stipulation of public interest is designed to protect human dignity and inhibit the sensational press.

Some problems, however, inhere in this formulation. Clearly, the phrase "of public interest" carries with it both a normative prescription and an actual description. It may refer either to what ought to be of public interest, in, for example, the good society, or to what actually interests people here and now. If the latter criterion (actual interest) is followed, then the noble and educational motive of the law is obstructed. If the former (ideal public interest) is preferred, then there are serious ramifications for freedom of the press, since reporters must not only report the truth and what they consider to be of public interest, but must also keep in mind judicially articulated standards.[161] Furthermore, even if the courts strive to articulate objective standards, it is highly probable that their standards will reflect conventional values. This will thwart the primary purpose of the principle of free expression, which is to protect the unconventional view of what is or should be of public interest.

The peculiar defense of truth, however, has not been the target of much litigation. It is the third defense—that of good faith[162]—that received interesting judicial interpretations, casting more light on the Court's conception of the press and its role in society.

The defense of good faith can apply if two conditions are fulfilled. It must first be established that the publication was made in good faith. Section 16 of the Defamation Law creates a presumption of good faith if, *inter alia,* the publication was reasonable under the circumstances. It creates a presumption that negates good faith if, *inter alia,* no reasonable means to verify the truth were employed. These latter presumptions could enable the Court to incorporate press ethics into the law of defamation by, for instance, holding that an effort to verify the truth through checking with an independent source constitutes reasonable means.[163] Thus far, however, the Court has not taken this course.

Second, in order for the defense of good faith to apply, it must be shown that the circumstances of the publication conform to one of 11 categories enumerated in section 15.[164] One of these categories provides that the defense obtains if the relationship between the defamer and the reader imposed a legal, moral, or social obligation to publish.[165]

In 1969, the Court declined to recognize a social obligation to keep the public informed as a defense under section 15.[166] The Court held that newspapers should have neither more nor fewer privileges to publish than private individuals, and that "the ordinary relationship between a newspaper and its readers does not impose on the newspaper any specific obligation to publish information of public interest and therefore does not give it a special privilege to shield its inaccurate publications."[167] At first glance, the holding looks as if it is a part of the authoritarian trend, which seeks to limit the legal defenses of free expression. This is true in terms of the result which denied the press an important defense. However, the philosophy underlying this result is classical liberalism, not authoritarianism. Under authoritarianism, the press is an extension of the government, and ought to accept governmental judgments as correct. Liberalism, on the other hand, is based on a separation between the government and the people. In extreme form it tends to reduce individuals, including journalists, into self-serving beings, devoid of any sense of social responsibility. The holding which equates private individuals and newspapers can therefore be viewed as the logical consequence of liberal theory.[168]

Yet, this is only the tip of the iceberg. The tension between the authoritarian result—no protection to the press when it criticizes official conduct—and the libertarian justification—the press is neither more nor less obligated to expose official misconduct than are private individuals—indicates a problem. On the one hand, by recognizing reputation as an important attribute of social interaction, it promotes a conception of the individual as a social being. On the other hand, it fails to recognize the social dimension of the mass media, which is as pertinent to the community as to the individual. The Court's decision missed an opportunity to establish an equilibrium between the obviously noble purpose of the defamation law to preserve human dignity (via the preservation of reputation), and the social function of the press, which strives ultimately to serve the same goal.

Another important way in which the Court narrowed the good faith defense as applied to the press was in its interpretation of the term "comment." Three of the categories enumerated in section 15 require that the defamatory publication constitute a comment about, for example, the conduct of the defamed in his or her official capacity.[169] The crucial legal question, then, is how the Court should treat the distinction between fact and opinion. Two models are possible. The Court could adopt a rigid distinction between fact and opinion, requiring that facts be true and separated from opinion, in order to shelter the opinion by the defense of good faith. Or the Court could accept that the dividing line between fact and opinion is subtle and not easily discerned, and that as a consequence the publication should be classified as fact or opinion according to its predominant character when read as a whole. If classified as opinion, the falsity of some facts would not eliminate the defense. Both models call for judicial discretion. Adoption of the first model requires a measure of interference with editorial discretion and tilts the balance against press freedom. Adoption of the second model favors the press by allowing more creativity and freedom in the choice of words and the structuring of a publication.

In a recent case, the Supreme Court in a four-to-one decision opted for the first model and interpreted a newspaper article's concluding phrase, "in fact, the Electric Company is not interested in selling the car," as a statement of fact. Since the newspaper could not prove the statement's truth, the Court held that the defense of good faith could not apply, and found the newspaper liable for defamation.[170] The Court's rigid approach to the distinction between fact and opinion not only reflects the formalistic jurisprudential trend[171] but also displays an authoritarian tendency in the insistence on rigid rules of public discourse. In a similar vein, a 1977 decision held that calling a person "anti-Zionist" amounts to a statement of fact and hence cannot be protected by the defense of fair comment.[172]

Finally, section 17 specifically removes the defense of fair comment from the press if the defamed requested and was denied a right of reply. The section provides that a defamed person may require the newspaper to publish a correction or a denial of material related to the defamed that had previously been published in that newspaper. The newspaper is required to publish the correction or denial in a manner similar to the one in which the defamatory material was published, and with reasonable speed. The newspaper is entitled to demand that the defamed sign the request, that the reply not contain defamatory or other material the content of which may be illegal, and that the length of the reply be reasonable under the circumstances.[173] Israeli newspapers do occasionally publish corrections; it is quite likely that they are spurred to do so by section 17. Beyond that, we know very little about the sociology of the right to reply in Israel. It is important to note, however, that the Israeli right of reply does not arise in lieu of a defamation suit, but rather as a necessary condition to be met before the press can argue that the defense of good faith applies.

Defamation suits may be either criminal or civil. An interesting feature of the Israeli law of defamation is the private criminal complaint, whereby private individuals may bring defamation suits through the criminal process.[174] In recent years there has been a proliferation of such complaints, some of which are filed by public figures against newspapers. The method is cheaper and speedier than the civil suit and these factors may account for its popularity. However, one cannot request damages in this type of procedure. Notwithstanding the disadvantage, the popularity of this method indicates that it is considered an efficient device to vindicate one's reputation and to generate public attention about the indignation felt by the defamed. Presumably, this remedy is more valued than the potential recovery of damages. But it is also important to note that the initiation of a private complaint does not preclude a civil action for damages. Most such suits are settled out of court.

In addition to the remedies applicable against all defamers (monetary awards and up to one year imprisonment in case of criminal conviction), the law provides for a specific remedy against newspapers. The Court may prohibit the circulation, or order the confiscation, of the issues in which the defamation was published, and may order the publication of a correction, a denial, or the opinion of the Court.[175]

Israel's defamation law is a symptom of the authoritarian trend in Israel's free speech jurisprudence. Both the statute and its interpretation by the courts reflect oversensitivity toward individual reputations and undersensitivity to the sociopolitical role of the press and to the sociology of criticism. Thus, in the area of defamation, the legal system does not reflect the equilibrium between libertarianism and authoritarianism (albeit delicate and precarious) that typifies other areas reviewed so far. Ironically, it was the very planning of an authoritarian defamation law that raised the consciousness of the press and strengthened its confidence and enabled it to function well as a watchdog of the government.

## Privacy

In 1981, the Knesset passed a statute making the violation of privacy a tort and a misdemeanor.[176] The process of enactment was rather hasty. Both the government and the public had deliberated for several years. In 1976, a blueprint for a bill on privacy was proposed. It met with strong press opposition and seemed to have been shelved. Why it was suddenly revived and promptly enacted is not clear. The reasons may have been rooted in political and instrumental considerations—the then-embattled Begin government resented the press, which it identified as the cause of its ailing public support. Partially, though, the new statute also reflected deeper undercurrents of Israeli intolerance of free speech.

The Privacy Act contains 37 sections and regulates both data banks in general and violations of privacy in particular. The liability of newspapers is specifically regulated.[177] Section 30 provides that criminal and civil liability for publication of a violation of privacy rests on the person who brought the information to the newspaper, the editor, and the person who actually made the decision to publish. A publisher is exempt only from criminal liability.[178]

Under the statute, a person's privacy cannot be violated without his or her explicit or implicit consent.[179] The long list of matters that constitute a violation of privacy opens with "monitoring or following a person in a manner which may be disturbing" and closes with "a publication about the intimate private life of a person, his health or private behavior.[180] On its face, this elaboration should be hailed as an exemplary protection of human dignity and an admirable aspiration for high standards in public discourse. An obvious target is the sensational press.[181] Arguably the statute does not aim at the establishment press. On close examination, however, it seems that the political and intellectual press is no less vulnerable. First, the Act effectively curtails investigative journalism by conditioning an inquiry upon the consent of the parties involved. Second, the statute obstructs the important function of the press as a watchdog of official behavior. The prohibition on the disclosure of private information does not except public officials. Thus, the public is denied information that may be crucial in any evaluation of official performance and public morality (e.g., information about the health of the Prime Minister).[182] Furthermore, it is interesting, although hardly surprising, to encounter again the Israeli belief that one may effectively distinguish between public and private behavior, and that private conduct is irrelevant to public conduct. This approach is symptomatic of the deeply rooted Israeli formalism; it in turn exposes a connection to authoritarianism, as reflected in the Act's potential for curtailing political and intellectual speech.

The defenses provided by the Act could mitigate its potential chilling effect on the press. One defense protects a violation of privacy if it is done "in circumstances where the violator was under a legal, moral, social or professional duty to do so."[183] Another defense shelters the violation if it is related to the public interest.[184] To qualify for the latter defense, however, a newspaper must show not only that the violation was in the public interest, but also that the publication was not false.[185]

These defenses are sufficiently ambiguous to leave ample discretion to the courts to construe them in favor of or against press freedom. A court cognizant of the social importance of a free press may attribute to newspapers a professional, social or moral duty to inform. Similarly, it may construe broadly the defense of public interest and hold that the publication of information about public officials is presumptively justified. But a court may also construe the same defenses narrowly. Indeed, if one is to judge from the Court's previous application of the Defamation Law, it is much more likely to prefer a restrictive attitude toward the press.

Both the context and the language of the statute seem to reflect a certain hostility harbored by the Knesset toward the press which may, in turn, affect the Court's discretion. An authoritarian attitude can be discerned from the set of situations explicitly excluded as defenses. That reasonable means were taken to prevent the violation does not constitute a defense in civil proceedings.[186] That the publication merely repeated information aired previously and that an apology has been published subsequently constitute only mitigating circumstances, which the Court may take into account after the verdict, but they do not constitute a defense. These three situations have one thing in common—they all constitute aspects of editorial processes. Thus, the Act declines to recognize as *relevant to the defense* basic professional practices that are an organic part of journalism.[187] That this refusal to recognize the institutional aspects of the press indicates a certain hostility toward the press is buttressed by the linguistic asymmetry between the language of the defenses and the language of the mitigating circumstances. The defenses are couched in ambiguous terms that allow for either libertarian or authoritarian interpretation. The mitigating circumstances are highly structured and specific, thus tying the hands of the judge who wishes to treat the newspaper leniently. For example, to constitute a mitigating circumstance, a repetition of previously aired information must refer to the *source* that generated the information. Or, to constitute a mitigating circumstance, an apology must meet the following conditions:

1. The apology was accompanied by an effort by the publisher to stop the sale or distribution of the copy which contained the violation; *and*
2. The apology was published in the same place, form, and length as the previous violation; *and*
3. The apology was not qualified.[188]

From this perspective, Israel's Privacy Act is a step toward restricting press freedom. However, an assessment of the actual impact of the Act on the press is premature. Beyond the chilling effects, its actual impact will depend on both the willingness of private parties to utilize it and its interpretation by the courts.

## PRESS CONCENTRATION

The shift to sovereignty has brought about significant changes in the Israeli press structure. Prior to independence and through the fifties, Israeli newspapers were published by the diverse political parties and advocated their partisan positions. Of these, only the Labour Party's *Davar* and *Al-Hamishmar* are still viable enterprises. The rest have withered away due to lack of funds and public indifference. The remaining three major newspapers in the Hebrew language (*Ha'aretz*, *Ma'ariv*, and *Yediot Aharonot*) are privately owned. Another major daily is the *Jerusalem Post*, published in English. These publishers compete against each other and represent different editorial policies. They generally make an effort to reflect the broad spectrum of Israeli politics.

From this point of view, the problem of media concentration is not significant in Israel.[189] If there is a problem, it has not yet surfaced in the public consciousness or legislative deliberations. It should be emphasized, however, that not much is known about this issue. Cooperation between newspapers (e.g., joint advertising sections) exists to a degree, though its extent and ramifications are unexplored. Furthermore, in the past 20 years, attempts by independent publishers to publish new dailies all failed.[190] Partially, this failure can be attributed to readers' indifference. But some of the blame may also rest on shrewd efforts by existing publishers to stifle competition. So far, no serious effort to explore the dimensions of this problem has been undertaken.

## THE PRESS COUNCIL

The Press Council was founded in 1963 in response to a governmental offensive on the press. The context was the then-pending bill for a rather draconian Defamation Law. The government argued that such a bill was necessary in view of what the government considered irresponsible and abusive attacks on individuals. During its campaign to rally public support and prevent passage of the most restrictive provisions of the bill, the press established the Press Council.[191] Although it has never been conceded, it is clear that the Press Council was designed to counteract two central and interrelated governmental charges. First, by publishing a Code of Ethics, the Press Council attempted to refute the charge that the press pursues asocial and self-serving interests. Simultaneously, the code emphasized the fundamental value of press freedom for a democratic society, and affirmed the social functions of newspapers in providing accurate information to the public and in reflecting the public's view.[192] Second, the Press Council counteracted the government's call for press regulation by providing a mechanism for self-regulation.

The Code of Ethics contains 14 sections. It emphasizes the obligation of reporters to "provide the public with accurate information and inter-pretation compatible with the facts"; prohibits the publication of libel, personal incitement or unfounded charges, violation of privacy, and plagiarism; affirms the duty of the reporter not to disclose confidential information or sources; and prohibits any relationship between a reporter and other commercial or public enterprises which may affect journalistic integrity.[193]

The policymaking institutions of the Press Council are its council and its executive committee. They are composed of all the editors-in-chief, representatives of the publishers, and representatives of the reporters, as well as a minority of public figures. A complaint alleging that a newspaper has violated the ethical code may be initiated either by members of the council or by a private party affected by such a violation. The council's legal counsel may either dismiss the complaint or appoint an *ad hoc* investigative committee. Any conclusions reached by this committee are brought before the executive committee, which may require that the newspaper publish an apology or, after obtaining the plenary's approval, publish its own opinions or conclusions related to the case.

This mechanism of self-regulation suffers a number of shortcomings. The press serves as its own guard. The Press Council's institutions are dominated by representatives of the journalistic enterprise. The public's representatives are in the minority. Thus, in all cases, the press retains the power to decide whether a member newspaper has violated the ethical code. No disinterested third party reviews the controversy, and the doubt may always persist (whether warranted or not) that the council's decision preferred the press's self-serving interests over those of the public. The public's role in supervising the compatibility between the code and actual press behavior is further undermined by the fact that the right of standing is narrowly defined to apply only to parties who were actually injured by the publication. Finally, the mechanism has no teeth and depends entirely upon the good will of the newspapers. The question, of course, is whether a more vigorous mechanism would backfire by limiting press freedom.

The Code of Ethics remains largely a journalistic normative ideal. Its existence, however, and the enforcing mechanism accompanying it raise the press's consciousness to the imperatives of journalistic ethics and thereby raise the quality of Israeli journalism.

## CONCLUSION

Given historical Jewish consciousness, the immediate colonial legacy, and the ever-present threat to national existence, Israeli democracy, and with it the Israeli press, have shown remarkable resilience. The commitment to a democratic form of government and to libertarian values, characteristic of mainstream Zionist thought, has proved a sufficiently sturdy base on which a solid free press could develop.

As this essay makes amply clear, however, the birth of the Zionist state did not make intolerance and fear of dissent disappear. They persist. The continuous occupation of a sizeable hostile population—the Arabs of the West Bank—and consequently the continuous confrontation with a hostile press, which consciously and openly views itself as an arm of the Palestinian struggle, are a poisonous environment for both democracy and a healthy jurisprudence of free speech and free press.

A recent crisis, involving Israel's Broadcasting Service and the Supreme Court, illustrates the complexity of the situation. In 1982, the executive committee of the state-controlled Broadcasting Service prohibited the broadcasting of interviews with public figures who were identified as affiliated with the P.L.O. The prohibition reflected the volatility of the political situation, exacerbated by the official Israeli stimulation of Jewish settlement on the West Bank and the resultant political frustration of the Arab population. The prohibition was symptomatic of the increasing intolerance of the Israeli government toward opinions which are disagreeable to it. At the same time, one cannot deny that the Palestinian struggle for national liberation lacks a liberal spirit. The Palestinian leadership and the Palestinian press, which is identified with the Palestinian cause (just as the Hebrew press identified with the Jewish leadership prior to independence), are united in a determination to use all media, including the Israeli media of communications, in their struggle with Israel, and make no effort to be fair in their criticism of Israeli policies. They thus encourage the suppressive instinct of the Israeli authorities.

The Supreme Court was faced with the difficult task of preserving the spirit of liberalism—the right to free speech and the right to know—against the illiberal spirit which permeated both the Palestinian leadership and the present decision-makers at the Broadcasting Service. The justices unanimously invalidated the regulation. In so doing they scored a victory for Israeli liberalism and yet revealed the authoritarian-libertarian dialectic within Israeli free speech law. Permitting the stifling of free expression and thereby shutting off an important propaganda channel was, perhaps, intuitively perceived by the Court as winning the battle but losing the war by sacrificing an essential facet of Israeli democracy. The Court, then, invalidated the prohibition. But the grounds of the opinion reflected its ambivalence. The Court rested its opinion on the narrow ground that the term "public figures" was overly broad and vague. Two of the three justices thought that a more precisely defined regulation would withstand scrutiny. Thus, although libertarian in result, the reasoning of the majority opinion embraced themes from the authoritarian approach to free speech.[194]

It is doubtful that this ambivalence can be presently resolved. Israel's press law is in its formative years. Its profile in the years to come will depend largely on political developments which may either encourage or suppress the libertarian elements of Israeli culture.

## NOTES

1.  Hebrew for Jewish settlement.
2.  Yet the Israeli model of government also bears some resemblance to the French Third Republic. *See* A. Rubinstein, *The Constitutional Law of Israel*, (Jerusalem, 3rd ed. 1980) at 13–20.
3.  This does not mean that Zionism was a mere reflection of Enlightenment

values. Rather, its sociopolitical program reflected the disappointment in the failure of the Enlightenment to bring about meaningful liberation to the Jews. However, as children of Enlightenment thought, Zionist thinkers did embrace the basic values of the Enlightenment. For an interesting survey see S. Avineri, *The Making of Modern Zionism* (1981).

4.  M. Carmilly-Weinberger, *Censorship and Freedom of Expression in Jewish History* (1977).

5.  For a discussion of the impact of the common law on Israel's legal system see Friedmann, *Infusion of the Common Law Into the Legal System of Israel*, 10 Isr. L. Rev. 324 (1975).

6.  MacPherson, *Possessive Individualism* (1962).

7.  *See,* e.g., R.H. Soltan, *French Political Thought in the 19th Century* (New York, 1931); L. Krieger, *The German Idea of Freedom.* For the background of the justices of Israel's Supreme Court see E. Rubinstein, *Shoftey-Eretz* (1980) (in Hebrew).

8.  *See generally* Lahav, "American Influence on Israel's Jurisprudence of Free Speech," 9 Hastings Const. L. Q. 21 (1981).

9.  The 1977 shift to the Likud (right-wing) government brought about a de-emphasis of the socialist legacy but, if anything, the statist element was strengthened.

10.  *Kol Ha'am* v. *Minister of the Interior,* 7 P.D. [law reports of the Israeli Supreme Court] 871 (1953) (in Hebrew). [Editor's note: The official English translation of *Kol Ha'am* appears in 1 *Selected Judgments of the Supreme Court of Israel* 90 (1948–1953). All citations to *Kol Ha'am* v. *Minister of the Interior* will be made to the official translation, hereinafter cited as 1 *Selected Judgments.*]

11.  *Electric Co.* v. *Ha'aretz,* 32(3) P.D. 337 (1978), (*Ha'aretz* II) reversing 31(2) P.D. 281 (1977) (*Ha'aretz* I).

12.  The *Kol Ha'am* case arose when the Minister of Interior suspended publication of the Israeli Communist Party's two newspapers, one of which was *Kol Ha'am* (The People's Voice). The two papers had published editorials denouncing an alleged policy of the Israeli government to support the United States with Israeli troops in the event of war between the United States and the Soviet Union. Pursuant to his powers under section 19 of Israel's Press Ordinance, the Minister suspended both papers for periods of 10 and 15 days on the grounds that the editorials were likely to endanger the public peace. The two papers challenged the order in the High Court of Justice. *See* 1 *Selected Judgments* at 91–93.

13.  The Court regarded freedom of the press as a particular form of freedom of expression. *Id.* at 94.

14.  *Id.* at 97.

15.  32(3) P.D. 337 (1978).

16.  *Id.* at 346.

17.  *Id.* at 347.

18.  *Id.* at 344. In equating the right to life with the right to reputation the court relied on the Jewish halachic holding that "whoever insults his friend in public is likened to one who bleeds him."

19.  *Kol Ha'am,* 1 *Selected Judgent* at 97.

20.  *Id.* at 100.

21. *Ha'aretz II,* 32(3) P.D. at 343, 344. Notice the juxtaposition of "liberty" and "right."

22. *E.g.,* Basic Law: The Knesset and Basic Law: The Government, regulating the structure and powers of the Legislative and Executive branches of government, respectively. With the exception of a few entrenched provisions, these statutes do not enjoy a normative status that is higher than any ordinary laws. The usage of the term "basic law" for a constitution is uniquely German and reflects German influence on Israeli law.

23. For the text of the Bill of Rights and commentary see Ratner, "Constitutions, Majoritarianism, and Judicial Review: The Function of a Bill of Rights in Israel and the United States," 26 Am. J. of Comp. L. 373 (1978). The planned Israeli Bill of Rights differs from its German counterpart in at least one significant respect: it validates, wholesale, legislation enacted prior to the passage of the Bill and which restricts civil liberties (*id.* at §20).

24. Bill of Rights §11, *reprinted in* Ratner, *supra* note 23, at 395.

25. Several decisions prior to *Kol Ha'am* asserted the right to free expression and free press. *See,* e.g., *Goraly* v. *Attorney General,* 5 P.D. 1145 (1950); *Bloy* v. *Minister of Interior,* 2 P.D. 136 (1949).

26. Declaration of the Establishment of the State of Israel, 1 Laws of the State of Israel [L.S.I.] 3 (1948), *reprinted in Official Gazette* no. 1 (1948).

27. *Kol Ha'am,* 1 *Selected Judgments* at 105. This is a judge-made rule of interpretation and is not always followed by the courts.

28. Courts Law 5717–1957, at §7, 11 L.S.I. 157 (1956–1957).

29. *See* Law and Administration Ordinance 5708–1948, 1 L.S.I. 7 (1948). Section 11 provides: "The law which existed in Palestine on...(14th May, 1948) shall remain in force, insofar as there is nothing therein repugnant to this Ordinance or to the other laws which may be enacted...and subject to such modifications as may result from the establishment of the State...." *Id.* at 11.

30. Defense Emergency Regulation art. 87 (1945), *reprinted in Palestine Gazette* no. 1442, at 1058 (Supp. II 1945).

31. *See* Lahav, "Governmental Regulation of the Press: A Study of Israel's Press Ordinance" (pts. I & II), 13 Isr. L. Rev. 230, 489 (1978). Following an aborted attempt to re-enact a new version of the Press Ordinance, the Minister of Justice appointed a commission to reconsider the issue of a press law for Israel. So far the commission has not submitted its recommendations.

32. The chapter on sanctions also contains sanctions for the violations of other laws, e.g., for violation of the criminal law against seditious libel.

33. *Supra* note 30, as amended.

34. Section 4 of the Press Ordinance provides: "No newspaper shall be printed or published in Palestine unless the proprietor...obtain[s] a permit under the hand of the district commissioner...." Press Ordinance §4 (1933), *reprinted in* 2 R. Drayton, *Laws of Palestine* 1215 (1933). Section 30(1) requires the printer to obtain a similar permit. *See id.* §30(1), *reprinted in* 2 R. Drayton, *supra,* at 1228. Section 2 defines newspaper as "any publication containing news, intelligence, reports of occurrences, or any remarks, observations or comments, in relation to such news, intelligence or occurrences, or to any other matter of public interest, printed in any language and published in Palestine for sale or free distribution at

regular or irregular intervals...." *Id.* at § 2, *reprinted in* 2 R. Drayton, *supra*, at 1214–1215.

35.   *Id.* § 22, *reprinted in* R. Drayton, *supra* note 34, at 1226–1227. In *Kahooji* v. *Attorney General* 14(3) P.D. 1929 (1960), a group of Arab nationalists (members of the El-Ard group, later outlawed in Israel, *see also infra* notes 46 & 55) were convicted of having published a newspaper without a permit. The sociology of the press law demonstrated by this case is interesting. The group had published six "one time editions," each using the name of one of the defendants as editor, and each using a different title which resembled the words "El-Ard." The Court declined to recognize the practice as a legitimate exploitation of a loophole in the press law.

36.   Press Ordinance §5(1)(b) (1933), *reprinted in* 2 R. Drayton, *supra* note 34, at 1217. Under section 5(5) the Minister of Interior has discretion to waive this requirement. *Id.* at §5(5), *reprinted in* 2 R. Drayton, *supra* note 34, at 1218.

37.   *Id.* at § 5(1)(d), *reprinted in* 2 R. Drayton, *supra* note 34, at 1218. In theory this requirement could be used to stifle the expression of persons who lack adequate financial means. However in present-day Israel it is a toothless formality.

38.   *Id.* at § 8(1), *reprinted in* 2 R. Drayton, *supra* note 34, at 1219.

39.   *Id.* §§ 11(1), (2), (3), 12, 16 *reprinted in* 2 R. Drayton, *supra* note 34, at 1220–1221, 1222, 1224.

40.   *Id.* § 6, *reprinted in* 2 R. Drayton, *supra* note 34, at 1219.

41.   M. Stein, *Publisher of the Democratic Newspaper* v. *Minister of Interior,* 6(2) P.D. 867, 870 (1952). (The permit of the Yiddish language *Democratic Newspaper* was cancelled for failing to meet the minimum frequency requirement for daily papers.)

42.   *Id.* at 872.

43.   *Bloy* v. *Minister of Interior,* 2 P.D. 136 (1949); There may have been other cases which did not reach the court.

44.   The bureaucracy may sometimes obstruct the process of permit-issuance by pedantically insisting on the requirements of the black-letter law. There is no empirical information on the question of whether these formalities actually deter press freedom. However, it does seem that there are no high-level political decisions behind the red tape.

45.   Article 94 provides:

94.—(1)   No newspaper shall be printed or published unless the proprietor thereof shall have obtained a permit under the hand of the District Commissioner of the District in which the newspaper is being, or is to be printed.

(2)   The District Commissioner, in his discretion and without assigning any reason therefor, may grant or refuse any such permit and may attach conditions thereto and may at any time suspend or revoke any such permit or vary or delete any conditions attached to the permit or attach new conditions thereto.

(3)   Any person who contravenes this regulation or the conditions of any permit thereunder and the proprietor and editor of the newspaper in relation to which the contravention occurs shall be guilty of an offense against these Regulations.

Defense Emergency Regulation art. 94 (1945), *reprinted in Palestine Gazette* no.

1442, at 1079 (Supp. II 1945). Notice, that in order to block judicial review and circumvent the rule of law, the regulation explicitly absolves the government from the need to reason any denial of permit.

46. *El-Ard* v. *Dist. Commissioner,* 18(2) P.D. 340 (1964). In *Kahooji, supra* note 35, members of the same group were prosecuted for having failed to obtain a permit under the press ordinance. Now they applied for a permit. The Defense (Emergency) Regulations rather than the Press Ordinance were invoked here because under the latter there was no discretion to deny a permit.

47. *El-Assaad* v. *Minister of Interior,* 34(1) P.D. 505 (1980).

48. *Id.* at p. 513 (author's translation). Notice that Israeli law is applied here since East Jerusalem is within Israel's jurisdiction.

49. *Id.* at 514–515.

50. *Mahoul* v. *Jerusalem District Commissioner,* P.D. (1983, in press).

51. Press Ordinance §10 (1933), *reprinted in* 2 R. Drayton, *supra* note 34, at 1220.

52. *Id.* §17, *reprinted in* 2 R. Drayton, *supra* note 34, at 1225.

53. *See,* e.g., *id.* at §§15(2), 21, 22, 36 *reprinted in* 2 R. Drayton, *supra* note 34, at 1224, 1226, 1226–1227.

> 54. 19. (1) The High Commissioner may cause the proprietor or editor of any newspaper or both such persons to be warned that certain matter appearing in such newspaper is, in the opinion of the High Commissioner, likely to endanger the public peace and that, if the publication of such matter in the newspaper is continued, the High Commissioner in Council will consider the question of suspending publication of the newspaper under the provisions hereof.
>
> (2) The High Commissioner, either with or without having caused the proprietor or editor of a newspaper to be warned under subsection (1), may, if any matter appearing in a newspaper is, in the opinion of the High Commissioner in Council, likely to endanger the public peace, by order, suspend the publication of the newspaper for such period as he may think fit and shall state in the said order the period of such suspension.
>
> (3) Any copy of a newspaper which has been suspended under the provisions hereof may be seized by a police officer, customs officer or officer of the post office.
>
> (4) Any person who publishes a newspaper the publication of which has been suspended under this section is guilty of an offence and is liable to imprisonment for six months or a fine of one hundred pounds or both such penalties.

*Id.* at §19 (1933), *reprinted in* 2 R. Drayton, *supra* note 34, at 1225. A second sanction of importance is that imposed pursuant to a conviction of seditious libel. *See infra* text accompanying notes 85–88.

55. See *supra* notes 35–46; and *Jiryis* v. *Haifa District Commissioner,* 18(4) P.D. 673 (1964); *Yardor* v. *Elections Committee* 19(3) P.D. 365 (1965).

56. In March 1967, two-and-a-half months prior to the 1967 War, King Hussein of Jordan, then-ruler of East Jerusalem, closed down all Palestinian newspapers in an effort to tame Palestinian nationalism. Ironically, therefore, present day Palestinian newspapers in East Jerusalem owe their existence to the

Israeli government. While these newspapers are printed in East Jerusalem their readership is mostly on the West Bank and the Gaza strip. See M. Negby, *Justice Under Occupation*, 148–149 (Jerusalem, 1981) (in Hebrew).

57.    By contrast to El-Ard which had been a fledgling movement.

58.    Lahav, *supra* note 31, at 509 (Part II).

59.    *Omar International Inc., N.Y.* v. *Minister of the Interior*, 36(1) P.D. 227 (1982). The articles described a period of violence and disorder on the West Bank, the assassination of President Sadat of Egypt, and the assassination of a Palestinian dignitary who had allegedly collaborated with the Israeli authorities.

60.    *Kol Ha'am*, 1 *Selected Judgments* 90 (1953).

61.    *Omar International*, 36(1) P.D. at 234.

62.    *I.e.*, the radical Zionists and radical Palestinians each deny the other's legitimate right to self-determination.

63.    *See Kol Ha'am*, 1 *Selected Judgments* at 105–107; *Ulpaney Hasrata* v. *Garry*, 16(4) P.D. 2407 (1962); *see infra* text accompanying notes 117–121.

64.    Defense Emergency Regulations art. 98 (1945), *reprinted in Palestine Gazette* no. 1442, at 1080 (Supp. II 1945).

65.    *But see* concluding paragraph of this section.

66.    *See* D. Goren, *Secrecy and the Right to Know*, 102 (1979).

67.    *Id.* at 91, 98.

68.    *Id.* at 103.

69.    Censorship Accord §2 (1966), *reprinted in* D. Goren, *Secrecy, Security and Freedom of the Press*, 213 (1976) (in Hebrew). Sections 1 and 2 state in full:

1.    The purpose of censorship is to prevent the publication of security information which might aid the enemy or damage the defense of the state.
2.    Censorship is based on cooperation between the military authorities and the press in order to implement the above purpose.

70.    *Id.* at §1.

71.    *Id.* at §4.

72.    *See 1979 Journalists Yearbook, Free Expression and Security Needs by an Intelligence Officer*, 110 (Tel-Aviv, 1979) (in Hebrew).

73.    For example, in 1979 two military officers were tried and convicted for shooting South Lebanese villagers during operation Litany. Publication of the circumstances of the incident as well as the military court decisions were withheld by the censor. *Jerusalem Post*, Nov. 13, 1979.

74.    In this fashion, information about plans for Jewish settlements on the West Bank is kept secret, D. Goren, *supra* note 66, at 163–164; Lahav, "Political Censorship—Some Reflections on its Validity in Israel's Constitutional Law," 11 Is. L. Rev. 339 (1976).

75.    Section 5(6) of the Accord states:

The Committee's deliberations shall be kept secret. Its decisions are publishable, except for cases related to, or to the extent that security considerations, as defined in 1, require secrecy and this matter will be within the Committee's discretion.

Censorship Accord §5(6) (1966), *reprinted in* D. Goren, *supra* note 69, at 213.

76.    See Cody and Ramati, "Covering the Invasion of Lebanon," *Washington*

*Journalism Review,* Sept. 18, 1982. The position of Israel's then-chief-of-staff, Lt. Gen. Raphael Eytan, was made clear even prior to the 1982 War: "Nothing which might give satisfaction to an Arab, should be allowed to be published by the Israeli news media." Cited in Goren, *Secrecy and the Right to Know* (1979), p. 164.

77.    Penal Law, 5737–1977, at   103 L.S.I. (special volumn) 35 (1977).

78.    Ordinance to prevent terrorism, Sepher Ha-Houkim 980 at 187 (1980). Section 4(2) prohibits the dissemination "in writing or orally, words of encouragement, [or] support" of a terrorist organization. Section 4(7) prohibits any "conduct which displays identification or support of a terrorist organization by raising a flag, displaying a symbol or a slogan or by uttering a hymn or a slogan...in public...." The sanction is a prison term of up to three years or a fine or both.

79.    As an illustration of the manipulability of legislation for purposes of stifling dissent, at least on the normative level, compare the prohibition against disseminating defeatist propaganda, *supra* note 77, enacted in 1957 as part of the state security law, and probably traceable to a European source (*see supra*, e.g., a similar Swedish provision in Strömberg's essay, "Press Law in Sweden," n. 91), with the 1981 statute against terrorism, *supra* note 78, which is an independent Israeli formulation, designed to outlaw gestures of sympathy to the P.L.O. and reflecting the escalation of the Israeli-Palestinian conflict and a decrease in the level of tolerance by the Israeli government.

80.    It is also important to note that §123 of the Penal Law, L.S.I. (special volume) 42, requires the consent of the Attorney General to any criminal prosecution pursuant to the state security law.

81.    Penal Law 5737–1977, at §113(a), L.S.I. (special volume) 38 (1977). Section 113 states in full:

(a)    A person who delivers any secret information without being authorised to do so is liable to imprisonment for fifteen years.

(b)    A person who delivers any secret information without being authorised to do so and with intent to impair the security of the State is liable to imprisonment for life.

(c)    A person who obtains, collects, prepares, records or holds possession of any secret information without being authorised to do so is liable to imprisonment for a term of seven years; if he thereby intends to impair the security of the State, he is liable to imprisonment for fifteen years.

(d)    In this section, "secret information" means information whose contents, form or mode of keeping indicate or indicates that the security of the State requires its being kept secret and information relating to a class of matters which the Government, with the approval of the Foreign Affairs and Security Committee of the Knesset, has, by order published in *Reshumot,* declared to be secret matters.

(e)    It shall be a good defence for a person charged with an offence under subsection (c) that he did nothing unlawful to obtain information in so far as it was secret information and that he obtained, collected, prepared, recorded or held possession of it in good faith and for a reasonable purpose.

82.    Trials related to matters of national security may be held *in camera* and be kept secret. Penal Law 5737–1977, at 128, L.S.I. (special volume) 43 (1977).

83.    D. Goren, *supra* note 66, at 124.

84. *Haaretz*, Aug, 13, 1980, at 1 (in Hebrew).

85. *Kol Ha'am, 1 Selected Judgments* at 94–95.

86. Penal Law, 5737–1977, §136, L.S.I. (special volume) 145 (1977).

87. *Id.* at §137, L.S.I. (special volume) 145.

88. Press Ordinance §23(1) (1933), *reprinted in* 2 R. Drayton, *supra* note 34, at 1227–28.

89. *Attorney General* v. *Biletsky,* 7 Psakim 231 (1952).

90. 16 P.D. 1023 (1962).

91. This magazine has irritated Israeli governments almost since its inception, more than 30 years ago. Unlike *Bul,* it has enjoyed a measure of influence on Israeli society and its publisher, Mr. Uri Avnery, was twice elected to Israel's Knesset.

92. 16 P.D. at 1026.

93. *Id.*

94. *Id.* at 1028.

95. One opinion, per Olshan J., 16 P.D. at 1029, even invoked the "rule of law" as a justification. Ironically, the rule of law—the very embodiment of reason conceived to curb arbitrary will—was used to justify the most flagrant discrimination and to legitimate limitless executive "will."

96. My friend Dr. Ruth Gavison points out that the crucial error in the opinion is the very requirement that the petitioner proves a right. Under Israeli law one need not assert anything beyond the right to receive nondiscriminatory treatment from the authorities. This interpretation shares the Court's positivistic approach. Its shared implicit premise is that it is not the task of the judiciary to recognize the special role of the press in disseminating information and therefore it is not necessary to create a right of access.

97. Essentially, the message to other reports was "behave or your accreditation will be revoked."

98. The important role played by the Israeli press in bringing about the Commission of Inquiry which probed into the September 1982 massacre of Palestinians in Lebanon is proof of the press's independence.

99. Section 288 of the Penal Law provides:

> A person who by gesture, words or acts insults a public servant or a judge or officer of a religious court or a member of a commission of inquiry under the Commissions of Inquiry Law, 5729–1968, whilst engaged in the discharge of his duties or in connection with the same is liable to imprisonment for six months.

Penal Law 5737–1977, at §288 L.S.I. (special volume) 79 (1977). Yet no prosecution involving the press is known to have taken place.

100. *See New York Times* v. *Sullivan,* 376 U.S. 254 (1964).

101. 32(3) P.D. 337 (1978), *rev'd* 31(2) P.D. 281 (1977).

102. 31(2) P.D. at 186–187.

103. *Id.* at 294 (Shamgar, J.).

104. 32(3) P.D. 337 (1978) (Landau, J.).

105. *Id.* at 345–346, citing G. Gately, *Libel and Slander,* 223 (7th ed. 1974).

106. 32(3) P.D. at 346–347.

107. *Id.* at 347 ("fair comment" is a technical term for a defense in libel cases).

108. *See supra* text accompanying note 105.

109. The Court does not seem to refer to a notion of journalistic responsibility which is self-determined *by journalists* but to a notion of responsibility shaped by either the judges or the political elite—both *subjects* of press criticism. This follows from the factual context of the case. *Ha'aretz,* which published the article, is an establishment newspaper. It followed the canons of investigative journalism, checking with two sources prior to publication. It sought, and was refused, comment from the electric company. The court did not address itself to the newspaper's demonstration of responsibility in this context. A propos the conception of press responsibility, which implies a sense of civic duty, compare the courts' conception of the press as a "private trade" in the *Shalom Cohen* case, *supra* text accompanying notes 90–94. Thus Israel's court has an incoherent conception of the press's role in society. When the press claims rights or privileges it is rejected on the grounds that it is merely a private trade. When its obligations are considered it is called upon to develop public responsibility.

110. I. Galnoor, "Government Secrecy in Israel," in *Government Secrecy in Democracies,* 156 (I. Galnoor ed. 1977).

111. Penal Law, 5737–1977 at 117 L.S.I. (special volume) 39 (1977).

112. *Id.* 117 (d)(2), L.S.I. (Special Volume) 40 (1977). To be non-classified, the information should "not concern the security or foreign relations of the state" and not be in violation of the public interest or a private right. *Id.*

113. Basic Law: The Government 5728–1968, at 28; Section 28 states in full:

(a)  The deliberations and decisions of the Government and of the committee of the Ministers on the following matters are secret and their publication is prohibited:

(1)  the security of the State;

(2)  foreign relations of the State;

(3)  any other class of matters whose secrecy the Government regards as vital to the state and which it has proclaimed, by order, for the purposes of this section;

(4)  a matter which the Government has decided to keep secret: Provided that the disclosure and publication of such a matter shall only be prohibited to a person who knew about the decision.

(b)  The provisions of subsection (a) shall not apply to things whose publication has been permitted by the Government, the Prime Minister or a person empowered by it or him in that behalf or is required under any law.

The section also enables the government to declare its deliberations as secret and subject any coverage thereof to both the military censor and the criminal law by technically declaring itself the "committee on matters of national security." See Goren, *supra* note 66, at 127. In this fashion matters related to the statistics of Jewish immigration to Israel, movement of oil tankers to Israel, and political talks with foreign officials were declared secret.

114.   Archives Law, § 10, Sepher Ha-Houkim 171, at 14 (1955). According to the Archives regulations of 1966 (as amended, Kovetz-Takanot 3937 at 524 (1979)), historical material related to national security or foreign relations or material related to personal matters may be kept secret up to 50 years and other material may be kept secret up to 20 years.

115.   Except for one case, in the sixties, in which a government employee was prosecuted and convicted for having sold to the press official correspondence between the Attorney General and the police. The case was not published. Recently, the government's spokesman was found guilty in internal disciplinary proceedings for having offered official information to the German magazine *Der Spiegel. Ha'aretz,* Oct. 29, 1982, at 10.

116.   I. Galnoor, *supra* note 110, at 189.

117.   *Ulpaney Hasrata* v. *Garry,* 16 P.D. 2407, 2415 (1962); *see also id.* at 2426 (Silberg. J.).

118.   In the sense that it was willing to consider openly the social and political context of censorship.

119.   16 P.D. 2419.

120.   *Id.* at 2414.

121.   Ironically, it is the arrogant paternalism, so characteristic of the Labor party of the fifties and sixties, which pushed the mostly working class Afro-Asian Jews to vote for the even more authoritarian right wing Likud.

122.   16 P.D. at 2415.

123.   *Id.* at 2414. Such associations were more likely to be raised in the censor's or another Jewish-European mind than in the mind of the "volatile" Afro-Asian audience.

124.   *Id.* at 2414. However, political censorship of films is not always banned by the court. *See Ein-Gal* v. *Censorship Board,* 32(1) P.D. 274 (1979). The Court sustained the Board's decision to deny a permit to show the film "The Struggle for the Land—or Palestine in Israel." The film presented a one-sided version of the Arab-Israeli conflict in a way which was biased against the Zionist cause and pro-Palestinian. The Court agreed that the film constituted incitement of both Israeli Arabs and Jews to support the Palestinian cause and terrorist activities and that therefore the permit was properly denied. *Id.* at 278.

125.   *Itzhaki* v. *Minister of Justice,* 28(2) P.D. 692 (1973). The book was cleared for publication and published in 1981.

126.   In contradistinction to the public right of access, which as a matter of law is not recognized in Israel, the legal system does recognize an individual right to know. The Administrative Procedure Amendment (Statement of Reasons) Law, 5719–1959, 13 L.S.I. 7 (1958–1959) orders public employees to give reasons for denying the request of a private individual to exercise his power (§ 2 (a)). Section 3, however, grants public employees broad discretion to decline to give reasons. In 1983 the Court invalidated a regulation issued by Israel's broadcasting authority, which prohibited the broadcasting of interviews with "public figures who consider the P.L.O. the sole or legitimate representative of the Arabs in Judea, Samaria or Gaza." The invalidation rested on the narrow grounds that the term "public figure" is overbroad and should be narrowly defined, but *in dicta* two of the three justices emphasized the centrality of the right to know in Israel's legal system. *Zichrony* v. *Israel Broadcasting Service,* March 23, 1983.

127.   Courts Law 5715–1957, at §38, 11 L.S.I. 157 (1956–1957) (as amended).

128.   In addition the court is permitted to close a trial if the public forum may deter a witness from giving testimony. *See also* Youth Care and Supervision Law 5728–1968 at §24(a)(b) 22, L.S.I. 261 (1967–1968); Penal Law 5737–1977, at §128, L.S.I. (special volume) 43 (1977), permitting the exclusion of defendants or their counsel from the trials. In recent years the Israeli legislature has been toying with the idea of prohibiting the disclosure of names of suspects prior to conviction, but a statute to this effect has not yet been enacted. *See generally* Gavison, "A Minimal Area of Privacy—Israel," Israeli Reports to the Tenth International Congress of Comparative Law.

129.   Penal Law 5737-1977, at §251, L.S.I. (special volume) 72 (1977). Section 251 provides:

A person who by any means of publication publishes in bad faith an incorrect report of proceedings in a court or in a commission of inquiry under the Commissions of Inquiry Law, 5729–1968, is liable to imprisonment for six months.

130.   *Id.* at §255, L.S.I. (special volume) 72 (1977). Section 255 states in full:

A person who says or writes anything concerning a Judge, whether of a secular or religious court, in respect of his office with intent to impair his status or publishes any invective against a Judge, whether of a secular or religious court, with a view to bringing the administration of justice into suspicion or contempt is liable to imprisonment for three years; but the discussion with candor and decency of the merits of the decision of a Judge in a matter of public concern shall not be an offence under this section.

131.   *See*, e.g., *Weil* v. *Attorney General*, 3 P.D. 93 (1950); *Sternhal* v. *Attorney General*, 6 P.D. 119 (1952).

132.   E. Harnon, *Contempt of Court by Disobedience*, 38–39 (Jerusalem 1965).

133.   Courts Law 5715–1957, at §41, 11 L.S.I. 157 (1956–1957). But the clause does not apply to an item published in good faith about something which had been said or had happened in open Court.

134.   Repealed by court order and the Court's Law.

135.   17 P.D. 169 (1963). The article read: "Only one word had [the defendant] to say . . . when asked if he were guilty of the murder . . . [but his attorney responded for him 'not guilty']. . . . Except for [the defendant] nobody would ever know if the negative answer was the one he prepared. Previously, prior to the beginning of the trial, he responded differently to the answer of a reporter. . . ." *Id.* at 173.

136.   Relying, for example, on *Patterson* v. *Colorado,* 205 U.S. 454 (1907); *Bridges* v. *California*, 314 U.S. 252 (1941); and *Pennekamp* v. *Florida,* 328 U.S. 331 (1946). 17 P.D. at 179, 178, and 175 respectively.

137.   17 P.D. at 179. The Court supported this choice by relying on the language of the statute.

138.   *Id.* at 181.

139.   E. Harnon, *supra* note 132, at 39–40. The *Disenchik* case may signal a

slight preference for the stricter British standard over the more permissive American approach. However, this has not been a consistent trend. *See,* e.g., Justice Cohn's dictum in *Bourkan* v. *Minister of Treasury,* 32(2) P.D. 800, 803 (1978):

> Where a case is *sub judice,* then appeal to the media of communications and public opinion constitutes contempt of court. This does not mean that we shall follow the English Common Law.... We have grown accustomed to the American approach....

140.   17 P.D. at 175, 181, 184. Fourteen years later, in *Sibony* v. *The State of Israel,* 31(2) P.D. 828, 829 (1977), the court, while rebuking the press for threatening the fairness of the judicial process, expressed reservations about the immunity of the judge to adverse public opinion and inflammatory press coverage. See also dictum in *Foka Hirsh* v. *State of Israel,* 30(3) P.D. 197, 202 (1976), where the Court emphasized the importance of the appearance of justice.

141.   17 P.D. at, 180. The court dismissed this issue by observing: "[T]he public may know what transpires in the courtroom...but how does the publication that a defendant confessed his guilt to a reporter serve the public interest? Such publication merely raises the tension and might satisfy the passion for sensations." *Id.*

142.   *Id.* at 185 (Berinson, J.).

143.   They do so notwithstanding the journalists' Code of Ethics which regulates the matter. In 1966 a district court judge was brought to trial for having allegedly received bribes. During the trial a Tel-Aviv theatre presented a play, the details of which were similar to the facts of the trial. The Censorship Board refused to revoke the theatre's permit and the Attorney General petitioned to the High Court of Justice, arguing that the matter was *sub judice.* The court, applying the *Dissenchik* doctrine, *supra* note 135, revoked the permit to perform the play for the duration of the litigation. *Attorney General* v. *Censorship Board,* 20(4) P.D. 757 (1966).

144.   *Foka Hirsh* v. *State of Israel,* 30(3) P.D. 197, 200 (1976).

145.   32 P.D. 800 (1978).

146.   *Id.* at 803–04 (Cohn, J.): "A petitioner...must keep silent outside the courtroom, lest his appeal to the press be interpreted as a lack of confidence in this court...either because he distrusts the court's ability or willingness to help or because he thinks that the court will be influenced by the publication or public opinion."

147.   The police manage such information by disclosing or leaking, selectively, information about certain investigations or individual suspects.

148.   Commissions of Inquiry Law, 1968, Sepher Ha-Houkim 548 p. 28, §24, 25(6) links the status of a member to that of a judge and 18(a) applies the contempt of court provisions, *supra* note 133, to a commission's proceedings.

149.   "The Agranat Report," the Commission of inquiry into the Yom-Kippur War, pp. 60–65 (1975) (in Hebrew).

150.   2 E. Harnon, *Evidence* 127 n. 29 (Jerusalem 1977).

151.   *See* Hershkovitz, "Journalist's Shield Against Disclosure of Sources," 1980 Bar-Ilan Univ. L. Rev. 251, 252 (citing both cases); Harnon, "Confidential Communications: Should the Journalist's Privilege be Recognized?" 3 Tel Aviv

Univ. L. Rev. 542 (1973); *see also* Press Council's Code of Ethics, *infra* text accompanying notes 193–96.

152.  *See infra* at §VI.

153.  More accurately, the press became a critical organ in matters of domestic affairs. It retained its reserve and self-censorship in matters of national security, but its independent and aggressive reaction to the 1982 war in Lebanon may signal a shift in its approach.

154.  Defamation Law 5725–1965, §§1, 3.

155.  *Id.* at §§ 11, 12.

156.  Section 11(b) protects the editor, in criminal defamatory proceedings, if he or she utilized reasonable means to prevent the defamatory publication and did not know about the publication. Section 12 assigns liability to the printer and distributor of the defamatory material, in both criminal and civil proceedings, but only if they either knew or had to know that the publication was defamatory.

157.  *Id.* at §4.

158.  *Id.* at §13.

159.  *Id.* at §14. The section explicitly provides that the defense of truth will apply even if the truth of trivial details which are not damaging in themselves was not proven.

160.  *Id.* at §16.

161.  And thereby editorial discretion is controlled by judicial discretion.

162.  Called the defense of fair comment in most common law jurisdictions.

163.  Section 16 provides:

(a)  If the accused or defendant proves that he made the publication under any of the circumstances referred to in section 15 and that it did not exceed what was reasonable under such circumstances, he shall be presumed to have made it in good faith.

(b)  The accused or defendant shall be presumed to have made the publication otherwise than in good faith if—

(1)  the matter published is not true and he did not believe it to be true; or

(2)  the matter is not true and he had not, prior to publishing it, taken reasonable steps to ascertain whether it was true or not;

(3)  he intended to inflict greater injury by the publication than was reasonable in defending the values protected by section 15.

*Id.* at §16.

164.  *Id.* at §15. See, e.g., subsections 15(8), (10) and (11), which provide:

15.  In a criminal or civil action for defamation, it shall be a good defence if the accused or defendant made the publication in good faith under any of the following circumstances:

. . . .

(8)  the publication was a complaint against the injured party in a matter in which a person to whom the complaint is submitted was a superior of the injured party, by law or contract, or a complaint submitted to an authority competent to receive complaints against the injured party or to investigate the matter which is the subject of the complaint;

. . . .

(10)   the publication was made for the sole purpose of denouncing or denying defamatory matter published previously;
(11)   the publication was merely the delivery of information to the editor of a newspaper in order that he might examine the question of its publication in the newspaper.

165.   *Id.* at §15(2):

[T]he relations between him and the person to whom the publication was addressed imposed on him a legal, moral or social duty to make the publication. . . .

166.   *Electric Co.* v. *Ha'aretz,* 23(2) P.D. 87 (1969) The facts are the same as in the principal *Ha'aretz* case, *supra* note 101–102.
167.   *Id.* at 94.
168.   *See generally.* Unger, *Knowledge and Politics* (New York 1975).
169.   Sections 15(5), (6) and (7) provide that the defense obtains if:

(5)   the publication was an expression of opinion on the conduct of the injured party—
    (a)   as a party, the representative of a party, or a witness at a public session in a proceeding as referred to in section 13(5), provided that the publication is not prohibited under section 21, or
    (b)   as a person whose case is the subject of an inquiry, as the representative of such a person or as a witness at a public session of a commission of inquiry as referred to in section 13(6),
or on his character, past, actions or opinions as revealed by such conduct;
(6)   the publication was a criticism of a literary, scientific, artistic or other work which the injured party had published or publicly exhibited, or of an act he had performed in public, or—in so far as pertinent to such a criticism—an expression of opinion on the character, past, actions or opinions of the injured party as revealed in such a work or act;
(7)   the publication was an expression of opinion on the conduct or character of the injured party in a matter in which the accused or defendant was a superior of the injured party, by law or contract, and the publication was justified by his being a superior as aforesaid. . . .

*Id.* at §§15(5), (6), (7).

170.   *Electric Company* v. *Ha'aretz,* 32(3) P.D. 337 (1978). A reading of the text makes rather clear that this was the opinion of the reporter. *See* further discussion *supra* at notes 101–109.
171.   The formalism of this approach stems not from the reliance on textual interpretation but from the belief that the separation of fact from opinion is attainable and fortifies the objectivity and scientific nature of the profession.
172.   *Committee of Sephardic Community* v. *Arnon,* 32(2) P.D. 183, 185 (1977). The Court held that had appellants argued that appellee's willingness to negotiate with the Palestine Liberation Organization amounts to anti-Zionist activity, it could be held a comment. But the mere assertion that one is anti-Zionist

amounts to a fact, and a reasonable person could not understand from the statement that it is an opinion.

173.   Interestingly, Section 17(b) provides that if the defamation was published in a magazine, the defamed may demand that the correction be published in a daily newspaper. It is likely that this section was aimed at *Ha-Olam Hazeh* (see *supra* note 91 and accompanying text). Section 10 gives the court discretion to order the publication of a denial or a correction.

174.   Defamation Law 5725–1965, §8.

175.   *Id.* at §§9, 10. Section 21 permits the court to issue a temporary gag order to prohibit the publication of information about the trial.

176.   March 11, 1981 Sepher Ha-Houkim 1011, p. 128 (1981).

177.   *Id.* at §30. "Newspaper" is given the same broad definition that appears in the Press Ordinance, *see supra* note 34.

178.   And provided that he or she employed reasonable means to prevent such publication and had no knowledge of it, *id.* at §30(b). Notice the similarity to the Defamation Law, *supra* note 163.

179.   Section 1 provides that "[a] person will not violate the privacy of another without the other's consent." *Id.* at §1 Section 3 defines content as either explicit or implicit. *Id.* at §3.

180.   *Id.* at §2.

181.   In addition, it regulates private investigators and private or governmental data banks.

182.   Blasi, "The Checking Value in First Amendment Theory," 1977 Am. B. Found. Research J. 521.

183.   March 11, 1981 Sepher Ha-Houkim 1011, p. 128 (1981, §18(2)(b).

184.   *Id.* at §18(3).

185.   This is not an exhaustive list. Six defenses are enumerated in section 18. Section 19 provides a defense if the violation were done by a security related authority in the course of performing its duties.

186.   But it does constitute a defense in criminal proceedings, *see id.* §30(2).

187.   *See also id.* at §28, which excludes any evidence about the nature, history, or personality of the plaintiff.

188.   *Id.* at §22(1)(2) (emphasis supplied).

189.   It is a recognized problem in the electronic media, which are run by the state. The relative independence of radio and television triggered cries of protest by the government now in power. Those presently in power feel that the journalists in the electronic media are biased against them. It is not clear how much of this is true and how much should be attributed to efforts by the government to suppress free criticism.

190.   *E.g.,* Moshe Dayan's failure to establish *Hayom Hazeh* as a competitive daily.

191.   First bill of defamation law, *Hatzao't Hok* 142 (1962) (in Hebrew).

192.   §1 of the Press Code of Ethics (in Hebrew).

193.   *Id.* at §§2, 6, 8, 5, 11, 12, respectively.

194.   *Zichrony* v. *Israel Broadcasting Service, supra* n. 126. Justice Bach's concurring opinion was noteworthy for its libertarian spirit, which affirmed the *Kol Ha'am* legacy established by Justice Agranat 30 years earlier.

# Seven

<hr>

# Press Law in Japan

**Masao Horibe**

## GENERAL FRAMEWORK

### The Jurisprudence of Free Speech

Until the end of the Second World War, the Japanese press was subject to legal restrictions and governmental pressures. Moreover, the ascent of militarism, a movement which triggered Japan's involvement in the war, was characterized by the stifling of free expression in general and dissident expression in particular. The suppression of free speech can, consequently, be seen as concomitant to the rise of militarism. Indeed, during the Second World War the press and broadcasting media served as government propaganda organs. This experience made the Japanese press determined not to repeat the errors of the past and sensitized it to the value of free speech. This history provides the genuinely Japanese justification of free expression.

Other justifications for free expression reflect strong Western influence on Japanese political and legal thought in the last century. The prevailing justifications are: (1) that it is an essential factor in the maturing of human personality; (2) that it serves as the best method for discovering truth by setting up a free market of ideas; (3) that it guarantees self-government; and (4) that it coordinates the social needs for stability and change.

The postwar conception of free expression has also shaped governmental policies toward the press. As a result, contemporary Japan is considered to be one of the few countries that effectively guarantees the principles of free expression.

## The Constitution

The Japanese Constitution, adopted on November 3, 1946, took effect on May 3, 1947. Enacted under the aegis of the Occupation, it superseded the Meiji Constitution—the constitution of the Japanese Empire of 1889.[1] Article 21 of the 1946 Constitution explicitly guarantees freedom of expression, including that of the press: "1. Freedom of assembly and association as well as speech, press and all other forms of expression are guaranteed. 2. No censorship shall be maintained, nor shall the secrecy of any means of communication be violated."[2] The Meiji Constitution provided that "Japanese subjects shall, within the limits of law, enjoy the liberty of speech, writing, publication, public meetings and association."[3]

In contrast to the Meiji Constitution, which recognized free expression only "within the limits of law,"[4] the 1946 Constitution seems to guarantee unlimited press freedom. The Supreme Court's teaching, however, is that reasonable and necessary restrictions, designed to protect the public welfare, may constitute valid limitations on the press.[5]

## Role of the Courts

Under the Constitution of 1946, the Supreme Court is the guardian of the Constitution. Article 81 vests the Court with broad powers of judicial review: "The Supreme Court is the court of last resort with power to determine the constitutionality of any law, order, regulation or official act."[6]

The ambiguous language of Article 81 was fertile ground for questions concerning the nature of the Japanese power of judicial review. One issue was whether inferior courts, as well as the Supreme Court, could exercise this power. In 1950, the Supreme Court ruled that inferior courts could also consider a statute's validity.[7] Another question was whether the court was empowered to comment on abstract problems of constitutionality as does the German constitutional court. The Supreme Court ruled that "courts do not possess the power, in the absence of such a concrete legal dispute, to hand down abstract decisions covering the future and relating to doubtful disputes concerning the interpretation of the Constitution and other laws, orders, and the like."[8]

Although the Supreme Court has never declared a statute restricting press freedom as unconstitutional, the courts, as shall be reviewed below, have played a significant role in developing the jurisprudence of free speech.

## THE PRESS AND THE GOVERNMENT

### Press Laws

From 1869 to 1949 the Japanese legal system contained special statutes which regulated the press.[9] For instance, the first such statute to be passed—the Newspaper and Publication Regulation—provided:

1.   Each newspaper must have its own title.
2.   On receipt of an official permit for publication, the publisher is not required to obtain authorization stamps on every issue before publication, but he shall submit two copies of each issue to the authorities concerned.
3.   Each issue of the newspaper must bear the date and place of publication, the name of the editor or publisher, and its own number.
4.   If a probe into items published is necessary, the editor shall be required to justify their publication. If he fails to do so, he shall be fined.
5.   The newspaper shall publish news items concerning natural calamities, prices, commercial and administrative laws (indiscrete criticism is not permitted), military affairs (when the editor fails to change his misled opinions, he shall be responsible), fires, weddings, deaths, births, arts and literature, parties, clothing, eating and drinking, the official gazette, translation of foreign books, miscellaneous foreign stories, and all things unharmful to the public.
6.   The authors of books, articles, or criticisms shall be identified when their books, articles, or criticisms are published (with the exception of poems whose writers are not known).
7.   Publication of items making a false charge against persons is prohibited.
8.   Indiscreet publication of items on religious doctrines is prohibited.[10]

Subsequent ordinances and acts contained similar provisions.

During the Occupation, press censorship was introduced. With the enactment of the 1946 Constitution, however, all general press laws were repealed. Nevertheless, restrictions on press freedom persist. For example, the law of defamation, the Election Act, and other statutes to be discussed below[11] restrict press freedom.

### National Security

#### *Genuine National Security Interests*

To understand the distinctive Japanese approach, it is useful to distinguish between matters related to external security and matters related to internal security. External security matters, i.e., those related to the carrying on of a war or the maintenance of an effective defense, raise the greatest controversy in Japan. This controversy stems from the feature most characteristic of the Japanese Constitution—the renunciation of war in Article 9:

1.  Aspiring sincerely to an international peace based on justice and order, the Japanese people forever renounce war as a sovereign right of the nation and the threat or use of force as a means of settling international disputes.
2.  In order to accomplish the aim of the preceding paragraph, land, sea, and air forces, as well as other war potential, will never be maintained. The right of belligerency of the state will not be recognized.[12]

Despite this constitutional provision, the government established the Self-Defense Forces in 1954.[13] At the outset, the government tried to rationalize this form of rearmament on the ground that it did not constitute a "war potential." In recent years, however, the government, as well as the ruling Liberal Democratic Party, have abandoned that justification. Instead, the government relies on the clear approval given by a majority of the Diet to the Self-Defense Forces Act which authorized the establishment of these forces. Thus, it is the Act, buttressed by a presumption of constitutionality, which justify the Self-Defense Forces. By this reasoning, the government and the Liberal Democratic Party have recognized the domain of external security to constitutionally restrict freedom of the press.

In contrast, although differing in their methods of reasoning, the predominant majority of constitutional law scholars and some opposition parties, especially the Japan Socialist Party and the Japan Communist Party, consider the Self-Defense Forces Act a violation of Article 9 of the Constitution.[14] Therefore they do consider security-based limitations on press freedom, which are valid under the Act, as invalid due to the Act's unconstitutionality.

When, however, external security matters concern the pursuit of foreign relations, both the government and opposition parties more or less approve of restricting the freedom of the press.[15]

### Censorship

Paragraph 2 of Article 21 expressly prohibits censorship by providing that "[n]o censorship shall be maintained, nor shall the secrecy of any means of communication be violated." Although the second half of the paragraph refers only to the means of communication, such as letters, telegrams, and telephone messages, it should be interpreted as prohibiting all censorship of speech and publication. This broad protection stands in sharp contrast to the various types of prior restraint permitted during the era of the Meiji Constitution.[16] In contemporary Japan there is no security-related censorship in a legal sense.

### Criminal Statutes

In addition to the prohibition against defamation,[17] several other criminal provisions directly regulate the press.[18] For example, the Special Criminal Act to Implement Agreement under Article 6 of the Treaty of Mutual Cooperation and Security between Japan and the United States of America regarding Facilities and Areas and the Status of the United States Armed Forces in Japan[19] prevents disclosure of United States military secrets. In addition, the Secrecy Protection Act Accompanying the Japan-U.S. Mutual Cooperation and Security Treaty[20] safeguards secret defense information of the United States. Significantly, each Act refers to secrets of the United States; neither purports to protect the secrecy of the Japanese government.

The most important statutory provisions which can arguably be applied against the press are articles 100 and 111 of the National Public Employees Act of 1947. Article 100 mandates that "[g]overnment employees shall not leak secrets that become known to them through their official duties"[21]; Article 111 makes it a criminal offense to induce a civil servant to commit a crime.[22] A famous case before the Supreme Court juxtaposed both the legitimacy of keeping secrets related to foreign affairs[23] and the obligations of public employees to protect the confidentiality of governmental information.[24]

At a meeting of the House Budget Committee on March 27, 1972, a Socialist representative disclosed three secret cablegrams exchanged between Japan and the United States during the negotiations over the return of the Okinawan islands to Japanese control. In the cablegrams, the government pledged to pay four million dollars to Okinawan landowners in compensation for property damage resulting from the United States military presence. This commitment conflicted with the publicly announced agreement specifying that the United States would pay the compensation. The dietman* charged that the government had concluded a "secret deal" with the United States government over Okinawa's reversion to Japan; the government insisted there had been no such secret promise.

In April 1972, a political reporter for the *Mainichi Shimbun*, one of the three largest newspapers in Japan, was arrested along with a female employee in the Foreign Ministry. The public employee was indicted for

---

* A *dietman* is a member of the Diet, the general legislative assembly of the Japanese government.

alleged violations of Article 100 of the National Public Employees Act (divulging secret information); the reporter was charged with violating Article 111 of the Act (inducing a civil servant to commit a crime). The prosecution charged that, by using his "intimate" relations with the employee between May and June 1971, the reporter had persuaded her to give him copies of the three cablegrams which the reporter then gave to the dietman.[25] The reporter admitted obtaining the cablegrams and arranging to transmit them to the Socialist Party opposition (the dietman had not revealed his source), but claimed that his actions were part of his newsgathering activities and that a conviction would infringe on freedom of the press.

The Tokyo District Court found the former employee guilty of leaking government secrets. The newsman, who had resigned upon his arrest, was acquitted. The court found that the ministry documents constituted "substantial secrets"[26] and if disclosed would interfere with the conduct of foreign affairs. Thus, the employee's conviction was merited by the possible dangers to the national welfare. In order to find a violation under Article 111, however, two requirements had to be met. First, that "substantial secrets" were obtained by illegal acts of persuasion. Second, that the inducement consisted of acts which would cause an independant determination in another party to commit an illegal act.[27] Thus, the court recognized that inducement occurred even though the employee reached the same decision independently. However, the court found the reporter's acts, which otherwise might have been punishable, protected as justifiable conduct in light of the value of freedom of the press in a democracy. Balancing the need to protect the secrets in question against the interests of newsgathering activities, the court concluded that the reporter's actions were justifiable as part of the public information function of the press.[28]

On appeal by the prosecution against the newsman's acquittal (the employee did not appeal her conviction), the Tokyo High Court reversed, finding the reporter guilty of violating the National Public Employees Act. The court emphasized that freedom of newsgathering activities did not extend to inducing public servants to cooperate affirmatively with those activities. Nor could the imposition of a duty upon public servants to keep secrets be considered as a restriction on that freedom. It further criticized the balancing approach adopted by the district court as lacking objectivity or as apt to fall into arbitrary judgment. While interpreting "inducement" more strictly than the lower court, the high court still ruled that the reporter's acts constituted inducement.[29] The former reporter was given a six-month suspended sentence.

The reporter appealed to the Supreme Court. On May 31, 1978, the First Petty Bench of the Supreme Court[30] affirmed the judgment below. The Court held that a "secret" is a fact unknown to the public, considered worthy of being protected substantially, and the classification of which is subject to judicial review; it found the leaked cablegrams worthy of protection. Further, the Court construed "inducement" as acts of persuasion, made with the intent of causing a public employee to reveal secret information and sufficient to invoke an independent determination in that employee to commit the illegal act. While finding that the former reporter's acts did constitute inducement, the Court recognized, in general terms, the importance of freedom of the press in informing the public about government activities. The Court stated that when the press is investigating state secrets, its newsgathering activities may conflict with a public employee's duty not to disclose those secrets. Therefore, such activity can be justified if motivated by a "genuine desire" to inform the public and if the means used are warranted to be right in light of socially accepted ideas. The court concluded that the reporter's activity could not.[31]

This case demonstrates that even civil service laws can be invoked against the press. The Supreme Court's judgment is thus open to criticism for its chilling effect on press attempts to discover and reveal government secrets. Still, the approach of balancing between press-related interests and the need of governmental secrecy, adopted by the Supreme Court, may prove a useful doctrine for protecting press freedom in future cases.

At the present time, the Criminal Code does not prohibit public employees from disclosing secret information. The Draft of the Revised Criminal Code, proposed by the Legislative Council of the Ministry of Justice, does, however, make it a crime for former or current public employees to disclose government secrets; the proposed penalty is a maximum three years' imprisonment.[32] Despite the drafters' explanation that they have merely transferred to the Draft the prohibition contained in the National Public Employees Act, the press as well as many academics and practicing lawyers strongly oppose this proposal. I think that prohibiting disclosure of secrets and penalizing violations of employment rules under the civil service laws are entirely different from making disclosure a crime under the Criminal Code.

Furthermore, it seems that formal mechanisms of control, such as the one suggested by the Draft of the Penal Code are unnecessary, in view of the self-discipline which generally characterizes the Japanese press.

### Abuse of National Security and Seditious Libel

Generally, the Japanese government may try to invoke a public official's duty to keep secrets in order to conceal governmental corruption or abuse of power. The Secret Cablegrams Leak Case, discussed above, is a good example of abuse of national security. The Lockheed scandal, revealed in the United States in February 1976, is another flagrant illustration.

Although in some cases the press seems to refrain from publishing news or criticism under the pretense of preventing harm to national security, there is inadequate information to evaluate the actual performance of the press.

Since the repeal in 1947 of the Criminal Code's provision prohibiting criticism of the Emperor or his Empire, Japan has had no provision corresponding to seditious libel.

## The Reputation of Public Officials

The Japanese legal system provides no special protection for the reputation of public officials. Indeed, the Criminal Code distinguishes between ordinary defamation and defamation involving public figures.[33] Thus, under Article 230, truth is not a defense in the case of private defamation, and the defamer may be punished by fine or imprisonment.[34] In contrast, truth is recognized as a defense in matters of public interest. Article 230.2, added in 1947, states that if the allegedly defamatory statement relates to matters "concerning a public employee or a candidate for elective public office and, upon inquiry into the truth or falsity of the alleged facts, the truth is proved, punishment shall not be imposed."[35]

The Supreme Court has interpreted Article 230.2 as reconciling the need to protect an individual's reputation with the need to guarantee freedom of speech.[36] In particular, the doctrine of popular sovereignty—one of the most important principles of the Japanese Constitution—provides justification for less protection for public officials because they are "servants of the whole community" and "the people have the inalienable right to choose...and to dismiss them."[37]

The prevailing Japanese view on this point has been succinctly put by the Hiroshima High Court, when it decided a libel suit brought by an elected public official against a newspaper. The court stated that "in a democratic society, the press bears the responsibility of publicly criticising elected public officials tinged with criminal conduct."[38] However, the court will not protect information unrelated to official conduct. Thus, a newspaper's comment on the physical disability of an elected official was ruled as unrelated to official conduct and therefore not protected against a libel suit.[39]

## Access to Governmental Information

My understanding of the status of governmental information is that it belongs to the people and therefore should be kept open, unless there are legitimate justifications to keep it secret. This is also the popular conception in Japan. The government, however, is likely to embrace a different philosophy, according to which the government is the proprietor of the information and thus the information remains confidential unless the government, in its discretion, releases it.

Although Japan has no equivalent to the American Freedom of Information Act,[40] there is scholarly support and judicial mention of the "right to know" or "freedom to know."[41] Moreover, citizens, as well as the press, have urged central and local governments to enact similar laws. On March 29, 1980, the Movement for Legislating the Public Disclosure of Information Act was established to campaign for the legislation. Prior to the movement's organization, the opposition parties had pledged similar legislation, after confronting a wall of secrecy in the series of government scandals and corruption cases concerning aircraft companies and politicians. From 1980 to 1981 each of the opposition parties introduced its own bill in the Diet; unfortunately, lack of consensus on the scope of disclosure exemptions, especially regarding the exemption of national defense secrets, divides the opposition.[42] At the local level, most prefecture governments have been studying the system of free information, and some of them seem to favor enacting freedom of information laws.[43] As of April 1, 1983, two prefectures as well as one city and four towns passed freedom of information ordinances.

It is noteworthy, however, that utilization of any freedom of information laws by the press is doubtful. The Japanese press has developed independent informal mechanisms to obtain information skillfully, and its reliance on formal channels may not be substantial.

## THE PRESS AND THE JUDICIAL PROCESS

### Free Press and Fair Trials

Except in certain circumstances, the Japanese Constitution mandates public trials:

> 1.  Trials shall be conducted and judgment declared publicly.
> 2.  Where a court unanimously determines publicity to be dangerous to public order or morals, a trial may be conducted privately, but trials of political offenses, offenses involving the press or cases wherein the rights of people as guaranteed in Chapter III of this Constitution are in question shall always be conducted publicly.[44]

No Japanese law prohibits the press from reporting pretrial, trial, or posttrial proceedings, including the testimony presented and the circumstances surrounding the case. Pursuant to the Juvenile Act, however, the press may not report the names of juvenile suspects. The Act prescribes that with respect to a juvenile who has been on quasi trial in a Family Court or a person against whom public prosecution has been instituted on a crime he or she has committed while a juvenile, such articles or photographs as to enable other persons to infer that he or she is the criminal involved in the said case, from his or her name, age, occupation, residence, appearance, etc. therein shall not be published in newspapers or other publications.[45]

Violation of this provision carries no criminal sanction.

In 1958 the Japan Newspaper Publishers and Editors Association established its own model standard. The standard requires self-control by the press and prohibits publishing the names, photographs, or other information capable of identifying a juvenile.[46] It modifies the Juvenile Act by allowing the press to report a juvenile's name and other pertinent information, if the press considers the public interest in the case to outweigh the interest in protecting the identity of the juvenile suspect. Special cases might involve a juvenile who is wanted by the police and considered likely to repeat a felony such as arson or murder.

Actual press reporting of trials has provoked much hostile criticism from lawyers, focusing particularly on reports concerning criminal suspects. Critics claim that the press treats suspects as if they had already been found guilty, thereby violating the presumption of innocence. Despite this harsh criticism, the press continues to report freely on trials. That it can do so rests on the absence of a jury system in Japan, and on the concomitant belief that professional judges are not apt to be influenced by the news reports.

Generally, the Japanese press prefers self-restraint to legal regulation. Two examples of self-restraint are the voluntary omission of the victim's name in a rape case and the practice of not reporting kidnapping cases when the life of the kidnapped person may be endangered by the reportage.

## Reporters' Privilege

Of most significance in Japan is whether reporters have a constitutional or statutory right to keep their sources, notes, tapes or films, confidential. In the absence of any express statute protecting the confidentiality of newsmen's sources, the jurisprudence of a reporter's privilege has been developed by the courts.

The first notable case arose in 1949 when a reporter for the *Asahi Shimbun,* one of Japan's three largest newspapers, refused to testify about the identity of his news source. He was convicted of violating article 161 of the Code of Criminal Procedure,[47] which makes it a crime for any person to refuse to be sworn or to testify without good reason, and was fined. After the high court affirmed his conviction, the reporter appealed to the Supreme Court, asserting free press claims.

In 1952, the Court dismissed the appeal.[48] The Supreme Court's unanimous opinion did recognize certain exceptions to the statutory duty to testify. But the privilege against testifying granted to some individuals, for example, medical doctors, nurses, practicing attorneys, and government officials, was explicitly guaranteed under the Code of Criminal Procedure.[49] Declining to extend the statutory exceptions to include newspaper reporters, the Court stated:

> [Article 21, paragraph 1 of the Constitution] guarantees the freedom of expression equally to all the people; it does not provide reporters with any special guarantee. Consequently, if we were to adopt the logic of the appeal, all persons would be guaranteed the freedom of sources under Article 21, even in the drafting of articles and essays, and, as a result, they would end by having the right to refuse to testify concerning the sources used. Constitutional guarantees impose considerable restrictions on the legislative power of the National Diet by making it impossible to easily restrict such guarantees, even by Diet-enacted legislation; but such guarantees are not open to infinitely wide interpretation, as in the argument for appeal.
>
> The guarantee of the above constitutional provisions means that everyone must be allowed to say what he wishes to the extent that it does not interfere with the public welfare. This absolutely cannot be interpreted as a guarantee of the right to refuse—even before one has decided what he wishes to write—to testify about a source of material that will be used later on, thus sacrificing the duty to testify, indispensable to the proper operation of the judicial process, which is of the highest importance to the public welfare.[50]

Another case presenting claims of a reporter's privilege involved the submission of television news films to the Fukuoka District Court. The films had recorded students demonstrating against the visit to Japan by the U.S.S. *Enterprise*, an American nuclear-powered aircraft carrier. The students who were arrested alleged excessive use of force by the police. After the prosecutor refused to indict the police for abuse of their authority, the students petitioned the district court to initiate "quasi-prosecution procedure." As part of its investigation into whether there were sufficient grounds for trial, the district court requested the television companies to produce the films because they were indispensable evidence of what had occurred. They refused, asserting that to submit the films would interfere with future newsgathering activities. The television companies argued further that if they were compelled to produce the films, the public might distrust the press since their films would be used for purposes other than merely reporting the news. The television companies based their refusal on the public's "right to know," which, they argued, was guaranteed by Article 21 of the Constitution. The district court disagreed and issued an order compelling production of the films. After the Fukuoka High Court upheld the order, the four television companies appealed to the Supreme Court.

In their appeal before the Supreme Court, the appellants argued:

The freedom to report news occupies an important place under Article 21 of the Constitution. It is one of the bases of a democratic society, for which the Constitution of Japan stands. In order to fully guarantee the freedom to report news, the freedom of news-gathering activities should also be guaranteed. As a matter of fact, the freedom of news-gathering activities has so far been widely enjoyed by the press. This is because those in the press have kept it in mind that their news-gathering activities should have as their sole purpose news-reporting and that the product of their activities should not be used for any other purpose, and also because the public has placed confidence in this principle of morality in news-gathering. However, if the court order demanding the submission of these news films for the purpose of using them as evidence in a criminal trial is upheld and the news media is obliged to obey the order, public confidence in the press in this respect will be lost and it will become much harder to secure public cooperation in news-gathering activities. This will in turn obstruct the exercise of the freedom to report the truth. Thus the general public will not have enough data upon which to base their judgments, which are necessary for the exercise of their sovereign power. Further, their "right to know," which should accompany freedom of expression, will be hampered....[51]

The court agreed with this analysis stating:

In our democratic society, as is pointed out by the appellants, news reports offer important material upon which the people may make their judgments when they participate in the governmental process. News reports thus serve the people's "right to know." Therefore, it goes without saying that the freedom to report news, together with the freedom of expression of thoughts, is guaranteed under Article 21 of the Constitution, which provides for freedom of expression. For the purpose of securing the accuracy of the news reported by the press, and in the light of the policy behind Article 21 of the Constitution, the fredom of news-gathering activities as well as of news reporting is to be respected.[52]

Nonetheless, the Court, sitting as the Grand Bench, unanimously affirmed the decision below. It emphasized that the guarantee of a fair criminal trial was one of the basic principles of the Constitution, and, in this case, outweighed press freedom. Any disadvantage which the press might suffer after submitting the films would not relate directly to the freedom of news reporting, but only to the possible detrimental effect on future newsgathering activities.

Some commentators assign great weight to the general proposition in the opinion concerning the people's "right to know" and the freedom in gathering news, praising it is as an important development in Japanese press law.

The most recent reporter's privilege case once again involved a newsman's refusal to disclose the identity of his sources. On June 24, 1977, the *Hokkaido Shimbun*, the seventh largest newspaper in Japan, published an article reporting that teachers at a nursery had abused some pupils. One of the teachers brought a libel action against the *Hokkaido Shimbun*. The staff writer on the newspaper's city desk, who wrote the article, testified as a defense witness. When cross-examined by attorneys for the plaintiff, he refused to disclose his news source on the ground that it was a reporter's duty to protect news sources. The plaintiff requested the court to decide whether the newsman had a privilege to refuse to testify. On May 30, 1979, the Sapporo District Court ruled that the newsman could refuse to reveal his source.[53] The court based its ruling on article 281 of the Code of Civil Procedure, which allows a witness to refuse to testify on matters relating to "technical or trade secrets."[54] The court interpreted "trade secrets" to include the information source of a newsman, charged with a social mission to inform the public. To require disclosure of the news source might have a detrimental effect on future newsgathering activities. Although the district judge also recognized some limitations on this privilege, he held that the refusal would not deprive the plaintiff of an opportunity to offer counter-evidence.

The plaintiff filed an immediate appeal, asserting that the refusal to testify was an abuse of the reporter's privilege. On August 31, 1979, the Sapporo High Court upheld the district court ruling, stating that the extent of a restriction on the refusal to testify is to be determined by balancing the interest of securing a fair trial against the interest in protecting the process of news gathering.[55] The Supreme Court, on March 6, 1980, dismissed the special appeal against the decision of the lower court on procedural grounds.[56]

It is significant that the highest court has, for the first time, implicitly recognized a reporter's privilege to refuse to reveal his information source in a civil action. Whether the privilege extends to the criminal process is not yet settled.

This decision, which was welcomed by the press, also supports the prevailing constitutional view of the newsman's privilege. But it should be emphasized that the journalist's privilege will not be allowed to override the public interest in ensuring that no reporter invades the rights of others through reprehensible conduct.

## THE PRESS AND THE INDIVIDUAL

### Defamation

Because Japan has no general press laws, defamation is one of the most important subjects in the field of press regulation. Japanese law defines defamation as reducing the respect of another in the community or lowering him in the estimation of his fellows. Japan has no group libel in the strict sense of the word. Both criminal and civil defamation are prescribed by the Japanese codes. Professor Lawrence Beer succinctly explained the Japanese situation:

> As a matter of doctrine, civil suit is the preferred remedy, except in extreme cases. However, in practice criminal prosecution or recourse to the Civil Liberties Bureau are the useful avenues in Japan, in those instances in which any public remedy is sought at all. Costs, in time and fees, are greater in civil litigation than in criminal prosecution; the civil damages awarded are generally nominal; and the injured party is usually more interested in prompt vindication than in monetary compensation. It may be that aggrieved parties are led by knowledge at the relatively high rate of conviction in criminal cases to assume greater certainty of vindication by that route, an assumption not clearly warranted by experience in criminal defamation cases.[57]

Under paragraph 1 of Article 230 of the Criminal Code, "[a] person who injures the reputation of another by publicly alleging facts shall, regardless of whether such facts are true or not, be punished by imprisonment with or without forced labor for not more than three years or by a fine of not more than one thousand yen.[58] Paragraph 2 further provides that "a person who injures the reputation of a dead person shall not be punished unless such defamation is based on a falsehood."[59] On request of the defamed party, the prosecution may indict the defamer. The prosecution, however, retains discretion on whether to bring the case to court.

As mentioned earlier,[60] the Criminal Code distinguishes between ordinary defamation and defamation involving the public interest. If indicted, the press attempts to prove truth under Article 230.2 of the Criminal Code. That Article stipulates:

1. When the statement as defined in paragraph 1 of [Article 230] relates to matters of public concern and has been made solely for the purpose of promoting the public interest, the person making that statement shall not be punished if the truth thereof is established upon inquiry into its truth or falsehood.
2. In applying the provision of the preceding paragraph, facts concerning the criminal act of a person against whom prosecution has not yet been instituted shall be deemed to be facts which relate to matters of public concern.
3. When the statement as defined in paragraph 2 of [Article 230] relates to facts concerning a public employee or a candidate for elective public office, the person making that statement shall not be punished if the truth thereof is established upon inquiry into its truth or falsehood.[61]

Truth as a defense is thus permitted only in cases in which the allegedly defamatory statements relate to "matters of public concern" and have been made "solely for the purpose of promoting the public interest." Generally speaking, matters are of public concern if by their nature they are of public or national importance, or if they have attracted public attention or criticism. The press claims that the very fact of publication creates a presumption that the matter is of public concern. In a 1953 decision the Tokyo High Court disagreed, holding that a magazine article, reporting a rumor that executives of several press companies had been bribed in order to keep certain criminal scandals secret, did not constitute a matter of public concern.[62]

A recent Supreme Court judgment in a libel case involving the leader of a religious organization created great interest in the press.[63] The case arose when articles in the March and April 1976 issues of the monthly magazine *Gekkan Pen* (Monthly Pen) charged the president of a Buddhist lay organization with having had intimate relations with two female members of the organization. The magazine editor was arrested and prosecuted for criminal defamation and, in June 1978, received a 10-month suspended sentence by the Tokyo District Court.[64] Although unsuccessful in his appeal to the Tokyo High Court,[65] the First Petty Bench of the Supreme Court remanded the case to the Tokyo District Court. In its judgment, the Supreme Court formulated a new test for "matters of public concern." The Court stated that even the private behavior of a private person could be of public concern, depending upon the nature of a person's social activities and the degree of his influence on society through those activities.

For the press, the defense of truth has been the central issue in criminal and civil defamation cases. Since 1969, however, the press has not been required to prove the truth of statements in criminal defamation actions. The case relaxing this requirement arose in February 1963 when the *Yukan Wakayama Jiji* (Evening Wakayama Times) published a series of articles entitled "The Sins of the Vampire, Tokuichiro Sakaguchi." (Sakaguchi published an allegedly sensationalist newspaper, the *Wakayama Tokudane* [Wakayama Exclusive]. One of the articles attacked Sakaguchi for attempting to corrupt public officials by offering to suppress stories of their misdeeds in return for money. The Osaka High Court sustained the lower court's conviction of the editor of the *Yukan Wakayama Jiji*. Dismissing the judgment, the unanimous Grand Bench of the Supreme Court set forth a new rule to be applied in criminal defamation suits against the press. Proving the truth of defamatory statements was no longer required as part of the press's defense. Rather, the press need only show that a statement was made under the mistaken but reasonable belief, based on reliable materials and a reliable source, that it was true.[66] Thus, if a statement were made in good faith, the court would not impute to the speaker a criminal intent, and, absent a criminal intent, there would be no crime of defamation.

Under the Civil Code, defamation is a tort.[67] Pursuant to Article 709 of the Code, the defamer is required to compensate for the resulting damages.[68] In addition, Article 710 requires compensation "even in respect of a non-pecuniary damage, irrespective of whether such injury was to the person, liberty, or reputation of another or to his property rights."[69] These two articles protect an individual's reputation and are the most comprehensive of the 16 articles concerning tort law.

Other remedies for defamation are available under Article 723:

> If a person has injured the reputation of another, the court may, on the application of the latter, make an order requiring the former to take suitable measures for the restoration of the latter's reputation either in lieu of or together with compensation for damages.[70]

One such suitable measure is to require the person to apologize publicly in a national or local newspaper. The apology does not necessarily imply personal recognition of wrongdoing, and is frequently used both in and out of court to settle disputes.

In contrast to Article 230.2 of the Criminal Code, the Civil Code does not explicitly exempt defamatory statements which relate to matters of public concern, which are made solely in the public interest, and which allege facts later found to be true. But in 1966 the Supreme Court held the principle of the Criminal Code provision applicable to civil cases. It therefore banned tort actions where the defamatory statements are proved to be true, are related to matters of public concern, and are made solely in the public interest. Moreover, proving the statements' truth is unnecessary if the defamer had reasonable grounds to believe they were true.[71]

Because civil damage awards are small, they do not deter newspapers from reporting. So far as I know, the highest award given in a civil case was 1,500,000 yen (approximately $7,500).[72]

Since the repeal in 1949 of the Newspaper Act,[73] Japan has had no statutory provision recognizing the right of reply. Nevertheless, Article 723 of the Civil Code, which permits a court to order "suitable measures for the restoration of [an injured party's] reputation,"[74] may provide a basis for asserting this right. Indeed, the Japan Communist Party (JCP) raised such a claim in a defamation suit brought against the *Sankei Shimbun*, Japan's fifth largest newspaper. The newspaper had published an advertisement by the Liberal Democratic Party which ridiculed the JCP and charged it with making a proposal contradictory to its party platform. Although the district court stated in general terms that the constitutional right to freedom of speech included the right of reply, and acknowledged further that Article 723 provided a basis for this right, it refused to grant the plaintiff's demand unless the original advertisement was found to be libelous.[75] The Tokyo High Court, however, deleted the section of the district court's opinion which discussed the right of reply.[76] This case raised some important issues, including, for example, the principle of equality in communication—a complicated matter because of the policy of neutrality toward political parties adopted by most of the Japanese press.

## Privacy

The Japanese language has no equivalent for the word "privacy." Legal scholars, who have researched the development of the American right to privacy, have tried to translate it into Japanese, but no translation has yet prevailed. Japanese speakers usually use the word "puraibashi" in *kataka-na* (one of the two Japanese alphabets) for "privacy."

The legal basis for a right of privacy can be found in Articles 709 and 710 of the Civil Code, due to their comprehensive scope. The right was judicially recognized in 1964 by a Tokyo District Court Judgment, in a well-known case usually called "After the Banquet."

Hachiro Arita, an unsuccessful socialist candidate for the 1959 Tokyo gubernatorial election and a one-time foreign minister, sued Yukio Mishima for invasion of privacy. Mishima had, without Arita's consent, written a *roman à clef (After the Banquet)* based on Arita and his former wife. On September 28, 1969, the Tokyo District Court awarded Arita most of his requested damages of 800,000 yen (then approximately $2,200), which at that time was the largest damage award ever assessed in a privacy or defamation action.[77]

In establishing this new right, the district court declared that respect and protection of an individual's dignity in a society of mass communications was no longer merely a matter of ethics. Rather, this personal interest was elevated to a legal right, to be protected against unlawful infringement. The court defined the right of privacy as "the legal right and assurance that one's private life will not be unreasonably opened to the public." Moreover, it found that the right was recognized in statutory provisions covering certain aspects of privacy, and was guaranteed under the constitutional requirement that "all of the people shall be respected as individuals."[78] The word "privacy" came into widespread use in Japan and the case promoted scholarly research into the American and other foreign legal systems' approach to the right of privacy.

Although welcomed by lawyers, the judgment was criticized by the literary community. As far as I know, newspapers have not been sued for invasions of privacy; however, several cases involving magazines or movies based on living persons (*model movies*) have raised privacy and freedom of expression issues. The Japanese press is attempting to respect the right of privacy as a matter of public morality, while at the same time emphasizing the importance of press freedom. In general, the prevailing opinion is that because both privacy and press freedom are important social interests in a democracy, the facts of a particular case will determine which interest will be paramount.


## PRIVATE ARRANGEMENTS WHICH AFFECT THE ROLE OF THE PRESS IN SOCIETY

### Individual Access to the Media

Japan recognizes no legal right of access to the media. But, because of American influence, over the past decade we have discussed whether to establish such a right.[79] While some proponents insist on establishing a legal right of access, the press claims this would violate its right to editorial freedom. Needless to say, if the press accedes voluntarily to the demand, then the difficulty of reconciling an access right with press freedom can be avoided.

Over the past decade, the Japanese press has also increased the space available to the public for editorial advertisements. In particular, the *Mainchi Shimbun,* one of Japan's three largest newspapers, professes itself to be an "open newspaper," based on the public's increased demand for access to the press. Thus, the press can no longer disregard individual access to the media.


### Media Concentration

Media concentration is not considered an urgent problem in Japan because there has been no tendency toward press monopolization. One of the characteristics of the Japanese press is that there are three major newspapers, *Asahi, Mainichi,* and *Yomiuri,* each very influential in every field. For example, as is shown in Table 1, the *Yomiuri Shimbun* has a daily circulation of more than eight million. Besides these three, there are two other national newspapers, three major block papers, and many local ones. According to the Japan Newspaper Yearbook of 1980, the total daily circulation in 1979 was 45,851,852, in which the largest three newspapers held a market share of approximately 45 percent. The three major newspapers will continue to expand as further technological innovations are introduced. Despite a high market share, however, the Anti-Monololy Act[80] is inapplicable because each newspaper is in a competitive position.

The major newspapers in Japan are affiliated with four major commercial broadcasting networks throughout the country. This recent trend of affiliations and mergers points to media concentration as an increasingly important issue.

**Table 1.    Daily Newspaper Circulation in Japan**

|  | 1967 | 1973 | 1979 | 1981 |
|---|---|---|---|---|
| Total* | 32,447,141 | 39,847,332 | 45,851,852 | 47,256,150 |
| **National Newspaper** | | | | |
| Yomiuri | 3,273,908 | 6,368,717 | 8,388,315 | 8,740,664 |
| Asahi | 5,350,372 | 6,517,912 | 7,502,150 | 7,470,028 |
| Mainichi | 4,260,639 | 4,883,095 | 4,585,316 | 4,537,907 |
| Sankei | 1,948,272 | 1,885,550 | 1,940,149 | 2,014,036 |
| Nihon-Keizai | 987,465 | 1,516,661 | 1,805,086 | 1,904,375 |
| **Block Newspaper** | | | | |
| Hokkaido | 741,785 | 809,451 | 993,957 | 1,031,443 |
| Chunichi | 1,824,808 | 2,270,891 | 2,691,292 | 2,777,011 |
| Nishi-Nihon | 671,098 | 606,466 | 657,935 | 700,347 |
| Big Three | 12,884,919 | 17,769,724 | 20,475,781 | 20,748,599 |
|  | (39.7%) | (44.6%) | (44.7%) | (43.9%) |
| National Five | 15,820,656 | 21,171,935 | 24,221,016 | 24,667,010 |
|  | (48.8%) | (53.1%) | (52.8%) | (52.2%) |
| Major Eight | 19,058,347 | 24,858,743 | 28,564,200 | 29,175,811 |
|  | (58.7%) | (62.4%) | (62.3%) | (61.7%) |

* This total includes the daily circulation of all member newspapers of the Japan Newspaper Publishers and Editors Association. Therefore, this figure includes the circulation of newspapers in English, sports newspapers, and special subject newspapers, as well as that of general newspapers. It is estimated that approximately 90 per cent of the above-listed figure is attributable to the circulation of general newspapers.
*Source:* Newspaper Yearbook 1968, 1974, 1980, and 1982

## Self-regulation

Japan has no mechanism equivalent to a press council. The Japan Newspaper Publishers and Editors Association (*Nihon Shimbun Kyokai*), organized in 1946 by Japan's daily newspapers, large and small, has, however, formulated as its moral charter the Canons of Journalism.[81] The code's preamble recognizes the important role of the press in rebuilding a democratic and peace-loving nation. To accomplish that task, adherence to a high ethical standard is necessary, thereby elevating the profession's prestige. The canons provide for (1) freedom of the press, (2) a sphere of news reporting and editorial writing, (3) the principle of editorial comment, (4) impartiality, (5) tolerance, (6) guidance, responsibility, and pride, and (7) decency. For example, the paragraph concerning decency states:

A high sense of public decency is naturally required of newspapers because of their share in influencing public opinion. Such a standard of decency can be achieved by abiding with the above-mentioned principles. Newspapers and journalists, when they fail to observe those principles, will invite public condemnation and disapproval by other papers and journalists and in the end will be unable to operate or work. Therefore, all members of the Nihon Shimbun Kyokai should make efforts to cooperate and maintain a higher ethical standard by promoting their moral unity, guaranteeing free access to news material and assisting each other in newspaper production. Thus, the association of newspapers which strictly observe the Canons of Journalism shall be able to accelerate and ensure the democratization of Japan and simultaneously elevate Japanese newspapers to world standards.

Although anyone may notify the association that a newspaper has violated the rules of ethics, the Canons of Journalism provide no enforcement mechanism for violations. Under its Articles of Association, the association has the power to expel a newspaper from membership for violating the rules of ethics; however, the association has never exercised this power.

In conclusion, Japan is certainly a paradise for the press.

## NOTES

The author wishes to acknowledge the assistance of Takeshi Kamada, a graduate student at Hitotsubashi University School of Law.

*Note on citations:* For the form of citation of Japanese legal materials, see *The Japanese Legal System: Introductory Cases and Materials* 30–35 (H. Tanaka, ed. 1976).

1.  *See* Takayanagi, "A Century of Innovation: The Development of Japanese Law, 1868–1961," in *Law in Japan: The Legal Order in a Changing Society* 6 (A. von Mehren ed. 1963). The Meiji Constitution of 1889 was modeled on the Prussian Constitution.

2.  *Kenpo* (Constitution) art. 21, *reprinted in VII Constitutions of the Countries of the World* (A. Blaustein & G. Flanz eds. 1973).

3.  *Constitution of the Empire of Japan* 1889, art. 29.

4.  Under the Meiji Constitution, the judiciary had no power to review the constitutionality of a diet act. Great Court of Judicature Judgment, March 3, 1937, 16 Keishu 193 (in Japanese).

5.  The Court views the public welfare justification as permitting limited restrictions on the exercise of freedoms. Article 12 of the Constitution states that "[t]he freedoms and rights guaranteed to the people by this Constitution shall be maintained by the constant endeavor of the people, who shall refrain from any abuse of these freedoms and rights and shall always be responsible for utilizing them for the public welfare." Article 13 provides that "[a]ll of the people shall be respected as individuals. Their right to life, liberty, and the pursuit of happiness shall, to the extent that it does not interfere with the public welfare, be the supreme

consideration in legislation and in other governmental affairs." Similar limitations upon the exercise of certain economic freedoms are contained in Articles 22 and 29. Recent Supreme Court decisions suggest that the constitution permits or requires greater restriction on economic freedom than on civil liberties such as freedom of expression.

6.   *Kenpo* (Constitution) art. 81, *reprinted in* A. Blaustein & G. Flanz, *supra* note 2.

7.   Supreme Court Judgment, February 1, 1950, 4 Keishu 88 (in Japanese).

8.   Supreme Court Judgment, October 8, 1952, 6 Minshu 783, translated in J. Maki, *Court and Constitution in Japan: Selected Supreme Court Decisions, 1948–60*, 362 (1964).

9.   *E.g.*, Newspaper and Publication Regulation 1869; Press Ordinance 1869; Press Ordinance 1875; Newspaper Ordinance 1883; Press Ordinance 1887; Press Act 1893; Newspaper Act 1909.

10.   The regulation was issued on February 2, 1869; its English translation appears in Ito, "History of the Japanese Press," *1949 The Japanese Press 4.*

11.   *Keiho* (Penal Code), Law No. 45 of 1907 (hereafter *"Penal Code"*), art. 230 (defamation); *id.* art. 175 (prohibiting distribution or sale of obscene publications); *Minpo* (Civil Code), Laws No. 89 of 1896 and No. 9 of 1898 (hereafter *"Civil Code"*), art. 709 (defamation); Election of Public Officials Act, Law No. 100 of 1950, art. 148 (guaranteeing press freedom to report and comment truthfully on elections); Juvenile Act, Law No. 168 of 1948, art. 61 (prohibiting publication of information identifying juvenile criminal suspects). *See* text accompanying notes 45, 57–71 *infra*.

12.   *Kenpo* (Constitution) art. 9, *reprinted in* A. Blaustein & G. Flanz, *supra* note 2.

13.   Prior to establishing the Self-Defense Forces, Japan had maintained the National Security Forces, which, in turn, had reorganized the National Police Reserve. The National Police Reserve had been established in 1950 pursuant to cabinet authorization. Although a leader of the Socialist Party of Japan attacked the Reserve's constitutionality under Article 9 of the Constitution, the Supreme Court dismissed the case on the ground of standing. Supreme Court Judgment, October 8, 1952, 6 Minshu 783, translated in J. Maki, *supra* note 8, at 362.

14.   On September 7, 1973, Sapporo District Court held the Act unconstitutional. 712 Hanrei Jiho 24, noted in 6 *Law in Japan* 175 (1973). But, on August 5, 1976, the Sapporo High Court vacated this ruling on technical grounds. 821 Hanrei Jiho 21, noted in 9 *Law in Japan* 153 (1976). The First Petty Bench of the Supreme Court affirmed the judgment below on September 9, 1982. 1054 Hanrei Jiho 16.

15.   *See* text accompanying notes 21–31 *infra*.

16.   No formal system of censorship existed in the era of the Meiji Constitution; however, the Minister of Home Affairs regularly censored publications pursuant to his nonreviewable authority to prohibit the sale or distribution of newspapers. *See* Newspaper Act, Law No. 41 of 1909.

17.   *See Penal Code,* art. 230; text accompanying notes 56–65 *infra*.

18.   The Anti-Subversive Activities Act, Law No. 240 of 1952, enacted notwithstanding pervasive opposition, is not directly concerned with the press.

19.   Law No. 138 of 1952.

20.   Law No. 166 of 1954.

21.   National Public Employees Act, Law No. 120 of 1947, art. 100.

22.   *Id.* at art. 111.

23.   *See* text accompanying notes 12–15 *supra.*

24.   For a more extensive discussion of this case see Brown, "Government Secrecy and the 'People's Right to Know' in Japan: Implications of Nishiyama Case," 10 *Law in Japan* 112 (1977).

25.   The reporter did write an article concerning the compensation plan, which was published in the evening edition of the *Mainichi* on June 18, 1977, the same day the reversion plan was announced. The article referred to the plan only in vague terms, with no mention of the cablegrams; it therefore brought no public reaction. Because the reporter was prosecuted not for publishing the newspaper article, but for inducing the public employee to commit a crime, this case is not a classical press case.

26.   Earlier court decisions in government secrecy cases had established a standard distinguishing between "formal" and "substantial" secrets. Formal secrets were those matters officially designated by the government as protected by national interests; substantial secrets included matters commonly accepted as actual secrets. *See* Brown, *supra* note 24, at 119. In response to the government often not submitting the disputed documents to judicial scrutiny, though at the same time claiming they were formally designated as secrets, the courts developed the category of substantial secrets and used indirect evidence to evaluate whether particular documents were substantial secrets. *See id.* at 123.

27.   *See* Brown, *supra* note 24, at 133.

28.   Tokyo District Court Judgment, January 31, 1974, 732 Hanrei Jiho 12 (in Japanese).

29.   Tokyo High Court Judgment, July 20, 1976, 820 Hanrei Jiho 26 (in Japanese).

30.   There are fifteen justices of the Supreme Court. They divide themselves into three petty benches each consisting of five justices (three being the quorum), except in (i) cases on appeal involving a constitutional issue where there is no existing precedent of the Supreme Court, (ii) cases on appeal concerned with a nonconstitutional point of law on which a petty bench has found it appropriate to overrule a precedent of the Supreme Court, (iii) other cases which petty benches have referred to the grand bench because they considered them of great importance, or (iv) cases where the opinions of the petty bench justices have ended in a tie. In these exceptional cases, all the justices of the Supreme Court sit together as the grand bench.

*The Japanese Legal System: Introductory Cases and Materials* 48 (H. Tanaka ed. 1976).

31.   Supreme Court Decree, May 31, 1978, 32 Keishu 457 (in Japanese).

32.   *See* Hirano, "The Draft of the Revised Penal Code: A General Critique," 6 *Law in Japan* 49, 62 (1973).

33.   *See* text accompanying notes 57–66 *infra.*

34.   *Penal Code*, art. 230.

35.   *Id.* at art. 230.2(3).

36.   Supreme Court Judgment, June 25, 1969, 23 Keishu 975 (in Japanese).

37.   *Kenpo* (Constitution) art. 15, *reprinted in* A. Blaustein & G. Flanz, *supra* note 2.

38.  Hiroshima High Court Judgment, Octobr 14, 1954, 7 Kosai Minshu 885 (in Japanese).

39.  Supreme Court Judgment, December 15, 1953, 7 Keishu 2436 (in Japanese). *See* discussion relating to defamation and privacy at text accompanying notes 57–72 and notes 77–78 *infra*.

40.  5 U.S.C. §552 (1976).

41.  *See* e.g., Osaka District Court Judgment, August 30, 1958, 9 Gyosaireishu 1662; Supreme Court Judgment, October 15, 1969, 23 Keishu 1239; Supreme Court Decree, November 26, 1969, 23 Keishu 1490 (in Japanese); text accompanying notes 51–52 *infra*.

42.  The bills of the Japan Socialist Party, the Japan Communist Party and the four middle of the road parties differ in their treatment of national defense secrets.

43.  Article 94 of the Constitution permits local public entities to "enact their own regulations within law," *Kenpo* (Constitution) art. 94; article 14(1) of the Local Autonomy Act provides that local assemblies can enact local ordinances subject to the provisions of any act of the Diet and any order issued by the national government. Law No. 67 of 1947, art. 14(1).

44.  *Kenpo* (Constitution) art. 82.

45.  Juvenile Act, Law No. 168 of 1948, art. 61.

46.  The Japan Newspaper Publishers and Editors Association Policy for Dealing with Article 61 of the Juvenile Act (December 16, 1958).

47.  Code of Criminal Procedure, Law No. 131 of 1948 (hereafter *"Code of Criminal Procedure"*), art. 161.

48.  Supreme Court Judgment, August 6, 1952, 6 Keishu 974, translated in J. Maki, *supra* note 8, at 38.

49.  *See Code of Criminal Procedure,* art. 149.

50.  J. Maki, *supra* note 8, at 41–42.

51.  Supreme Court Decree, November 26, 1969, 23 Keishu 1490, translated in Tanaka, *supra* note 30, at 741.

52.  *Id.*

53.  Sapporo District Court Decree, May 30, 1979, 930 Hanrei Jiho 44 (in Japanese).

54.  *Code of Civil Procedure,* Law No. 29 of 1890 (hereafter *"Code of Civil Procedure"*), art. 281(1).

55.  Sapporo High Court Decree, August 31, 1979, 937 Hanrei Jiho 16 (in Japanese).

56.  Supreme Court Decree, March 6, 1980, 956 Hanrei Jiho 32 (in Japanese).

57.  Beer, "Defamation, Privacy and Freedom of Expression in Japan," 5 *Law in Japan*, 192, (1972).

58.  *Penal Code,* art. 230(1). The Act for Temporary Measures Concerning Fines, Etc., Law No. 251 of 1948, raised the fine to 200,000 yen.

59.  *Penal Code,* art. 230(2).

60.  *See* text accompanying note 33 *supra*.

61.  *Penal Code,* art. 230.2.

62.  Tokyo High Court Judgment, February 21, 1953, 6 Kosai Keishu 367 (in Japanese).

63.  Supreme Court Judgment, April 16, 1981, 1000 Hanrei Jiho 25 (in Japanese).

64.  Tokyo District Court Judgment, June 29, 1978, 978 Hanrei Jiho 132 (in

Japanese).

65.    Tokyo High Court Judgment, December 12, 1979, 978 Hanrei Jiho 130 (in Japanese).

66.    Supreme Court Judgment, June 25, 1969, 23 Keishu 975 (in Japanese).

67.    *Civil Code,* art. 723.

68.    *Id.* at art. 709.

69.    *Id.* at art. 710.

70.    *Id.* at art. 723.

71.    Supreme Court Judgment, June 23, 1966, 20 Minshu 1118 (in Japanese).

72.    Tokyo District Court Judgment, September 28, 1964, 15 Kakyu Minshu 2317 (in Japanese). This award was given in a privacy invasion case; articles 709 and 710, the civil defamation provision, also provide the principal statutory basis for privacy claims. *See* text accompanying note 77 *infra.*

73.    Newspaper Act Law No. 41 of 1909. I understand that the right of reply provision was derived from French law.

74.    *Civil Code*, art. 723.

75.    Tokyo District Court Judgment, July 13, 1977, 857 Hanrei Jiho 30 (Japanese). The case was of further interest because the District Court recognized an "actual malice" standard similar to that adopted in *New York Times Co.* v. *Sullivan*, 476 U.. 254 (1964). This doctrine is not yet popular in Japan.

76.    Tokyo High Court Judgment, September 30, 1980, 981 Hanrei Jiho 43.

77.    Tokyo District Court Judgment, September 28, 1964, 15 Kakyu Minshu 2317. *See* Ito "Issues in the 'After the Banquet' Decision," 1 *Law in Japan* 141 (1967); Beer, *supra* note 57, at 204.

78.    *Kenpo* (Constitution), art. 13.

79.    *See* e.g. M. Horibe *The Right of Access* (1977) (in Japanese); M. Horibe, *What is the Right of Access—Freedom of Speech and Mass Media* (1978) (in Japanese).

80.    Anti-Monopoly Act, Law No. 54 of 1947.

81.    The Canons of Journalism, Japan Newspaper Publishers and Editors Association, adopted July 23, 1946.

# Conclusion:
# An Outline for a General
# Theory of Press Law in Democracy

Pnina Lahav

## INTRODUCTION

Freedom of the press is woven into the texture of modern democracy. Its development has been integral to the historical struggle for democracy and the rule of law. The invention of the printing press was a turning point in Western history; the printed word played a key role in the process of unfettering the bonds of the dark ages. It made unorthodox thought accessible to broader social groups. It popularized both the challenge to authoritarianism and the ascendance of liberalism during the Enlightenment and since. The industrialization of the press during the nineteenth century, and the consequent emergence of modern journalism, accompanied the democratization of Western societies and served as a ferment to both the ideal and the institutional aspects of mass democracy. In political theory, the press is presented in multifaceted roles—as a vehicle for self-expression, as a reflection of public opinion, as an informer of the public, as a participant in the formation of public opinion, and as a watchdog of the government. These roles do not necessarily complement each other and are not all even compatible with one another, yet each seems vital for a democratic system of government in mass society.

In the introduction to this book I presented three groups of democracies: the Anglo-American, the Continental, and the non-Western. All share the ideology of liberalism and a commitment to press freedom, but they differ in their form of government, in their historical experience and cultural heritage, and in the characteristics of their legal systems.[1]

The concentration, in this volume, of so much material on the legal conceptualization of a free press facilitates an inquiry into a general explanatory theory of press law. In this essay I will delineate the beginning of a theory to explain the relationship between modern democracy and a free press as well as the form which this relationship takes.

First I shall discuss two elements which clearly distinguish between the various legal systems in this volume: the presence of a written constitutional commitment to press freedom, and the existence of a special legal regime for the press. Then I shall discuss the kinds of legal regimes that have emerged under different circumstances.

## THE CONSTITUTIONAL DIMENSION

Commitment to press freedom exists in all the countries reviewed here, but the kind of control varies in substance and form. Formally, some of the liberal democracies under review have neither written constitutions nor normative constitutional commitments to press freedom. England and Israel are such countries.[2] They describe themselves as having "a living constitution" and consider the principle of freedom of speech and of the press as part of this tradition. Operationally, this means that the British and Israeli courts lack power to invalidate statutes violating the principle of free expression. However, as a guideline for statutory interpretation, the principle of free expression may be used by the courts to disarm potentially suppressive statutes. Thus, even absent the power of judicial review, courts willing to protect free expression can, through interpretation, render the law less harmful.[3]

Countries with formal constitutions, such as the United States, Sweden, and Japan, share an explicit normative commitment to liberty of speech and press. The nature of the constitutional commitment, however, reflects both their respective constitutional histories and their philosophical conceptions of press freedom. One method of differentiating between the various types of formal commitment is by the historical period in which the commitment was made. There is a difference between the constitutional language of France, Sweden, and the United States, dating back to the late eighteenth and early nineteenth centuries, and the constitutional language of Japan, the Federal Republic of Germany, or India which are typical of the twentieth century. The earlier constitutional commitments are couched in broad and general language and are relatively short compared to the elaborate and specific constitutional provisions of the twentieth century.

The difference may reflect stages of sociopolitical development. Twentieth century constitutional law reflects the postindustrial, bureaucratic, and hence highly elaborate mode of government, in contrast to the simpler structure of the late eighteenth century. Yet, the twentieth century commitments to free expression draw on earlier traditions among which there are also differences. It may be useful to compare the American and French approaches.

Consider the American Bill of Rights of 1781 and the French Declaration of the Rights of Man of 1789. The First Amendment to the United State Constitution is conceived in absolute and negative terms:

> Congress shall make no law...abridging the freedom of speech, or of the press....[4]

The language is both absolute in its prohibition of normative limitations on the press (this does not mean that American law rejects limitations on press freedom; I shall discuss this point below), and negative in the sense that it does not affirm the positive right to speak, but rather prohibits limitations on this right. By contrast, Article 11 of the French Declaration is positive in its assertion of the central importance of free speech in society, and at the same time qualified:

> The unrestrained communication of thoughts or opinions being one of the most precious rights of man, every citizen may speak, write and publish freely, provided he be responsible for the abuse of this liberty, in the case determined by law.[5]

There are several explanations for the contrast between the absolute/negative American phraseology and its qualified/positive French counterpart. The absolute prohibition on press restrictions may simply manifest American federalism. It is arguable that the framers of the Bill of Rights wished to prohibit the federal legislature from restricting press freedom, but would permit the states to do so.[6] The negative language manifests the pragmatic, empirically oriented spirit of the common law, which dominated American legal thought, in contradistinction to the more theoretical and conceptual spirit of the civil law. Arguably, the First Amendment reflects the pragmatic spirit simply by prohibiting measures associated with the oppressive colonial regime and by postulating that in the absence of legal restrictions liberty of speech is secure. The conceptual French Declaration, on the other hand, finds it necessary to declare explicitly the principle as "a precious right." These explanations have a grain of truth in them, but they are not entirely satisfactory.

American constitutional thought of the late eighteenth century was not uniform. Some state constitutions followed the model of the Federal Bill of Rights whereas others preferred the French approach.[7] For example, the Massachusetts Constitution of 1780 reads:

> The liberty of the press is essential to the security of freedom in a State; it ought not, therefore, to be restrained in this commonwealth.[8]

It may be misleading to place too much emphasis on the explicit subordination of press freedom to law in the Continental model, by contrast to the absolute protection of the American formula. Even where the commitment is phrased in absolute terms—so the argument goes—it cannot in reality be absolute. Within any liberal legal system, no right is absolute. Freedom of the press conflicts with other equally imperative principles such as privacy, reputation, and national security. It is evident to any student of the American legal system, on both the federal and state levels, that the First Amendment coexists with certain limitations on the press. The distinction, however, may be meaningful in terms of legal thought and operationally in terms of doctrine.

From the perspective of legal thought, both models rest upon the natural law tradition within liberalism. From that tradition, Western culture derived the belief in the importance of individual self-expression, and in the legitimacy of radical criticism of existing social arrangements. Most importantly, modern democracy is rooted in the idea that "all men are created equal," hence capable of participating in the political decision-making process. It is not difficult to see the link between these notions from natural law and the liberal justifications for free expression: the quest for individual self-fulfillment, the marketplace of ideas, the search for truth, and participatory democracy.[9]

But while the American First Amendment and Article 11 of the French Declaration stem from the same natural law tradition, they differ in their conception of the legal system; this difference may shed some light on the choice of an absolute or a qualified model. The French Revolution upheld the ideal of majority rule and nourished faith in the action of the legislature which represents the people. At the same time it harbored suspicion of judges and judicial discretion, which during the *ancien régime* were the vehicles for arbitrary rule and capricious oppression.[10] The subordination of the "precious right" of free expression to statutes, therefore, was associated with confidence in a legislature capable of distinguishing between right and wrong for the good of society. Restrictions adopted by a democratically elected legislature, were viewed as compatible with the preservation of the principle of free expression.[11]

By contrast, American legal thought, as part of the common law tradition, did not share so pervasive a suspicion of judicial power.[12] Moreover, American political theory placed a premium on a system of checks and balances in which each power could neutralize the other,[13] hence the absolute terms of the First Amendment, leaving the exact nature of the limitations on free expression to an interplay between Congress (which obviously was expected to pass *some* law limiting freedom of speech), the state legislatures, the courts, and other countermajoritarian forces.

This explanation, helps us understand another salient distinction between the American and the French legal systems—the existence of a regime of press law in continental Europe and its absence from the United States and England. France, Sweden, and the Federal Republic of Germany have *press laws*, i.e., statutes devoted specifically to matters concerning the press. The difference between the American and European approaches stems in part from the Contiental preference for legislative planning, in contrast to Anglo-American legal thought, which preferred to let the courts work out doctrines regulating the press incrementally, within the framework of ordinary laws which apply to everybody.

A review of twentieth century constitutions reveals that most preferred the French (positive/qualified) to the American (negative/absolute) model.

For example, Article 5 of the Basic Law of the Federal Republic of Germany provides:

> 1.   Everyone shall have the right freely to express and disseminate his opinion by speech, writing and pictures and freely to inform himself from generally accessible sources. Freedom of the press and freedom of reporting by radio and motion pictures are guaranteed. There shall be no censorship.
> 2.   These rights are limited by the provisions of the general laws, the provisions of law for the protection of youth, and by the right to inviolability of personal honour.[14]

Article 5 divides the norm into two parts: a *most ringing assertion of the right*, followed by a list of legitimate limitations. In contrast to the French or Swedish eighteenth century declarations, which subject the press to law, the modern approach specifies categories in which restriction is permissible.[15] A similar model appears in India's constitution, in the European Convention of Human Rights, and in Israel's draft for a Bill of Rights.[16]

Variations within the positive model may have enormous effects on the press. The qualifying section may be phrased in a way that leaves very little to the core principle of free expression.[17] Also, the availability of judicial review, i.e., the power of the court to invalidate statutes which violate the Constitution, as well as the level of judicial activism, are crucial for an evaluation of the normative protection which the press gets in any legal system.[18]

From the comparative perspective, the important question is how much of a difference do these distinctions make? Does the absence of a formal constitutional commitment and judicial review in England indicate that the British press is less free than the German press? Does the explicit list of limitations contained in the German Constitution make the German press more or less free than the Swedish or the French press?

Clearly, one critical variable in any attempt to analyze this question is the court. A court within any democracy, given a healthy and substantive commitment to free speech, can protect the press by conventional methods of statutory interpretation. Indeed, even with a formal constitution and judicial review, the bulk of the judicial work is in interpreting rather than invalidating statutes. The level of judicial activism, and the judges' belief in basic philosophical justifications for free expression, may provide more accurate clues in comparative study. At the same time, the judicial awareness of the liberal justifications of a free press and the acceptability of those justifications as part of the legal argument, may depend on and be encouraged by the formal constitutional commitment to press freedom.

## PRESS "LAWS"—A SPECIAL REGIME FOR THE PRESS?

> [T]he revolutionists of France...borrowed their ideas about...liberty of the press from England and [believed]...that...free expression...and...the "liberty of the press" are fundamental doctrines of the law of England.... Yet this notion...is essentially false.
>
> A.V. Dicey[19]

### An Initial Comparison between Anglo-American and Continental Press Law

In his classic, *Introduction to the Study of the Law of the Constitution*,[20] the noted nineteenth century English scholar A.V. Dicey compared and contrasted the press laws of England and France. His description of the press law of England identified components which were also present in American law[21] whereas the components he identified as French were also typical of other continental legal systems. His analysis, therefore, is a good testing ground for comparing the Anglo-American law with continental law.[22]

Dicey observed the historical similarities between England and France up to the seventeenth century. During this period both systems shared an authoritarian approach to the press. In England, there were restrictions on printing, censorship, and special press offenses, which were tried by the Star Chamber. France of the *ancien régime* experienced an absolute monopoly over printing and sales of publications as well as censorship, all fortified by very severe penalties for those caught violating any of the restrictions.[23]

The passage from authoritarianism to liberalism was different in each country. England experienced a gradual evolution. The Star Chamber fell in 1641. Censorship was legalized during the Restoration, through the enactment of the Licensing Act in 1662, but was terminated in 1695. Since then, English press law has contained no formal mechanisms of censorship, and the press has been regulated through the law of defamation and seditious libel. Quoting Macaulay, Dicey emphasized that the termination (rather than the abolition) of the Licensing Act had been a chronological and pragmatic rather than a philosophical turning point in England's press law. The Commons voted to terminate the Act for practical and commercial reasons, not because they came to recognize the value of arguments such as those advanced by Milton in the *Areopagitica*.[24]

In France, events were different. The French revolutionary commitment to freedom of the press found its way into the Declaration of the Rights of Man, yet suppressive policies persisted:

> One government after another has, with curious uniformity, proclaimed the freedom and ensured the subjection of the newspaper....[25]

English tolerance, Dicey observed, gradually became part of the political culture, despite the absence of a constitutional commitment to free speech. France, its formal commitment to freedom of speech notwithstanding, persisted with an authoritarian approach. Given the historical similarity betweeen the two systems, how could these differences be explained? Dicey identified two major factors which differentiated modern England from modern France: the rule of law and political liberalism.

Dicey summarized liberty of the press in England as a symptom of the idea of the rule of law:

> The liberty of the press...is in England simply one result of the universal predominance of the law of the land.[26]

This symptom translated into the fact that there was no special legal regime for the English press. England recognized neither privileges nor special duties for the press. Rather, the ordinary law applied equally to the press as to everyone else. Dicey further analyzed this situation in England into two components. First, English law rejected the legitimacy of censorship, and accepted only subsequent punishment. Only judicial application of the (mostly criminal) law could suppress speech. Thus British law could not require a deposit from a publisher as a prior condition to permitting publication. Nor could the government seize or suspend a paper prior to its publication. Second, the prosecution of a newspaper was not handled by special courts (e.g., the historical Star Chamber) but by the ordinary courts. Hence the substantive equality of the press was compounded by an institutional aspect—the ordinary court and the jury.

These manifestations of British press law were nonexistent in France. France of the nineteenth century did recognize the legitimacy of preventive measures such as licensing, seizure, and suspension. Moreover, nineteenth century France tried press related offenses in special press courts. This contrast led Dicey to conclude that there was a causal connection between the absence of a special press regime for the press and the liberty of the press; and furthermore, another causal connection between the rule of law and the relatively less suppressive attitude toward press freedom in England, compared to France.[27]

Dicey may have been correct in his observation of a nexus between the rule of law and liberty of the press, for the reason that both are facets of liberalism. However, his case for a connection between the absence of a press law and de facto press freedom is more problematic.

## Press Regimes and Liberty of the Press

In France, the Federal Republic of Germany, and Sweden, special press statutes regulate the press. Britain and the United States, on the other hand, do not recognize a difference between the press and other institutions or individuals, and apply their free speech law uniformly to all. Dicey attached critical theoretical importance to this difference,[28] considering the press regime itself a hindrance to the liberty of the press. This idea was not peculiar to Dicey. Interestingly, it was implied in a recent concurring opinion by Warren Burger, Chief Justice of the United States Supreme Court.[29] However, the theory that a special press law in itself constitutes a threat to press freedom, has merit only if a special press regime is identified with an authoritarian press regime, such as obtained in France during the nineteenth century.[30] A different theory may be derived from examination of the Swedish experience. Since the eighteenth century Sweden had enjoyed both a formal constitutional commitment and a specialized press statute. As Professor Strömberg's essay (this volume) demonstrates, the statute—including a "catalogue of press crimes" and a special adjudicatory process for the press—has not prevented meaningful press freedom in Swedish political reality. The Swedes even see the specialized press regime as both a manifestation and a guarantee of press freedom.

Clearly, there are different types of press regimes. There is an authoritarian press regime, described by Dicey, which has indeed predominated in most countries. Yet there is another type overlooked by Dicey—the neutral, or even the benevolent press regime, epitomized by the Swedish model. Both may exist in a democracy, although the authoritarian model does contradict the spirit of press freedom.

The authoritarian press regime was typical of nineteenth century Europe. The Imperial German press laws (recall the vociferous critiques of the young Marx against the oppressive press laws of his native Germany),[31] and the French press laws prior to the 1881 press statute, as well as some of the post-1881 amendments, are two examples of this phenomenon. In the twentieth century, England introduced authoritarian press laws to its colonies, in an effort to control and influence native public opinion. Israel received such a statute, and retains it to this day. Japan's Imperial press law closely resembled the German Imperial press code. The authoritarian press laws have essentially had the same characteristics:

1. Licensing. A publisher is required to obtain a permit prior to publication.
2. Qualifications. Not every person qualifies as a publisher or editor.[32]
3. Publication requirements. Permits are conditioned on meeting requirements concerning frequency of publication and may be revoked if these requirements are not met.[33]

4. Executive discretion. The executive branch may suspend a publication or seize all copies of it.
5. Special punishment. Certain convictions may have special punishments attached to them. For example, a conviction for seditious libel may be followed with an exclusion from journalistic activity for a period of time.

All the countries compared in this volume have experienced the authoritarian approach. However, while some have experienced it in the distant past (England, the United States, and Sweden) and some had to live with it until the Second World War (Japan, Germany, and France [with modifications]), some retain it to this day (Israel) trying to maintain an uneasy balance between the draconian features of the law and a democratic commitment to press freedom.

Clearly, however, such abuse of the press does not stem from the press law as a form, but from its normative content. A press law is an instrument. It may be utilized to suppress or enhance press freedom, depending on the values it reflects. The Anglo-American fear of a press law, as such, reflects the libertarian rejection of authoritarianism. It is a historical aversion, but analytically, a press law need not necessarily supress speech. The Swedish press law, for example, protects contributors to publications by absolving them of legal responsibility, and guarantees authors the right to remain anonymous while designating the editor as solely responsible for the publication.[34]

In the United States, where the idea persists that a law defining the press is inherently dangerous, we nonetheless have seen modern legislation dealing specifically with the press. Reporters' privilege statutes, for example, define the term "press" and regulate the privilege in a fashion reminiscent of the continental press statutes. Like the Swedish statute, these mini-press-statutes are libertarian in the sense that they strive to strengthen press freedom by shielding the newsgathering process from state intervention.[35]

Thus, the press law of a particular country is not so much determined by the existence of a particular type of constitutional commitment, or by the presence of a special press statute, as by the particular political philosophy which animates it.

## SOME THEORETICAL REFLECTIONS ON THE LEGAL REGULATION OF THE PRESS IN A DEMOCRACY

The law of the press in modern democracies reflects two separate yet interrelated sets of tensions. First, it reflects the tension between universal liberal values and the state. Universal liberal values are epitomized in the commitment to free expression, whereas the nation state is typically manifested in arguments designed to curb expression in the name of national or collective interests. Second, it reflects the tension within journalism between the press as a partisan fourth estate and journalism as a profession. As the fourth estate, the press is conceptualized as a pressure group within the democratic market place, hence as possessed with a political character. On the other hand, the concept of journalism as a profession emphasizes the objective and apolitical nature of reporting.

## Universal-Liberal Values and the Nation-State

> Persecution for the expression of opinions seems to me perfectly logical. If you have no doubt of your premises or your power and want a certain result with all your heart you naturally express your wishes in law and sweep away all opposition.... But when men have realized that time has upset many fighting faiths, they may come to believe...that the ultimate good desired is better reached by free trade in ideas...and that the truth is the only ground upon which their wishes safely can be carried out.
>
> Oliver Wendell Holmes[36]

The emergence of the state preceded the ascendance of liberalism and the concept of the rule of law. Prior to the Enlightenment, the attitude of the state toward the press was authoritarian. When the printing press was invented and its potential understood, the state considered the press as a tool to advance its own notion of the public good. Since those in power identified the public good with the rulers' self-interests, the press was conceived as a tool to advance the rulers' point of view. Other views, or information not disclosed by the government, were considered dangerous, illegitimate, and unworthy of publication.[37] Alongside the authoritarian conception of the press, there existed in the preliberal state an instrumental conception of public law. Public law was conceived as a set of tools to be used at the discretion of the rulers, in order to satisfy their power interests.[38] The combination of the authoritarian theory of the press and the instrumental conception of public law yielded a legal system of extensive press control complete with licensing, censorship, and powers of suspension and forfeiture. The philosophical justification for suppression was authoritarian—speech was a weapon, therefore it should be monopolized by the state. Only the rulers knew what was in the public good, and any challenge to official policy should be suppressed since "the serpent should better be killed while still in the egg."[39] The legal implementation of this philosophy took the form of extensive suppression of speech through the use of naked executive powers, unbound by notions of due process and fairness.

With the advent of the Enlightenment, two important developments affected the press. First, there developed the libertarian justifications for free expression. The libertarians argued that the press should be free of governmental control, and developed justifications for press freedom such as the justification from self-fulfillment, the justification from the search for truth (a free marketplace of ideas would facilitate the search for truth), and the justification from self-rule.[40] Alongside the libertarian conception of the press, the liberal state developed a different conception of law. The conception of the rule of law prescribed that the legitimacy of governmental action depended on the principles of the generality of law and uniformity in adjudication.[41] These two conceptions—the principle of free speech and the principle of the rule of law—challenged the legitimacy of the authoritarian/instrumental conception of press law.

The best illustration of the shift from the authoritarian/instrumental theory to the libertarian/constitutional theory is the doctrine against prior restraint. The doctrine, announced by Blackstone in eighteenth century England, provided that legal limitations over press freedom cannot be applied prior to publication. It thus delegitimized the licensing and censorial mechanisms which typified authoritarian regimes:

> The liberty of the press is indeed essential to the nature of a free state; but this consists in laying no *previous* restraint upon publications, and not in freedom from censure for criminal matter when published. Every freeman has an undoubted right to lay what sentiments he pleases before the public; to forbid this, is to destroy the freedom of the press; but if he publishes what is improper, mischievous, or illegal, he must take the consequence of his own temerity.[42]

The principle of free expression was embedded in this doctrine, in the sense that the doctrine rested on the premise that people should be permitted to say anything without previous administrative control. The doctrine reflected the liberal conception of law in its insistence that speech could be regulated only by statute (by subsequent punishment), not by administrative devices.

The doctrine served as the cornerstone of English and American press law and was imported to legal systems such as those of Israel and Japan, which were subjected to Anglo-American influence in one form or another. However, the very same ideas appeared in Sweden and in France, although in different form. In both Sweden and France, the advent of the Enlightenment brought about an aversion to censorship and an insistence that only the law, that is, a process of legislation and adjudication, could legitimately suppress speech. In the Federal Republic of Germany, this process was delayed, since the acceptance of liberalism was generally delayed there, but the principle is presently incorporated into the German basic law.[43]

However, it would be a mistake to think that this description of the passage from an authoritarian/instrumental conception to a liberal/constitutional conception of the press reflects a historical reality in which the former conception was abandoned by Western democracies. The instrumental conception of the press did not disappear. To the contrary, it has been very much present in all the legal systems reviewed here. What did happen was a transformation of this conception to fit the new requirements of a liberal legal order. Governments adjusted to the new reality by complying with the new philosophy in form. They either drafted laws which gave ample discretion to the government to suppress the press,[44] or utilized the criminal law of seditious libel which, by a clever combination of legal presumptions and the bad tendency test, operated to suppress dissent.[45]

These tools of regulating the press for instrumental purposes pretend to comply with the rule of law, but do so only in form, not in substance. The appearance of judicial supervision and generalized uniform legislation is retained, but the breadth of executive discretion authorized by these schemes discloses their true character as norms which recognize neither the societal value of freedom of the press nor the liberal facets of a constitutional order.

In modern democracies, the tension between the authoritarian/instrumental and libertarian/constitutional conceptions reappears, in the form of the tension between the nation state and universal liberal values. The state, typically invoking arguments of national security or public peace and order, seeks to gain more discretionary power to regulate speech.[46] The press resists by appealing to universal values.

This dialectic between universal values under a liberal constitutional order on the one hand, and the state with its instrumental conception of public law and speech on the other hand, is the key to the understanding of press law in democratic societies. In all the modern democracies reviewed here there exists a real tension between the two approaches to law and the two conceptions of the press. It is the form this tension takes in the various societies that distinguishes them. Each has its own unique combination, peculiar to its history, philosophy, and political culture. The manifestations of the particular combination, the causes which contributed to its formation, and the results, in terms of the degree of freedom enjoyed by the particular national press, have not yet been adequately explored, and herein lies the challenge to scholars of comparative press laws. For example, in the United States the liberal/constitutional theme is so strong that it generally keeps the instrumental approach subdued, although it does not manage to overcome it altogether. In Europe as well as in Israel, it seems that the interests of the state are assigned greater weight. A good illustration is the law of defamation. American defamation law is unique in the protection it gives false statements about the public conduct of governmental officials, as long as those statements are not published with actual knowledge or reckless disregard of the truth. This rule, announced in the decision of *New York Times* v. *Sullivan*[47] reflects a preference for the liberal justification of self rule over the interest of the state in protecting the reputation of rulers (since rulers are our representatives, we must be able to criticize them even if their reputation is tarnished). Other legal systems, such as the French, prefer the interest of the state in the reputation of its officials over liberal justifications.[48]

Another example is the involvement of foreign nationals in press enterprises. France has an extensive system which controls and sometimes excludes foreign participation in protected expressive activities.[49] The fear and therefore the ban on foreign speech has been an element in the press laws of most democracies.[50] It is a manifestation of the compromise between the nation-state and universal liberal values. The nation-state accepts the value of freedom of speech, but only within the limits of its own borders and as applied to its own nationals. Foreigners may still be subject to an instrumental/authoritarian treatment. In the Anglo-American legal systems the regulation of foreigners has not been as pronounced as it has been on the continent. However, when the tension between the nation-state and universal liberal values intensifies, as occurred in the United States during the McCarthy era, the ban on foreign expressive activities may reappear.[51]

Generally speaking, during the nineteenth century the instrumental conception was rather strong in all the countries represented in this book which were committed to a liberal-democratic form of government. It is only in the mid-nineteenth century that John Stuart Mill developed his articulated and complex defense of free expression, and only in 1881 that France enacted a relatively liberal press law.[52] Similarly, in the United States, it was only at the beginning of the twentieth century that the American Supreme Court began to pour liberal content into the First Amendment, and to articulate doctrines which would make the courts guardians of free speech.[53] This development parallels the growth of the modern press. There is a historical correlation between the growth of modern newspapers and the democratization of politics, between the expansion of a market economy and the growing authority of an entrepreneurial urban middle class, and the development of modern press law.[54] The growth of a democratized mass society and its increasing dependence on the press for information have encouraged the emergence of the press as a powerful institution, as an essential intermediary between the government and the people that keeps the people informed about the government and informs the government what the people think and want, or where "the shoe pinches." From this vantage point, the press sees itself as an actor in the democratic marketplace, or as another pressure group in society.

The shift in the power and self-image of the press has produced a new locus of tension in the dialectic. Historically, the press was assigned a special status within the state. The government's perception of the press as a potentially threatening instrument resulted in a special legal order for the press. During this period the press had a negative status and operated under rules that were more harsh than those applied to ordinary citizens. With the rise of the liberal state, the press struggled to be relieved of this special status. For the press to be treated like everyone else, in accordance with the rule of law, was a sign of progress. In the second half of the twentieth century this perception has changed. The press, aware and confident of its societal and political role in democracy, has sometimes come to demand a privileged status, except that now it aspires for a positive status. When journalists ask for a reporters' privilege, or for an editorial privilege, or for a special right of access, they are asking for a privileged legal status within the legal order.[55] This demand produces a tension within the liberal values themselves. It makes journalists call for an absolute conception of a free press, a conception that contradicts the rule of law and the notion that journalists should be treated like ordinary citizens. This conflict between free speech and the rule of law appears in all modern democracies. Again, the particular form of the dialectic distinguishes between the various legal systems.

For example, in the Federal Republic of Germany there is a qualified privilege. In the United States mini-press-laws provide for a reporter's privilege and immunity to search in the newsrooms, but the statutory right of reply has been declared unconstitutional.[56] Yet, it is interesting that, so far, courts in all the countries compared here have resisted the requests to carve out a special status for the press, and even among journalists themselves there is a debate about whether a special positive status for journalism is warranted.

## Journalism as the Fourth Estate and Journalism as a Profession

"If you ask me," Cain explained, "the most that any newspaper should try to do is choose sides in a fight, and then fight as hard as it can, even when it secretly wishes the fight were going a little differently. But you are always trying to dredge up basic principles. In a newspaper it won't work. For example, turn to music. A piano has eight octaves, a violin three, a cornet two, and a bugle has only four notes. Now if what you've got to blow is a bugle, there isn't any sense in camping yourself down in front of piano music."

"You may be right," Lippman retorted, "But God damn it, I'm not going to spend my life writing bugle-calls!"[57]

The industrialization of the newspaper has transformed it from a vehicle which merely transmitted a political party's voice into an independent institution.[58] At the same time, the growth of newspapers has encouraged the self-image of journalists as professionals.

As a profession, journalists proclaim the ideal of objectivity—the notion that reporting can and should separate facts from values and the idea of social responsibility, that journalists serve the public interest, not their own self-interest.[59]

Such self-images of the press are contradictory. On the one hand, the press is a political and commercial organ in a market society. On the other hand, the press is a neutral and objective medium. The increasing public awareness of the press as a powerful organ has led to public pressure to regulate the autonomy of the press, by curbing press monopoly, by passing laws to protect individual privacy and reputation from journalistic intrusion, and by enacting statutes that guarantee a right of reply. The press resists these regulatory efforts by warning that such legislation is but another form of the old authoritarian conception of the press, which will ultimately end in muzzling freedom of speech. At the same time, it attempts to emphasize its objective role, and its commitment to social responsibility, by introducing reform, e.g., op-ed pages in many newspapers, ombudsmen, and press councils. Many of the countries represented in this volume have press councils which issue codes of professional ethics and attempt to regulate violations of their voluntary rules. It is also interesting to note that in none of the modern democracies reviewed here was the institution of a press council successful in fostering a public opinion that perceives journalists as objective professionals. This phenomenon seems to be but another symptom of the inherent contradiction between the press as a political organ and the press as an objective medium.

Another manifestation of the same contradiction is the increasing awareness, within most of the democracies reviewed here, that press monopoly is turning the old ideal of a free marketplace of ideas into a hollow concept. When a state considers legislation to correct the situation, the press resists. The state claims that only by breaking centralization can an affinity between public needs and journalism be maintained. The press, opposing such steps, argues that only a strong centralized press can have the political and financial resources to stand up to the swelling bureaucracy and fulfill its public obligations. Similarly, the press opposes legislation protecting privacy, or providing for a right of reply (which would give either private individuals or the government a right of access to the newspaper in order to correct a perceived bias). At the same time the press may be quite vocal in its demand for a reporter's privilege, editorial privilege, and the right of access to information.

This dialectic, like the one between universal values and the nation-state, is typical of the press laws of modern democracies. The tension between journalism as the political, sometimes partisan fourth estate and journalism as a profession permeates all modern democratic press law. Again, the various systems differ as to the particular form by which the tension is resolved. In continental Europe, for example, there is a statutory right of reply, but little enthusiasm about a reporter's privilege. Conversely, the American Supreme Court considers the right of reply a violation of the First Amendment, but is rather ambivalent about the issue of a reporter's privilege.[60]

## CONCLUSION

The search for understanding the law of the press cannot focus exclusively on forms of regulation. It must transcend the form and inquire into the political theories that underpin the systems of regulation.

Contemporary press laws reflect both the ideas embedded in authoritarianism and the ideals of the Enlightenment. Historically, press freedom was achieved through the struggle against authoritarianism. However, in modern democracies, the eminence acquired by the press revived the demands for press regulation by the state. In this context, libertarians are caught in the middle. On the one hand they recognize that a newspaper is more than an ordinary citizen and that the press is an important social institution with a legitimate need of certain privileges that will facilitate its work. On the other hand, they are suspicious of regulatory measures designed to correct press abuse of its powers, lest such measures open the door to a new authoritarianism.[61] Increasingly, modern press laws are responding to the social responsibility theory of the press. This theory, developed by Theodore Peterson, asserts that

> Freedom carries concomitant obligations; and the press, which enjoys a privileged position under our government, is obliged to be responsible to society for carrying out certain essential functions of mass communication in contemporary society. To the extent that the press recognizes its responsibilities and makes them the basis of operational policies, the libertarian system will satisfy the needs of society. To the extent that the press does not assume its responsibilities, some other agency must see that the essential functions of mass communication are carried out.[62]

The challenge to contemporary press laws lies in their ability to translate this theory into coherent legal terms, which will safeguard against both press and state authoritarianism.

## NOTES

1. See *supra* pp. 000–000. For a general discussion of comparative law see M.W. Glendon and C. Osakwe, *Comparative Legal Traditions* (1982) and K. Zweigert and H. Kötz, *An Introduction to Comparative Law*, 2 vols. (T. Weir, tr.) (1977). There is very little material available about comparative press law. For recent works see G.T. Kurian, ed., *World Press Encyclopaedia* (1982), D. Nimmo and M.W. Mansfield, eds., *Government and the News Media* (1982) and J. Leftwich Curry and G.A. Dassin, eds., *Press Control Around the World* (1982).

2.   Recall Dicey's assertion, made in the late nineteenth century with his characteristic stiff upper lip:

> Freedom of discussion is, then, in England little else than the right to write or say anything which a jury, consisting of twelve shopkeepers, think it expedient should be said or written. Such "liberty" may vary at different times and seasons from unrestricted license to very severe restraint....

A. Dicey, *Introduction to the Study of the Law of the Constitution* 246 (10th ed. 1965), (hereinafter cited as Dicey, *The Law of the Constitution*).

Today, however, the situation may have changed due to England's membership in the European community which subjects it to the European Convention of Human Rights. *See* Supperstone, "Press Law in the United Kingdom," *supra* p. 10. Since 1973, Israel's parliament has been considering a Bill of Rights which would guarantee press freedom. *See* Lahav, "Press Law in Israel," *supra* p. 268.

3.   Note, for example, how the Israeli Court neutralized the power to suspend newspapers by interpreting the relevant statute to mean that the Minister of the Interior must determine that there is a probable danger to the public peace prior to ordering suspension. Lahav, "Press Law in Israel," *supra* p. 268.

This practice of statutory interpretation also is common in countries where judicial review obtains. Most of the cases decided by the Supreme Court of the United States focus on statutory interpretation rather than invalidation of statutes. *See* Wellington, "The Nature of Judicial Review," 91 Yale L.J. 486 (1982). Also, the Japanese Supreme Court, which is vested with the power to invalidate statutes, has never done so. It prefers interpretive methods. *See* Horibe, "Press Law in Japan," *supra* p. 316.

4.   U.S. Const., amend. I.

5.   French Declaration of the Rights of Man, art. 11 (1789), *reprinted in* I. Brownlie, *Basic Documents on Human Rights* 9 (1971).

6.   Note that the Amendment reads "*Congress* shall make no law...." (emphasis supplied). *See* L. Levy, *Legacy of Suppression; Freedom of Speech and Press in Early American History* (1960), and Anderson, "The Origins of The Press Clause," 30 UCLA L. Rev. 455 (1983). *See also Gitlow* v. *New York*, 268 U.S. 652 (1925).

7.   However, state constitutions of the nineteenth century are more reflective of the qualified model. *See*, e.g., Minn. Const., art. I §3; Or. Const., art. I §8.

8.   Mass. Const., art. XVI §17. *See also* Va. Const. art. I §12. That section reads:

> [T]he freedom of the press is one of the great bulwarks of liberty, and can never be restrained but by despotic governments....

9.   *See generally* T. Emerson, *The System of Freedom of Expression* (1970); Emerson, "Toward a General Theory of the First Amendment," 72 Yale L.J. 877 (1963); Baker, "Scope of the First Amendment Freedom of Speech," 25 U.C.L.A L. Rev. 964 (1978); Blasi, "The Checking Value in First Amendment Theory" A.B. Found J. 521 (1977); F. Schauer, *Free Speech: A Philosophical Enquiry* (1982).

10.   M. Cappelletti and W. Cohen, *Comparative Constitutional Law* 25, 26 (1979).

11. Interestingly, the Swedes, enacting their constitutional commitment to free speech in 1809, while adopting the qualified model, were much more careful than the French in delineating the contours of legislative discretion:

> Press freedom means the right of every Swedish man to issue publications without any obstacles previously laid by the public power, to be, afterwards, prosecuted for their contents only before a lawful court, and to be punished therefore in no other case than if these contents be contrary to a clear law, given to preserve general peace without restraining general enlightenment.

*See* Strömberg, "Press Law in Sweden," *supra* p. at 229.

12. This point may explain another difference in American First Amendment law —that between congressional enactment and the common law. The theory is that while the founding fathers feared statutory restrictions, they did not oppose common law restrictions on press freedom such as the law of defamation or the law of seditious libel. *See* L. Levy, *Legacy of Suppression; Freedom of Speech and Press in Early American History* (1960).

13. *See*, e.g., J. Madison, *The Federalist* No. 10. For a discussion see Wellington, "The Nature of Judicial Review," 91 Yale L.J. 486 (1982).

14. Federal Republic of Germany, Basic Law, art. 5, (1949), *reprinted in* I. Brownlie, *Basic Documents on Human Rights* 19 (1971). For the interpretation of the term "general laws" in Article 5(2) see Kohl, "Press Law in the Federal Republic of Germany" text accompanying notes 49–50, *supra*.

15. But note that Article 19 of the Basic Law limits the power of the legislature to pass laws which will in fact vitiate the right under the guise of Article 5(2).

Article 19

1. Insofar as under this Basic Law a basic right may be restricted by or pursuant to a law, such law must apply generally and not solely to an individual case. Furthermore, the law must name the basic right, indicating the Article.

2. In no case may a basic right be infringed upon in its essential content.

3. The basic rights shall apply also to domestic juristic persons to the extent that the nature of such rights permits.

4. Should any person's right be violated by public authority, recourse to the court shall be open to him. If no other court has jurisdiction, recourse shall be to the ordinary courts.

*Reprinted in* I. Brownlie, *Basic Documents on Human Rights* 23–24 (1971). Clearly, however, these safeguards depend, *inter alia*, on the interpretations of the German Constitutional Court.

16. *See*, e.g. Constitution of India, Art. 19.

Article 19

1. All Citizens have the right:
   (a) to freedom of speech and expression....

2. Nothing in sub-clause (a) of clause I shall affect the operation of any existing law, or prevent the State from making any law, in so far as such law imposes reasonable restrictions on the exercise of the right conferred by the said sub-clause in the interests of the sovereignty and integrity of India, the

security of the State, friendly relations with foreign States, public order, decency or morality, or in relation to contempt of court, defamation or incitement to an offense.

*Reprinted in id.* at 32.

Article 10 of the European Convention on Human Rights reads:

Article 10

1.  Everyone has the right to freedom of expression. This right shall include freedom to hold opinions and to receive and impart information and ideas without interference by public authority and regardless of frontiers. This article shall not prevent States from requiring the licensing of broadcasting, television or cinema enterprises.

2.  The exercise of these freedoms, since it carries with it duties and responsibilities, may be subject to such formalities, conditions, restrictions or penalties as are prescribed by law and are necessary in a democratic society, in the interests of national security, territorial integrity or public safety, for the prevention of disorder or crime, for the protection of health or morals, for the protection of the reputation or rights of others, for preventing the disclosure of information received in confidence, or for maintaining the authority and impartiality of the judiciary.

*Reprinted in id.* at 743.

17.   This becomes evident when one compares the Indian and West German provisions. *Supra* notes 14–16.

18.   For example, in France there is only review *prior to* the final process of legislation. *See* Errera, "Press Law in France," *supra* p. 139.

19.   Dicey, *The Law of the Constitution, supra* note 2 at 239.

20.   *Id.* In England, the exclusive privilege of printing was given to 97 London stationers who constituted a guild that had power to seize all publications issued by outsiders. *Id.* at 260.

21.   However, one important difference is that the United States constitution did recognize liberty of the press as a fundamental doctrine of American law.

22.   A caveat is needed here. Dicey's discussion of the positive laws of England has been attacked by scholars since the first appearance of his book. However, there is a consensus that his insights are important. *See generally* R. Cosgrave, *The Rule of Law: Albert Venn Dicey, Victorian Jurist* (1981). Whatever the shortcomings of Dicey's descriptions may be, they certainly represent the general English perception of the differences between English and Continental law at the time. It is this perception which is of importance here.

23.   Dicey, *The Law of the Constitution, supra* note 2 at 254–255, 260.

The penalties of death, of the galleys, of the pillory were from time to time imposed upon the printing or sale of forbidden works. These punishments were often evaded; but they...retained practical force until the very eve of the Revolution. The most celebrated library works of France were published abroad.

*Id* at 254.

24.   Dicey, *The Law of the Constitution, supra* note 2 at 261, 262. Also, two

years after the Revolution, the Commons considered, but did not enact, a bill to prohibit unlicensed publication of the news.

25.  Dicey, *The Law of the Constitution, supra* note 2 at 257. The present French Press Law of 1881 was enacted during the liberalization which came with the establishment of the Third Republic. However, for an account of how the law failed to block suppressive policies in the twentieth century, *see* Errera, "Press Law in France," *supra* p. 158.

26.  Dicey, *The Law of the Constitution, supra* note 2 at 251.

27.  *Id.* at 250.

28.  "[U]ntil quite recently, the idea that press offenses were a peculiar class of offenses to be dealt with in a special way and punished by special courts was accepted by every party in France. *This is a matter of extreme theoretical importance.* It shows how foreign to French notions is the idea that every branch of law ought to be dealt with by the ordinary law of the land." *Id.* at 259.

29.  *First Nat'l Bank of Boston* v. *Bellotti*, 435 U.S. 765, 801 (1978) (Burger; C.J., concurring):

> The second fundamental difficulty with interpreting the Press Clause as conferring special status on a limited group is one of definition. The very task of including some entities within the "institutional press" while excluding others, whether undertaken by legislature, court, or administrative agency, is reminiscent of the abhorred licensing system of Tudor and Stuart England—a system the First Amendment was intended to ban from this country.

30.  In addition to failing to look beyond France, Dicey may have committed the error of generalizing on the basis of the particular British experience. In England, the Star Chamber's arbitrary and suppressive treatment of civil liberties created the suspicion of all specialized institutions. However, the Swedish press courts, with their jury system and relatively loyal commitment to press freedom, illustrate the notion that press courts, in and of themselves, are not an important factor.

31.  K. Marx, *On Freedom of the Press and Censorship*, S.K. Padover, ed. and tr. (1974).

32.  Requirements vary. They may include nationality (thus excluding foreigners), age (older age usually indicates an increase in one's willingness to accept the current regime), solvency (to ensure payment of fines and damages), and education (thus barring members of the working class from full participation in the press enterprise).

Such a requirement puts the publisher under financial pressure to keep publishing or lose the permit, and prevents the storing of spare permits to be used if the original permit is revoked or suspended.

34.  *See* Strömberg, "Press Law in Sweden," *supra* p. 235. The German press law follows the same route. Kohl, "Press Law in the Federal Republic of Germany," *supra* p. 193.

35.  *See* Soifer, "Press Law in the United States," *supra* p. 113.

36.  *Abrams* v. *United States*, 250 U.S. 616, 630 (1919) (Holmes, J., dissenting).

37.  *See generally* Siebert, "The Authoritarian Theory of the Press," in *Four Theories of the Press* 9 (1956).

38.  R. Unger, *Law in Modern Society* 56 (1976).

39.  Z. Chafee, *Free Speech in the United States* 23 (1969).

40.  *See* T. Emerson, *Toward a General Theory of the First Amendment* (1963).

41.  *See* Unger, *supra* note 38 at 53.

42.  W. Blackstone, Vol. 4, *Commentaries*\* 151–152.

43.  *See* Kohl, "Press Law in the Federal Republic of Germany", *supra* p. 13.

44.  Examples are the suspension powers in the French press law or the power given to the Postmaster General to deny a newspaper access to the mail by the American Espionage Act of June 15, 1917, c. 30 §3, 40 Stat. 217, 219.

45.  *See,* e.g., Supperstone, "Press Law in the United Kingdom," *supra* p. 000 (discussing the Official Secrets Act and Seditious Libel); the American Espionage Act as amended, May 16, 1918, 40 Stat. 553 (repealed in 1920). For a discussion of the bad tendency test *see* Z. Chaffee, *Free Speech in the United States* 23–30 (1969).

46.  Another manifestation of this phenomenon is the growing sophistication of the techniques of news management.

47.  376 U.S. 254 (1964).

48.  *See* Errera, "Press Law in France," *supra* p. 158.

49.  See Errera, "Press Law in France," *supra* p. 151.

50.  It appears in the press law of Sweden, Strömberg, "Press Law in Sweden," *supra* p. 234 and in §20 of Israel's Press Ordinance (1933) *reprinted in* R. Drayton, 2 *Laws of Palestine* 1215 (1933) giving the executive branch complete discretion to ban the import of foreign newspapers into Palestine, now Israel.

51.  See e.g., the regulations which preceded the United States Supreme Court decision in *Lamont* v. *Postmaster General* 381 U.S. 301 (1956). For an interesting discussion of efforts by the Reagan administration to ban foreign films and foreign speakers on political grounds see Floyd Abrams, "The New Effort to Control Information," *The N.Y. Times Magazine*, Sept. 25 1983.

52.  J. Mill, *On Liberty* (R. McCallum 1948); Errera, "Press Law in France," *supra* p. 137.

53.  Rabban, "The First Amendment in Its Forgotten Years," 90 Yale L.J. 514 (1980).

54.  M. Schudson, *Discovering the News, A Social History of American Newspapers* 6 (1978).

55.  *See* Lewis, *"A Preferred Position for Journalism,"* Hofstra L. Rev. 595, (1979); Lewis, "The Right to Scrutinize Government: Toward a First Amendment Theory of Accountability," 34 U. Miami L. Rev. 785, 793 (1980); E. Baker, "Press Rights and Government Power to Structure the Press", 34 U. Miami L. Rev. 785, 819.

56.  *See* Kohl, "Press Law in the Federal Republic of Germany" *supra* p. 210; Soifer, "Press Law in the United States," *supra* p. 115.

57.  R. Steel, *Walter Lippmann and the American Century* 210 (1980).

58.  In most liberal democracies, the press originally was a party newspaper. The passage into a fourth estate signifies the separation of newspapers from political parties, hence the political independence of the press. But notice that this independence is still political. *See* Siebert, *supra* note 47 at 60.

59. M. Schudson, *Discovering the News, A Social History of American Newspapers* 121–159 (1978).

60. *See* Errera, "Press Law in France," *supra* p. 169. Strömberg. "Press Law in Sweden," *supra* p. 242; Soifer, "Press Law in the United States," *supra* p. 112.

61. The possibility that well-intentioned regulation of the press will result in the revival of old authoritarian themes in a new garb, accompanied by modernized rhetoric, has become real as illustrated by the announcement of the UNESCO proposals concerning the press. *See* "International Commission for the Study of Communication Problems," *Many Voices One World* (1980); for later developments *see Boston Globe*, Dec. 19, 1982, at A22, col. 4.

62. Peterson, "The Social Responsibility Theory," *Four Theories of the Press* 73, 74 (1956).

# Index